The Bad Taste of Others

The Bad Taste of Others

JUDGING LITERARY VALUE IN
EIGHTEENTH-CENTURY FRANCE

Jennifer Tsien

UNIVERSITY OF PENNSYLVANIA PRESS *Philadelphia*

THIS BOOK IS MADE POSSIBLE BY A COLLABORATIVE GRANT
FROM THE ANDREW W. MELLON FOUNDATION.

Published by University of Pennsylvania Press
Philadelphia, Pennsylvania 19104-4112
www.upenn.edu/pennpress

Printed in the United States of America
on acid-free paper

10 9 8 7 6 5 4 3 2 1

Library of Congress Cataloging-in-Publication Data

Tsien, Jennifer Shianling, 1971–
  The bad taste of others : judging literary value in
eighteenth-century France / Jennifer Tsien.—1st ed.
    p. cm.
  Includes bibliographical references and index.
  ISBN 978-0-8122-4359-8 (hardcover : alk. paper)
  1. French literature—18th century—History
and criticism. 2. Aesthetics, French—18th
century. 3. Culture in literature. 4. Civilization in
literature. I. Title.
PQ265T75 2011
840.9'005—dc23
                              2011025527

CONTENTS

Introduction

Everyone expresses opinions about taste, but almost no one can define it; in fact, it may be easier to say what good taste is *not* than to give a formula for what it is. As the anthropologist Mary Douglas remarks about the choices made by present-day consumers, "Taste is best understood by negative judgments. The discourse of dislike and ugliness is more revealing than the discourse about aesthetic beauty."[1] For this reason, examples of bad taste may tell us more about a society's conception of manners, fashion, and artistic value than any rules of good taste. In our day, many would claim that society is so fragmented that no overarching rules of taste exist.[2] Yet museums, art galleries, magazine editors, shoppers, nightclub doormen, judges of television reality shows, and university professors make decisions based on taste every day. In many cases, these decisions determine the social status of individuals or the success of a business, or they may shape the cultural legacy of an era.

While our society is not always conscious of the influence of taste, the eighteenth-century literary world was very openly preoccupied with matters of taste or *goût*, if we are to judge by the frequency with which it is mentioned and by the number of works on the subject. For instance, a quick overview of works from 1700 to 1750 in the catalogue of the French National Library yields the following sample: *Le Bon goût de l'éloquence chrétienne; Le Passe-temps des gens de goût; Discours sur l'origine de la poésie, sur son usage et sur le bon goût; Trois lettres sur la décadence du goût en France; Les Principes de la morale et du goût; Le Dénonciateur du mauvais goût; Les Adieux du goût*; and numerous others. To eighteenth-century France, good taste was a necessary component of human nature and of national influence. Luc Ferry, in *Homo aestheticus*,[3] even puts innovations in theories of taste on par with the early modern revolutions in epistemology and politics. One could even say that the difference between good and bad taste was as important in the eighteenth century as the difference between good and evil or between truth and illusion. In all of these areas of human experience, philosophers attempted to resolve the problematic relationship between subjectivity and authority, and they sought to mark the difference between a savage and a civilized man.

To a large extent, eighteenth-century theories of taste developed together with other areas of philosophy: for critics such as Dubos and Diderot, for example, arguments about taste and beauty were closely intertwined with new conceptions of sensibility, ethics, subjectivity, and even the workings of the human body. In other ways, reflections about artistic judgment seemed to diverge sharply from other Enlightenment ideas, particularly in matters of equality, cultural relativism, and human perfectibility.

Given the importance of taste in this period, it is not surprising that it produced significant new ways of thinking about the artistic experience. Because the discussion of taste rose to the foreground so conspicuously in the eighteenth century, many present-day scholars have seen this period as the cradle of modern aesthetic thought. Why do scholars focus on this period as "The Century of Taste"? While one could mark 1750 as the birth of aesthetics, based on the fact that the term first appeared as the title of a book by Alexander Baumgarten, the meaning of the term—either perception through the senses or the judgment of beauty—was hardly new.[4]

Since antiquity, thinkers had speculated about the nature of sensory perception and of beauty, and at least since the seventeenth century many had tried to determine the nature of taste.[5] It may be impossible to pinpoint a clear break between premodern and modern reflections on beauty, especially if this break is identified with the second half of the eighteenth century.

Some scholars have seen the so-called birth of aesthetics as the product of a new configuration in the relationship between the creator, his patrons, and the public. For instance, Annie Becq, in her monumental work *La Genèse de l'esthétique française moderne*, sees the second half of the eighteenth century as the time when the science, or the true philosophy, of aesthetics emerged. She explains that this event resulted from the increased autonomy of writers and of artists through their liberation from the constraints of courtly patronage and a shift to a more market-based relationship with their public: "The increasing autonomy of the intellectual and artistic field created the conditions necessary to conceive of the aesthetic order, strictly speaking, and it consequently favored the emergence of modern aesthetics."[6] While the correlation between the market system and the birth of modern aesthetics described by Becq may seem plausible in some respects, the rise of the authorial autonomy was neither linear nor simple, as she acknowledges herself. For instance, Geoffrey Turnovsky has demonstrated in *The Literary Market*[7] that it is impossible to demarcate exactly when the system of courtly patronage was transformed into the market system because in many cases the two existed simultaneously; that is, authors depended on a variety of sources for their income at any one time.

Annie Becq may have inherited her views regarding the new creative autonomy and its effects from Habermas's *Structural Transformation of the Public Sphere*, though she does not cite him explicitly. Habermas maintains that in the period when artists and writers depended on a small and powerful elite (namely the king, his circle, his institutions, and in some cases the church) who had the "monopoly of interpretation,"[8] there was no need to argue about what was good art. It was only when there was a growth in the number of people who were interested in the arts—not elites but sufficiently educated individuals of all social backgrounds—and when the bourgeois public sphere emerged that cultural products became accessible on the open market.[9] Consequently, everyone felt that they had the right to make judgments about paintings and books: "The 'taste' to which art was oriented from then on became manifest in the assessments of lay people who claimed no prerogative, since within a public everyone was entitled to judge."[10] From these circumstances, Habermas claims, the art critic was born, in order to speak for the public as its "mandatary."[11]

Habermas's optimistic faith in open discussion, however, is belied by the elitist statements contained in actual eighteenth-century treatises on taste, many of which express horror at the notion that "everyone was entitled to judge." Habermas does hint at an inherent problem in the art critics' self-appointed role as "spokesmen for the public": these critics also presumed to be the public's educators[12] and in some cases, these critics "could turn against the public."[13] But in

Habermas's view, the ultimate judgment finally resulted from public debate, so that each opinion would eventually submit to a better-argued one. Even though Habermas's Enlightenment society relied on the use of reason in debates about art and literature, in reality, reason was not always the deciding factor. More often, critics claimed a number of other qualities that made them better judges of artistic productions than other people: their degree of sensibility, which is unverifiable and unmeasurable; their authority, based on greater erudition; and that supremely intangible quality, taste, which in some cases they deemed to be the domain of the chosen few.

Regarding the critics' relationship to the public, Habermas claims that at times, groups of thinkers wished to form exclusive cliques, but this proved impossible because the public debate about art always became accessible to a "more inclusive public of all private people."[14] I agree that the eighteenth century saw constant tension between those who wished to establish themselves as the exclusive authorities of taste and the large number of consumers of art who also wanted a say in these matters. Since the line of demarcation between expert and non-expert was always in flux, perhaps aspirants to the status of critic needed to fend off all encroachments to their position through the language of exclusivity. While Habermas puts the emphasis on the happy outcome of this struggle, in this study I will concentrate instead on the efforts made by critics to discredit the public's choices, even while announcing the universality of taste.

One problem inherent in the concept of taste was that its elusive nature made it difficult, if not impossible, to bridge the gap between one person's subjective perception of beauty and its wider application to a nation or to humanity in general. The majority of the writers I deal with in this study declared that the standards of taste were universal, even though actual differences in opinion forced them to explicitly reject the taste of others. Batteux, for one, affirmed that "there can be but one only good taste in general . . . therefore those who are not pleased with beautiful nature, must necessarily have a bad taste."[15] This ideal of taste supposedly transcended class, nationality, and history—yet the ideal of taste these philosophers upheld undoubtedly depended on their own subjective preferences.

To a certain extent, disagreements about who had the right to judge cultural productions are already inherent in the word *public*. This key concept for Habermas has been destabilized by more recent scholars such as the art historian Thomas Crow, who finds deep discrepancies between various conceptions of what constitutes a public in the writings of the eighteenth century. On the one hand, officials such as the leaders of the Académie Royale de Peinture et de Sculpture claimed that "public" acclamation gave legitimacy to certain painters and subjects. In doing so, they assumed that the population would passively accept established notions such as the moral didacticism of art, the hierarchy of genres, and artistic conventions. This idea of the "correct" judgment being supported by an imaginary consensus is analogous to the idea in literature, expressed by Dubos, Batteux, and others, that the "public" eventually agrees with those people who have superior taste.

As Thomas Crow indicates, however, this imaginary, passive public did not coincide with what he calls the "audience"—the actual crowds of people who looked at the art in the Louvre's salons and who bought paintings in the outdoor markets.[16] For example, historical and mythological paintings, which represented the top level of the hierarchy of painting, did not please consumers as much they were meant to. Instead, people often chose to admire, and to buy, paintings that were not meant to edify them: for example, modest interiors by Chardin and frivolous *fêtes galantes* by Watteau. Like the leaders of the Académie Royale de Peinture et de Sculpture, the *philosophes*, self-appointed leaders of the literary world, were frustrated when the reading public became unruly and chose different works that they would have desired, especially from what they saw as the tasteless genres of fairy tales, chivalric novels, biblical poetry, or magazines. When the people who constituted the actual ensemble of consumers expressed their preferences for the "wrong" art or the "wrong" texts, they challenged the critics' assumption that the majority of the public would eventually consecrate the works that the experts had deemed most worthy of passing on to posterity. Despite the difficulties involved in identifying a public and determining its exact effect on the birth of aesthetics, it is still very probable, as Habermas assumes, that the increasing size of the public had a significant bearing on the conceptions of taste of the eighteenth century. The rise in literacy and the growing access to culture, as we can see in the opening of the Louvre's salons to all, surely made it possible for anyone to consider himself or herself a judge of the arts, whether this status was acknowledged by others or not.

This growth of the public for art and literature, which Habermas sees in a positive light, caused critics such as Dubos, Diderot, and

Marmontel to react with horror. But their motivations, they claimed, were not merely self-serving or elitist; in fact, they were protecting the public from itself—or rather, they were protecting their abstract, idealized public from the actual, less manageable public. More specifically, these philosophers portrayed themselves as protectors of a national cultural legacy that was constantly under the metaphorical threat of either decadence or barbarian invasion. They claimed that after the eras in which Italy and Spain had dominated European culture and French culture had wallowed in an inchoate state, French letters were now ready to rise to the top rank. This intense focus on French pride may seem surprising when one considers the well-known cosmopolitanism of these same authors in other areas, such as customs, morals, and religion. Nevertheless, these critics, particularly Marmontel, reconciled their nationally centered view of culture with their interest in the outside world by elaborating theories of a supposedly natural process by which the world gradually looked to one country to set the standard of taste. In their view, France had reached a point at which it could take its position as the leader in matters of taste.

This ambition explains, for example, the *philosophes'* anxious desire to safeguard the advances made during the previous century in establishing correct French usage and in expunging so-called tasteless words, which they judged to be too foreign, archaic, or vulgar. Eighteenth-century critics expressed the need to sweep away foreign influences not only on vocabulary (for example, Italian-style diminutives) but on literature as well, as we can see in Dubos's denunciations of Spanish farce or Voltaire's mockery of "Oriental" biblical style. Even the supposedly shameful parts of France's literary past, such as Frankish words, *gaulois* humor, or *préciosité*, had to be purged from the canon that would be handed down to posterity. La Harpe's survey of literature, from the Greeks to Voltaire, contained in his *Lycée, ou Cours de littérature ancienne et moderne*, consecrated this eighteenth-century view of the French literary *patrimoine*, especially in an era when the study of French literary history had not previously existed as a discipline.

While critics such as La Harpe often connected the foreign with the tasteless, they saw ancient Greeks and Romans not as foreigners but as the ancestors of French culture.[17] This perceived kinship was central to the Quarrel of the Ancients and the Moderns, which was just ending as the first eighteenth-century treatises on taste, those by Dubos and Crousaz, were beginning to appear. Although the Quarrel remained unresolved, I believe that its influence could be seen in French writers' self-image as both the inheritors of Greek and Roman culture and as the founders of a new and better culture, as we will see in the discussion of Corneille's *Horace*.

A strong and civilized society, as opposed to barbarism or decadence, was the ambition of these eighteenth-century thinkers: it was not the France that they saw around them but the France that they aspired to. Good taste played an important part in creating this national self-image. The concern with the national literary legacy can be compared with the call for the heroic "grand goût"[18] in the visual arts during the same period. In both cases, writers of treatises blamed the petty, the feminine, and the foreign for bringing about the bad taste that would weaken the French nation.

The aspiration to establish France as the new world leader in matters of culture underlies many of the calls to crush examples of bad taste in their midst. In order to accomplish their goal, eighteenth-century critics needed not only to set the standard of good taste but also to assume the authority to pass judgment. Among these critics, it is important to distinguish two connected groups. The first group belonged largely to the first half of the eighteenth century and the other the second half, though in some cases the two overlapped. In Chapter 2 I will provide more detailed discussions of each particular author, but for the moment I will explain, in broad outlines, what each group represented and what was at stake in their conception of taste.

In the first group, one can include critics such as Dubos, the marquise de Lambert, and Montesquieu. Whether noble or bourgeois, they frequented elite social circles, and the marquise de Lambert even hosted a literary salon attended by partisans of both the ancient and the modern camps during the Querelle d'Homère. These critics owed much to their seventeenth-century predecessors' ideal of good taste, which emanated from worldly politeness. They also inherited the *honnête homme*'s disdain for those they saw as pedantic, including philologists, pedagogues, and, in Dubos's case, even artists themselves. Despite their connection to the recent past, however, these critics from the early eighteenth century truly innovated in the realm of taste and aesthetics by concentrating on the functions of the viewer's mind as he or she reacted to a work of art. This particular kind of taste depended on an extremely fine-tuned sensibility or an innate sense of "tact," both in the sense of touch and in the sense of politeness.

In their works, we can see that the focus on sentiment does not imply a belief in egalitarianism but rather in a closed community of the ultra-sensible. The marquise de Lambert, in her *Réflexions sur le goût*, describes taste as depending on "an extremely delicate sensibility in the heart, and a great justness in the [the mind]."[19] She says it cannot be learned, but instead, "nature gives us what we have of it, we never can acquire it, and the more refined part of the world alone are acquainted with it in any degree of perfection."[20] Similarly, the abbé Dubos proves his faithfulness to the *honnête homme* ideal in his *Réflexions critiques sur la poésie et sur la peinture* by granting the authority to judge art exclusively to the "public," which, he makes clear, does not refer to the *peuple* but to a polite and educated elite. He also explicitly bypasses the opinions of critics who write "dissertations"[21] and even the producers of art, calling the latter *artisans* rather than *artistes*.

We can see how this insistence on feeling contains the seeds of the trend in sensibility that would flourish in Europe during the late eighteenth century. But inherent in the concept of sensibility is the problem of exclusiveness and inclusiveness. One could see sensibility as a democratizing trend, in which people of all backgrounds who can feel strongly may claim membership in an elite of the heart, as Rousseau would try to demonstrate, for example, with himself as a model of a low-born man of feeling or with his hero Saint-Preux in the novel *La Nouvelle Héloïse*. One could even be led to assume that sensibility is an aspect of human nature that is common to all. But this application of the concept of sensibility was far from the thoughts of high-society denizens such as Lambert and Dubos. I believe that they intended this concept of sensibility as way of distinguishing the refined from the vulgar, a distinction that they assumed would naturally coincide with the person's social station.

In the realm of visual arts, the early eighteenth-century *mondains* correspond to the *amateurs* whose influence has been documented by scholars such as Thomas Crow, René Démoris, Florence Ferran, and Charlotte Guichard. These amateurs were private collectors of art, mostly aristocrats, who claimed that their *goût exquis* and their active support of artists sufficed to give them the authority of taste, especially when government patronage was on the wane. These amateurs, who frequented some of the same circles as Dubos, Lambert, and Montesquieu, demanded and received a semi-official role to play in the Académie Royale de Peinture et de Sculpture. These were surely the types of amateurs to whom Dubos referred when he defined the true public as the educated elite, neither professional artists nor critics. But these amateurs' influence would come under fire when a new generation of thinkers came to dominate artistic discourse.[22]

This new generation largely coincided with what we call the *philosophes*, the most prominent among them being Voltaire, d'Alembert and Diderot.[23] They came from a wide variety of social backgrounds, ranging from the rank of artisans to the high bourgeoisie, but they sought to transcend their past to create a new society of men of letters, or a "société de gens de lettres," as a number of them identify themselves in the title page of the *Encyclopédie*. These authors wished to take their distance, on the one hand, from the *mondains* who were previously in the ascendant and, on the other, from hermit-like pedants. In the article "Philosophe" of the *Encyclopédie*, for example, the anonymous author points to the difference between the mere society wit and the true *philosophe*: "The world is full of intelligent people and very intelligent people, who always judge; they always guess, because to judge without a sense of when one has a proper reason to judge is to guess. . . . The philosopher . . . judges and speaks less, but he judges more surely and speaks better."[24] In this passage, this writer seems to be attacking the position of Dubos and Lambert, who granted the members of "le monde" (a common abbreviation for "le beau monde" or high society) the right to judge spontaneously by instinct rather than by study. Nevertheless, the author insists later in this article that a *philosophe* is also an *honnête homme*, in the sense that he is not dishonest and that he does not isolate himself from society.

To mark a further distance from the high-society *mondains*, the *philosophes* stated that the authority to judge literature no longer depended only on sentiment; it also depended on rigorous training. As Voltaire asserts in his article "Gens de lettres" of the *Encyclopédie*, a true man of letters possesses a deep understanding of a number of fields; he can "pass from the thorns of Mathematics to the flowers of Poetry, and [can] judge equally well a book of Metaphysics and a play."[25] This type of man also differs from the *beaux-esprits* of elite circles because these are incapable of true "culture" and "philosophy": "A man of letters is not what is called a 'wit' [*un bel-esprit*]. Wit alone assumes less culture, less study, and requires no philosophy; it consists primarily of a brilliant imagination, pleasant conversation, assisted by general reading. A wit can easily not deserve the title of man of letters at all; and the man of letters may not at all claim the brilliance of the wit."[26] Thus the *phi-*

losophes of the eighteenth century, even while admiring many aspects of the aesthetic of the *honnêtes gens*, were intent on showing that they were a new breed of thinker—more erudite, more profound, and less intent on pleasing their social circle.

On the other hand, several passages by Diderot and Voltaire show us that they also wished to distinguish themselves from the pedants that the *honnêtes gens* disdained so much. In *Le Temple du goût*, for example, Voltaire shows his contempt for mere philologists; on the way to the eponymous Temple of Taste, he passes by a cluster of dust-covered scholars who do not even have an interest in approaching the temple. He lists some by name, such as André Dacier,[27] and others by comic pseudonyms, such as Lexicocrassius and Scriblerus,[28] and he describes them as follows:

> Their faces wan, their fire quite spent,
> With pouring o'er Greek authors bent.
> Soon as the squalid troop I spied,
> I raised my voice, and to them cried,
> "To Taste's famed Temple do you bend?"
> "No, sir, we no such thing intend.
> What others have with care expressed,
> With accuracy we digest,
> On others' thoughts we spend our ink,
> But we for our part never think."[29]

Instead of writers who have the ability to please, or philosophers who can judge, these men merely compile, and they keep their distance from matters of taste.

While Voltaire shows a spatial separation from these pedants in the *Temple of Taste*, leaving them behind in the dust, Diderot and d'Alembert separate themselves chronologically from the pedants in their Preliminary Discourse to the *Encyclopédie*. In the section of this text that contains an imagined history of knowledge, Diderot and d'Alembert maintain that the order of succession was as follows: memory, imagination, and reason. Memory is represented by the compilers, or the scholars who rediscovered ancient texts during the Renaissance; imagination refers to the authors of the seventeenth century who embellished literature; then, in the final stage, that of reason, the philosophers appeared. In Diderot's and d'Alembert's view, the present-day philosophers benefit from the erudition of the first group and the style of the second, but they have surpassed them intellectually.

These *philosophes* declared their autonomy from the previous patronage system, as Annie Becq states in *La Genèse de l'esthétique française moderne*, but they also cast a look of suspicion on the market system that would dominate literature in future centuries. We can see that their new independence existed, to some extent, on a purely rhetorical level. As Geoffrey Turnovsky demonstrates in *The Literary Market*, royal pensions, aristocratic influence, sinecures, and honorary positions all contributed to writers' economic survival, even if they would have liked to see themselves as independent *gens de lettres*.

To conceive of their new place in society, they looked for models in the past, particularly from antiquity and the seventeenth century, pointedly ignoring the Middle Ages and the French Renaissance. They appropriated a number of erudite predecessors while keeping their distance from those they saw as pedants. They also looked to worldly models in more recent decades while disdaining mere society wits. For instance, they praised and frequently quoted from Quintilian, who had earned his living as a teacher; they drew inspiration from seventeenth-century *mondains* such as Bouhours and Vaugelas and from more pedagogical types such as the grammarians of Port-Royal. From the early part of the eighteenth century, they praised the worldly Dubos, but they also picked up ideas from theology professors André and Crousaz, who described the judgment of beauty as a science.

Despite their defense of what they considered good taste, Voltaire and his partisans did not necessarily practice it themselves at all times. For example, while Voltaire denounced obscure writing, he still reveled in nonsense language and riddles in his *contes philosophiques*. While Diderot called order a natural necessity in his treatise on beauty (the article "Beau" of the *Encyclopédie*), many of his writings experiment with a meandering style that follows the capricious functions of the mind. In some cases, such as Voltaire's, one may see the disjunction between theory and practice as a way of reinforcing his principles through parody. In other cases, however, one can simply see a divide between this ideal of good taste in the eighteenth century and the actual practice of literature, no matter who represented each side in the battle of taste.

Nonetheless, the *philosophes*' self-identification as the new judges of taste necessitated the exclusion of others, even as more and more members of the increasingly literate public wished to participate in the world of letters. One could see part of the title of the *Encyclo-*

pédie, "par une société de gens de lettres," as declaring this new status. The word *société* can commonly designate a group of people who
assemble to enjoy each others' company, but this definition would
better describe the previous model of aesthetic judgment. Instead, the
type of *société* represented by the Encyclopedists conformed more to
the limited sense of a commercial company or a religious order rather than the egalitarian, open Republic of Letters praised by scholars
such as Habermas. The commercial and the religious definitions of
société suggest the image of the Encyclopedists as a closed sect backed
by institutions, less devoted to pleasure than to the business at hand.

In establishing their authority to judge literature, this *société des
gens de lettres* needed the expression *bad taste* to help them police the
border between the "real" writers and those who merely aspired to
this status. As Pierre Bourdieu remarks about the use of exclusion in
the literary world, the formation of a class of self-designated writers
implies the negation of others' claim to the title: "One of the central
stakes in literary (etc.) rivalries is the monopoly of literary legitimacy,
that is, among other things, the monopoly of the power to say with
authority who is authorized to call himself writer . . . the monopoly
of the *power of consecration* of producers and products."[30] Although
Bourdieu refers, in *Les Règles de l'art*, to the nineteenth-century literary landscape, he still has some relevant insights for the eighteenth
century, especially for their construction of a metaphorical barrier
between professionals and non-professionals in the field of literature.
The *philosophes* could use their self-created authority to shape the
French literary legacy as they wished to see it, and the label *bad taste*
would prove useful in removing elements from the past and present
that did not correspond to their vision. It is ironic to consider how
the ascendancy over public opinion that *philosophes* like Diderot and
Voltaire so desired paralleled the rule of an absolutist monarch over
the people. Although the *philosophes* are known for denouncing the
abuses of the monarchy and its institutions, in many ways they expressed the desire to rule over the literary world in an unchallenged
way, even to the extent of excluding the works they disapproved of,
just as the king's government could censure books that did not meet
with its favor.

In the chapters that follow, I will discuss the efforts of the eighteenth-century critics, in their capacity as authorities on taste, to rein
in what they saw as the excesses of the book world. For this reason,
I will begin Chapter 1 by establishing that there was a perception

among critics that the field of literature suffered from a deluge of books. This excess provided a major motive for imposing criteria of taste that would distinguish the good from the bad in the realm of the intellect. In Chapter 2, I discuss these criteria of good taste, specifically in the treatises of Dubos, Batteux, Voltaire, Marmontel, Diderot, and their contemporaries. The next four chapters explore different aspects of so-called bad taste that were to be rejected: the barbarism of other time periods, the vulgarity emanating from other countries, and the dangers of obscurity and disorder brought by various popular genres. Once these elements could be purged, the critics thought, the French literary legacy would be worthy of being passed down to posterity.

CHAPTER ONE

Too Many Books

According to one commonly held view of the eighteenth century, the printing press spread Enlightenment to the masses and made democracy more possible than ever before. This was an idea promoted by writers of the Revolutionary era such as Condorcet and Benjamin Franklin, and it is an idea that appeals to our present-day sensibilities. But if generalized literacy was so beneficial, what should we make of the number of authors of the eighteenth century who warned against the deluge of unworthy people, writers and readers, who supposedly overcrowded the literary world?

As I will demonstrate, the growing literary public was, in fact, the object of much scorn in France during the eighteenth century. Rather than rejoice over the widening frontiers of the book market, a number of writers made the case for restraining the numbers of books, readers, and authors to enhance their own role as producers of material and judges of quality. According to acerbic satires from Voltaire to Louis-Sébastien Mercier, the access to books drove the majority of the reading public insane, and in the worst cases, it drove them to believe they could become writers themselves. In these critics' view, this state of affairs could only lead to the corruption of taste in the Republic of Letters. They identified their enemy behind the anarchic growth of the book market as the spirit of *bad taste*, also known as *mauvais goût* or *faux goût*. This evil force could be countered with two weapons: treatises on taste in which they laid down the rules of good writing—yet coming just short of making formulas one could follow because the crucial quality, taste, was ultimately indefinable—and satire, in which bad examples of literature were punished.

This chapter will examine what imaginary excesses the spread of literature produced. I will focus first on the figure of the bad reader: the gullible and overly enthusiastic consumer who values books for everything but their intellectual content. I will then examine the deplorable follies that bad readers supposedly committed, especially that of attempting to become writers. Finally, I will situate the complaints of excessive numbers of books within the debates about the progress or decadence of civilization occasioned by the printing press.

ON BIBLIOMANIA

If one is to believe certain writers of the era, the eighteenth century was threatened by a serious plague, that of bibliomania: regular people ruined themselves collecting whole libraries full of rare books, old books, any kind of book, but in many cases neglecting to actually read them. According to these writers, the line between bibliophiles and bibliomaniacs was a blurry one, for love could easily turn into insanity. The problem is mentioned by a number of authors, but one of the most extensive texts devoted exclusively to this subject is the essay *De la bibliomanie* by Louis Bollioud-Mermet of the Académie de Lyon. First published in 1761, the essay warns the public: "Never have there been so many books of all kinds, in all forms, and never have there been so few readers whose true aim is serious study and solid instruction."[1] He deplores at once the excessive numbers of books and the ignorance of those who buy them.

Looking at the problem of bibliomania transhistorically, Bernhard Metz writes in "Bibliomania and the Folly of Reading"[2] that the first French usage of the term *bibliomanie* appears in a 1654 letter by Guy Patin. Even when the term *bibliomanie* is not used, however, according to Metz, authors from antiquity to the present day have mocked people who are obsessed with amassing books without understanding their content. To support his claim, Metz cites passages from, among others, Seneca, La Rochefoucauld, La Bruyère, Gustave Flaubert, and Robert Musil, as well as the authors that will concern us in this section, Bollioud-Mermet and d'Alembert. Nevertheless, it is surely significant that the term *bibliomanie* came into usage in the mid-seventeenth century, since scholars tend to see this period and the eighteenth century as important stages in the developing book market, especially the commerce of luxury books.[3]

In regard to Bollioud-Mermet, Metz particularly notices the medical language that permeates his essay. While it is difficult to believe that *De la bibliomanie* can claim any true medical credentials, the rhetorical casting of bibliomania as an illness that must be cured certainly enlivens Bollioud-Mermet's text with a sense of mock urgency. Aside from an amusing metaphor, however, the reference to medicine recalls that eighteenth-century medical discourse sometimes dealt with the physiological dangers of excessive reading. Recent research, notably Alexandre Wenger's *La Fibre littéraire: Le discours médical sur la lecture au XVIIIe siècle*[4] and Natania Meeker's article "*Lire et devenir*: The Embodied Reader and Feminine Subjectivity in Eighteenth-Century France,"[5] explains how writers of medical treatises warned against the health and moral hazards of irresponsible reading. Wenger specifically addresses the perception in the eighteenth century that there were too many books and too many aspiring authors. As Wenger sees in the treatises of a number of physicians, the pathological dangers of reading come from the "democratization of letters," since the ability to read puts an ever larger number of susceptible people are at risk. Physicians also place some blame on the number of books: "It's the quantity—the *excess*—that creates the epidemic, since the works that flood the market awaken the curiosity of new readers every day—readers who are deprived of any particular critical competence."[6] The ability to read, joined with the inability to judge, and eventually the desire to write would form a dangerous combination.

These medical treatises supplemented the traditional religious denunciation of books; as Jean Marie Goulemot reminds us, "penitential and confessional manuals pay attention to the importance of reading, and the censure can only be understood in relation to the literature that was tacitly implied, and to its (negative) influence."[7] Taking these findings into account, one could trace three sources for the skepticism, if not hostility, toward the potential excesses of reading. The first source would comprise the medical studies that sought to expose how books caused bodily weakness; the second source would include religious texts that denounced the immoral influence of literature. Third, I would include the writings by the *philosophes* and their followers who called for a restriction of the number of books for reasons of taste.

These discourses, though often representing conflicting ideologies, nevertheless bore some common traits. For instance, all three advocated a careful selection of books and tried to establish a distinction between useful and dangerous reading practices. The medical, religious, and philosophical commentaries on reading had other points in common. All concerned certain types of readers classified as more "at risk" than others. According to Wenger, those who formed the at-risk population were those who had not received the solid education necessary for being able to properly select and judge books: specifically, manual workers, women, and young people.[8]

Like the medical and religious discourses, treatises on books by the Enlightenment *philosophes* showed a dread of the potential problems caused by the availability of books. If we look at the unattributed article "Livre" of the *Encyclopédie*, we can find a number of ideas that are further explored by the authors I will treat in this chapter. Instead of defending the virtues of the book, as one may expect, this article warns us against books for the following reasons:

1. They make us neglect our duties in society.

2. They keep us from learning through our own experience.

3. Bad authors can corrupt us with their "errors, fables, and follies."

4. The "excessive multitude" of books.

5. There is no measure of quality: "few fixed and universal rules."

6. Too much disparate material in books: for example, one work may attempt to cover the subjects of theology, mathematics, grammar, etc.[9]

The author of this entry returns several times to the issue of excessive quantity and suggests reducing one's library to one or two books, for example, the Bible or the Koran, but concedes that this would be an extreme measure.

Were the fears of bibliomania justified? The historian Roger Chartier confirms, in *Lectures et lecteurs dans la France d'Ancien Régime*, that there was a new proliferation of readers in eighteenth-century France. The numbers of books had increased not only among aristocrats and bourgeois but also among the "petit peuple"[10]—artisans, merchants, and even servants. Another historian of the book, Henri-Jean Martin, points out some methodological problems in Chartier's methods of measuring literacy, but he nevertheless confirms the growth of the production of books and of the number of literate people in France. Martin's statistics show that "the French printing trade experienced a new period of prosperity. Financiers and *nouveaux riches* rushed to buy books, which they preferred in luxurious formats, well illustrated, and concerned with secular, or even frivolous, topics,"[11] all which were matters of concern for Bollioud-Mermet.

In our day, this growth in literacy would receive unqualified praise; why were there warnings about the dangers of the spread of learning in the eighteenth century? One of the central problems with bibliomania was the question of *value* and the two ways in which one could understand the term. Bollioud-Mermet states that the experts, namely the *gens de lettres*, know that value depends on the quality and usefulness of the book's content. The knowledge contained in the book, however, is sometimes in direct opposition to its other value, its monetary value. He describes crazed collectors as choosing the latter over the former: "They boast of possessing an immense number of volumes. I would infinitely prefer to see them possessed of genius, talents and learning; and what is better still, of good sense, simplicity and virtue. These, however, are not, like books, for sale, and if they were I doubt if they would find many purchasers."[12] In his opinion, bibliomania emerged from a foolish misunderstanding of books as objects of luxury, "mere curios" or "meubles de pure curiosité"[13] that contributed to ostentatious displays of wealth.

Bollioud-Mermet elaborates on this idea of books as furniture when he deplores the characteristics that added to books' monetary value but not to their artistic value. Rarity, for example, increases a book's price. Bollioud-Mermet, however, counters that a book may be rare only because an accident may have happened to destroy the other books of the series or because the book may belong to the category of those "which the press never cares to draw from their obscurity, and of which the scarcity can only be attributed to the contempt in which they are held!"[14] In other words, these books may be rare only because they were so bad that no one wanted to reprint them.

He continues with his ironic dissociations between the price of the object and the content of the text by discussing features of luxury books such as extra-wide margins and unusual formats. In reference to the trend in books with very large margins, he accuses booksellers of making people pay for mere paper, while anyone who seeks real instruction would surely prefer actual text to blank space. Addressing the problem of excessively large and excessively small formats, he remarks that the latter has such small type that it harms the eyes of the reader, and the former is just inappropriate for certain texts. The examples he gives are a monstrously large version of *Imitation de Jésus Christ*, which really should be an intimate manual, and a folio edition of La Fontaine's *Fables*, nominally written for children but so large that no child could actually lift it. Going further in his criticism of expensive books, he cites the highly prized but impossible-to-read books whose pages are uncut and must remain uncut in order to preserve their monetary value.

The contrast I have just described between the two concepts of value can also be expressed in the contrast between the exterior and interior of a book. Bollioud-Mermet states, "Few are lovers of learning or wisdom; all they care for is the book and its cover."[15] For instance, he claims that he would be much happier to read Demosthenes, Virgil, or Bossuet in a humble edition than a mediocre text bound in leather and lavished with gilt. To cover up inferior writing with luxurious ornamentation, he claims, is as absurd as crowning slaves with flowers or covering a prostitute with a queen's apparel. It is obvious, from his point of view, that the book buyer's sense of judgment simply cannot be trusted.

Furthermore, these readers' desire for luxurious bindings is in contrast with their hunger for low-quality content, according to Bollioud-Mermet. Certain genres especially attracted his ire by their novelty or alleged strangeness; he describes these as "books of an odd or peculiar character from which nothing is to be gained for instruction, nothing to be hoped for the cultivation of the mind, nothing even for the amusement of refined and delicate readers."[16] He lists these as "fables, tales, romances, histories of chivalry, adventures, burlesques, facetiæ, macaronic poems, treatises on magic, witchcraft and divination, memoirs of scandalous procedures, slanderous chronicles, defamatory libels and hosts of other writings inspired by an ill-regulated imagination or a cynical license."[17] Many of these genres and subgenres constitute the *Bibliothèque bleue* that has occupied recent historians of the book.

Another critic, Pierre de Villiers, in his *Entretiens sur les contes de fées, et sur quelques autres ouvrages du temps pour servir de préservatif contre le mauvais goût*,[18] expresses a similar contempt toward chivalric tales and other bad books or "mauvais bouquins," including the *Roman de la Rose* and *Chevaliers de la Table Ronde*, as well as the poems of Ronsard and Marot. According to Bollioud-Mermet and Villiers, it was only the bad taste of the public and the dishonesty of the publishers that made these books successful. In many cases, the so-called bizarreness of these publications was due to their status outside the hierarchy of genres, since they could be classified as neither tragedies nor heroic poems nor old or new comedies. Any non-classical genres that came along, such as chivalric novels, could only represent a degeneration of taste. In their view, the public, in its perverse desire for new things, was easily seduced by these writings.

In his treatise denouncing the bad literature of his day, Pierre de Villiers concentrates further on the gullibility of buyers, who respond automatically to certain inducements. His text is in the form of a dialogue, and his interlocutors complain that certain titles nearly always guarantee success, such as those ending in the suffix -*ana*: *Menagiana, Arliquiniana, Fureteriana,* and *Chaevraeana.* The two interlocutors also denounce the parasitical publications whose success depends on their titles' resemblance to a famous work. Specifically, they discuss La Bruyère's *Caractères ou les mœurs de ce siècle* and the authors who hope to ride on the famous moralist's coattails. One speaker cites several works whose authors and publishers cynically decide to "stuff in the book titles, one way or another, the terms *caractère, mœurs,* and *ce siècle.*"[19] He even cites one author who goes so far as to call his book *Livre dans le goût des Caracteres des Mœurs de ce Siècle.* From these references to printers' manifold strategies for making money, one has the impression that the scent of fraud hovers over the whole book industry. In fact, Villiers and Bollioud-Mermet show literature's vulnerability to the trickery that was potentially a part of any commercial transaction of the time.

Although the book trade may have been rotten and the people unable to distinguish good from bad, Bollioud-Mermet offered one possible justification for collecting books, dependent on the status of the buyer himself. A great nobleman or a prince could justify owning a large number of books if he shared them with the rest of the public. This exception did not apply to bourgeois private citizens who amassed books, since they had money to buy books but did not have any aristocratic duties to the public. Thus in Bollioud-Mermet's view, bourgeois collections could not be justified on the same terms as many princely collections, which were, under certain conditions, accessible to scholars in the eighteenth century and which have been handed down to us today as national libraries, such as the branches of the French National Library at Richelieu and the Arsenal. Bollioud-Mermet insists on this distinction based on social rank. Luxurious books "are only for princes or nobles. The grievance is that in this case, as in so many others, a private individual should presume, in matters of taste, to indulge so foolish an ambition."[20] One of the many faults of the bibliomaniac is thus revealed to be his pretension to rise above his social rank, even to set himself on par with the king.

D'Alembert, in his article "Bibliomanie" of the *Encyclopédie*, also allows for this aristocratic exception to book collecting, but he also makes a concession for another type of elite, the *philosophes*: "The love of books is estimable in only two cases: 1. when one knows how to esteem them for what they're worth, when one reads them as a philosopher in order to profit from the good that they could contain and to laugh at the bad; 2. when one possesses them for others as much as for oneself and when one shares them with pleasure and without reserve."[21] Those who read must do so as a philosopher ("en philosophe") and those who own must play the public role of sharing their books, the acknowledged role of princes and communities rather than private citizens.

Metz, in his article on bibliomania, draws our attention to another related article from the *Encyclopédie*, "Bibliotaphe" (defined as "enterreur de livres" or "burier of books"), in which Jaucourt exposes the problem of hoarding books and preventing others from enjoying them. As alternatives to "burying" books through private ownership, the Encyclopedists and Bollioud-Mermet presumably envisaged either the aristocratic model of a *grand seigneur* collecting books that he makes available to his subjects or the newly emerging system of lending libraries. It is difficult to determine whether they looked backward with nostalgia to aristocratic patronage or forward toward the public access to books that would occur in the future. In any case, a parallel could be drawn between this railing against the private ownership of books, except for "philosophes" and "les grands," and Diderot's disapproving attitude toward private purchase and display of paintings.[22]

Bollioud-Mermet went further than d'Alembert in providing reasons why a single citizen should abstain from bibliomania. A community, he claimed, could make reasonable use of a wide variety of books, but an individual could not because each person can only specialize in one thing: "The number of books necessary for each citizen is limited. All that exceeds, becomes superfluity or overweening ambition."[23] The reason, he claims, is that no one can know all subjects with any convincing degree of profundity. While some have more aptitude for sciences, others for engineering, others for history, no one can successfully embrace all aspects of human knowledge. This idea alone sounds reasonable, but it assumes a rigid set of limitations for each potential reader based on his or her social background. Bollioud-Mermet draws out the implications of this limitation: "Nothing seems more out of place than theological treatises in the library of a mathematician, or works on physics in that of a rhetorician."[24] The assumption underlying such statements is that individuals cannot freely choose to read about a field outside their training.

An insufficiently educated person in the field of letters, or "the unlettered man,"[25] is thus trapped within the limits of his formal schooling, which is itself determined by the social circumstances he is born into. We can imagine the sort of person Bollioud-Mermet has in mind when he cites an example of a man "who by commerce or financial operations has amassed a great fortune and acquired by purchase a title of nobility" and who now wants to appear as a "man of universal tastes."[26] He has nothing but scorn for men who "by a defective education [are] debarred from the advantages of study, whose very occupation deprive[s] them of leisure and taste, [and] who none the less make pretensions to form libraries."[27] Bibliomania, in the case of the nouveaux riches, constitutes one aspect of their social climbing. If they lack a solid educational background, Bollioud-Mermet ridicules any attempt to fill gaps of knowledge through the acquisition of books. Admittedly, he may have targeted specific types of people who bragged of their book collections without reading or understanding the texts—surely a reasonable complaint. However, *De la bibliomanie*'s view of the human being assumes that anyone who wished to explore literature outside his own profession, especially those of humble backgrounds, was subject to a fit of delusional arrogance. This injunction that every member of society stay in his or her place finds its parallel in exhortations to ordinary people who aspire to become writers, such as Voltaire's *Pauvre diable*, in which he tells bad poets to get a real job, so to speak.

By pushing aside the "homme non lettré," Bollioud-Mermet and the Encyclopedists establish the authority of the professional in judging intellectual matters. The scholar or the *philosophe*, according to the treatises above, deserves access to books because only he is capable of absorbing the intellectual value of the book. As Metz remarks in his study of bibliomania through the ages, "The bibliomaniac is the counterpart of the scholar; he is the oppressed and excluded other of scholarship."[28] This distinction is surely reinforced by the fact that institutionally affiliated scholars were the ones writing these treatises—Bollioud-Mermet was the secretary of the Académie de Lyon and d'Alembert could boast of his position as member and secretary of the Académie Française, among other credentials.

Furthermore, Bollioud-Mermet concludes that only *gens de lettres* can act as gatekeepers of all disciplines; their profession "should be exempt from the contagion" so that they can control the disease of bibliomania that would otherwise "invade every other profession."[29] The texts on bibliomania imply, then, that the *gens de lettres* have an obligation to control the rising tide of bad books because people of other professions cannot do it for themselves. Only philosophers, scientists, and other self-appointed experts have the judgment and education to discern the good from the bad.

In these writers' opinion, one step that intellectuals can take toward the restitution of good taste involves the elimination of large quantities of books. For instance, in "Bibliomanie," d'Alembert gives us an exemplary account of an intellectual who wisely chooses the best pieces of literature and burns the superfluous pages: "I have heard one of the most intelligent men of this century say that he had managed to create for himself, by a singular method, a very well-chosen and somewhat abundant library, which does not occupy much space. If he buys, for example, a work in twelve volumes, in which there are only six pages that deserve to be read, he separates these six pages from the rest and throws the rest in the fire. This way of creating a library would suit me well enough."[30] The same impulse to burn unnecessary pages of books for the sake of universal improvement appears in Louis-Sébastien Mercier's futuristic utopian world of *L'An deux mille quatre cent quarante*. He recounts how society was saved though a massive book burning,[31] in which a pile of dictionaries, novels, poems, funeral orations, and other texts were collected into a "Tower of Babel." They were then set on fire as an "expiatory sacrifice to veracity, to good sense, and true taste."[32] This supposed liberation from bad books is cited by Roger Chartier in his *Lectures et lecteurs dans la France d'Ancien Régime*, but Chartier claims that Mercier's sentiments were unfamiliar to his contemporaries, in particular the idea that "the book can be an obstacle as much as an aid in the search for truth."[33] But as we have just seen, these sentiments had been expressed in the satires of bibliomania.

This reduction of libraries to a minimum implies that readers— ordinary readers, not *gens de lettres*—needed to be saved from their own bad taste. Bewildered by the large quantities of texts surround-

ing them, readers could supposedly do no more than grab the first
things they laid their hands on or be dazzled by deceptively enticing
titles or pretty bindings. Since the majority of readers had not undergone the training necessary to be professional thinkers, according to
the latter, they lacked the judgment to penetrate through the multitude of books and find those few pages of true wisdom and beauty.

These writings about bibliomania evoke several trends that belie
the popular view of the Enlightenment. They demonstrate to us that
the idealized progress of learning, advocated by philosophers such as
Francis Bacon, actually met with doubt among certain eighteenth-
century writers. Even the invention of the printing press, widely
hailed by modern intellectuals as an important step toward Enlightenment, provoked ambiguous reactions from Bollioud-Mermet and
his fellows. Even though he starts his treatise by paying his respects
to the "advancement of study" and to the "art, as ingenious as admirable, of printing,"[34] his treatise emphasizes the negative aspects
of the printing press far more. He reflects: "It is still a moot question
whether the invention of printing has contributed more to the progress of letters and the perfection of ethics than to their injury."[35] The
idea that humanist learning is open, and advisable, to people of all
classes and professions is more recent than we tend to think. By contrast, these texts arguing against the proliferation of books show us
a hostile sense of protectiveness in regard to knowledge and a view
of human beings as locked in their profession and class. For instance,
Bollioud-Mermet compares the bibliomaniac to a blind man: "As well
might one born blind devote himself to the collecting of paintings
and expect you to regard him as a connoisseur of art."[36] However,
Bollioud-Mermet would never take into consideration that though a
blind man may be blind forever, an aspiring connoisseur, with some
effort and will, could one day break into the realm of the intellect.

METROMANIA: FOOLISH READERS BECOME WRITERS

If the public had to be discouraged from their book-buying frenzy, it
was only for their own good, according to certain critics. After all,
when those afflicted with bibliomania reached an advanced state of
illness, they were subject to the even more pernicious effects of *métromanie*, or the rage to write verse. In this scenario, ordinary people,
driven mad with enthusiasm for books they could not understand,
started to believe they could be authors themselves. The phenomenon

can be compared to Don Quixote's misguided enthusiasm for knight-errantry, Bouvard and Pécuchet's awkward attempts to participate in high art, or the improbable aspirations among young people in our day to become actors or models. Literature allegedly held an equal fascination for the imagination of the eighteenth-century public. In all the examples above, but most pertinently for the aspiring writer, such ambitions held several dangers. First, according to critiques, the majority of aspirants were doomed to fail because they lacked both training and good judgment. Second, in pursuing a chimera, they sacrificed the modest but solid advantages of their worldly position. And finally, they left themselves open to the ridicule of the satirical observer, through whose eyes we witness their fall.

Alexis Piron satirized this frenzy in his 1738 comedy *La Métromanie*, in which he depicts an advanced case of a foolish reader-turned-writer. In this play, the protagonist, Damis, abandons his bourgeois life to pursue his dream of becoming a full-time poet and playwright. His respectable uncle Baliveau tries to convince him that the poetic career is a miserable state in which one belongs to no class and performs no useful service to society. Baliveau exclaims:

> So he will versify! What a great way to live!
> To become famous, but only for his madness!
> To be, so to speak, a man outside of any rank
> And the titled plaything of the small and the great!
> Consider the members of the profession he has chosen.
> Either laziness or vanity has produced this race.
> Amidst idle people, it can triumph,
> But in a well-regulated state, it should be suffocated.[37]

The moral of the play is that instead of yielding to this sickly rash,[38] Damis should accept the fortune, the familial duties, and the marriage that are due to him.

His folly is echoed and amplified by another character, Francaleu, the elderly man who takes on the persona of a female poet in the pieces he submits to the journal *Mercure de France*. Ironically, Damis himself criticizes the older Francaleu's obsession with poetry, calling it "an itch / That brings shame to rhyme as much as to reason."[39] In the end, Damis is punished by the humiliating revelation that the lady with whom he had been having a platonic but flirtatious exchange of poetry in the *Mercure* is in fact Francaleu himself. The final blow to Damis's ego comes with the news that his play has failed on the first night, a disappointment that leads him to reenter the place he was meant to occupy in the world, according to his family. Thus the metromaniac is duly corrected.

While Piron's satire focuses on aspiring poets and playwrights, Charles Palissot de Montenoy's 1760 comedy *Les Philosophes* attacks those who fall under the spell of the famous philosophers of his day. Although Palissot declared war on the *philosophe* party, with the exception of Voltaire, his message paradoxically leads in the same direction as his enemies' texts that warn against the excesses of reading. The plot and, to some extent, the message of Palissot's play imitate the model of Molière's comedies that ridicule inappropriate learning, such as *Les Femmes savantes* and *Les Précieuses ridicules*. Palissot presents a foolish reader, Cydalise, an ignorant but wealthy lady who becomes so obsessed with the writings of the *philosophes* that she starts to believe she can be one herself. Like the *femmes savantes*, Cydalise is seized with an extravagant passion for knowledge but is unable to fully absorb it.

Her understanding of philosophy (for which the *philosophes* are blamed) makes her renounce all conventions, an attitude Palissot exaggerates in order to convince the audience of her general error. For instance, she presents her daughter Rosalie with rational arguments against maternal love and against loyalty to her dead husband, all "vulgar ties."[40] She supposedly incurs the disapproval of the audience (if one is not already upset that she opposes the marriage plans of the two virtuous youths, Rosalie and Damis) by denouncing the arbitrary nature of loyalty to one's country and by declaring the uselessness of keeping one's word. In short, her love of philosophy has led to her escape from constraints that the reader or spectator presumably respects. With her contempt for these ideals, this character confirms the dangers of reading.

Perhaps if she met Palissot's standards for true intellectualism, her unconventional opinions might seem more justified, but Palissot demonstrates that her self-proclaimed erudition is nothing but a badly digested consumption of books, encouraged by unscrupulous *philosophes* who scheme to get her money.[41] When called upon to express an idea, she is incapable of using clear terms or rational thought:

> I believe, in fact,
> That an excellent work shows itself in the smallest trait.
> It's a *je ne sais quoi* . . . that seizes our soul . . .
> You feel it . . . well, it's the attraction of genius.[42]

Rather than using the aesthetically sanctioned expression *je ne sais quoi* as Bouhours or Pascal theorized it,[43] she literally does not know what to say. All she can do is resort to trendy catchwords and to a vague appeal to emotions that her interlocutor supposedly shares. Perhaps more dangerously, Cydalise wishes to become a philosopher in her own right. She lacks the necessary training, however, as we see when one of the other characters teases her about her philosophical background, unbeknownst to her:

Carondas: But tell me then how all this happened.
You must know everything that's been written . . .
What? You haven't read the erudite Vossius?

Cydalise: No, never.

Carondas: Casaubon?

Cydalise: Even less.

Carondas: Grotius?

Cydalise: Not at all. Are those works by a woman? . . .

Carondas: You at least know Thales, Anaxagoras?

Cydalise: No.

Carondas: *The Natural Son?*

Cydalise: Oh, that one, okay.
Those are the writings that you should mention right at the beginning.[44]

Once again, her only recourse is to sensibility, since the one text she knows is the *comédie larmoyante* of Diderot. Carondas's interrogation of Cydalise demonstrates the idea that a good reader, and even more a respectable writer, must build upon a certain educational foundation. In political theory, that foundation would include precisely the writers above: Vossius, Casaubon, and Grotius. Like many foolish readers depicted in satire, Cydalise believes she can appear upon the intellectual scene without any special training and with exposure only to the most trivial kinds of works (or those that Palissot judges to be trivial): Diderot's comedies and works by women, supposedly sentimental novels.

Her deficient education leads her to wander aimlessly in various fields of knowledge under the illusion that she can cover all of them. Just as Bollioud-Mermet frowns upon any ordinary person who tries to master a large number of disparate disciplines, Palissot shows us Cydalise's misguided desire to embrace all knowledge. In her book, she claims,

I concisely treat the mind, good sense,
The passions, laws and governments;
Virtue, mores, climate, customs;
Civilized peoples and savages;
Apparent disorder, universal order,
Ideal happiness, and real happiness.
I carefully examine the principles of things,
The secret chain of causes and effects.
I have written a profound chapter expressly for you;
I want to entitle it: *Duties as they are.*
Well, it's an encyclopedia of morals,
And Valère calls it a work of genius.[45]

In this long list of subjects, Palissot evokes the idea of excess—too many subjects, too many words, just as there are too many books falling into the wrong hands.

If Cydalise is blind to her own incompetence, she is abetted by the *philosophes* who frequent her salon and try to charm her into giving them money. While she brags about the book she is writing, they secretly laugh at her because they are the ones who are dictating ideas and words to her. Palissot's satire aims at the gullibility of the Cydalises of the world as well as those who use philosophy as a cover for dishonest motives. As in Bollioud-Mermet's essay, the idea of a swindle has a prominent place in the critique of foolish readers and writers. If non-experts insist on participating in the world of letters, Palissot seems to say, they can only fall prey to unscrupulous producers of false knowledge.

In texts such as Palissot's, literature becomes a market in which anyone can trick another for profit. To illustrate their dishonesty in the most concrete terms, one of the *philosophes* actually picks the pocket of another while the latter harangues him on the virtues of self-interest. Later, in planning how they will make Cydalise's future book successful, the *philosophes* Carondas and Valère overtly mock the reading public as easily manipulated. When Carondas asks whether they can make the public believe the merits of a bad book, Valère responds, "We know how to prescribe / How it must think, speak, judge, write; / We will easily make up its mind."[46] Their parasitical nature recalls Villiers's complaint that publishers deceive people into buying books by imitating the titles of famous works. The charlatans in Palissot's comedy are finally unmasked in the end when they are discovered, by means of a lost letter, to have plagiarized their works directly from ancient writers.

In considering these texts that ridicule bibliomania and metromania, we can see several common traits emerge: first, the necessity of confining people within their social category and protecting them from the destabilizing influence of reading, and second, the fearful evocation of the literary world as a market, one that unfairly dissociates value and price. One suggested solution is to limit the numbers of books—though it is hard to gauge the seriousness of satirists and other writers when they call for the destruction of books through burning. In any case, they express a general preference for ignorance over false erudition. The availability of books apparently gives people the false impression that they can transcend their caste, sex, and educational limitations. But without the proper training, the love of books can become an illness or a madness, which can make people sacrifice their real social interests to follow an improbable career, as in the case of the protagonist of *La Métromanie*, or to reject social obligations, as in *Les Philosophes*. What the texts discussed above imply is that people should tend to what is useful in their social station, such as marriage and procreation, rather than attempt to reach the higher realm of the intellect.

This lack of judgment among foolish readers can be seen as a lack of taste, if taste can be defined as the ability to discern good from bad literature. These texts place a rigid barrier between those who understand literature and those who merely own books; they convey the message that taste is something that certain people lack, and these tasteless hordes are essentially different from those who have taste. In fact, the tasteful few hardly even appear in the comic works I cite above. The sympathetic characters depicted in the plays by Piron and Palissot are not *savants* but limited people (the bourgeois uncle in *La Métromanie*, Cydalise's daughter Rosalie in *Les Philosophes*) who joyfully accept their humble role in life.

THE CURSE OF THE PRINTING PRESS

These texts by Bollioud-Mermet, d'Alembert, Piron, Palissot, and others effectively enjoin the public to keep its distance from literature: this message contrasts remarkably with Condorcet's description of the triumphal spread of learning in his 1795 treatise *Outlines of an Historical View of the Progress of the Human Mind*. How can we explain these opposing views? While historians of the book such as Henri-Jean Martin tend to cite laudatory comments about the book trade from eighteenth-century writers, they assume that the opinions expressed during the Revolutionary period represent those of the whole century. For instance, in *Le Livre français sous l'Ancien Régime*, Martin cites a number of statements about Gutenberg and the invention of printing from the fifteenth to the twentieth centuries. After quickly passing over the eighteenth century, he jumps to Revolutionary harangues calling for the sanctification of Gutenberg among the great men of the Pantheon. In Martin's narrative, there is no negative reaction to the proliferation of books until the nineteenth century.[47]

If one puts secondary sources aside, however, one can see in the words of eighteenth-century writers that their attitudes toward printing were actually ambivalent. Their views can be sorted into two tendencies: enthusiastically pro-books (arguing that democratized reading spreads Enlightenment) and anti-books (calling for a restriction in the number of books, writers, and readers). The first opinion is expressed not throughout the century but mostly around the time of the Revolution. The second position is represented mostly in the earlier part of the eighteenth century in the works of the satirists and essayists I mentioned above and in works by the most prominent *philosophes*, such as Rousseau, Voltaire, and Diderot.

Montesquieu is one of the rare voices from early in the century that hailed the printing press as a means for people to inform themselves, in defiance of their leaders' secretive policies: "The invention of printing, which has put books into the hands of all the world; the improvements in engraving, which have made geographic charts so common, in a word, the establishment of political papers, give every individual a knowledge of a general interest, sufficient enough to instruct him in all the private transactions [*des faits secrets*]."[48] This idea would reappear much more frequently at the end of the century, especially in the writings of Condorcet and Germaine de Staël.

In fact, Condorcet makes the very history of humanity, in his *Outlines of an Historical View of the Progress of the Human Mind*, hinge upon the invention of the printing press: "In short," he exclaims, "is it not the press that has freed the instruction of the people from every political and religious chain?"[49] For Condorcet, this groundbreaking event marks the emergence of the world from medieval ignorance, which keeps the people subjected to tyranny, to the modern era, which is ready to march toward universal Enlightenment. In contrast to the idea of decadence that was more often evoked earlier in the century, Condorcet famously makes the case for progress. Specifically, his enthusiasm for widespread literacy refutes every aspect of bibliomania, since he insists on the advantages of seeing persons of all classes with a book in their hand: "The art of printing had been applied to so many subjects, books had so rapidly increased, they were so admirably adapted to every taste, every degree of information, and every situation of life, they afforded so easy and frequently so delightful an instruction, they had opened so many doors to truth, which it was impossible ever to close again, that there was no longer a class or profession of mankind from whom the light of knowledge could absolutely be excluded."[50] Even autodidacticism, which is condemned by Bollioud-Mermet, is celebrated here: "That instruction which is to be acquired from books in silence and solitude can never be universally corrupted."[51]

Equally enthusiastic is Germaine de Staël when she goes so far as to declare, "Printing has founded the human race,"[52] in her 1797 essay *Des circonstances actuelles qui peuvent terminer la révolution et des principes qui doivent fonder la république en France*. In Staël's view, the rise in literacy and the access to books are closely tied to the idea of the "perfectibility of the human mind"[53] because they set humankind's scientific discoveries on firm grounding and consequently allow people to build upon previous knowledge.

Perhaps similarly swept away by Revolutionary fervor, Louis-Sébastien Mercier seemed to change his views about books toward the end of the century. After having expressed his book-burning fantasies in *L'An 2440*, he wrote numerous statements of enthusiastic support for printing ten years later in another publication, *Le Tableau de Paris*. He remarks that "the invention of printing is a divine present given to men"[54] precisely for the same reasons Montesquieu cited decades earlier: printing can reveal the truth and prevent corrupt leaders from deceiving their subjects. It is difficult to explain Mercier's turnaround on the proliferation of books, and he offers none himself.

Although Mercier (in his later works), Condorcet, and Staël took different ideological positions in relation to the actual Revolution and its successive governments, they all asserted that the perfectibility of man through reading was desirable in the new society that was being founded. All looked upon readers and writers with indulgence, without discriminating between educated or uneducated readers or between grave scientific treatises and popular novels.

Expressing a high regard for the spread of books and literacy is hardly surprising to us in the twenty-first century, since this viewpoint is now widely accepted in our society. Significantly, the French and American republics were founded exactly at the time when writers were expressing unbounded trust in the spread of learning, and this enthusiasm has remained, for example, in educational policy. These ideas should therefore seem familiar to us; it is the opposing view that tends to be overlooked: the deep distrust, even among the most well-known *philosophes*, of proliferating books and readers.[55]

While the printing enthusiasts commonly affirmed that access to knowledge prevents leaders from deceiving their subjects, those who denounce printing had an interesting variation on this idea, namely, that it is the printed books that deceive the public. Voltaire takes this complaint to an extreme by calling libelous publications the worst vice of the eighteenth century, claiming that no other century in history has suffered from them so much. For example, in his 1749 pamphlet "Des Mensonges imprimés" ("Of Printed Lies") he rages against those who produced a spurious *Testament de Richelieu*. He blames the unscrupulous Dutch printers, who, as merchants, simply commissioned works that would sell, without any regard for truth. Authors, meanwhile, were so abject that they needed to prostitute their pen—an idea Voltaire also expressed in the preface to his 1759 *Histoire de l'empire de Russie sous Pierre le Grand*, in which he explains why so many lies have been printed about historical figures: "A Dutch bookseller orders a book to be written, just as a manufacturer gives directions for weaving a piece of cloth; and unhappily there are authors to be found, whose necessities oblige them to sell their labors to these dealers, like workmen, for hire; hence arise these insipid panegyrics, and defamatory libels, with which the public is overrun, and is one of the most shameful vices of the age."[56]

Voltaire conjures up the image of the book trade as no more sublime than the fabric trade, particularly when he stubbornly refuses to use the term *belles lettres* and refers instead to "this trade of printed paper"[57] in "Des Mensonges imprimés." He questions even the motivations behind the public's desire to read: "Now every person reads, either to cultivate or adorn his mind, or, at the least, that he may be able to boast of his reading."[58] While the printers were guilty of rapaciousness, according to Voltaire, the readers and writers were no less guilty.

Like Mercier's book-burning episode in *L'An 2440* and d'Alembert's distillation of the bibliomaniac's library to a minuscule remnant, Voltaire's "Des Mensonges imprimés" presents the image of "an im-

mense library, without ten pages of truth in the whole collection."[59]
Is printing ever worthwhile? Certainly, he admits, though one has to
know how to wade through the mire of bad books of the past and
present: "amongst all those lies, are there no truths? Yes, such a proportion as of gold dust in the sands of some rivers."[60] With the image
of a few flecks of gold in the muddy sediment of a river, he transmits
to us a pessimistic idea of the rarity of good literature among the
pseudo-intellectual dross.

Sympathetic to this idea that printing has done more harm than
good are Diderot's and d'Alembert's narrations of the progress of human thought. Diderot, known far and wide as the author of inspiring
treatises on the equality of humankind and against tyranny (for example, the article "Autorité politique" in the *Encyclopédie*), also com-
plained about too many books. For example, in his 1763 *Lettre sur le
commerce de la librairie*, he calls for a legal limitation of the number
of publishers in France, which will raise, he claims, the intellectual
level of printed works. To make his argument, he takes the time to
explain what he calls the history of printing. In Gutenberg's time, he
writes, printers who established themselves in France produced only
small, inferior works: "it was not with Homer, or with Virgil, or with
any author of this caliber that the nascent art of printing took its first
steps. It began with small works of little value, of little scope, and
in the taste of a barbarian century."[61] These works of low intellectual value, such as the *Rule of Saint Francis* (the guide for Franciscan
monks), Diderot tells us, sold well because the public was intrigued
by the novelty of having books at all. He even refers to himself as a
bibliomane who collects these curious objects for their historical rarity rather than their content.

Subsequently, printers decided to print good works, which he calls
"esteemed works" or "learned books."[62] Unfortunately, only true *savants*, who tended to be poor and restricted in number, bought these
volumes, and the book trade could not sustain itself by selling just
the works of the greats, whom he lists as Corneille, Racine, Voltaire,
Bayle, Moréri, Pliny, and Newton. Therefore, the book trade had to
resort to printing less-than-respectable books to survive, such as religious pamphlets implicated in controversies and other ephemeral
works. The overly numerous publishers, desperate to sell any productions of dubious quality, caused the downfall of literature, a situation
that leads him to call for reform in this particular treatise. Whatever
his strategic purpose in writing this treatise may be, it does not have a

demagogic aim but an exclusivist one. The perfectibility of the human race never plays a part in this work, since Diderot creates an essential separation between intellectuals ("érudits"), who are rare in number, and the ignorant general public.

The history of printing in the Preliminary Discourse to the *Encyclopédie* by Diderot and d'Alembert shows us an even more elaborate view of printing as a mixed blessing, based on the ideas of excess and restraint. Gutenberg's invention marked the period when Europe began emerging from the "dark times"[63] of ignorance, the authors state. At the same time, ancient Greek and Latin texts were rediscovered, but in this early period, people were only capable of compiling and copying the ancients in a servile way, without discernment. It was easy to accumulate knowledge, claimed the authors dismissively, just as the treatises on bibliomania disdained the excess number of books. They claim that once the Age of Reason arrived, the *érudits* decided to use this new faculty to sort through the mass of knowledge and choose only the worthwhile portions: "The realm of erudition and of facts is inexhaustible; the effortless acquisitions made in it lead one to think that one's substance is continually growing, so to speak. On the contrary, the realm of reason and of discoveries is rather small. Through study in that realm, men often succeed only in unlearning what they thought they knew, instead of learning what they did not know."[64] In this text, the idea of large quantities of authors or texts is inimical to the idea of good literature: the sixteenth century produced "a multitude of Latin poets, orators, and historians,"[65] but for the *philosophes*, the culmination of intellectual progress would involve purging the excessive number of books that characterized the earlier stage of development.

Rousseau went further than his peers and represented a particularly extreme case of book-hating, which seems to be at odds with the egalitarianism of his political essays. The idea of too many of books provoked his ire, and in his 1750 *Discours sur les sciences et les arts*, he persuades his readers that humankind would be better off without "the art of perpetuating the extravagances of the human mind."[66] His principal motive, as he explains in the rest of his essay, concerns the unfortunate recourse to books instead of the more salutary use of personal experience to gain philosophical knowledge.[67] This view also appears in the *Encyclopédie* article "Livre" as one of the disadvantages of books. But Rousseau's harangue against books, inferior authors, and ignorant readers takes the Voltaire/Diderot/d'Alembert line of argument a step further and denounces the whole realm of arts and sciences, to which he himself belonged.

Rousseau's denunciation of intellectual activity, upon closer scrutiny, depends on a hierarchization of superior writers, inferior writers, and the multitude of readers: "But if the development of the sciences and arts has added nothing to our true felicity, if it has corrupted our morals, and if the corruption of morals has impaired our purity of taste, what shall we think of that crowd of elementary Authors who have removed the difficulties that blocked access to the Temple of the Muses and that nature put there as a test of strength for those who might be tempted to learn?"[68] In this passage, taste is an important factor in his chain of deplorable events, since he blames the arts and sciences for corrupting our morals, and, as an ultimate consequence, the "purity of taste" is compromised. He describes his ideal of literature as a "Temple des Muses" whose access is barred by the metaphorical barriers of "difficulties," placed there by Nature herself. This ideal has been destroyed by scheming sub-authors, who invent ways to vulgarize knowledge (for example, through compilations) and to let the profane multitudes enter the temple: "What shall we think of those Compilers of works who have indiscreetly broken down the door of Sciences and let into their Sanctuary a populace unworthy of approaching it; whereas it would be preferable for all who could not go far in the career of Letters to be rebuffed from the outset and directed into Arts useful to society. He who will be a bad versifier or a subaltern Geometer all his life would perhaps have become a great cloth maker."[69] In Rousseau's vision, the writers are just as guilty as the readers, the "unworthy populace" ("populace indigne"). Like Voltaire, he degrades the book trade by putting it in the same category as other types of commerce—again, cloth manufacturers. Furthermore, Rousseau claims that posterity will reproach him and his contemporaries for allowing the production of bad books. He imagines future generations crying out to their God, "deliver us from the enlightenment and the fatal arts of our fathers, and give us back ignorance, innocence, and poverty."[70] Rousseau proposes ignorance as a preferable alternative to excessive, inappropriate knowledge. Although Rousseau and Diderot are associated with Revolutionary ideals of equality, they actually asserted an elitist belief in a strict, almost sacred separation between culture and the "populace." In their view, communication between the two had to be controlled by the *philosophes*, lest vulgarizers of scholarly works do it wrongly and consequently corrupt the public.

The place of the writer in, or rather outside, society as described in Alexis Piron's *La Métromanie* recalls the problematic situation in the texts on bibliomania. Can one be an artisan, a bourgeois, and still read and write poetry? The answer in these texts is no. The question of how true poets and philosophers fit into the social hierarchy remains unanswered. Instead, Voltaire, Diderot, and their fellows upheld the idea that only true *gens de lettres* like themselves had the right to act as intermediaries between the realm of the mind and the mass of readers. These authors insisted on their special training that set them apart from the majority of the public[71] and on their intangible sense of judgment or taste, which remained elusive to others. For an ordinary person to attempt to practice literature was, in their view, as impracticable as for that person to practice cutlery or clock-making without the proper apprenticeship. The abbé Dubos, writing several decades before Diderot and d'Alembert, also discouraged people from the writing profession, comparing a writer's training to that of a navigator or a doctor: "He that is not a pilot, says Horace, ought not to stand at the helm. Those who have not studied the virtue of simples, should not pretend to make up medicines. None but physicians ought to prescribe bleeding to patients. Even the very meanest trades are not practiced 'till after an apprenticeship; but every body, capable or incapable, will dabble in verses."[72] What solution did these writers propose to clear the Republic of Letters of inferior writers? They would institute some sort of law: the ideal of taste. Consequently, numerous treatises of the period served the double purpose of defining good taste and crushing any dissent through disapprobation and ridicule. The ideal of taste was a useful way for certain writers to claim the power to judge the whole literary world, since the requirements of taste included a set of rules to which the less-favored aspirants to the status of intellectual would be held, but these rules would also be vague enough that even if one followed all the rules, one could still be found wanting.

The writings that separated good taste from bad revealed many assumptions about readers, especially regarding what he (and often she) lacked in order to make judgments. Various aesthetic theories, such as those of Batteux and Voltaire, purportedly granted the authority of judging art, including literature, to the public. However, they eventually make it clear that by "public" they are in fact referring to an elite, and one that agrees on the merits of works of art. Once the critics laid the groundwork for proving that the literary world was overcrowded with ignorant people, these critics could start dictating rules for exclusion on the grounds of taste.

A NOTE ON KITSCH

Several people have asked me whether the bad taste that I deal with in this study can be considered as kitsch. It is reasonable to make the connection between bad taste and kitsch, since they both concern the ugly, the tacky, the vulgar, and the devalorization of art through popular consumption. But can one apply the concept of kitsch to the problems of bibliomania and metromania? The first problem that comes to mind is anachronism. Theodor Adorno, Max Horkheimer, and Clement Greenberg, as well as Matei Calinescu, author of *Five Faces of Modernity*, have all assumed that kitsch objects (such as Disney movies or miniature reproductions of Michelangelo sculptures) must be the product of a modern age in which objects are reproduced mechanically. For this reason, their field of inquiry begins only in the industrial revolutions of the nineteenth century. Nevertheless, if one extends the idea of mechanical reproduction to the production of books, then the issues of kitsch can perhaps be transposed to the early modern era, since the printing press allowed a mass production of sorts. Furthermore, when dealing with books, Greenberg does focus on industrialization as much as the growth in literacy. He muses: "Kitsch is a product of the industrial revolution which urbanized the masses of Western Europe and America and established what is called universal literacy."[73] Although universal literacy had not been achieved in eighteenth-century France, the large increase in literacy surely had a major influence in the issues of taste that the *philosophes* grappled with.

Thus if one accepts the printing press as an early instance of mass production, kitsch and its repercussions do seem to apply to the book trade of eighteenth-century France. For example, critics in the early modern and modern eras deplore the use of art as a mere leisure activity. Greenberg specifically explains the existence of kitsch as the introduction of art, in a debased form, into the worker's daily life. Since this man's heavy burden of labor leaves him only a small amount of leisure, he requires art that is easily digestible and immediately gratifying. He does not have, Greenberg states, "enough leisure, energy and comfort to train for the enjoyment of Picasso."[74] By contrast, it is up to the experts to study difficult or avant-garde art. The opposition

Greenberg makes between these two different types of consumers of art and their capabilities recalls the eighteenth-century critics' insistence on the necessary distinction between the *érudits* and the rest of the population. The importance of "training" to understand Picasso also parallels Voltaire's insistence that the aesthetic experience be partially based on training—in the rules of theater or in ancient languages, for example.

Another explanation for kitsch concerns Thorstein Veblen's idea of "conspicuous consumption," which certainly reverberates in Bollioud-Mermet's *De la bibliomanie*. As an example of this type of kitsch, Calinescu refers to people who built their modern homes in the form of miniaturized castles and filled them with artistic objects, in imitation of what they believed to be the aristocratic life. Calinescu cites this very example from Tocqueville's visit to America. According to this explanation of kitsch, the nouveaux riches, Calinescu remarks, are "trying to imitate the old aristocracy and its patterns of consumption. . . . The art they liked, created and bought mainly as a sign of social status, no longer had to perform its difficult aesthetic function."[75] In this passage, Calinescu offers a definition of kitsch that is related to bibliomania: the confusion of art and luxury. Likewise, Bollioud-Mermet specifically criticized social climbers who wanted to give themselves the semblance of taste and aspired to amass private libraries in imitation of the *grands seigneurs* but without understanding the content of their books.

Finally, like Adorno and Greenberg, the eighteenth-century critics assumed that the public made its choices in a passive way, thus becoming prey to unscrupulous manipulation in the market. Villiers worried that dishonest booksellers could pass off worthless copies of books that purported to be in the style of La Bruyère, while Horkheimer and Adorno deplored the second- and third-rate film experiences offered by the cliché-ridden Donald Duck films.[76] It is ironic that the twentieth-century Marxists Adorno and Greenberg, as well as the Enlightenment *philosophes* who questioned political authority, denied that the masses could be trusted to select their own art.

CHAPTER TWO

What Is Good Taste?

It would be impossible to undertake a discussion of bad taste without first considering the standard of good taste, a term that was notoriously difficult to define, even among its self-appointed defenders. The *Dictionnaire de Trévoux*, an authority on matters of erudition in the eighteenth century, gives us a glimpse of the confusion surrounding the word *taste*. The author of the article "Goust" ("Taste") points out, "it is much easier to say what is not taste, good and bad taste, than to mark precisely what it is."[1] He equates taste with "judgment" or "discernment," while explaining to us what taste is *not*: "it is not difficult to establish that *esprit* and taste are not the same thing. . . . It is also easy to see that taste does not come from learning; one can have a lot of knowledge, a brilliant mind, and very bad taste."[2] In the 1721 edition, the author also includes a formidable list of quotations about taste by various writers of the previous century.[3] For instance,

> [Madeleine de Scudéry]. Good taste is a natural sentiment that one cannot learn or teach; it must be inborn. Consequently, we should not look down on those who do not have it; we do not have the evidence in our hands to prove to them that they are wrong. [Saint-Evremond]. Good taste comes only from an exquisite and precise knowledge of how to judge good from bad, concerning matters of propriety and charm of all sorts; one only acquires it with a great deal of care and reflection. [Chevalier de Méré]. Bad authors spoil the taste of the public by accustoming it to bland and insipid things.[4]

The overwhelming amount of information he presents in this dictionary entry, with its multiple, sometimes contradictory quotations from various authors, leaves us without any certainty about the concept. However, the litany of quotations reveals both the continued dialogue between seventeenth- and eighteenth-century thinkers and the impossibility of deciding on an all-encompassing definition of taste.

To approach the definition of taste from another angle, let us enter the intimidating temple of taste (as Voltaire's and Alexander Pope's allegories depict it) through a small side door, guided by a little-known writer with whom we are by now familiar, Bollioud-Mermet. Aside from his anti-bibliomanie treatise, he penned an essay against his contemporaries' taste in music, *De la corruption du goust dans la musique française*, or *On the Corruption of Taste in French Music*. In this text, his enraged disapproval gave him the impetus to attempt to define the term *good taste*: "good taste is what *conforms to nature*; what is approved by *reason*; what is *neither exaggerated nor affected*; what pleases *our senses*; what seduces our *heart*; what *interests* us; that in which we find *nothing that shocks us, nothing that revolts us*; what *famous artists have most universally practiced*; what *true connoisseurs admire*. Everything that does not have these qualities can only be in bad taste" (emphasis added).[5] This passage contains, in a nutshell, many of the elements that theoreticians and celebrated writers attempted to develop in their discussions of taste. Bollioud-Mermet's definition, with its vagueness and circular reasoning, illustrates the challenge that he and his contemporaries faced in trying to define taste.

First, he demands that art conform to nature, an idea that he also expresses negatively by rejecting its opposite, the affected. But what nature does he refer to? The literary critics of the eighteenth century, following their immediate predecessors in the seventeenth century as well as the ancients, codified "nature" and "the natural" in highly specific ways that defy our present-day expectations about the meaning of this word. The word *nature* is a perfect example of a polemical term disguising itself as a term of universal consensus. Batteux, as I will explain later in this chapter, would enjoin poets and painters to copy nature but not to choose just any object to depict because the objects in our midst may happen to be ugly or damaged. The artist must choose an ideal example of the species or an assemblage of the perfect parts of several models, as in the legend of Zeuxis,[6] but this requirement sends us back to the problem of what ideal the model should be held up to.

Jean Ehrard addresses precisely this problem in *L'Idée de nature en France à l'aube des Lumières*. Regarding Batteux's injunction to "imitate beautiful nature" or "imiter la belle nature," Ehrard asks, "But how do we choose what aspect of Nature should be reproduced? How do we decide that one 'part' is more beautiful than another if we have not defined beauty to begin with? So we return to the beginning point, and thus Batteux's whole work is reduced to a tautology—in order to be beautiful, a work of art must imitate beautiful nature—unless we admitted once and for all that antiquity possesses the privilege of [determining] good taste."[7] Other conceptions of "nature," such as that found in Boileau's *Art poétique*,[8] rely on a classical principle that the author should meet the audience's expectations about a character's personality, as it is already known or as it is expected from his social category. For example, Achilles should be angry, young men should be impetuous, and servants should be cowardly. When Bollioud-Mermet, Batteux, and others call for artists to imitate nature, the entreaty brings us back to the conventional ideals of beauty, which are in turn founded on past conceptions of good taste. If we try to discern on what basis these past conceptions of good taste were founded, we return to the original problem: What is good taste?

Aside from the unresolved question of what *nature* means, Bollioud-Mermet's definition of good taste brings up a second problem. His concept of good taste depends on how art should touch us emotionally, as he indicates with his use of the words *heart* and *interest*.[9] In his opinion, our appreciation of good art should spring spontaneously from us, while looking at bad art should give us an instinctive feeling of "shock" and "revulsion." But how does he know that what touches his heart also touches that of others?[10] By referring to "us," Bollioud-Mermet invents a community of people who agree with each other—and with him—but if I feel my heart moved by the sight of a Rubens painting, or if Virgil bores me, can my feelings be wrong? As we will see, the answer is yes: one's spontaneous feelings can be wrong.[11] Nevertheless, the sentiment prompted by art played an important role in the theories of taste, as a complement to learned expertise.

Finally, Bollioud-Mermet's definition of taste defers to a certain authority based on the consensus of an elite. Good taste, he implies, is what people of good taste practice, including the "best" artists and the "true" connoisseurs. The obvious problem here is that the very designation of these people as such depends on how good taste is defined. What I find especially important in this passage is the way in which Bollioud-Mermet, like others who define taste, simply invests himself with the authority of choosing the objects of good taste. Everything else "ne peut être que de mauvais goût."

One thing that he and the other critics agree on is that the concept of taste transcends rules. For example, many eighteenth-century definitions of taste insist that the enjoyment of a work of art must spring spontaneously from the viewer. This spontaneity, however, must be accompanied by training in distinguishing the details that compose the work of art. A person of taste must have a high degree of emotional sensitivity and knowledge of rules, so taste is sometimes said to be learned and sometimes said to occur naturally in a person. However, lest we imagine that the newly established importance of subjectivity of the viewer leads to complete arbitrariness, the tastemakers always return to the idea of correct and incorrect judgment of each work of art. According to theorists, there is only one correct way to feel about each work of art. "To each his own taste" is not an option for them.

This combination of rules and spontaneous feeling serves to exclude certain producers and consumers of literary works. An appropriate analogy would perhaps be the Jansenist idea of the necessary combination of good works (equivalent to knowing the classical literary conventions) and God's elusive grace (equivalent to the instinctive sense of taste) in order to get into heaven.[12] On the one hand, a writer could fail by disregarding rules of art such as the Aristotelean unities, Horatian decorum, or the constraints of genre, either deliberately or out of ignorance.[13] For writers to know these rules and for the reader to recognize them, they each needed to have a certain classical background, which presupposed certain social conditions that would make this education possible. Even if the writer knew to follow these rules, his work could still fail if his instinctive sense of taste, sometimes called the *je ne sais quoi*, was faulty.

Although good taste may have been difficult or even impossible to define, a number of authors and critics of the eighteenth century set themselves up as authorities on taste. It would be useful at this point to discuss the major figures among them, in particular to demonstrate what ideas they shared and how they explained the presence of bad taste in the world.

THE TASTEMAKERS

In this study, the authors whose opinions I will refer to are bound together by one common trait: they each attempted to prove that their definition of taste was universal and therefore rejected the supposedly bad taste of certain writers, styles, and genres. In other words, I will focus on authors who, in their publications, make a distinction between good and bad taste and seek to impose it on others. The group includes major and minor figures, ancients and moderns, academicians and non-academicians, those whom Cassirer calls empiricists and those he calls Cartesians, those who possess what Pascal calls *esprit de finesse* and those who possess *esprit géométrique*.

Who are these writers? Among the most prominent authors of the period, we find Montesquieu, Voltaire, Diderot, d'Alembert, Buffon, and Marmontel—who benefited from international fame, mutual respect for each other, and the security of institutional status, such as membership to scholarly academies and royal appointments. Of course, their status vis-à-vis the French government was often precarious: the court prevented Diderot's accession to the Académie Française, and most of these *philosophes* found themselves, at some time during their lives, in danger of censorship and arrest. However, their success and their intellectual preeminence could hardly be disputed during their lifetime.

While the *philosophes* often addressed the general public, perhaps in an effort to educate it, another group of thinkers did not attempt to popularize their ideas but instead addressed a restricted audience of educated people. This group includes Jean-Pierre de Crousaz, Yves-Marie André, François Cartaud de la Vilate, the marquise de Lambert, and Louis Bollioud-Mermet. Slightly more well-known theorists include Anne Dacier, Jean-Baptiste Dubos, and Charles Batteux. These authors' considerations about taste, while not necessarily known to the general public and while rarely mentioned in present-day scholarship, still exerted an important influence on aesthetic thought of the eighteenth century.

In this study I will also include the opinions of what one could call the foot soldiers of the war of taste. These writers lived on the fringes of literature; they sought to ingratiate themselves with more successful writers such as Voltaire but never really attained their status: for example, Louis-Sébastien Mercier, Charles Palissot de Montenoy, and Alexis Piron. Robert Darnton describes their plight in *The Literary Underground of the Old Régime*,[14] specifically in the chapter "The Low-Life of Literature." As Darnton points out, they espoused the ideology of the great *philosophes*, as we see in Piron's *Métromanie*, even though the *philosophes* usually looked down upon them and even considered them part of the riffraff trying to break into the world of letters. Nevertheless, these aspiring critics, who ultimately failed in their attempts to belong to the more prominent group, served a particular purpose. They put the abstract ideas of the Enlightenment philosophers and of the academic theorists into an entertaining form, which brought out the absurd implications of bad taste. Since these satirists did not leave behind any coherent theories of good taste but only attacked specific examples of what they saw as bad taste, I will not include them in the discussion of individual theories later in this chapter. Instead, they will instead make their appearance in the chapters that concern various types of perceived bad taste.

What binds all the different types of writers mentioned above is a web of cross-references: the *philosophes* constantly made generally approving references to each other and they often cited the lesser-known theorists that I cite above as authorities in the field. The lowbrow writers, by contrast, did not enjoy reciprocal praise—their admiration was mostly one-sided. For example, while Mercier or Palissot may have praised Voltaire, the latter largely ignored such minor figures.

An important link among all of the writers I discuss is the evocation of their common ideals and common enemies. In general terms, one could summarize the characteristics that critics most often mention as typical of good and bad taste—respectively, consensus versus the bizarre; Greco-Roman roots versus "gothic" or "barbarian" (the latter terms could refer to Celtic, Gaulish, African, Asian, or Middle Eastern origins); proportion versus excess (the appropriate "size" or importance of metaphors, which they explain in terms of architecture); order versus disorder; and clarity versus obscurity. The same names appear repeatedly as examples of bad taste to be avoided: for example, Pradon, whose *Phèdre* once rivaled Racine's version in public opinion; Ronsard and Marot; and the journal *Mercure de France*.[15] Similarly, all of the writers tended to refer to the same textual sources of good taste. The main touchstones were Aristotle's and Horace's *Poetics* and occasionally Quintilian's *Insitutio oratoria*. More recent predecessors whom they constantly cited include Nicolas Boileau and Dominique Bouhours. Among English sources, the names of Shaftesbury, Francis Hutcheson, and Alexander Pope appear from time to time as common influences.

Ernst Cassirer, in his eminent 1932 study *The Philosophy of the Enlightenment*,[16] attempted to classify authors who grappled with the question of beauty into two conflicting groups: the rule-based "Cartesians" such as Boileau versus the emotion-based "empiricists" such as Dubos. In Cassirer's view, the conflict between the two resolved itself in Germany, specifically in Immanuel Kant's *Critique of Judgment*. Instead of showing Kant's ideas as merely chronologically succeeding those of French eighteenth-century theorists, Cassirer tries to convince us that Kant's ideas transcended the others.[17] In his attempt to force the eighteenth-century history of ideas to fit into a dialectical schema, Cassirer exaggerates the opposition between the aesthetics of rules and that of sentiment, making them seem mutually exclusive. But as Claude Chantalat points out in *A la Recherche du goût classique*,[18] the partisans of the rules and the partisans of the heart were never strictly divided in the seventeenth century. I would add that neither were they in the eighteenth century. The most systematic of theoreticians of beauty, such as Yves-Marie André, still reserved a place for emotion, while Dubos, partisan of sentiment, still laid down rules, for instance about the proper choice of subject for a tragedy.

Rather than granting undue importance to Kant's influence on eighteenth-century France, I would like to focus on the main outlines of theories of taste before Kant. I will also avoid discussion of eighteenth-century British philosophers, despite their strong influence on eighteenth-century French thought, because their ideas have been amply and skillfully covered in numerous recent studies.[19] I will therefore limit my inquiry to French writers of the eighteenth century. In the following pages, I would like to examine several questions: how exactly was good taste defined by the critics mentioned above, where did bad taste fit into their systems, and finally, one problem that will become indispensable to my study of bad taste: if taste is universal, why do people still disagree?

Since the professed rules of good taste in the eighteenth century were not, at first glance, radically different from those of the seventeenth century, or, for that matter, from the poetics of Aristotle and Horace, innovations appeared rather on the level of psychological observation. What happens in the mind and the heart of the viewer when he or she contemplates the sacrifice of Iphigenia on stage? How does an artist experience the act of creation? These were questions to which writers such as Dubos and Diderot sought answers.

Before I proceed to the description of the theories of individual writers, however, I need to make two preliminary remarks. First, because of the proteiform use of the word *taste* in the pre-Kantian eigh-

teenth century, I am obliged to follow this model when I refer to taste
as it applies to the viewer, the object of art, or the creator. At the end
of the eighteenth century, Kant established that the idea of taste re-
sided in the mind of the individual who observes, not in the thing
observed. This idea had already been expressed decades earlier by
theorists such as Dubos, Montesquieu, and Hutcheson, but in fact the
word *taste* continued to be used in a fluid way by people of the eighteenth century. Taste could refer to a faculty of the mind, as in a connoisseur's taste, or it could be a feature of an object, such as a tasteless
comedy or painting. It could also be a feature of the creator's mind:
Diderot, for example, discusses the tension between genius and taste
in the act of writing. As Claude Chantalat remarks in *A la Recherche
du goût classique*, "so we see that that same word [taste] is used at
once to suggest the merits of judgment and those of the object being
judged, in the same way as, in the literal sense, it evokes the delicacy
of the palate and the exquisite flavor of the foods that please it."[20]
The multiple uses of the word *taste* in the primary texts will therefore
make it impossible to consistently impose the limited, Kantian definition of the word.

Second, one may well ask why I should include treatises on beauty
in a discussion of taste. The connection between taste and beauty is
more complicated than it seems. While the majority of critics, such as
Voltaire, maintain that taste is simply the ability to perceive beauty, a
few others, such as Dubos, Montesquieu, and the marquise de Lambert, separated taste from beauty. The latter two define taste not as
the search for beauty but as the search for *agrément* or pleasure. Lambert explicitly draws a line between taste and beauty, declaring: "The
agreeable [*l'agréable*] is the proper object of taste. Hence also it is not
to be reduced to rules; since, though beauty has rules, agreeableness
has none. The fine without the agreeable can never give us a delicate
pleasure; the agreeable is the native subject of taste, and it is thence that
it pleases us infinitely beyond the fine; and it is as arbitrary and variable, even as the taste itself."[21] Montesquieu, in his *Essai sur le goût*,
sees taste in a similar way, distinct from and even opposite to beauty,
as I will explain in the section devoted to his essay. Crousaz and André,
in turn, discuss the matter of taste in particular sections within their
larger studies of beauty. In any case, although taste does not always
involve the recognition of beauty, the characteristics of good taste and
the characteristics of beauty often coincide and make use of exactly the
same terms that I listed above, such as order and proportion.

We can begin our consideration of individual theories of taste and beauty with Jean-Pierre de Crousaz, who, according to Wladyslaw Folkierski, published the first theory of beauty in eighteenth-century France in 1715.[22] I will place him together with Yves-Marie André, who published his work on beauty in 1741, because these two thinkers are linked by their insistence on reason as a sine qua non of artistic judgment. The names of Crousaz and André, virtually forgotten today, feature prominently in Diderot's article "Beauté" as some of the most influential theorists of beauty in the eighteenth century. Both were at once theologians and mathematicians who also wrote about beauty; Crousaz was a Swiss Calvinist and André was a French Jesuit. Both Crousaz and André were avid fans of Descartes (even though André's university officially banned the teaching of this philosopher) and attempted to derive theories of beauty from his methods of reasoning.[23] Nevertheless, despite the unavoidable presence of logic in their aesthetic systems, these two authors insisted that the perception of beauty also depended on an instantaneous feeling.

In regard to beauty and reason, Blaise Pascal had previously mocked the idea of a *beauté géométrique* in the *Pensées*.[24] We cannot qualify things such as medicine or geometry as beautiful, he claimed; instead, we say that they are salutary or true. Meanwhile, he remarks that we use the word *beautiful* as a much vaguer term to describe things whose value cannot be measured with certainty, such as a poem or a painting. In short, Pascal scoffed at the idea of beautifying math—of trying to approach math with such an indefinite category as *beautiful*. André and Crousaz, on the other hand, attempted to do the opposite: they mathematized beauty, so to speak, by describing the rationality behind our perception of art.

Jean-Pierre de Crousaz first published his *Traité du beau* in 1715 while he was a professor at the Academy of Lausanne in Switzerland.[25] He begins this systematic treatise by establishing that some objects appeal to our heart and other objects appeal to our minds, but real beauty must do both: "At first, good taste makes us admire with our sentiment something that our reason would have approved of, after it had had the time to examine it well enough to judge it based on the right principles."[26] In looking at certain works of art, we spontaneously feel enjoyment, but eventually this feeling has to be confirmed by reason. He enumerates the qualities in visual objects that have the ability to please both the heart and the mind. These include order, proportion, and a balance between variety and uniformity—qualities that appear frequently in other treatises, such as Montesquieu's *Essai sur le goût.*

He then proceeds to explain how these rules apply to the aesthetic judgments of various things, some of which we may be astounded to see in a treatise on beauty, such as personal appearance, human behavior, and geometric shapes. For example, the heart and the mind are pleased, according to Crousaz, by the sight of an isosceles triangle because it balances uniformity and variety.[27] He affirms that the same type of judgment can be made of a human face that is white with pink cheeks, or of a body that is neither too fat nor too thin. In terms of architecture, Crousaz also insists on the proper proportions of buildings and their ornaments and condemns the "gothic trinkets"[28] of medieval cathedrals.

In Crousaz's system, what accounts for bad taste? Most people, he claims, are not accustomed to using their reason at all, so they erroneously tend to call things beautiful that merely appeal to their heart. "Bad taste . . . makes us enjoy what reason would not approve."[29] Furthermore, people can be swayed from the right path by different forces, which he lists as temperament, vanity, habit, passions, and flightiness ("légèreté"). But that does not mean, Crousaz warns us, that preferences influenced by these forces have the right to be called beautiful.

Like Crousaz, Yves-Marie André specialized in theology and mathematics, and was able to make these subjects compatible with his thoughts on beauty. The père André, as he is often referred to, spent most of his career as a professor of mathematics in Caen. In 1741 he published his *Essai sur le beau*, which Diderot describes in his article "Beau" as "the most accepted system, the most widespread, and with the best argumentation that I know."[30] André's particular system divides beauty into three categories: essential beauty (*beauté essentielle*), which was the best; natural beauty (*beauté naturelle*), which was good; and arbitrary, artificial, or conventional beauty (*beauté arbitraire/artificielle/de convention*), which was dubious. André defines the highest form of beauty, *beauté essentielle*, as an almost mathematical concept, since it would be true even if no examples of it existed.[31] It is not important whether it exists or whether it pleases the senses of actual human beings as long as it has the *right* to please: "What I call beautiful, in a work of literature, is not what pleases the imagination at first glance, when the faculties of the soul or the bodily organs are in certain particular states, but rather what has the right to please reason and reflection by its own excellence, by its light or by its justness, and, if one allows me this term, by its intrinsic appeal."[32]

When it comes to examples, he becomes vague and resorts to words that are difficult to define, such as *harmony* and *proportion* in literary style. This is Diderot's main objection to André's treatise: "Father André divides with lots of sagacity and philosophy the beautiful into its different sorts; he defines them all with precision: but nowhere in his book can be found the definition of the genre, or of the beautiful in general."[33]

The next category, *beauté naturelle*, is a physical manifestation of the *beauté essentielle*; it is supposedly created by God to please humans. André states: "In second place, I say that there is a natural beauty, which depends on the will of the Creator but is independent of our opinions and our tastes."[34] According to André, *beauté essentielle* satisfies our reason, while *beauté naturelle* appeals to our senses. He gives us several examples of *beauté naturelle* that can we can perceive with our eyes, including the azure of the sky and the greenness of fields. While he describes *beauté essentielle* in terms of lines, he mostly dwells on color when showing us examples of *beauté naturelle*.

Where does bad taste reside within André's system? In the last category, of course, because the first two are supposedly unassailable. The idea of an inferior *beauté arbitraire* accounts for fashion and novelty, as well as differences in taste from country to country or from era to era. A salient problem with André's system is the following question: what prevents him from elevating his own "arbitrary" preferences (or those of his country, of his time, or of his social milieu) to the level of *beauté essentielle*? While there may be some consensus about, for example, the correct proportions of a building, one could argue that these proportions are still ultimately based on subjective notions.

One worry that underlies André's whole system is the desire to avoid aesthetic "Pyrrhonism" that would ensue from granting each person the right to determine what is beautiful. Translated into political terms, this would result in anarchy; translated into metaphysical terms, it is tantamount to a radical skepticism. Analogously, the ideal of beauty must be upheld in order to keep the arts from descending into chaos.

While André and Crousaz defended their aesthetics, which depended on a Cartesian ideal of geometrical perfection that transcended our experience, another professor came into prominence in Paris with a system that was more based on observation. The abbé Charles

Batteux constructed his idea of beauty on the relationship between the work of art and the world. "Imiter la belle nature" or "Imitating beautiful nature" is the principal message of Batteux's *Beaux-arts réduits à un même principe* of 1746, but to understand this idea, one must consider the problem of defining *nature*, as I briefly mentioned earlier. In this work, Batteux rejects the idea that any object, selected at random, can be worthy of being depicted in art. "What should we think," he exclaims, "of a painter who should represent his men dwarfs, emaciated, hunch-backed, lame, etc. because they are often found so in nature?"[35] Instead, he insists that the artist choose the best example of that type of object, but that brings us back to the question of how to choose what is most beautiful and whose standards of beauty are the criteria.

Where is bad taste in Batteux? He first attempts to account for the differences in various styles. If various writers treat a subject in different ways, he reassures us, all views are valid, just as several artists, scattered around a studio, can sketch the same model from different points of view—or the same model can change poses: "as the position of the same model may be varied ad infinitum, and as these variations may be again multiplied by the different points of light they fall under, which are likewise infinite; it follows, that the same object may be represented under an infinite number of appearances, every one different, and yet each regular in itself, and entirely conformable to nature and good taste."[36] In practical terms, Batteux applies this analogy to several examples: if Cicero and Sallust recounted Catilina's plot from different perspectives, or if Italian and French music are dissimilar, it does not mean that one is superior to the other.

Ultimately, however, Batteux upholds the belief that there is only one universal standard of good taste, without getting into particulars: "So there can be but only one good taste in general . . . therefore those who are not pleased with beautiful nature, must necessarily have a bad taste."[37] As in Bollioud-Mermet's definition of good taste, Batteux claims that this standard is determined by an elite. Their judgment is such, he states, that everyone, including those who do not initially agree, eventually submit to it.

> Is this now the voice of man, or is it not rather that of nature, which works such surprising changes? . . . Let a person of finished taste be attentive to the impression he receives from any production of art; let him form a clear and lively conception of it; in consequence of this let him give his opinion touching it; it is next to an impossibility but

every one else should subscribe to his judgment, since they would
feel the same sentiments as himself; and tho' perhaps, in not quite so
high a degree, yet still would they be of the same nature; and however
strongly they might have been biased by false taste or prejudice, yet
would they willingly yield to the impulse of nature, and pay her a secret homage.[38]

In short, those with bad taste are sometimes blinded by ignorance or
by prejudices, but they must finally acknowledge good taste, which,
like nature and truth, is irrefutable.

At the same time that the professors Crousaz and André were lay-
ing the foundations for a quasi-mathematical, quasi-theological system of beauty and Batteux was promoting his idealized version of nature, authors from another segment of society were judging works of
art from a different perspective. While the three authors mentioned
above belonged to the academic world, the other group frequented
high society; consequently, their writings theorize art according to
conceptions of politeness, pleasure, and elitism. The latter group,
which includes the abbé Dubos, the marquise de Lambert, and Montesquieu, were latter-day continuators of seventeenth-century salon
culture and at the same time precursors of the trend in sensibility.
Despite the differences of all the writers in method and social position, however, they came to very similar conclusions about good and
bad taste.

The abbot and diplomat Jean-Baptiste Dubos, one of the most innovative thinkers among these *mondains*, devised new ways of approaching the judgment of art, specifically by focusing on the effect
of art on human emotions. In *Réflexions critiques sur la poésie et
sur la peinture*, first published in 1719, his radical emphasis on sentiment led him to reject certain considerations that previous critics had
seen as inseparable from the judgment of taste, such as morality and
reason. He is known for introducing the idea of a sixth sense, that of
artistic reception, which briefly preceded a similar idea elaborated by
Francis Hutcheson in England. Other proponents of sentiment, who
frequented the same society as Dubos, include the marquise de Lambert, the abbé Trublet, and Cartaud de la Vilate. Dubos and Lambert
in particular remained faithful to a conception of taste that they inherited from the previous century, which compared a certain instinctive sense of taste to aristocratic politeness.

As a proponent of emotion, Dubos asks provocative questions such
as: why does an action that would horrify us in real life, such as a

murder, please us when we see it in a painting or a play? He places great importance on the pleasure that art gives to viewers, in open defiance of the classical principle that art must both please and instruct. His interest in the sensual perception of art even leads him to him inquire about the role of the body in artistic experience. In Dubos's text, the effect of art on the human body is not limited to tears or trembling; each human being's physical makeup also determines to what degree he or she is capable of perceiving and creating art. For example, the ideal artist must have "a happy arrangement of the organs"[39] and, using terms from ancient science, Dubos claims that this artist must have the appropriate temperature. He remarks: "I have supposed here, that the composer's blood is heated; for indeed painters and poets cannot invent in cool blood; nay 'tis evident they must be wrapt into a kind of enthusiasm when they produce their ideas."[40] By contrast, those who are too "cold" are mediocre, and those whose blood is overheated will simply produce chimeras.[41]

In the present day, Dubos is sometimes cited as a proponent of equality in matters of taste. This idea is based on statements from his *Réflexions* such as "the subject which comes under my examination, is most obvious and intelligible. Every man is possessed of a standard rule applicable to my arguments."[42] If one reads further, however, one comes to realize that when he refers to "every man" or "tout le monde," he refers to high society, or what one could call "le beau monde": "'Tis that I do not mean the lower class of people by the public capable of passing judgment on poems or pictures…. The word public is applicable here to such persons only, as have acquired some lights, either by reading or being conversant with the world."[43] In this elitist strain, he also insists on downplaying the role of professional critics (among whom he does not include himself) and even of the artists themselves in judging works of art, reserving this privilege for his social circle.

However imaginative and daring some of Dubos's ideas may be, as Ehrard points out, other aspects of his treatise are extremely conventional. For instance, when Dubos turns to specific examples from literature in which he discerns good taste from bad, he often returns to the same rules previously stated by critics. Indeed, his comments on the proper composition of tragedies and other genres hardly deviate from the ideas expressed in the previous century. His praise of writers such as Homer, Virgil, Corneille, and Bossuet also conform to the opinions of many of his contemporaries.

Dubos's insistence on emotion could be seen as a liberation—from the authority of the past, from rigid rules of composition—but what he proposes is not something radical. He does not proclaim everyone's right to feel as they wish in reaction to a play or a painting. Instead, Dubos assumes everyone's spontaneous emotion will eventually lead them to the same universal judgment, as he makes clear in his long discussion of the merits of Homer's *Iliad* and Virgil's *Aeneid*, in which he invalidates any possible reasons why a reader would *not* admire these works. He remarks that scientific theories may be rendered obsolete by successive generations, but the great works of poetry will always be received equally well by people of all eras, paradoxically, because of personal sentiment: "those opinions whose extent and duration are founded on sense, and on the inward experience, as it were, of such as have always adopted them, are not subject to be exploded."[44]

This is exactly the type of idea that Terry Eagleton questions in *The Ideology of the Aesthetic*. Focusing especially on later eighteenth-century texts, such as Rousseau's political writings and Kant's aesthetics, Eagleton advances the idea that, as opposed to a law that is imposed on individuals (in terms of either political power or artistic rules), some eighteenth-century thinkers proposed a different way for people to internalize and submit to a general rule. Eagleton states, "The liberated subject is the one who has appropriated the law as the very principle of its own autonomy, broken the forbidding tablets of stone on which that law was originally inscribed in order to rewrite it on the heart of the flesh."[45] In other words, the individual is told that he is free, but he is free so that he can *feel* the necessity of following the communal law and so that he can "freely" consent to it. He is even more subject to the law because he has internalized it. I believe a similar transference can be seen in Dubos's new focus on the body and the heart as the sites for artistic experience but that results in merely reinforcing the consensus about previously consecrated painters and literary figures. Although Dubos's aesthetic system does offer the promise of experiencing art in a new way, he ultimately dismisses the radical consequences that his ideas could lead to.

Still, one can count Dubos as the most prominent and most inventive figure in a group of critics who placed great emphasis on emotion in the reception of art. With his *Réflexions*, he may have cleared a new path in aesthetics that made it possible for future theorists, such as Diderot and then Diderot's admirers in Germany, to formulate their own aesthetic systems. Certainly, Dubos's thoughts on the connection between art, sentiment, and the body could be seen as anticipating the movements of sensibility and even Romanticism.

Like Dubos, Montesquieu's theories of taste tended toward worldliness and pleasure.[46] Both also concentrated less on abstract definitions of beauty and more on the ways in which taste affects the viewer internally. In Montesquieu's words, "the sources, therefore, of beauty, goodness, &c. lie within us; and of consequence, when we inquire into their causes, we do no more than investigate the springs of our mental pleasures."[47] In *Essai sur le goût*, he first lists six elements that please the viewer: the ability to provoke curiosity, then order, variety, symmetry, contrasts, and the ability to provoke surprise. These are found in the objects that we look at, including literature and architecture, and even in another human being. He then adds other qualities in our minds that affect how we experience these objects: sensibility, delicacy, and the je-ne-sais-quoi (some editions add "le naïf").

Montesquieu's essay is innovative in some ways, but in other ways it merely repeats statements made by critics of previous decades. His focus on the viewer's experience certainly marks him as a member of the new philosophical generation, which looks at taste from the inside of the human mind. However, Montesquieu treads a familiar path in calling for classical proportions in architecture and in defining taste as a combination of education and an innate sense of judgment. One feature that makes Montesquieu's *Essai sur le goût* stand out is the emphasis above all on pleasure, to the extent that Ehrard, in *L'Idée de nature*, aptly calls him a hedonist philosopher. In fact, Montesquieu even breaks with the definition of taste as the judgment of beauty, since for him, taste signifies the search for pleasure, while beauty is set aside as a secondary concern. Designating the objects of his inquiry, he promiscuously mixes art with games: "Poetry, painting, sculpture, architecture, music, dance, different sorts of games—in short, the works of nature and of art—can give pleasure to the mind. Let us see why, how, and when they give it; let us give explanations for our sentiments: this may contribute to forming our *taste*, which is nothing more than the advantage of discovering, with promptness and finesse, the amount of pleasure that each object should give to men."[48] While Dubos, Voltaire, Kant, and others also emphasize the importance of pleasure in the aesthetic experience, they leave us with an abstract understanding of pleasure as a mental experience. By contrast, Montesquieu gives us the concrete examples of pleasures that some of his more pious contemporaries might call vices, such as gambling, seduction, or dancing. Toward the end of his essay, in discussing his perception of feminine beauty, he even distinctly rejects physical perfection in favor of surprise, wit, and seductive dress. This "hedonistic" theory of taste seems all the more remarkable in contrast to the treatises of Crousaz and André, which include large sections devoted to beauty in moral behavior. The latter's insistence on such qualities as modesty and good deeds can be partly explained by their status as clerics, but their ideas of moral behavior are also integrated into their whole aesthetic systems, just as Montesquieu's love of flirting is built into his.

In Montesquieu's *Essai sur le goût*, where does bad taste fit in? Objects can displease when they violate Montesquieu's six principles of good taste. For example, a gothic cathedral's ornaments can have too much variety and not enough order, or a human face with perfect beauty can bore the viewer from lack of surprise.

The fact that Montesquieu's treatise on taste appeared together with those of Voltaire and d'Alembert in the *Encyclopédie* article "Goût" makes him an excellent transitional figure between the first half of the eighteenth century, divided between the professors and the *mondains* that I have discussed here, and the group of writers who formed what some scholars call the "philosophical party." The latter includes d'Alembert, Diderot, Voltaire, Marmontel, and Rousseau,[49] writers whom Annie Becq has shown as practicing a new rhetoric of intellectual autonomy, which marked an important step in the transformation of the status of writers from hired artisans to the independent creators who were idealized in the nineteenth century. While the patronage system was far from obsolete, as Geoffrey Turnovsky demonstrates in *The Literary Market*, it was the writers' portrayal of themselves at a midpoint between the frivolous *mondains* and the dusty pedants that influenced their aesthetic theories. As we will see, their theories of taste will borrow from Dubos, Batteux, and the others, while emphasizing their own authority as professional, erudite men of letters.

Voltaire wrote extensively about taste in a number of works, many of which Sylvain Menant has collected and commented on in *L'Esthétique de Voltaire*.[50] What are the principal outlines of Voltaire's thoughts on taste? Menant emphasizes aspects of his style such as rapid pacing, faithfulness to ancient genres and themes, and a sense of playfulness that would appeal to his aristocratic friends. Menant's predecessor in this field, Raymond Naves, author of *Le Goût de Voltaire*, describes

Voltaire's taste as a balance between the rules and a spontaneous, case-by-case judgment: "he opposes the judgment by convention with a complete impressionism, founded on the independence of the connoisseur, the freshness and the acuity of his impression."[51] By staking out this middle ground, states Naves, Voltaire avoids the two tasteless extremes of pedantic dogmatism and frivolous trend-chasing.

While I will refer later to Voltaire's pronouncements on taste in relation to specific genres that he makes in other works, I would like to concentrate for the moment on his explicit definition of taste as it appears in his article "Goût" for the *Encyclopédie*. In this article, he begins with a concentration on the immediate, instinctive side of taste, which brings it close to the literal meaning of the physical sensation of a flavor on the tongue: "It discriminates as quickly as the tongue and the palate, and like physical taste it anticipates thought. In common with physical taste it is sensitive to what is good and reacts to it with a feeling of pleasure, it refuses with disgust what is bad."[52] Immediately afterward, though, he introduces a disruptive element by mentioning that this sense can sometimes be wrong and it must somehow be corrected. Aesthetic taste, he claims, often resembles sensory taste, since it is "frequently uncertain and misleading, at times it cannot even tell whether something is pleasant or not, and sometimes it needs practice to develop discrimination."[53] This potentially errant sense of taste can only be stabilized with a strong educational foundation.

As Voltaire explains, taste depends on a spontaneous, almost physical reaction to art, but this does not suffice. One also needs training in order to discern the various elements of the work of art in order to understand why one has that spontaneous reaction. He illustrates this idea with the following example: "A young man who is sensitive but untutored . . . the first time he sees a beautiful tragedy he will be moved, but he will be unable to discern either the effect of the unities. . . . Practice and reflection alone will make it possible for him to experience immediate pleasure from elements that formerly he could not distinguish at all."[54] To put it briefly, Voltaire defines taste as a combination of rules and sentiment—an idea that is far from original. The interest in reading his statements on taste, however, lies in the specific ways in which he describes taste going astray. In fact, Voltaire tends to dwell on the negative aspects of taste as often as he does on the positive. In his definition, taste is "the discernment of beauty and flaws in all the arts."[55] So it is as important for taste to perceive the beautiful as it is to reject the ugly.

One can compare Voltaire's description of good taste to the scene in Molière's *Bourgeois gentilhomme*, where an aristocrat is capable of describing the excellence of a meal in astonishing detail and can thus show his superiority to the bourgeois upstart. The idea is also compatible with the anecdote from *Don Quixote* that David Hume retells in his essay "Of the Standard of Taste."[56] In this story, two connoisseurs who sip wine claim to taste elements of leather and metal, which surprises onlookers until the connoisseurs are proven right when someone finds a key with a leather strap inside the cask. Good taste, specifically delicate taste, thus involves the ability to instantaneously react to an object and at the same time to be able to break this reaction down into its component parts.

It is important to note that Voltaire pairs sentiment not with reason but with an awareness of certain literary conventions. Unlike André, he does not claim that beauty is an abstract, immutable concept comparable to Descartes's understanding of truth. Instead, Voltaire is more impressionistic, as Naves describes him, in the sense that his idea of good taste depends on many circumstantial factors, such as the rules appropriate for a specific genre or the possibility of allowing for various types of exceptions, as we can see in his ambivalence toward Milton, Molière, and Shakespeare.

Voltaire's critique of bad taste is in some ways close to that of Anne Dacier, the most prominent representative of the Ancient party in the later part of the Battle of the Ancients and the Moderns. Her most famous work, *Des Causes de la corruption du goust* (1714), mostly defends the *Iliad* against criticism, but it also addresses a general decline in taste, as she indicates in the title. She specifically blames the popularity of two genres, opera and the novel, for destroying French taste. Unlike theorists such as Montesquieu or Batteux, she does not formulate an abstract ideal of good taste; rather, she attacks specific instances of what she sees as bad taste, as Voltaire does. And like Voltaire, she expresses deep skepticism for new genres, although Voltaire defended the newly created art of opera.

Voltaire's influence extended to his many protégés and admirers, including the literary critics La Harpe and Marmontel, who helped disseminate many of his literary opinions in their own works. Jean-François de la Harpe began his career as a Swiss student of obscure origins and rose to win a number of academic prizes in rhetoric. His admiration for Voltaire was rewarded with the latter's protection, resulting in La Harpe's election to the Académie Française. During the

Revolution, he converted from anti-clerical skeptic to zealous Catholic and publicly renounced his ties to the *philosophes*. He wrote his best-known work, the sixteen-volume *Lycée, ou Cours de littérature ancienne et moderne*, as a series of lectures on literary history. Despite his conversion, La Harpe's *Lycée* demonstrates to us how the *philosophes'* general statements regarding taste can be applied in a detailed way to specific works of literature from antiquity to the end of the eighteenth century.

La Harpe is one example of a new breed of literary critics who wrote treatises that situated themselves at an equal distance between traditional pedagogical manuals and more high-flown aesthetic philosophy. In an article about eighteenth-century poetics, Annie Becq cites Nicolas-Charles-Joseph Trublet's distinction among three types of treatises: "He confirms, in 1754, the existence in his own century of a new kind of rhetoric and poetics: 'The first, scholastic and detailed . . . the second, general and limited to exposing the first principles of the art. The third, philosophical and containing fine reflections on the causes of pleasure or disgust given by works of eloquence and poetry.'"[57] The first category, the school manuals, has been thoroughly studied by Daniel Mornet in *Histoire de la clarté française* and by Marc Fumaroli in *L'Age de l'éloquence*, and the third category comprises precisely those philosophers, such as Dubos or Crousaz, who reflected on wider issues of perception and artistic imitation, for example. Let us consider the middle category, in which we can include critics such as Dumarsais, the chevalier de Jaucourt, and in some instances d'Alembert and Buffon.[58] These authors offered general rules of style without creating larger systems of what we, in the present day, would consider philosophy. The term that Becq uses to refer to these critics is *philosophe-grammairien*, which also appears in an 1818 edition of Dumarsais's *Des Tropes*. In this text, the editor's preface refers to Dumarsais as a philosopher-grammarian and characterizes him as an intellectual descendant of Arnaud and Nicole, who established the grammar and logic of Port-Royal.[59]

All of these philosopher-grammarians addressed specific matters of correct style and, more intangibly, good taste in writing. As opposed to school manuals, the writings of these philosopher-grammarians addressed a general public rather than just schoolboys. D'Alembert and Jaucourt, for example, exposed their views in articles of the *Encyclopédie* on such issues as elegant metaphors or heroic verse, which is perhaps surprising if we consider their training in mathematics and medicine, respectively. Among the topics classified as literature or rhetoric that Jaucourt undertook for the *Encyclopédie*, we find "énigme," "fabuliste," "génie," "lecteur," and "orateur," some of which I will explore in subsequent chapters.

Among the philosopher-grammarians referred to by Annie Becq, perhaps the most celebrated during his time was Jean-François Marmontel, author of two texts that established his ideal of good writing: the *Poétique française* (1763) and *Eléments de littérature* (1787). The latter includes, as a preface, his *Essai sur le goût*. Aided by powerful protectors such as Voltaire and the marquise de Pompadour, Marmontel had an enormously successful career as a poet, novelist, opera librettist, contributor to the *Encyclopédie*, and ladies' man. He won entry into the Académie Française[60] with the publication of *Poétique française*, which he later augmented and reorganized by alphabet to produce *Eléments de littérature*. The latter resembles Dumarsais's *Des Tropes* in that it describes the skills that the poet must master in order to write well, but it has a much wider range, from Aristotle's conception of *inventio* to the rhyme patterns for different types of French verse forms.

In *Essai sur le goût*, Marmontel reshapes the idea of taste to conform to Rousseau's theories of human nature. Rousseau never created a system of aesthetics, and his comments about taste were mostly limited to denunciations of his contemporaries' love of luxury and of the development of arts and science in general. Nevertheless, Marmontel, who was his colleague and admirer, attempted to derive principles of taste from Rousseau's writings. Marmontel begins *Essai sur le goût* sounding like Batteux: "There is only one supreme judge, a single judge who, in matters of *taste*, is without appeal: it is nature. Fortunately, almost everything submits to this universal arbiter."[61] Soon afterward, however, he applies the word *nature* to a three-level schema of human development and, of course, of taste.

First there are the savage men or *hommes sauvages*, who, Marmontel claims, actually express themselves with good taste. Imagine, he says, listening to the words of a savage who has just lost his son: "he feels everything that he should feel, he feels it to the degree he should feel it, and as far as his language permits it, he says it as he should say it. No turn of phrase that does not express the movement of his thought; not a single ambitious or superfluous epithet; not a single excessive hyperbole; not a single false metaphor, even though everything is in images; not a single trait of sensibility that is not exact and penetrating;

why is that? Because nature is always true, and everything that is exaggerated, mannered, forced, out of place belongs to art."[62] Although Marmontel claims that savages speak in figurative language, their directness and simplicity ensure that their speech is always tasteful. It is not clear whether this scenario of a mourning native was based on his experience, his readings of travel accounts, or his imagination.

The second level of taste is that of uncultured or barbaric man (*l'homme inculte* or *barbare*), the man of bad taste, who prefers artifice over nature, or the convoluted over the simple. He is too affected by custom, opinion, and whim. Then the third stage of taste is that of *l'homme civilisé*, a man who once again returns to the primitive values of simplicity: "Between the state of savage man and civilized man, and in the transition from one to the other, is the state of barbaric man. The savage, as I conceived of him, would be the man of nature; the barbarian, on the contrary, is a denatured man; his reason, his mores, his ideas, his sentiments, are perverted by conventions and by his habits, all as artificial as the fashions of luxury and vanity. . . . To pull these men out of barbarism is thus to begin to return them to nature."[63] To summarize the three-level development of man, we can list the stages of civilization as follows:

1. homme sauvage (good taste)
2. homme inculte (bad taste)
3. homme civilisé (good taste)

Marmontel thus locates bad taste in the *inculte* state when people are swayed by convention, a concept somewhat similar to the père André's description of *beauté arbitraire* or *beauté de convention*.

This process recalls Rousseau's depiction of humanity's political trajectory in *Discours sur l'inégalité* and *Le Contrat social*. The first stage is idealized as an enviable state of moral simplicity, then humans become corrupted by social convention, then in a final stage set sometime in the future, people revolt and then refound society according to the original principles. Rousseau and Marmontel situate their contemporaries in the second stage—that of corruption through social convention—suggesting that the return to the original goodness will take place in a vague future time.

Marmontel's fellow *philosophe*, Diderot, was less occupied with improving people's writing style and more intent on continuing the philosophical effort to define abstract beauty. In his various aesthetic writings, Diderot's ideas about beauty and taste can be difficult to grasp, partly because of their complexity and partly because he had no compunctions about contradicting himself from one moment to the next. His *Encyclopédie* article "Génie" ("Genius") appears for the most part as a pre-Romantic apology for the liberation of the creative forces of genius, which must fight against the constraints of the conventions of art, which he associates with the concept of taste. In this essay, taste plays the role of oppressing creativity and promoting the spread of general mediocrity.

On the other hand, in the article "Beau" for the *Encyclopédie*, Diderot remains close to the traditional definition of beauty as uniformity, symmetry, and so on without challenging it. In this article, he offers summaries of the aesthetic theories of his predecessors, from Plato to his own contemporaries. Once Diderot elaborates his own theory, he explains the concept of beauty with the term *rapports*: "I then call beautiful outside of myself, that which contains in itself what can awaken in my understanding the idea of rapports; and beautiful compared to me, everything that awakens this idea."[64] He repeatedly insists that beauty depends on the number of *rapports* one sees in objects, but he does not clarify this term entirely.

The concept of *rapports* may seem puzzling because of its vagueness. If readers wonder how the idea of *rapports* can be applied to literature, Diderot offers an explanation, using the line from Corneille's *Horace* that everyone in the eighteenth century seems to cite as the standard of good taste: "Qu'il mourût" ("For him to have died"). If someone hears the phrase as an isolated line, without any idea about its context, he claims, that person will judge it with indifference. However, the more the person knows about the story of *Horace* and the heroic circumstances that surround this reply, the more one will be affected by it:

> if I told him that this is the answer from a man who was asked what another man should do in a fight, then the person starts to see in the answerer some sort of courage, one that does not allow him to think that it sometimes is better to live than to die; and the "for him to have died" starts to interest him. If I were to add that the fighter is the son of the one that is asked the question; that this is the only son he has left; that this young man was facing three enemies, who had already killed his two brothers; that the old man addresses his daughter; that he is Roman: then the answer "for him to have died," which beforehand was neither beautiful nor ugly, increasingly becomes

beautiful as I develop the rapports it entertains with the circumstances, and ends up being sublime.[65]

We can see that Diderot's *rapports* are meant to reveal something
about, on the one hand, the creative process of the writer and, on the
other, the abilities of the viewer.

Concerning the writer, the ideal of *rapports* shows us that he has
mastered the art of conciseness, or of expressing a lot in a small number of words. As John Lyons describes the appeal of this famous
phrase, "Not only are there very few words but the huge significance
of the content is stated without acknowledgement of its extent."[66]

In regard to the viewer, the term *rapports* refers to the capacity
to discern more or less meaning in the piece, which in turn depends
on "the individual's innate gifts or limits," as Lester Crocker states
in *Diderot's Chaotic Order*. Crocker continues, "Diderot offers examples to show that the number or complexity of relationships the
individual can grasp and the character of the experiences in which,
according to the culture to which he belongs, he will discern relationships or be blind to them constitute the two variables of taste and
aesthetic judgment."[67] Therefore, since not all viewers will succeed
in perceiving the same number of *rapports*, one can see *rapports* as
a type of "taste test," if I may repurpose this term from advertising.
The higher the number of *rapports* a viewer can discern, the higher
his level of taste.

Diderot explains a concept very similar to that of *rapports*, but using other terms, in his *Lettre sur les sourds et les muets* of 1751. In
this text, he explains that good poetry is imbued with *poetic hieroglyphics* and *emblems*, which only "the man of taste" will be able
to see but to which "ordinary readers" will remain oblivious.[68] He
offers the example of a verse from Boileau's *Lutrin* and does what
we would consider nowadays as a thorough literary analysis of this
single verse. While the *rapports* described in his article "Beau" have
more to do with the characters' situation in the plot, Diderot's *emblems* and *hieroglyphics* in his *Lettre sur les sourds et muets* pertain
to aspects of prosody. Nevertheless, they share one thing in common:
they both contain a network of meaning that is visible to people in
varying degrees. Therefore, the quantity of meaning that one can see
determines, in Diderot's judgment, one's level of taste. Like Voltaire,
he emphasizes the small number of men of taste in the world: "there
are a thousand people of good sense for every one man of taste, and
a thousand persons of taste for each person with exquisite taste."[69]

Thus the concept of *rapports*, like his concept of *hieroglyphics* and *emblems*, serves to measure the taste of viewers and assumes only a small minority of the public will meet the standard.

THE SOURCES OF BAD TASTE

As we can see in these texts, not only Diderot but all the theorists of taste discussed above had to deal with a thorny problem: they tried to establish that taste was universal, true for all people of all nations at all times, but a commonsense objection is, "What if someone does not agree?" To explain why someone may make an error of judgment in art, Diderot lists no less than twelve reasons in his article "Beau," including prejudice, habit, and a lack of experience in viewing art that may or may not be remedied by education. Other critics confront this problem in terms of lack of sensitivity, bad eyesight, prejudice, or ill-nesses of taste. Nearly all use the term *nature* to establish their opinions as indisputable: good taste (their own) is natural; bad taste (those who disagree) is artificial.

In his *Réflexions*, Dubos has it both ways: in one section, he creates a hierarchy of better and worse discernment with the analogy of the senses, but in another section, he claims that people have different ways of perceiving art, which are equally valid. First, comparing taste to the senses permits him to ward off any doubt about the superiority of one level of discernment over another, since everyone agrees that sharper eyesight is better than duller. This metaphor works particularly well with concept of the "sixth sense" to refer to the suscepti-bility to beauty in art: "The sense here spoken of, is in all men; but as they have not eyes and ears of equal goodness, so their sense is not equally perfect. Some have it better than others, either because their organs are naturally better composed, or because they have im-proved it by frequent use and experience."[70] Consequently, those who have worse eyesight, metaphorically speaking, must eventually defer to the judgment of those with better eyesight: "It happens therefore, that short-sighted folks hesitate sometimes before they acquiesce to the sense of one that sees better than themselves; but as soon as the person who is moving forward, comes within a proportionable dis-tance, they are all of one opinion. In like manner all that judge by sense, agree at last with respect to the effect and merit of a work."[71] If this explanation makes sense, then any possible tension occasioned by conflicting opinions about works of art is smoothed out. The question remains, however: if two people disagree, which of them would identify himself with the aesthetically nearsighted person?

In another section of the *Réflexions*, Dubos contradicts this idea of sharper and duller senses, but he does this with a specific agenda. In this passage, we can see that he addresses the debate about the superiority of color or line in painting, which impassioned his contemporaries, and he defends the partisans of color.[72] To explain why one cannot dispute the preferences of various people, Dubos states that they have different faculties that are more developed than those of others. For example, one man could have a "more voluptuous eye,"[73] which is more sensitive to color, while another could have a heart that is more sensitive to "mouving expressions."[74] The viewer with the voluptuous eye is attracted to color, exemplified by the paintings of Titian, while another viewer can have a penchant for Poussin, who represents line. Opposing the idea that *poussinistes* represent the party of reason while colorists represent the irrational, he claims that they are different but equal: "The prepossession we have in favor of one part of painting preferable to another, depends no more on our reason, than the passion we have for one kind of poetry in preference to another. It depends intirely [*sic*] on our taste; and this on our organization, present inclinations, and the situation of our minds."[75] By defending his colorist opinions against the proponents of line, Dubos seems to be attacking the universalism of taste. Since he tries to impose his own preferences in other parts of the work, though, I believe one should view this momentary open-mindedness as a defense on one position in one particular debate.

Recalling Dubos's metaphor of eyesight, Batteux characterizes disagreements about taste in terms of obstruction. Wrong judgments, he asserts, must result from ignorance or prejudice, whose "noise" interferes with the sound of nature: "But as we are apt to consider this point with our minds prejudiced, we cannot distinguish nature amidst the confusion of objects that arise, and so often mistake false taste for true, [and] give [it] the same titles."[76] A man of taste, by contrast, hears and feels distinctly.

For other theorists, the right taste depends on the state of the viewer's faculties and almost his bodily health. Voltaire, for example, in his article "Goût" from the *Encyclopédie*, considers people whose taste is either bad or depraved, using the analogy of food.[77] Someone with bad taste, he claims, prefers overly spiced foods to simple, natural flavors (an analogy that makes sense in France but perhaps not in other parts of the world): "Just as having bad taste in the physical sense means deriving pleasure only from seasoning that is excessively piquant and unusual, so having bad taste in the arts is to enjoy only elaborate ornamentation and to be insensitive to la belle nature."[78] An even worse taste, which Voltaire calls "depraved taste," degenerates into an illness—that of eating things that most people find disgusting.[79] He does not specify further, but perhaps we can assume he refers to obsessions such as that of eating dirt; what then is the artistic equivalent of eating dirt? Well, enjoying burlesque and *précieux* styles, for example: "A depraved taste in the arts consists in enjoying subjects that are revolting to men of good judgment. Such taste leads us to prefer the burlesque to what is noble, and to prefer what is precious and affected to simple and natural beauty: this is a sickness of the mind."[80] Thus, rather than saying that bad taste is a mere deviation from his own taste, Voltaire relies on an analogy with the standard of mental health.

Other theorists, such as Cartaud de la Vilate and la marquise de Lambert, base their concept of taste mostly on the degree of sensibility each person has. Some people of taste, they assert, are simply more sensitive (*sensibles*); their emotions are more easily inflamed by artistic works. Before Buffon made the pronouncement "Le style est l'homme même" ("style is the man himself"), Cartaud de la Vilate, in his *Essai historique et philosophique sur le goût*, assumes that the bodily humors of the writer express his style (as someone can express juice from a fruit): "Style is an imprint of the soul, in which one sees the different characters of one's passions. The language of dogmatists is grandiose, that of Pyrrhonians is modest and circumspect. Plato spoke bombastically; Socrates was always moderate and tended towards raillery. . . . The marked contrast between these four famous men, Mr. Arnaud, Claude, Nicole, and Jurieux, is the effect of the contrariety of their humors."[81] Similarly, the reader reacts according to his particular bodily humor and the disposition of his organs; for this reason, there are often discrepancies between the opinions of men of taste and the rest of the multitude. Like critics of the seventeenth century, Cartaud de la Vilate designates the defining character trait as *délicatesse*: "delicate taste is an exquisite discernment that nature has placed in certain organs for sorting out the different virtues of the objects that pertain to sentiment."[82] Some people have it, others do not—and those who have it must sometimes suffer from their excessive delicacy: "If it is a misfortune to be hurt by the majority of ob-

jects that surround us, delicate taste is a fatal gift. The finest organs
are the most vulnerable. With ordinary eyesight, one can find certain
objects beautiful, but these objects would cause chagrin to someone
with sharper eyesight."[83] The marquise de Lambert also bases the correct judgment of art on emotion rather than reason; therefore, those
who do not immediately feel the pleasure occasioned by beauty are
simply excluded from the realm of taste: "There is certainly, however,
such a thing as a justness of taste. . . . But, as it is impossible to lay
down any certain rules on this head, so it is also impossible to convince other people of their errors in regard to it. When their sensibility
ceases to inform them, it is in vain for us to attempt to instruct them
in it."[84] The socially elitist cast of this passage is made more explicit
when Lambert compares her idea of taste, which is both inborn and
perfected in the right milieu, to the sense of politeness.

Whether theoreticians explain that people have different degrees of
good taste through the metaphors of eyesight, hearing, or sensibility,
they often reject the possibility that one who judges "wrongly" may
one day acquire good taste through education. In other words, if one
subscribes to these ideas, one must ultimately deny the idea of human
perfectibility through education, a belief that tends to be attributed
to the Enlightenment. Other theoreticians, however, place more emphasis on education, but to require lengthy exposure to great art still
denies those who have neither enough leisure nor enough early training the right to participate in the judgment of art—in spite of the purported universality of taste.

How did these theorists succeed in imposing their standards and
making all rivals look like they had bad taste? Rival aesthetic systems, as upheld in salons and as evidenced in best-seller lists, certainly
existed, but the difference is that these rival systems did not profess
their standards as universal, as the theorists mentioned above did.
The readers from humble milieus could not wield the pen as skillfully
as the *philosophes* to defend their choices in novels, and perhaps they
had also internalized the idea of their inferior judgment. In the case
of other potential opponents to the universalism of taste, oppositional
discourse was mostly absent; it would require medieval poets to rise
from the dead and foreign art critics to land on French shores to defend their conceptions of good taste.

The eighteenth-century critics whose theories I have summarized
in this chapter compared their own era to ancient Rome. While the

designation of this period, especially in England, as the Augustan Age is well known, the comparison between the two eras reveals much about the fears and aspirations of eighteenth-century French writers. Voltaire and his fellows describe their own society as emerging from past chaos and preparing itself for a battle with bad taste, which takes on the metaphorical form of barbarians, Goths, and Orientals. They uphold their ideal of taste, largely based on Greek and Roman models, as if the survival of their civilization depended on it.

CHAPTER THREE

The Barbaric, or
Of Time and Taste

When it comes to taste, some eras are indisputably better than others—so states the abbé Dubos: "the superior excellency of some ages, in comparison to others, is a thing too well known, to require any arguments to evince it. Our business here is to trace, if possible, those causes which render one particular age so vastly superior to others."[1] In other words, there is no need to ask *whether* some centuries are superior; instead, we would do better to discover *why* they are superior. If critics like Dubos looked back in time to judge French literary history according to their eighteenth-century standards, it was surely because they wanted to shape what would be defined for posterity as French culture. Inevitably, this shaping involved chiseling away the elements that they saw as unfit to represent their culture, even if they were influential or popular. In this chapter, I will examine how critics such as Dubos, Voltaire, Marmontel, and La Harpe looked at the history of French literature through the lens of taste.

Despite the Enlightenment's well-known tendency toward cosmopolitanism, especially in matters regarding customs and religion, the *philosophes* were interested in glorifying French culture. Their claim to greatness concentrated most of all on language and literature, since they conceded that in some cases the Italians may have excelled in painting or the British in philosophy. The critics mentioned above attempted to create an image of French literature that was coherent, unified, and, most important, tasteful by selecting certain works of French literature and either ignoring or ridiculing others. Rhetorically, their strategy involved making what French literature *was* coincide with what they thought it *should be*, meanwhile casting aside rival styles by labeling them "not French" or "not literature."

As Homi K. Bhabha states in his post-structuralist analysis of national discourses, "the origins of national traditions turn out to be as much acts of affiliation and establishment as they are moments of disavowal, displacement, exclusion, and cultural contestation."[2] And Bhabha does not neglect the importance of taste in the creation of a coherent national narrative: among the "narratives and discourses that signify a sense of 'nationness,'" he lists such things as social hierarchies, attitudes toward outsiders, institutions, political affiliations, and "the customs of taste."[3] In eighteenth-century France, as we will see, the creation of "French taste" by the *philosophes* depended on the invention of the Grand Siècle as much as on the rejection of certain elements—such as medieval romances, Marot's neologisms, and Pradon's *Phèdre*—from literary history.

THE IMAGINARY HISTORY OF TASTE

A considerable number of eighteenth-century writers recount the same imaginary history of Western civilization, from an eighteenth-century point of view.[4] With only a few small variations, the history is as follows: the world began as a morass of darkness and ignorance, from which emerged the shining beacon of ancient Greek civilization. This high point was followed by another, the Roman Age, specifically the Age of Augustus. The world was plunged into obscurity once again with the Fall of Rome at the hands of the uncouth barbarians of the North. So the earth remained shrouded in the errors of early Christianity, until the Italian Renaissance brought civilization into the light once again. A period of religious strife made the darkness return, which lasted until the last age of brilliance and glory: seventeenth-century France. The status of the authors' era, the eighteenth century, remains in doubt, because the forces of obscurity are struggling against the forces of light, and only the great writers and philosophers can keep society from falling into a state of barbarity once again.

This imaginary history of taste appears in a well-known passage by Voltaire from the *Siècle de Louis XIV*: "whosoever thinks, or, what is still more rare, whosoever has taste, will find but four ages in the history of the world. These four happy ages are those in which the arts were carried to perfection, and which, by serving as the era of the greatness of the human mind, are examples for posterity."[5] He then specifies what he means by these ages: the Greece of Plato and Aristotle; the Rome of Virgil, Ovid, and Horace; the Age of the Medicis; and the Age of Louis XIV. Voltaire also makes it clear in his *Temple du goût* of 1733 that the presence of Goths and barbarians marks the low points in the history of taste. In this work, good taste takes the allegorical shape of a temple that is built by the Greeks, then usurped by the Romans, then destroyed by invaders, and finally rebuilt by Richelieu and decorated by Louis XIV. The temple, of course, looks like a classical building, not "disgraced / With heaps of rubbish round it placed; / For once our sires, but little skilled, / Their Gothic structures used to build."[6] The high points of taste, according to Voltaire, coincide with the high points of "lumières" or Enlightenment values (such as religious tolerance, reason, and humanism)[7] that he describes in such texts as *L'Essai sur les mœurs et l'esprit des nations* because, in his view, taste has significant links to the development of society.

Voltaire's statements about the history of taste were by no means isolated—in fact, similar ideas had been sketched out in the previous century, though mostly in regard to language, by critics such as Bouhours and Fénelon.[8] In 1719, the abbé Dubos remarked: "History makes mention of four ages, whose productions have been admired by succeeding times. Those happy ages in which the arts attained to a perfection which they fell short of at other times, are, that which commenced ten years before the reign of Philip father of Alexander the Great, that of Julius Caesar and Augustus, that of Julius II and Leo X, and finally, that of our king Lewis the fourteenth."[9] Numerous later critics and satirists also continued to repeat this idea about the four great periods, including Marmontel in his *Essai sur le goût* and La Harpe in the fifth volume of the *Lycée, ou Cours de littérature ancienne et moderne.*

Charles Palissot, though the avowed enemy of d'Alembert, Diderot, and Marmontel, followed Voltaire's lead and included a negative version of this same imaginary history of taste in his mock epic poem, *La Dunciade.* In this poem, which is only loosely based on Alexander Pope's *Dunciad,* Stupidité appears in the form of a goddess who commands armies of inferior writers. In one key episode of Palissot's *Dunciade,* a character has a miraculous vision of the progress of Stupidité, as well as the victories and defeats of her troops throughout history. In this vision, Stupidité triumphs during the Fall of Rome when she leads the horde of "those brigands vomited by the North, / Desolators of a tearful Europe / and fierce enemies of the arts."[10] She then travels to the Orient, where she transforms herself into the Islamic religion; afterward, she returns to Europe, specifically to France, and oversees the "chaos of profound ignorance"[11] of the Middle Ages. She is responsible for instigating the Crusades and fomenting the growth of theological pedantry and the feudal system during this "age of barbarism,"[12] those "frightful centuries."[13] In the final showdown in the present day, Stupidité gathers her troops of bad modern authors (at least those whom Palissot disapproved of), including some female writers such as Mme Riccoboni and some *philosophes* such as Marmontel. Together, they attack Mount Parnassus in a mock epic battle of taste. Apollo finally triumphs, however, with the aid of the all-powerful whistle or "sifflet"—the authors are booed and they lose the battle.

Following the pattern of light and darkness I mentioned before, Palissot situates the goddess's origins in the chaotic darkness that preceded the birth of the Greek gods. Addressing her enemy, Apollo, she exclaims,

> Daughter of Chaos, I reigned before you;
> I commanded the whole of nature,
> When on Mount Pindus they did not yet know your laws.
> For a long time, darkness preceded light.
> And destiny had you be born after me.[14]

In this passage, she expresses the idea that the primordial state of the world, its default state, so to speak, is one of darkness and ignorance. For intelligence and good writing (as represented by Apollo) to emerge, the gods must make an extraordinary effort. This idea is expressed through the reference to Greek mythology's struggle for the creation of the world and in the battle that Palissot depicts between Stupidité and Apollo.

This is an important aspect of the rhetoric of the history of taste: the idea that the world can easily sink back into the darkness of ignorance if we are not vigilantly defending the advances of culture. The Fall of Rome is evoked by Voltaire and other critics with a frequency and a sense of urgency that suggest that, in their mind, the episode is not just a historical one but one that is eternally repeating itself. In Voltaire's historical essays, for example, one can see a tension between an optimistic belief in the progress of science and a fear of regression in issues of morality or taste. Enlightenment and good taste do not appear as inevitable goals that society is moving toward; they are the result of arduous work on the part of thinkers and leaders, who must struggle against their enemies.

These narratives show us that the trajectory of taste, with its ups and downs, is less a linear progress than a constant battle between darkness and light. Rémy Saisselin, in his study *Taste in Eighteenth-Century France,* also concludes from reading Voltaire and the abbé Dubos that "History might be viewed as a series of oscillations between an ever present and strong tendency toward the Gothic and those rare moments, the triumph of reason and will, which are those of perfection."[15] Although Palissot looks at the issue from the opposite side as Voltaire, he illustrates the same ideas about the history of taste. In this vision, the fall of Rome only marks the beginning of one era of bad taste, which is a primeval force that retreats at certain times and triumphs at others.

In reference to Voltaire's famous statement about history having only four bright moments of civilization, Diego Venturino, in "Généalogies du Grand Siècle," remarks that Voltaire saw the bright parts as uniform, as if they represented the same type of Enlightenment— an Enlightenment that is closely tied to the standard of good taste: "Voltaire seeks out his own kind, the bearers of the torch of reason in all times and in all places, that is, the principles and the values of enlightened modernity of his time, considered as universal."[16] This unchanging substance is either buried or uncovered in successive periods, as Venturino describes it. While this observation may be true for Enlightenment values, it is not so certain that Voltaire or his colleagues considered the good taste of ancient Greece as the same type of good taste that emerged in seventeenth-century France. In fact, these critics remark that seventeenth-century authors such as Corneille actually surpass the ancients. In this sense, Voltaire will help shape a specifically French patrimony of good taste, which is influenced by the Quarrel of the Ancients and the Moderns.

PROGRESS AND THE QUARREL OF THE ANCIENTS AND THE MODERNS

One may well ask how this oscillating view of the history of taste compares with the common assumption about the Enlightenment's belief in progress. As I mentioned in Chapter 1, the idea of progress only appeared commonly at the end of the eighteenth century,

most famously in the writings of Condorcet. In fact, during the rest
of the century, there was as much anxiety about decadence as there
was faith in progress. This ambivalence was reflected in the series of
Quarrels of the Ancients and the Moderns, which began in the seventeenth and continued into the early eighteenth century.[17] On the one
hand, the partisans of the ancients saw the trajectory of time as declining from the Golden Age of antiquity, and at best we could only
hope to successfully imitate the past. The moderns judged the present
more favorably, with the justification that the more recent centuries
had the advantage of building upon the accomplishments of the past,
which they expressed with the famous image of the dwarves sitting on
the shoulders of giants.

   After the final phase of the Querelle of the 1710s, involving Anne
Dacier's and Antoine Houdar de la Motte's rival translations of the *Iliad*, eighteenth-century critics tended not to subscribe wholly to either
position but to borrow ideas from both sides. I believe that the following statement from Voltaire sums up his position between the ancients and the moderns: "Both taste and reason seem to require that
we should, in an ancient as well as in a modern, discriminate between
the good and the bad that are often to be found in contact with each
other."[18] Accordingly, the image of the four flashes of light (Greece,
Rome, Renaissance Italy, the France of Louis XIV) against the darkness acknowledges the importance of ancient writers but also valoriz-
es the creations of the newly canonized French "classiques"—Bossuet,
Molière, Corneille, Racine, and others—as equal to the Greeks and
Romans. Many eighteenth-century writers also reconciled the ancient
and modern positions by pointing out that in the domain of astrono-
my, for example, advances had clearly been made after Aristotle but
that he had never been surpassed in the realm of poetics.

   In examining the eighteenth-century critics' judgments about other
periods of French literary history, we will see evidence of these combined ancient and modern stances. I will examine first the contempt
for the French Middle Ages and Renaissance, then the praise of selected seventeenth-century works, and finally the fear of decadence
in their day.

THE MIDDLE AGES: "BARBARIAN" AND "GOTHIC" TASTE

Eighteenth-century critics who wished to uphold the primacy of
the Greek and Latin models for their own ideal of literature fought

against any rival models by deeming them "barbaric" or "Gothic." These two epithets, representing two types of bad taste, on the one hand referred to the tribes that brought about the Fall of Rome[19] but on the other represented a more general judgment about civilization. I will explore both of these uses in this chapter.

First, the historical meaning of *barbaric* and *Gothic* tells us something about eighteenth-century thinkers' attempts to shape their own heritage. Their rejection of Celtic or Frankish influences appears with special prominence in discussions of the sound and the vocabulary of the French language. Second, the ahistorical distinction made between the barbaric and the civilized takes us to the heart of the issue of taste, since critics see good taste as proof that their society has successfully emerged from chaos, even if it is in danger of plunging back into it at any moment. This deliberate vagueness of the terms *Gothic* and *barbaric* can be seen in the often interchangeable use, among the writers of the ancien régime, of the names of various tribes such as the Goths, the Franks, the Vandals, the Gauls, and what Voltaire calls the "Welches." In these instances, the marauding Goth was more of a literary bogeyman whose features only sometimes coincided with those of the historical figure. For example, Montesquieu, in his unfinished 1734 essay "De la maniere gothique" ("Of the Gothic manner"), explicitly states that he does not exclusively associate the word *gothique* with the Gothic tribes: "The gothic manner is not the manner of a particular people; it is the manner of the birth or of the end of art."[20] Similarly, for Jaucourt in the article "Gothique (manière)" of the *Encyclopédie*, the term *gothic* referred not to a specific movement but simply to an absence of rules. He provides the following definition of *gothique*: "a manner that does not recognize any rules, that is not directed by any study of antiquity, and in which one only perceives a capriciousness that has nothing noble in it; this barbarian manner infected the Arts from 611 until 1450, the time that will be forever remembered, when one began to search for the beautiful in nature and in the works of the ancients."[21] This so-called infection of the arts by the medieval spirit will take on more specific characteristics when we examine the works that were not necessarily created by the so-called barbaric tribes but were associated with them.

In describing barbaric literary style, critics often evoke gothic cathedrals as metaphors for aesthetic faults. For Montesquieu, in his *Essai sur le goût*, Greek temples exemplify good taste while medieval churches represent excess: "A Gothic structure is to the eye what a riddle is to the understanding; in the contemplation of its various parts and ornaments, the mind perceives the same perplexity and confusion in its ideas that arise from reading an obscure poem."[22] He proceeds to explain that the churches' overwhelming number of details and lack of order tend to confuse and eventually bore the onlooker, just as a "poème obscur" will confound the reader to no good purpose. The complaint about overly ornamented buildings of the Middle Ages resonates throughout the writings of the eighteenth century. Crousaz remarks, for example, "It is for this reason that the gothic trinkets have fallen out of favor since taste has improved; one began to prefer simplicity in the parts, which allowed one to immediately see the proportions and how they relate to each another, to an infinite number of small ornaments and embellishments that amused, that distracted the attention from the main object."[23] In terms of literature, this overly ornamented architecture can be compared to a text that is overcrowded with rhetorical tricks.

Montesquieu refers to one specific rhetorical ornament that is overused by medieval writers: the antithesis.[24]

> certain authors, who, by perpetual antitheses, form a contrast between the beginning and the end of each phrase. Of this we find several examples in St Augustin, and others, who wrote during the low periods of the Latin language; and also in the writings of several moderns, particularly those of St Evremont. The same cadence or jingle repeated in every phrase is extremely disagreeable and fastidious. *Contrasts* thus multiplied, become intolerably uniform; and those oppositions that were designed to produce variety, degenerate, by perpetual repetition, into the most tedious symmetry.[25]

The particular objection that Montesquieu expresses against the dreaded *antithèse* is that, like excessive variety in architecture, it tries to surprise the reader with unexpected contrasts, but, paradoxically, it becomes uniform and tedious if used too often.[26]

It is typical of the anti-"gothic" discourse, as we can see in the passage above, that the author focuses first on an example of visual arts, the cathedral, and then immediately jumps to a seventeenth-/eighteenth-century author, Saint Evremond, without mentioning any actual French medieval literature. Aside from Saint Augustine, it is difficult to discern what texts the critics referred to, since titles and names of authors are rarely ever evoked. Instead of explaining to us what features of actual medieval writing they objected to, the critics of the eighteenth century often focused instead on discrediting one

seventeenth-century genre, namely modern epics that were set in the
Middle Ages.

To return to the historical use of the term *barbaric*, in terms of nationality, it is as if the critics attempted to reinvent their own history
by excluding anything that belonged to their Germanic or Celtic heritage. By doing so, they could claim the role of the direct descendants
of the Greeks and Romans, maintaining the tradition of *translatio
studii*, an idea they borrowed, ironically, from the Middle Ages. Defenders of eighteenth-century classicism resembled individuals who
find it advantageous to erase or ignore a whole branch of their family
trees.[27] Perhaps it is inevitable that an individual or a society would
be selective when looking at their past, but it is worthwhile, in any
case, to inquire into the reasons why eighteenth-century critics may
have wished to distance themselves from their "barbaric" ancestors in
favor of their Roman ones.

The idea of choosing one's history explains why many writers use
the words *barbaric* and *Gothic* with scorn, even if these writers were
descendants of so-called barbarian tribes. Critics such as Voltaire
and Marmontel even suggested that words derived from Germanic
or Celtic languages should be expunged from the French vocabulary.
In this matter as in many others, Voltaire and Marmontel followed
the satiric model of Boileau, a partisan of the ancients in the Quarrel
of the Ancients and the Moderns. In his *Art poétique* (1674), Boileau
mocks Frankish proper names when he derides epic poets who choose
barbaric heroes over Greek characters. While names such as Ulysse or
Hélène seem made for poetry, he exclaims,

> Such riches must condemn the surly writer
> Who names his hero Hildebrand. How frightful!
> One harsh, unpleasant, jangling name or title
> Can make bizarre what might have been delightful.[28]

This admonition tells us as much about Boileau's contempt for medieval names as it does about the threatening presence of his rivals,
the moderns, and their literary projects. His bile may have been specifically directed against Carel de Sainte Garde's epic poem *Childebrand*, but it is worth noting that in this passage of the *Art poétique*,
Boileau more generally attacks the trend in epic poems featuring
Frankish heroes, such as George de Scudéry's *Alaric* and Desmarets
de Saint-Sorlin's *Clovis*. In the passage above, Boileau's harsh judgment rests entirely on the opinion that Frankish-sounding names,

even if they are part of the French heritage, are harsh ("durs") or simply displeasing.

In eighteenth-century literature, even using words that referred to regions of France such as *bourguignon* or *breton*, named after the non-Roman tribes that settled them, obviously meant to bring shame to its natives and provoke hilarity among the public. This idea appears in Piron's play *La Métromanie*, in which one bad poet takes on the alias of a fictional bretonne woman named Mériadec de Kersic, whose name and origin (Quimper in Bas-Bretagne) are meant to render her automatically ridiculous to the public. Voltaire makes similar use of the Bretons in his story *L'Ingénu*, with the deliberately unharmonious name "Kerkabon" and the constant mention of Lower Brittany, with the adjective "bas-breton," to signify ignorance and provincialism. He could have chosen instead to set the story in a southern region of France, but I believe that the more Latinized names were not as funny to Voltaire or his audience.

In fact, Voltaire wrote a whole treatise in 1764 to express his scorn for the supposedly embarrassing non-classical aspects of the French language. It is entitled *Discours aux Welches*, and he refers to the "Welsh" without distinguishing them from Gauls, Franks, or other tribes that settled in France (unlike his more carefully researched chapters on medieval history in his *Essai sur les mœurs*). In the *Discours aux Welches*, he objects to the unpleasant sound of the non-Greek or Latin words that can be found in the French language. He disdainfully refers to the Fall of Rome at the hands of "Vandals, to whom you gave the sonorous appellation of Bourgonsions, or Bourguignons, people of great genius, and extremely cleanly, who rubbed their hair with strong butter."[29] He stresses the etymological variants of words such as *Bourguignon* and even *France*, surely because he wished to show the less familiar and less attractive sound of these Germanic variants. For instance, he remarks: "it was at that time that the Welsh country had the melodious name of Frankreich, the ancient name of France."[30] According to Voltaire, the French language is marred by "your ancient Welsh and Teutonic" or "dry and barbarous terms";[31] place-names strike him as particularly ugly and common, such as the rue Trousse-Vache or église Saint-Pierre-aux-Boeufs. Voltaire punctures French pride in the language by pointing out how grotesque and vulgar French words are in comparison to Greek.

Voltaire makes a similar point in the article that he significantly titled "Franc ou Franq; France, François, Français," of the *Diction-*

naire philosophique. In the title itself, he seems to offer his readers a choice between elegant modern French or "barbaric" French. In the section on the French tongue, he claims that the language of "the Celtic, or Keltic, people, a race of savages, of which we know nothing but the name,"[32] has practically disappeared from France, but "a remainder of the old patois is still conserved among some yokels in the [British] province of Wales, in lower Brittany, in some French villages."[33] This statement serves as a brief introduction to a long list of words that Voltaire cites for their Celtic provenance (later in the article, he admits that some may actually be of Frankish origin). Among these words, we find those in common usage, such as *acheter, parc,* and *rêver,* but it is significant that nearly half of the words suggest either dishonesty or vulgarity: *bagarre, fripon, ladre, rat, cracher, trognon, trousse.* In fact, many of the words that Voltaire claims are of Celtic or Frankish heritage contain the sounds (such as "gr" combinations and –g endings) that he uses to name unsympathetic characters in his writings, as we will see in the following chapter on foreignness and taste.

In "Franc ou Franq; France, François, Français," his stated purpose is not to delve into the origins of ugly words out of scholarly curiosity: "It is of little importance to know of these remains of barbaric ruins, a few words of a jargon that resembled, as the emperor Julian said, the cries of beasts. Let us think of conserving in its purity the beautiful language that we spoke in the great age of Louis XIV."[34] The important thing, he states, is to devise a purified and harmonious French language, perhaps resigning oneself to its "barbaric" sources but still trying to reach a certain level of decorum and harmony.

According to *Discours aux Welches,* the French language is rescued from total hideousness by a handful of its illustrious writers of the seventeenth century: "I am far from denying that Pascal, Bossuet, and Fénelon were extremely eloquent. It was upon the appearing of these geniuses that you ceased to be Welsh, and that you became French."[35] But now the times are threatened by "another plague," which is composed of "a set of rigid people who call themselves solid . . . men of learning, enemies to letters, who are forever banishing polite antiquity and fable."[36] The treatise ends with an exhortation to recognize the difference between good and bad writers: "Do not give ear to their insinuations, oh, Frenchmen! If you do, you will soon become Welsh again."[37] In this pastiche of a religious sermon, Voltaire commands readers to guard not against the devil or sin but against ugly words. If readers fail to do so, they may regress, even after their language has reached the high point of the seventeenth century. The idea of becoming French suggests that even though the Roman Empire has fallen and the remaining populations speak a corrupt mixture of "Gothic and Latin," the French nation can still refine itself enough to create an acceptable language. However, the standard of refinement must be maintained by removing unpleasant-sounding words, lest one return to that shameful state of linguistic barbarism.

As in the discourse against modern epics, the absence of actual references to medieval literature in the attacks on "barbaric taste" lead us to think that eighteenth-century critics were actually concerned with other threats, to which they gave the perfunctory designation of "the Middle Ages." The most obvious threat was religion; when Montesquieu insults Saint Augustine's style, for instance, he surely cannot be ignoring his Christian message. In fact, Montesquieu makes explicit connections between his contempt for the Middle Ages and the bad influence of Christianity in his *Pensées*:

> There is nothing as pitiful as the poetry of five or six centuries . . . there are only miserable works, made by people who had nothing more than ideas taken from Scripture. (The singular attention given to Scripture by a number of monks made others produce many bad profane works . . .) But, as soon as they began to read the Ancients, even if they lost a century commenting and translating them, they finally saw authors appear.[38]
>
> I believe that we were spoiled by the ideas from Scripture that people always wanted to transpose onto poetry.[39]

This rhetorical use of the Fall of Rome as a covert attack on Christianity is not unusual, as we can see, for example, in the work of eighteenth-century historians such as Edward Gibbon.[40]

At times, however, one is convinced that the complaints about the bad taste of the Middle Ages are truly about taste and do not merely disguise an attack on Christianity. Crousaz, for example, dedicates large sections of his *Traité du beau* to praising God's creation and to reflecting on the beauty of good Christian behavior. His dislike of gothic cathedrals surely does not proceed from any skepticism regarding religion, particularly since he was employed as a professor of theology, among other subjects. However, since he was a Protestant, perhaps one could suspect that his hostility toward gothic cathedrals proceeded from a specifically anti-Catholic sentiment. In any case, I believe that religion was sometimes the true target of the critiques of taste, but not in every case. Depending on the author, the "barbaric" could have represented other evils, such as the public's wayward reading preferences.

Bountiful evidence of anti-medieval hostility can be found in eighteenth-century texts, but some scholars, such as Lionel Gossman, have found proof that medieval historiography and philology still flourished in the eighteenth century. Certainly in the world of the novel, we can see that the Middle Ages enjoyed a great deal of success, even though the readers were, as Katherine Astbury remarks, less "worried with historical accuracy" than with seeing examples of the stereotypical knightly virtues.[41] In fact, the Middle Ages made their appearance in several guises during the eighteenth century: for instance, in the genre of fairy tales or as the setting for tragedies such as Du Belloy's *Le Siège de Calais* or Voltaire's *Tancrède*. Furthermore, the chivalric tales of Roland, Huon de Bordeaux, and Tirant lo Blanc had been transmitted from generation to generation, and this was no less true in the eighteenth century. Many of these chivalric tales were adapted and republished in the serial *Bibliothèque universelle des romans* from 1775 to 1789.[42] Lise Andries confirms the prominence of chivalric tales in the eighteenth century, specifically in the context of the *Bibliothèque bleue*.[43] While Andries focuses specifically on a lower-class readership, there is also evidence, from Gossman and others, that the appeal of chivalric novels reached all social ranks. As Gossman remarks in *Medievalism and the Ideologies of the Enlightenment*:

> Despite the jabs of eighteenth century novelists, the romances of Mlle de Scudéry, La Calprenède, and Honoré d'Urfé were still favorites with the reading public of the eighteenth century. Fontenelle and Rousseau, for instance, were both ardent readers of *L'Astrée*. There was thus a ready market for piquant versions of the old romances and *chansons* in the medieval or chivalric tradition—and several writers were kept busy supplying it. . . . The *Mercure* (from about 1743) and the *Année littéraire* (from about 1750) led the way in printing "medieval" or frankly pseudo-medieval novels and verse.[44]

It is interesting to see that Gossman follows the practices of eighteenth-century critics by making references to both actual medieval sources and seventeenth-century texts whose action takes place in the Middle Ages.[45] In any case, the presence, and even the popularity, of the Middle Ages in the eighteenth-century book market does not necessarily contradict the anti-medieval discourse among many of the *philosophes* but rather shows us the tension between popular tastes and the views of the critics I treat in this chapter. To disparagers of the Middle Ages, what did this period represent?

The abbé Dubos provides us with a few possible answers to this question. Even though he is considered a modern, Dubos devotes a considerable section of his *Réflexions* to praising Homer, and unlike the seventeenth-century moderns, he rejects medieval literature, purportedly for its vulgarity and the excessive importance it attributes to love. Like Boileau in *Dialogue des héros de roman*, Dubos makes a connection between gothicism and bad taste—specifically the bad taste that demanded the inclusion of too many love episodes in theater (a complaint of Voltaire's as well): "Romances of chivalry and pastoral tales have also encouraged among the French the pernicious taste of intermixing love with every thing."[46] Dubos also denounces bad taste in theater, and in his harangue he conflates the badness of foreign influences, of a vague "gothic" past, and of the lower classes. In chapter 21 of his first book, in which he explains his theory that the theater of one nation cannot be adapted to the tastes of another nation, he blames the introduction of Italian *buffoni* and Spanish farces to the French stage. We can no longer tolerate, he states, the operas of the abbé Perrin, which include buffoons. Even though the operas are of recent production, he claims, "these pieces, tho' written within these sixty-eight years, appear to us as Gothic poems composed five or six generations ago."[47] In regard to farces, he claims that the public has enough "bon goût" to reject the burlesque plays of *Dom Japhet* by Paul Scarron, whose sources were Spanish, since "those farces, whose constant subject is the course of life, which a particular class of debauched people perpetually lead, are as contrary to rule, as they are to decency and good manners."[48] Lest we misunderstand his frequent usage of the term *public*, we can see confirmation of Dubos's elitist conception of it in the following passage: "There is but a very small number of spectators, that have sufficiently frequented the company of the originals, whose copies are there exposed, so as to be able to judge whether the characters and events are treated with any resemblance of truth. One grows tired of bad company on the stage, as well as in private life."[49] To allow the inclusion of foreign and archaic elements in the French theater means, in Dubos's eyes, to lower the tone to a vulgar level.

We see, then, that eighteenth-century critics were concerned with eliminating elements from literature that they considered medieval, such as vulgar language and a lack of form. Yet their enemies were not actual literary works of the Middle Ages but more recent works that treated medieval subjects or whose style merely suggested that period.

THE RENAISSANCE IS NOT FRENCH

What is "wrong" with the Renaissance? One could suppose that the Renaissance and the Enlightenment shared enough common traits (secularism, admiration for antiquity) that eighteenth-century thinkers would consider the previous age as an illustrious ancestor. In fact, this was not the case. Although the Renaissance figured as one of the four high points in the Voltairian history of taste, it must be noted that he referred to the Italian Renaissance, not the French one. The third age of good taste, he claims, began when the Turks invaded Constantinople, forcing Greek intellectuals to take refuge in Italy and depend on the enlightened support of the Medicis. In Voltaire's opinion, other countries did not benefit as much as Italy from this exile of scholars because, metaphorically, their climates did not allow them to flourish, as he remarks in *Le Siècle de Louis XIV* (we will see a more literal discussion about the compatibility of certain climates and the arts in the next chapter). Among these unfortunate countries, he includes France: "The arts, always transplanted from Greece to Italy, found themselves in a favorable soil, where they instantly produced fruit. France, England, Germany, and Spain aimed in turn to gather these fruits; but either they could not live in those climates, or else they degenerated very rapidly."[50] Even though the French king François Ier may have tried to transplant great artists and architects from Italy, Voltaire claims, he failed to develop his country as a center for visual and literary arts. France could produce "no Michelangelo, nor Palladio" but, sadly, only Rabelais and "some epigrams and a few loose tales [that] made the whole of our poetry."[51]

Claude Faisant, in *Mort et résurrection de la Pléiade*, remarks upon Voltaire's intentional blindness to the French Renaissance: "Reducing the Renaissance to an exclusively Italian phenomenon, he saw in the 'Century of Louis the Great' the direct descendant of the 'Century of Pope Leon X' and of the Medicis. All his efforts were directed towards breaking the connection between our sixteenth and our seventeenth centuries, in order to isolate the latter for the national heritage and to inscribe it into the vision of the four great centuries of Humanity. At the same time, he threw the memory of our Renaissance into 'gothic' darkness."[52] In the history of taste, then, where do the literary figures of the French Renaissance fit, if not in the areas of illumination?

First of all, eighteenth-century critics tend to mention a small number of French names from the sixteenth century: Amyot (even though he was mostly a translator), Rabelais, Montaigne, Ronsard, and Marot. Others are rarely mentioned at all, as we can see, for example, in the comprehensive history of literature by La Harpe, who devotes only forty pages of his sixteen-volume *Lycée, ou Cours de littérature ancienne et moderne* to the period between the height of the Roman Empire and the advent of Louis XIV. In reference to this seemingly empty period, La Harpe states: "Descartes had not yet been born. The language had neither purity nor correctness. . . . French theater, which has since become the best in the world, did not exist. The prose of Amyot and the poetry of Marot distinguished themselves especially through a naive character, which is still felt among us; but the nobility and the regularity of an elevated diction, the conventions of style appropriate for the subject, were unknown qualities."[53] Like his mentor Voltaire, La Harpe counts Rabelais as an exception to this inferior era, although he admits that his merits are often hidden underneath a "bizarre and obscure language." In other words, "ultimately, he has, along with a great deal of mess and filth, some witticisms and even some passages that are full of satiric, original, and piquant verve."[54] The double-edged compliment draws our attention to Rabelais's qualities as much as to his reprehensible vulgarity.

Like his fellow Voltaire protégé La Harpe, Marmontel plunges both the Middle Ages and the Renaissance into oblivion when he remarks in his *Essai sur le goût*: "Between Euripides and Racine, some long periods of barbarism had to pass."[55] He elaborates on the characteristics of the art of this period that he finds so dreadful:

> The errors of the mind, the deviations of the imagination, the absurd fictions, the irregular compositions, were not the effects of ignorance but of depravity. . . . The coarsest sketches, the most shapeless productions of a nascent art, seemed marvelous to them. The poems of Ronsard, the tragedies of Jodelle were, in their time, inimitable masterpieces. . . .
>
> Art believed that its merit consisted in feats of skill, in vain subtleties, in puerile refinements, in a painful search for exaggerated sentiments, strange expressions, forced antitheses, extravagant hyperboles.[56]

Marmontel's emphasis on the "depravity" of Renaissance style recalls his description of the *homme inculte*, the intermediary figure
who lacks both the primitive man's instinctive eloquence and civilized
man's good taste.

Although the Middle Ages and the French Renaissance often seem
to be conflated in the critics' statements, when we look more closely, we can see that they tend to blame each period for two opposing
faults. While eighteenth-century writers such as Voltaire looked down
on the Middle Ages for getting too far away from the Greco-Latin tradition, they attacked the Renaissance for following this same tradition too closely. In Dubos's opinion, the French Renaissance failed to
produce good poetry altogether: "Is it because Ronsard and his contemporaries did not understand the learned tongues, they composed
works, whose taste has so little a resemblance with that of the better
sort of the Greek and Roman writings? No, so far from that, their
greatest defect is to have imitated them in too servile a manner, and
to have attempted to speak Greek and Latin with French words."[57]
Significantly, Dubos suggests that good taste in ancient Greece and
Rome cannot simply be transposed to French literature, since it becomes bad taste in this new context.

In a similar vein, d'Alembert and Diderot depict the Renaissance as
a necessary but awkward stage in French history in the Preliminary
Discourse to the *Encyclopédie*. Once the French had emerged from the
"Dark times" ("tems ténébreux") (I:xx) just after the Fall of Rome,
they were fortunate to rediscover the texts of the ancients, the authors
claim. But, they continue, the Renaissance scholars approached these
texts the wrong way: they accumulated and deciphered ancient works
servilely, indiscriminately worshiping all ancient authors. Referring to
their division of knowledge into three faculties—imagination, memory, and reason—Diderot and d'Alembert attribute the more pedes-
trian faculty of memory to these Renaissance scholars, but they claim
the superior faculty of reason for later scholars, including themselves.

Furthermore, Diderot and d'Alembert state that this erudition
without judgment led to bizarre changes in the French language, since
Ronsard and his fellows tried to integrate Latin and Greek to create what we now call Middle French: "they began by distorting the
French tongue instead of enriching it. Ronsard created a barbarous
jargon, bristling with Greek and Latin; but fortunately he made it
so unrecognizable that it became ridiculous."[58] Eventually, however,
good taste came to the rescue and scholars began to make distinc-

tions of beauty when importing ancient words into the vernacular: "Men soon saw that it was the beauties and not the words of ancient languages which should be translated into our own. Guided and perfected by good taste, it rather quickly acquired an infinite number of pleasing and happy expressions."[59] In their opinion, just as too much of a barbaric influence could make French ugly, so could an awkward grafting of Greek and Latin words onto the vernacular.

Then, taking their lead from Boileau's famous statement "enfin Malherbe vint" ("finally, Malherbe arrived"),[60] Diderot and d'Alembert give credit to this poet for bringing elegance to the French language: "Malherbe, nurtured by the reading of the excellent poets of antiquity and taking nature as a model as they had done, was the first to enhance our poetry with a harmony and beauty which it had never known before."[61] This conception of "Nature," not as arbitrariness but as the selection of the perfect model, recalls the specific meaning of Batteux's call to "imiter la belle nature." Thanks to Malherbe, the authors of the *Encyclopédie* remark, the French language received the boost it needed in order to be shaped into something that actually surpassed Greek and Latin (in this instance defending the moderns' point of view).

Voltaire agreed with this unfavorable view of Ronsard and his fellow Pléïade poets, as we can see when he complains in the article "Franc" in the *Dictionnaire philosophique* that "Ronsard spoiled the language by transposing the grafted words from the Greek that philosophers and physicians used," but "Malherbe repaired to a small extent the wrongs committed by Ronsard. The language became nobler and more harmonious through the establishment of the French Academy and it finally acquired, in the age of Louis XIV, the perfection to which it could be carried in all genres."[62] Voltaire even worries that in later periods, Marot can still reach out from the grave to impose his bad taste on French literature. Even though "Malherbe vint," Voltaire remarks about the early eighteenth-century poet Jean-Baptiste Rousseau in his *Siècle de Louis XIV*: "He would have corrupted the French language if others had imitated the *Marotic* style which he employed in serious works. But fortunately his adulteration of the purity of our language with the outworn forms of two centuries earlier proved only a passing phase."[63] Thus the French language was saved, for the moment.

In the eighteenth century, Ronsard and Marot are blamed for their choice of words, and like Montaigne, they are accused of using a language that is simply not French, but neither is it proper Greek or Latin. This prepares the way for a conception of good French taste that is inspired by but distinct from the ancients.

The conflict emerges from the tension between the wish to expand French vocabulary and to restrain it, which historians of the language have long discussed.[64] Among literary scholars, Daniel Mornet in *Histoire de la clarté française* and René Bray in *La Formation de la doctrine classique en France* have reflected on one particular phase of the history of the French language, the early seventeenth century. In this conflict, poets such as Malherbe represented those who preferred a purified, minimal vocabulary, while his contemporaries such as Marie de Gournay, editor of Montaigne's works, called for a richer variety of words. As Bray remarks, those who agreed with Gournay also tended to defend Ronsard's reputation. But Bray also shows us evidence that this latter party was on the wane while Malherbe and his partisans were on the rise. After all, Bray asks in regard to Marie de Gournay, "who took her seriously?"[65]—a sentiment that is also expressed in eighteenth-century works.[66] Other supporters of Ronsard, such as Régnier and Chapelain, were eventually ignored or ridiculed by Enlightenment critics for their alleged bad taste. By contrast, the laudatory references to Malherbe by Dubos, Voltaire, d'Alembert, and their fellow philosophers make it clear to us that when they looked back to this debate, they took the purists' side.

Among the objectionable words that others tried to introduce into the French language, they included diminutives. Dumarsais's article "Diminutif" in the *Encyclopédie* expresses unambiguous contempt for these derivatives:

> The Italians and the Spanish are more abundant in diminutives than we are; it seems that the French language does not like to be rich in trinkets and knick-knacks, says Père Bouhours. Today, we no longer use those words that have diminutive endings, like *hommelet, rossignolet, montagnette, campagnette, tendrelet, doucelet, nymphelette, larmelette*, etc. . . .
> The Italians and the Spanish make even more diminutives from the first diminutives; for example, from *bambino*, a small child, they made *bambinello, bamboccio, bambocciolo*, etc. That is how, in Latin, one made *homo* into *homuncio*, and from *homuncio, homunculus*, and even *homulus*. These three words are in Cicero. Père Bouhours says that these are pygmies that are multiplying and producing children that are even smaller than they are.[67]

In this passage, Dumarsais insists on the foreign provenance of these diminutives, which fits well with the rejection of the Spanish and Italian influences during the previous century. Another interesting aspect of the passage above is the choice of examples: the diminutives referring to small men are surely not chosen arbitrarily. In fact, they force the reader to associate effeminacy, foreign influences, and bad language choices.

Dumarsais continues his article by ridiculing those who favored the inclusion of diminutives into the French language—specifically Ronsard and Marie de Gournay, who "in their lifetime, neglected nothing to insert these terms into our language."[68] Through the words of the père Bouhours, Dumarsais depicts Gournay in particular as unhealthily obsessed with these words:

> she declared herself their high protector; yet our language did not accept these diminutives; or if it did at that time, it got rid of them immediately afterwards. Since the time of Montaigne, people have risen up against such cute [*mignon*] words, the favorites of his adopted daughter. It was useless for her to undertake their defense and to cry murder with all her strength; in spite of all that, the poor young lady still had the displeasure to see her dear diminutives banished little by little, and if she were alive now, I believe, continues the Père Bouhours, that she would die of chagrin at seeing them entirely exterminated.[69]

Dumarsais's choice of words, such as "adopted daughter ("fille d'alliance") and "poor young lady" ("pauvre demoiselle"), discredits this scholar by emphasizing her gender and by infantilizing her. In fact, Gournay's dismay at the exclusion of her "mignon" words appears, in this passage, to be nothing more than the reaction of a spoiled girl who has lost her favorite pets.

Furthermore, in this article Dumarsais defends his position as a purist by using expressions that suggest consensus, such as "the French language does not like" ("la langue française n'aime point") and "our language did not accept" ("notre langue n'a pas reçu"). These examples show how Dumarsais, like his colleagues, conflates the actual state of the language and the idealized vision of it—in spite of the lack of consensus revealed by the debates that he had just discussed.

Aside from problems with Middle French vocabulary, the eighteenth-century critics objected to the style of Renaissance prose writers, especially Montaigne.[70] This author provides an interesting case for the study of bad taste. Whereas one could believe that attacks on the so-called Gothic taste merely dissimulated attacks on Christian doctrine, the critics' condemnation of Montaigne's style was surely in conflict with the admiration they felt for his philosophy. In other words, one could easily separate Voltaire's and Jaucourt's remarks about Montaigne's bad taste from their affinity with his ideas.

According to many eighteenth-century texts, Montaigne's bad style was based on his use of archaic words, irrelevant Latin quotations, and excessive digressions. A more content-based criticism focused on his "indecent" frankness about bodily functions and his outrageous narcissism, which allowed him to talk about himself to an extent that was considered unacceptable in polite society. His qualities, which were sometimes cited by the same people who attacked him for the reasons above, were said to be a charming "naïveté" (a backhanded compliment, as if his words flowed without any reflection or intention on his part) and his "energy."[71] In Voltaire's judgment, "the French language acquired some vigor from the pen of Montaigne; but it did not yet have any elevation or harmony."[72] La Harpe also weighs the good and the bad qualities that he sees in Montaigne's writings: "Montaigne was doubtless a mind of superior caliber. . . . First, let us admit his faults: that's how we begin with people we love. . . . His diction is incorrect, even for that time, even though he's given the language some expressions and turns of phrase that it has kept as old treasures; he abuses his conversational liberty and loses sight of the question at hand."[73] With faults such as these, one radical solution that eighteenth-century critics proposed was to rewrite Montaigne. In *La Renommée de Montaigne en France au XVIIIe siècle*, Maturin Dréano discusses one revealing moment in the reception of Montaigne, when the critic Trublet proposed to translate the *Essais* into French. The debate that ensued in the *Mercure de France* shows us that, to critics like Trublet, Montaigne's language was so far removed from the ideal of acceptable style that one could hardly count him as a French writer—yet his ideas were evidently so important that critics did not want to dismiss him altogether.

Dréano documents the debate, which starts with Trublet's proposal to translate Montaigne, in the June 1733 issue of the *Mercure*: "His book is almost not a French book anymore."[74] In a later letter to the *Mercure*, Trublet elaborates on this thought, as Dréano reports: "The abbé Trublet returns immediately to discussing the language of Montaigne. 'This is what one commonly calls Gallic [Gaulois]. Now to change Gallic into French is basically to translate it. Formerly, Gallic words were considered French, but now they are no longer so, not any more than Italian or Spanish words are, with the exception of the word endings, which are still French.'"[75] This projected translation of Montaigne into French provoked so much opposition, as is documented in the letters to the *Mercure*, that Trublet decided to renounce it altogether. In regard to this debate, I would especially like to highlight the accusation that Montaigne is "not French" and the popular backlash against this type of judgment. It is significant that this debate took place in the pages of the *Mercure*, since this publication was much maligned among the Enlightenment *philosophes*, in my opinion, because it allowed readers to voice their opposition to the judgments of established men of letters.

Furthermore, as Sarah Benharrech points out in her article "Lecteur, que vous êtes bigearre!: Marivaux et la 'querelle de Montaigne,'"[76] Marivaux was one of the critics who defended Montaigne in the early eighteenth century. In this and other matters of literary aesthetics, Marivaux stood in opposition to many of the Enlightenment *philosophes*, who disparaged his style. Even when Marivaux praises him, though, he grants that Montaigne spoke his own language, which is not exactly French: "If Montaigne had lived in our day, how people would have critiqued his style! Because he spoke neither French, nor German, nor Breton, nor Swiss. He thought, he expressed himself according to a singular and fine soul."[77] Even his supporter could not bring himself to call him a French writer.

Ultimately, Montaigne presented a paradox to eighteenth-century readers and critics, with many unsure of how to reconcile his nonclassical taste with his appealing ideas. The dilemma of how to judge Montaigne could be compared to the French critics' puzzlement over Shakespeare and Milton, whose writings they considered full of vigor and even genius, yet whom they saw as committing major faults of taste.

THE SEVENTEENTH CENTURY: "QU'IL MOURÛT" VS. PRADON

In contrast to the tasteless Renaissance, eighteenth-century critics presented the seventeenth century as the Grand Siècle, the highest point of good French taste. It was the new golden age, which was better than antiquity because the French were able to build upon the achievements of their Greek and Roman predecessors. In *Le Siècle de Louis XIV*, Voltaire readily concedes that other countries may boast of their scientific and philosophical achievements, but in terms of literature, he claims that France at its best surpasses all others: "The philosophy of reason did not make such great progress in France as in England and in Florence. . . . All the discoveries and the great truths originated elsewhere. But in rhetoric, poetry, culture, didactic or merely amusing books, the French were the legislators of Europe. There was no longer taste in Italy. True rhetoric was everywhere unknown."[78] Other eighteenth-century critics agreed with Voltaire's high praise for the achievements of seventeenth-century writers, to the extent that it would be difficult to find an example of a dissenting opinion. In *Essai sur le goût*, Marmontel, for example, remarks of the period of Louis XIV's youth: "Let us conclude that the century of genius was also the century of taste; and let us add that it was more delicate, more refined, more enlightened taste than that of Rome or Athens."[79] But just as Antoine Compagnon demonstrates in his *Troisième république des lettres* that nineteenth-century critics and professors shaped the canon as we know it for the purposes of their political agendas, the Enlightenment critics invented the seventeenth century to serve their own ends, selecting certain aspects and pointedly ignoring others. For instance, they all agreed on a canon that included Molière, Racine, Corneille, and the religious orators Bossuet, Bourdaloue, and Massillon, but successful writers of the same century, such as Madeleine de Scudéry, Jean Chapelain, and Paul Scarron, were left by the wayside.

Marmontel addresses the problem of excluding authors from the seventeenth-century canon in his *Essai sur le goût*.

> One can well imagine that there was, at first, in the competition of writers and connoisseurs, an infinite number of failed pretentions and false glimmers of wit, talent, and taste. Each society had its predilections, each wit had his circle, each talent its enemies. . . . The most famous tribunals were often the most unjust. Here, Pradon had his patrons, and Racine his detractors; there, Chapelain was admired while reciting verses from *La Pucelle*; elsewhere, it was the Scudérys that were exalted, while Corneille was put down; Boursault had his partisans who preferred him to Molière. Everything seemed confused.[80]

In short, the period may have abounded in authors, even successful ones, but that does not mean that they had any merit. Marmontel blames these literary circles for their partisanship, as opposed to the "public," a term he uses rhetorically, much like Dubos, to give his particular preferences the appearance of consensus. He compares the resolution of these literary debates to the process of making wine and to purifying gold: "It was during this moment of fermentation and of trouble that the public spirit was becoming purified, like wine that emits some foam. All that opinion needs in order to be rectified, all that taste demands in order to become polished, is movement . . . partialies end, prejudices dissipate, opinion is finally set; and look at the bottom of the crucible, the truth remains, as pure as gold."[81] Like the père André, for whom essential beauty is as indisputable as a mathematical equation, Marmontel considers his idea of good taste as eternal and true, while he dismisses rival conceptions of good taste as ephemeral and partisan: "So it is not the ebb and flow of opposing sentiments, of scattered judgments, of heterogeneous opinions, that decide the taste of a century; it is their result, it is the whole and the sum of public opinion. Everyone was wrong, but the public was right in the end."[82] In this passage, however, Marmontel does not take into account the segments of the public (however he may define this term) who do not share his preferences in the end.

To justify the special place given to the authors of the seventeenth century, critics of the eighteenth century often looked to the same example. The line from Corneille's tragedy *Horace*, "qu'il mourût," practically became the motto of good taste in the eighteenth century. The line of the play is pronounced by the elder Horace in act III, scene 6, when he hears that his son, the younger Horace, ran away from his attackers during a battle. When asked what he would have wanted his son to do, the father responds, "Qu'il mourût"; he would rather his son die than betray his military honor. Dubos, Voltaire, Marmontel, and Diderot all cite these three words as the greatest example of good style. But what does this phrase tell us about good taste?

Boileau mentioned the *qu'il mourût* as an example of the sublime in the 1701 preface to his translation of Longinus's *On the Sublime*. The definition of the sublime that Boileau advances in this preface is one of terseness and simplicity, as we can see in his distinction between the sublime style and the sublime itself. In Boileau's conception, sublime *style* merely employs words of an elevated register, while the sublime itself, which he obviously prefers, may use simple words but still creates a feeling of awe. From ancient literature, he picks out the example from Genesis: "And God said, let there be light; and there was light,"[83] and from the corpus of French literature, he chooses one example, Corneille's "Qu'il mourût."

In this case, not only do words of a simple register create a major effect, but the terseness of the phrase also counts as an advantage. Voltaire, eternally finding fault even with his favorite authors, contrasts the beauty of the *qu'il mourût* with the more wordy phrase that follows it in the elder Horace's speech,[84] which continues, "that he had died / Or that a beautiful despair had saved him." In his *Commentaires sur Corneille*, Voltaire states in regard to this passage, "There is the famous *qu'il mourût*, this most sublime passage, this phrase to which none in antiquity can compare. The whole audience was so moved that they never heard the weak verse that followed."[85] For Voltaire, the *qu'il mourût* stands better on its own, presumably because its conciseness adds to its power.

The terseness and the simplicity of this line illustrate the ideal of good taste among critics such as Voltaire, specifically in conjunction with the discourse against ornamentation. The excesses of poetic ornament had been denounced repeatedly by authors ranging from Quintilian to Jean-Jacques Rousseau. These authors advocated a pared-down style, associated with masculinity and virtue. Corneille's *qu'il mourût* is a perfect example of this style, since the sentence is reduced to the very minimum, while the content expresses a conventionally manly sentiment: the suppression of familial love in favor of military honor. By contrast, eighteenth-century critics denounced the opposite of terseness, which they labeled *bel-esprit*, as convoluted language prized by the effeminate and the frivolous.

For Diderot, the famous phrase perfectly illustrates his theory of beauty, which is based on "rapports." As he explains in the article "Beau" of the *Encyclopédie*, it is not the phrase itself that is beautiful, but the more the reader knows of the circumstances of the plot that frame these words, the more striking and emotionally moving the phrase becomes, as I mentioned in Chapter 2. Tzvetan Todorov, in *Théories du symbole*, reflects on what this phrase means for Diderot's aesthetics: "*Qu'il mourût* is not beautiful in terms of what it imitates, but rather by the position it occupies in a network of relations."[86] Todorov thus concludes that in this instance, Diderot disregards the definition of good art as the imitation of nature, which many earlier critics, including Diderot himself, had defended.

Voltaire describes the line as "that line of Corneille's, unequalled by any in Homer, in Sophocles, or in Euripides."[87] It is important to note that the *qu'il mourût* is cited repeatedly as an example of literary beauty that is specifically French, not Greek or Roman. One might add that it is a particularly French phrase in the sense that it cannot be successfully translated, precisely because the verb *mourût* is in the imperfect subjunctive, a tense that does not exist in many other languages.

Just as the *qu'il mourût* exemplified good taste, the seventeenth-century text that is cited nearly as often in reference to bad taste was Pradon's *Phèdre*.[88] Jacques (a.k.a. Nicolas) Pradon's tragedy *Phèdre* first appeared in 1677, when it competed with Racine's play of the same title for public favor. We know that Racine's version has been consecrated as a masterpiece from the seventeenth century to this day, while Pradon's version remains obscure to specialists and unknown to the general public. Eighteenth-century critics remind us repeatedly that both plays deserved their different fates, although it is difficult to pinpoint why Pradon's version should be mentioned so much more often, in such hostile terms, than other tragedies of the period. Voltaire attempts, for example, to show us the difference of quality between the two authors in his preface to *Mariamne*, juxtaposing Racine's and Pradon's version of a speech by Hyppolite to Aricie. This judgment, however, always necessarily remains on the subjective level, so Voltaire's comparison fails to answer the question of why Pradon was so decried in the eighteenth century. In fact, I propose that the constant evocation of Pradon's *Phèdre* as a standard of bad taste has more to do with problems of the reception of literature.

In the preface to his tragedy *Mariamne*, Voltaire recalls the moment when both Racine's and Pradon's versions of *Phèdre* were competing for the public's favor and the score was tied, so to speak: "the two seemed at first to meet with an equal degree of applause; but the publication soon determined the real and intrinsic merit of each of them. Pradon, according to the usual practice of bad authors, came out with an insolent preface; accusing all those who had attacked his piece as unfair and partial critics; a trouble which he might as well have spared himself; for his tragedy, puffed as it was by himself and his party, soon sank into that contempt which it deserves."[89] The case of Pradon may serve as evidence to support the theory, shared by many critics (Dubos, Crousaz, André, David Hume, etc.), that explains how disagreements about taste resolve themselves over time. According to their optimistic view of the consensus on taste, prejudice and trends may sway the judgment of some susceptible members of the public, but the "right" judgment prevails in the end.

The constant reminders of the other *Phèdre* communicates to the public that there are moments when the inferior writers are prized as much as superior ones. I believe the eighteenth-century critics depict this as a fearful moment in which the "wrong" candidate actually has the possibility of winning. If the reading public's wayward judgments were not a threat, then these critics would not bother to discredit a forgotten writer. Dubos in particular conjures the ghost of Pradon as if to reassure us that he is really dead. Ironically, he reminds us of Pradon in order to tell us that he has been definitively forgotten, when he writes "of Pradon's Phaedra, which the public has now so great a contempt for, and which, to say something more, it has perfectly forgot."[90] Similarly, Voltaire remarks in the passage above from *Mariamne* that "if it were not for the 'Phædra' of Racine, the world would not know at this day that Pradon had ever written one."[91] He comes close to expressing a wish that Pradon would disappear from literary history, and in the specific space of *Le Siècle de Louis XIV*, he makes this wish come true simply by omitting Pradon's name from his catalogue of writers.

The enormous contempt that Pradon's name apparently inspires tells us about the eighteenth-century critics' assumption that the public is easily swayed, not only by the deceptive pleasures of novelty but by the power of *cabales*, which could be compared to lobbies in today's politics. In regard to *cabales*, Dubos remarks ominously, "As for Pradon's Phaedra, we still remember that a cabal formed of several partizans, among whom there were persons equally considerable for their wit and the rank they held in the world, had conspired to raise Pradon's Phaedra, and to humble that of Racine."[92] Voltaire, in his *Honnêtetés littéraires*, also blames the temporary success of Pradon's *Phèdre* on the backhanded maneuvers of *cabales*. He claims that Racine was right to be angry "at those who sent their lackeys to applaud Pradon's *Phèdre* and who reserved theater boxes for Racine's *Phèdre* just to leave them empty, to make people think that it had failed."[93] Whether their suspicions were true or not, the example of Pradon still serves as a warning against trusting public opinion without arbitration by critics such as themselves. One could well ask whether the classical defenders of good taste are not another type of *cabale*, an accusation they anticipate by claiming the indisputable prestige of "nature" and "eternal consensus" for their party.

While Pradon's name appears often to represent the bad taste of the seventeenth century, other writers, such as Desmarets de Saint-Sorlin, Paul Scarron, and Jean Chapelain, were also placed in the dark shadows of the Grand Siècle. Voltaire and his fellow critics claimed that these authors should be excluded because they wrote badly. We cannot presume to judge the quality of their writing, but we can consider various other motives that eighteenth-century critics had for defaming these particular writers. One motive surely related to their choice of medieval historical figures as heroes of their modern epic poems.

During the early Quarrel of the Ancients and the Moderns, certain moderns attempted to prove than one could write an epic poem based on Christian figures or on "barbarian" leaders, such as Saint Louis, Alaric, Clovis, and Joan of Arc. These works were met by much derision from their opponents among the ancients, such as Boileau and, later, Anne Dacier.[94] Voltaire and his fellows continued the attack on these epics of supposedly deplorable quality. One of many instances of Voltaire's scorn appears in his parody of Chapelain's *Pucelle d'Orléans*, through the very project of rewriting the *Pucelle* in a comic way but also in specific passages of this work. In canto 17 of his *Pucelle*, Voltaire depicts a magical castle inhabited by a "flighty, insipid" female phantom, and both the building and the spirit serve as allegories of bad writing. She holds "a babbling monster" ("le galimatias") in her arms like a pet, while "the lame enigma," "a host of silly lies,"[95] and other faulty uses of language fly around her like bats. Significantly, Voltaire mentions that she inspires bad literature and serves as a guide to "a Scudéry, Desmarets, and Le Moine."[96] In order to remove any possible ambiguity about his targets, Voltaire adds in a note: "[Georges de] Scudéry, author of *Alaric*, epic poem. Le Moyne, author of *Saint Louis*, or *Louisiade*, epic poem. Desmarets de Saint-Sorlin, author of *Clovis*, epic poem; these three works are terrible epic poems."[97]

Like Montesquieu, he also uses architecture to express bad taste: he describes the castle itself as a confusing mixture of ancient and modern and as an

> edifice accursed, howe'er it be,
> Constructed . . . with such dire industry,
> That all who entered were anon bereft
> Of every ray of reason they had left.[98]

Once again, bad taste takes the shape of a medieval building (since the action takes place during Joan of Arc's time), and although so-called gothic literature is under attack, only seventeenth-century depictions of the Middle Ages are mentioned.

THE EIGHTEENTH CENTURY: THE FALL OF ROME, AGAIN

Since French taste has supposedly emerged from the primeval chaos of the past, one could well ask: Why isn't the eighteenth century, in which these writers are living, the apogee of taste? I believe that the reason has to do with their need to use the present for rhetorical purposes, so they can refer to it as a time of strife and exhort the public to reject "false taste" in their midst, much like a preacher would admonish the public to fight continually against the devil. As I mentioned in an earlier section, the rejection of the barbaric ancestors takes a form that is both historical and non-historical. On the one hand, barbarians (Vandals, Franks, Visigoths, Ostrogoths) are those who sacked Rome in the fourth and fifth centuries, but on the other hand, barbarians (those who write badly) are those who threaten civilization at all times. The imaginary history of taste is less a historical narrative than a parable that teaches the readers a lesson: good taste and civilization are constantly threatened, and we must do what we can to defend these ideals.

Warnings of decadence pervade eighteenth-century writings about taste, despite the commonly held view, in our day, of the Enlightenment belief in progress. Scholars such as Jean-Claude Bonnet confirm the eighteenth century's obsession with decadence. He finds this topos or "lieu commun"[99] starting with the works of Anne Dacier at the beginning of the eighteenth century, then in a number of *éloges académiques* and in the works of Voltaire and La Harpe. As Bonnet explains, the perceived connection between the high point of the seventeenth century and the decline of the eighteenth was cast in terms of bodily strength: "This unprecedented effort was supposedly followed by a fatal lethargy. It was thus understood that the eighteenth century would be the fatigue or the repose of genius."[100] Another scholar, Marc-André Bernier, affirms in his article "Les Lumières au prisme de la décadence des lettres et du goût"[101] that Ernst Cassirer and more recent historians made the mistake of extending Condorcet's views on progress to the whole Enlightenment movement. By contrast, Bernier finds that "far from presenting an exalting, or even exalted, tableau of history, of the successive progress of enlightenment and good taste," the Enlightenment writers viewed their century as being "under the sign of *decadence*."[102] As evidence, he cites a number of eighteenth-century treatises on the corruption of taste, such as Rémond de Saint-Mard's *Trois lettres sur la décadence du goût* of 1734.

However, Bernier refuses to replace the idea of an overly optimistic eighteenth century with its opposite, that of a completely pessimistic one. One must in fact acknowledge that Voltaire saw advances in sciences and the standard of living[103] and that the moderns during the Quarrel of the Ancients and the Moderns did defend the idea of progress in the arts and in society. In Bernier's view, the *lieu commun* about decadence served a rhetorical purpose, but he stops short of explaining what this purpose could be. I propose that, rhetorically, the decadence of taste serves to exhort the public, the contemporaries of the critics, to choose correctly in matters of literature. The French nation will decline, they warn, if the public continues to allow bad writers to flourish—on the contrary, if they uphold the classical principles proposed to them by the *philosophes*, perhaps the decline can be staved off.

The theme of decadence, Bernier mentions, brings us to an important consideration in the history of taste, namely, the superposition of the eighteenth century on the Rome of the Augustan era. This popular way of creating parallels between the two periods allowed critics to draw the analogy between the great writers and the great leaders of both periods. Even though Voltaire, Marmontel, and others express the idea that the best French literature has surpassed ancient literature, they may still look to ancient Rome for a historical model. Specifically, the parallel between France and Rome permits the French writers to envisage their own civilization following the same trajectory as Rome: from primitive beginnings to a high point, then decadence, which leaves the nation vulnerable to attack by barbarians.

This is the case for many critics, including the classicist Anne Dacier, who finds that French literature was characterized by "coarseness" and "rusticity"[104] from the start, but the introduction of Greek and Latin models pushed it forward to the realm of good taste: "we crouched even longer in our state of barbarism because we did not take care to become acquainted with the perfect models that the Latins and Greeks had left us; and as soon as we began to study them, one could see this coarseness disappear little by little and the politeness and propriety of these originals drive away the rusticity and the poison from our works . . . it is only imitation that introduced good taste among us."[105] Unlike Voltaire and the Encyclopedists, she assigns only positive values to Renaissance erudition. Like her contemporary critics, however, she evokes the image of a rise and fall of taste, in which the end of a civilization returns to the obscurity or barbarity of its beginnings: "We have seen, in a convincing way, that it was the study of the Greeks and Latins that pulled us out of the coarseness in which we found ourselves; and we will see that it is ignorance and contempt of this same study that plunges us back into it. In fact, as soon as one neglected these excellent originals . . . one saw waves of bad works flood Paris and the rest of the kingdom."[106] This idea resembles the one expressed in Montesquieu's essay "De la maniere gothique," which I quoted earlier: "The gothic manner is not the manner of a particular people; it is the manner of the birth of or the end of art."[107] In other words, art in its infancy is thus equivalent to art in its dotage: according to the repeated warnings, eighteenth-century French culture, if it becomes perverse through an excess of refinement, will come full circle and return to its primordial chaos.

Several decades after Montesquieu, Marmontel expresses this idea with an agricultural metaphor. In both his *Poétique française* and his *Essai sur le goût*, he evokes the image of a field that has given up all its nutrients and is now infertile. In the latter text, he describes "the decadence of letters after a flourishing reign": "One could say that each climate was only able to give one single harvest and that, once the soil was exhausted by its own fecundity, there had to be centuries of repose before the soil was renewed and rendered fertile again."[108] In this era of decadence, according to Marmontel, good authors have already said what needed to be said, and now the public turns to the "bizarre" in a misguided search for something new.

La Harpe concurs with this idea that since good literature has already been produced, bad writers are resorting to desperate measures. In an era such as the eighteenth century, the "first masters" ("premiers maîtres") of the high point of civilization have already seized "what is most fortunate in art, what is most beautiful nature."[109] Like gleaners, those who follow them have to struggle to pick out the few things that remain. Meanwhile, those with inferior talents are tempted to find alternative paths, which lead to bizarreness and bad taste: "They throw themselves en masse on all the bizarre and monstrous innovations that bad taste can inspire and that caprice and novelty sometimes make successful. Then art, the artists, and the judges are equally corrupted; it is the era of decadence."[110] With all these references to decadence, it is implied that the trajectory of taste will parallel that of the French nation.

Do the ups and downs of French taste really reflect the political strength of their nation? Marc Fumaroli advances this thesis in "Le

Génie de la langue française," in which he refers to a late eighteenth-century text that explicitly links the rise of the nation and that of the language, Rivarol's essay *De l'universalité de la langue française.* In Rivarol's overview of the development of the French language, he links barbarism with political weakness, so that once the country gains strength and unity, the language becomes more stable and pure. Conversely, the French language will advance national interests by unifying the regions of France, and it will assert cultural domination over other nations by enthralling them with its good taste. Thus Rivarol gives readers yet another reason to uphold the progress of civilization and good taste and fight against the regression into barbarism. Just as the Roman Empire unified disparate peoples under one political and linguistic rule, historians of the French language have shown that France crushed regional differences as it imposed its political and cultural domination. The cultural weapon used to crush the enemies—those who resist the classical version of French taste—is public shame. As Domna Stanton proposes in her influential article, "The Fiction of *Préciosité* and the Fear of Women,"[111] the French government's suppression of the aristocratic revolts parallels the ridicule of the literary dissenters to the Académie's rules. Stanton focuses on women as the dissenters, but the same idea is valid, I think, for various kinds of groups whose aesthetic differed from the would-be official aesthetic.

CHAPTER FOUR

On Foreign Taste

The supposed universality of taste made it necessary for theorists to answer the question: Can other countries have good taste? To admit the possibility of different yet valid standards of artistic beauty in other countries called into question the whole basis of the universality of taste. If French taste were acknowledged to be merely one good taste among many, would that not lead to a dangerous relativism that would further break down the classical ideal, allowing different segments of the population to claim their own standards? Or if tastes were to be different for each country, could a French person simply choose to adopt the aesthetic standards of Persia or Peru? To prevent the breakdown of the universality of taste, the eighteenth-century critics found ingenious ways to answer the question about other countries' taste.

This metaphorical threat from other countries was a problem specific to the eighteenth century because of the new trends based on exploration and commerce with other parts of the world. In the previous century, French taste had to establish itself by disparaging the literature of Spain and Italy,[1] whose influence had until then dominated the literary realm. In the eighteenth century, the French public became more aware of the Americas and developed an immense hunger for everything "Oriental"—a vague term that could refer to anywhere from Morocco to Japan. This latter trend had existed in previous centuries,[2] but it received a new impetus from several sources, including the best-selling translation of *1001 Nights* by Antoine Galland, published from 1704 to 1717, and the encyclopedic sourcebook of Middle Eastern religion and literature by Barthélemy d'Herbelot entitled *Bibliothèque orientale* (1697). In addition, travel accounts by Jesuit missionaries in China[3] and by the merchants Jean Chardin and Jean-Baptiste Tavernier in Persia and India,[4] among many others, also fed the imagination of the French reading public. Thus the French people's overwhelming desire for descriptions of Egyptian pyramids, Aztec temples, and Chinese pagodas, as well as the influx of Far Eastern and Turkish commodities into European households, forced the critics to find a way to subsume foreign art into their own aesthetic system. But how?

I will consider three types of arguments that overtly or implicitly discredit the taste of countries outside Europe. As we will see, the denunciations of bad taste in literature most often focus on one geographical area: the Orient. For this reason, I will examine parodies of so-called Oriental language and consider some of the ideological motives behind these comic texts.

GEOGRAPHIES OF TASTE

The abbé Dubos fought against exotic trends by developing a theory of climate, especially its influence on the body, to prove that good art could only emerge from continental Europe. As I mentioned earlier, the human body played an important role in Dubos's treatise *Réflexions critiques sur la poésie et sur la peinture*. In this text, he demonstrates not only that the taste of the viewer manifests itself in a corporeal way but that the *génie* of the artist, whether he be a painter, writer, orator, or musical composer, depends on his physical constitution. In more specific terms, Dubos claims that the amount of genius that artists could command relied somewhat on training but also largely on their bodies: the appropriate warmth of their blood, how old they were (his optimal age for artistic production is thirty years old), their social origins (they had to be materially comfortable, since hunger diminished genius), and, most important for our present subject, their surroundings.

Let us examine the chain of cause and effect that Dubos draws between the individual's body and national taste. To begin with, he asserts that the earth releases a certain substance into the air, which varies from region to region. Since humans breathe this air, the inhabitants of different parts of the world will absorb these emanations that carry the particular traits of the earth on which they have stood. This is how people of different countries are physiologically different, according to Dubos.[5] While he proves with this line of argumentation that people are determined to bear the characteristics of their land, he does not assume that people of different races, for example, are essentially different; the important factor is where they live. Like grapes for wine, people are defined by the particular terrain on which they grow: "As two grains from the same plant, produce a fruit of a different quality when they are sown in different soils, or even when they are sown in the same soil but in different years; so two children born with their brains formed exactly in the same manner, will differ, when they grow up to the state of manhood, in sense and inclinations, if one of them be bred in Sweden, and the other in Andalusia."[6] Montesquieu later developed similar theories in regard to climate and political systems in his *Esprit des lois*, but Dubos concentrates more on the implications for art.

In the next step of his argument, Dubos turns his gaze on one part of the human body that he considers essential for artistic production: the blood. The earth releases its emanations into the air, and people inhale it, which in turn affects the quality of their blood. Consequently, people of different regions will have blood of different quality, plus the heat of their surroundings will affect the temperature of their blood. Dubos had stated earlier that a good artist must have healthy organs and blood of good quality, which will ferment to a temperature appropriate to artistic creation. For example, people from the cold climates of Scandinavia and Britain will have a cold imagination, which will prevent them from excelling in poetry and painting: "Every body knows, for instance, that we have never had from the extremities of the North but wild poets, coarse versifiers, and frigid colorists. Painting and poetry have never approached the pole nearer than the latitude of Holland."[7] While cold temperatures dull the imagination, Dubos describes the excesses of poetic fire caused by the other extreme in temperature. Hot blood, he claims in regard to poets such as Desmarets de Saint-Sorlin, leads to an "imagination brûlée" ("burnt" imagination), which can only produce "chimères bizarres"[8]—even though he lived in France.

In short, any climate that extends "beyond the fifty second degree of North latitude, nor nearer than five and twenty degrees to the line,"[9] has no hope of producing great art. To put it in other terms, the area of genius extends from France to Egypt, since the latitude of 52 degrees north lies just at the English Channel, while Dubos's border at the latitude of 25 degrees includes Egypt but excludes, for example, the Aztec empire. As we will see, Dubos does not necessarily remain consistent to these measurements, since he also criticizes East Asian furniture and Middle Eastern tales.

Thus Dubos claims that the world is composed of certain countries that can generate talent and others "in which arts and sciences do not flourish,"[10] just as human beings are born with different aptitudes. Since nature has distributed genius so unevenly, this diversity creates one large society of "mutual dependence."[11] As a result, Dubos can portray his unfavorable judgments of non-European cultures as a happy interchange in which Italy gives the world paintings, France gives it theater, and, in exchange, Incas and Scandinavians provide other resources.[12]

Dubos draws out the proto-colonialist implications of his system by comparing the native artistic superiority of certain countries and the advanced governing skills of Europeans: "'Tis observable, that the Europeans, and those who are born on the casts bordering upon Europe, have always been fitter than other people for arts and sciences, as well as political government. Wheresoever the Europeans have carried their arms, they have generally subdued the inhabitants."[13] He firmly refuses to yield any artistic or technical advantage to non-Europeans—with one exception I will mention later. For instance, he claims, if "chance" made the Chinese discover gunpowder and printing, the Europeans have now made better use of them. Most bizarrely, he claims that although Egyptians invented pyramids and sphinxes, these look better when copied by European hands: "If we happen to meet with a sphinx of surprizing beauty, 'tis probably the work of some Greek sculptor, who diverted himself with making Aegyptians figures, as our painters take a pleasure sometimes in imitating the figure of the basso-relievos, and the pictures of the Indies and China. Have we not had artists ourselves, who have diverted themselves with making sphinxes? There are several such in the gardens of Versailles, which are original pieces done by our modern sculptors."[14] Dubos only finds these shapes acceptable when they have been adapted to meet French expectations and have been emptied of all religious or cultural meaning—when they have become mere *divertissements*.

Turning to the arts of Mexican and Peruvian natives, he begins by praising them as "subtle" and "prodigious." Quickly afterward, though, he professes these works to be below the standard of European art:

> But as these people had no genius, they were, in spite of all their dexterity, very coarse artists. They understood neither the most simple rules of design, nor the first principles of composition, perspective, or

> chiaro-scuro. They did not so much as know how to paint with min-
> erals and other natural colors which come to us from their country.
> They have seen since that time some of the best pictures of Italy, a
> vast number of which have been sent by the Spaniards into the West-
> Indies. Their new masters have likewise shewn them how to make use
> of their pencil and colors, but have not been able to render them skil-
> ful painters.[15]

Indigenous art, measured by European rules of perspective and chiar-
oscuro, proves to be sadly deficient in Dubos's eyes. Nevertheless,
he makes an exception for these artists' ability to reproduce, even
surpass, "the vivacity of the colors"[16] of the Italian masters. It is significant that the only quality that Dubos grants to Peruvian painters
concerns color, since this term from painting also appears in the descriptions of foreign languages by several theorists, including Marmontel. Because certain regions tend to produce better artists than
others, these differences have an effect on the taste of the public of
each country. Dubos argues that because of the proliferation of good
painting in Italy and good theater in France, the people of these countries can develop a *goût de comparaison*, or good taste based on comparing works of art. He defines the latter faculty as follows: "By dint
of beholding pictures during our youth, the idea and image of eleven
or twelve excellent pictures is ingraved and imprinted deeply in our
yet tender imagination. Now these pictures, which are always present
to us, and have a certain rank, and fixt merit, serve, if I may say so,
for pieces of comparison, which inable us to judge solidly, how near
a new work approaches the perfection which other painters have attained, and in what rank it deserves to be placed."[17]

While Italians can judge painting because they are surrounded by
great examples, the French have more of an aptitude for judging writing: "As we have had a greater number of excellent poets than painters in France, the natural taste for poetry has had therefore a better
opportunity of improving, than that for painting."[18] Thus a country's geographical situation, which favors the development of genius
among artists, also fosters good taste among the consumers of art.

ANDRÉ AND MARMONTEL:
STAVING OFF AESTHETIC ANARCHY

The second argument that addressed foreign tastes, common to several eighteenth-century critics, began by deceptively granting legiti-

macy to a variety of aesthetic preferences but eventually circling back to the original stance on the single standard of taste, in the name of Nature. The père André and Jean-François Marmontel declared that true artistic beauty is the one that resembles nature the most, while on the other hand, social conventions only produce temporary, local standards, which are inferior. In this way, the theorists could explain away the fluctuations of fashion as well as the differences in taste among various cultures. They would surely deny that their version of the "natural" was itself based on their local French preferences.

To begin with Yves-Marie André, we can see that he was prepared to confront the question of cultural difference with his hierarchical system of three levels of beauty, which he develops in *Essai sur le Beau*. The highest form of beauty, *beauté essentielle*, exists on a metaphysical plane on par with mathematical truths, while the lowest form, to which he gives the pejorative label of *beauté artificielle* or *arbitraire*, depends on caprice. With his description of the chaos occasioned by the latter form of beauty, André warns us against aesthetic relativism: "How many arbitrary beauties have been invented . . . ! In Europe one wears earrings; in the Mughal Empire, one adds nose rings. In France, one powders one's hair and curls it into ringlets; in Canada one greases it and lets it hang over the shoulders. In the New World, one sees entire populations with their faces painted green, blue, red, yellow, a thousand foreign colors."[19] While the fleeting fashions of all countries, including France, may fall into the category of arbitrary tastes, André specifically associates colors with the Americas, just as Dubos had designated color as the one good quality of Latin American painting. As it emerged during the previous century's debate about color and line in painting, color connoted the passions, while line represented rationality.

To discover what is truly beautiful, *essentially* beautiful, in culture or in literature, André tells us that we must forget our personal penchants, our moods, our institutions, and instead submit to the "general taste." He sweeps aside cultural differences, ostensibly even those of the French, in order to get to the core of universal beauty. What do these truths engraved in our hearts look like if applied to literature? He writes, "What has one asked of them at all times, from the birth of letters to our day? what has one asked of them in all nations, from the extremities of the Orient, which saw the birth of eloquence, to the West, who raised it to perfection? and today, what does all the world ask of them, as if with the general cry of reason? Truth, order, propriety, and decency. There, Sirs (I do not believe that I will ever be belied by good taste), there is the essential beauty that we seek quite naturally in a work of eloquence."[20] With words such as *reason* and *naturally*, he justifies his description of essential beauty in literature as demanding truth, order, and decency.

The problem with the père André's system is that he is free to define the universal "general taste," which transcends all, according to his personal or national penchants. Readers may well grow suspicious of his reasoning in moments when he puts Africans' preference for dark skin in the category of local, therefore arbitrary, taste, while he attempts to prove that the *beauté essentielle* of pale skin, that of his own race, can be defended through indisputable logic. Other theorists of taste, such as Batteux and Crousaz, also establish the idea of a universal taste, supposedly untainted by the local preferences of other countries but that can in fact merely express their own personal or national preferences.

Marmontel also relies on assumptions about the meaning of "nature" when he develops an argument for a single standard of taste, while seeming at first to accept multiple ones. First, he claims, one person has a right to disagree with others about taste, just as small communities can hold opposing artistic opinions. But these small communities develop into larger societies and eventually into whole countries, each with a single standard of taste: "This society grows: it is no longer a circle, it is a town, a country, a whole population; and by a long coexistence, taste becomes uniform."[21] In this step of his argument, he assumes that all members of each society must necessarily agree with each other about taste.

Then, Marmontel explains, one society becomes culturally dominant, to the extent that others submit to its authority: "It is then that it begins to take on a sort of authority, and if the nation is really more enlightened, more cultivated than its neighbors; if it is more fertile in pleasing works, it will have some right to serve as a model in the art of pleasure and enjoyment."[22] But who decides which society will dominate aesthetically and which one will submit? Similar to Dubos's idea of interdependence among nations, Marmontel's idea of stronger and weaker cultures comes to an impasse if two nations both reject the role of cultural inferior to the other.

To address this potential conflict, Marmontel first seems to take a relativist position: "but each nation may still claim [*peut-elle prétendre*], for its own sake, to know what is appropriate for itself . . . its taste will not be the taste of its neighbors, but it will be its own good taste . . . it will not consider as proven that the dominant taste is better than its own."[23] His use of the word *peut* in the passage above allows for two different interpretations: one can read the first line as "each nation <u>can</u> claim," in the sense of "has the right to claim," which would allow one to read the subsequent phrases as statements of fact. Alternatively, one could attribute to the word *peut* the weaker sense of "each nation <u>may well</u> claim," merely mentioning a possible event. This meaning would then make more sense with the next sentences as free indirect discourse, in which Marmontel is speaking as if through the voices of the multiple nations but without espousing their cause.

Ultimately, though, he names the universal arbiter of these possible disagreements between nations: nature. He writes, "Thus the rules of propriety [*convenances*] that concern taste are not all accidental and artificial; some are unchanging, some are eternal, just like the essences of things . . . as for the essential and unchanging rules of propriety, there must be a taste that is, like them, independent of all sorts of convention; nature has established them, nature makes us feel them."[24]As in André's text, however, we are left with the problem of how a critic can define nature without being influenced by his own personal or national preferences.

André and Marmontel suggest that the alternative to their universal standard of taste is a dangerous state of chaos. André explicitly denounces aesthetic relativism as Pyrrhonism, or extreme skepticism, which he sees as a threat to philosophy in general and perhaps more specifically to his Catholic faith. The language he uses to describe the young fops and bad authors who would maintain that "there is no disputing about tastes"[25] hints at a kind of depraved behavior that denies all moral absolutes. Marmontel, in turn, refers to the possibility of political conflict between nations, which can only be resolved peacefully through submission to a single authority.

MARMONTEL, THE *ENCYCLOPÉDIE*, DACIER: THE GUILTY PLEASURES OF COLOR

The third way to address foreign tastes was more ambiguous; it involved praising one characteristic of foreign art but then questioning whether that characteristic had positive or negative implications. For instance, I mentioned earlier that Dubos conceded that Inca painters could surpass Italians only in the realm of color. This attribution of *color* to foreign artists appears in the texts of many critics, whether literally in terms of paint or metaphorically in terms of writing style. The painting terms *couleur* and *coloris* were applied to poetics to refer to figurative language. By analogy, perhaps we can suppose that its opposite, line, referred to plot (in a tragedy, for example), argument (in a sermon, a treatise), or abstract language—what Rousseau refers to, not unproblematically, as calling things "by their true name."[26] Just as in the debate among art critics about the preeminence of line over color or vice versa, one sees in discussions of literature that color is also associated with the passions and line with reason.

Marmontel, in his *Poétique françoise*, in the chapter entitled "Du coloris ou des images," links color with figurative language and eventually with foreign tastes. According to his definition, figurative or metaphorical language makes use of "sensible" things (things that can be perceived by the senses) from the external world to express more abstract inner states:[27] "It is an artifice of poetry to depict an idea with colors that are foreign to its object, in order to make this object sensible if it is not."[28] Far from excluding metaphors from literature, Marmontel admits that they give pleasure to the listener or reader—but ultimately warns that their persuasive powers lie precisely in their emotional effect, not on reason.

Along with his colleagues Jaucourt and Jean-Jacques Rousseau, Marmontel situates figurative language, with its poetic verve and its primitive irrationality, both chronologically and geographically. On the one hand, these critics imagine a progression from a state of savagery, in which ancient peoples (such as Jewish people, Egyptians, and Aztecs)[29] express themselves in highly imaginative visual metaphors, to an advanced state (French civilization) in which people have at their disposal a large vocabulary with which they can name objects and abstract concepts with precision. Jaucourt, in his *Encyclopédie* article entitled "Figure," makes it clear that rhetorical figures come from the lowest level of civilization: "Since the first men were simple, rough, and immersed in their senses, they could not express their conception of abstract ideas or the reflective operations of the understanding, except with sensible images that, through these applications, became metaphors."[30] Jaucourt characterizes early peoples who used figurative language as primitive or savage because they were unable to express abstract ideas.

More systematically, Rousseau imagines a successive order in which various languages developed: "Figurative language was the first to arise, proper meaning was found last. Things were not called by their true name until they were seen in their genuine form. At first, only poetry was spoken. Only long afterwards did anyone take it into his head to reason."[31] The pejorative characterization of this type of language is clear in Jaucourt's text, but it is more ambiguous in Rousseau. Since Rousseau does not equate "civilized" with "superior," it is difficult to know whether his association of the Orient with primitive language implies condemnation or praise.

The progression of languages would seem to involve a succession of periods from prehistory to the eighteenth century, in which figurative language, safely in the past, has been bypassed once and for all. Yet in reality the so-called primitive languages still coexisted with the so-called civilized ones, since Rousseau, Marmontel, and their fellows compared French with the languages of various parts of the world in their time.[32] The "Oriental" languages, namely of the Middle East, were most frequently the targets of this accusation of primitivism, as we can see in the treatises of Rousseau and in the *Encyclopédie*.[33] Marmontel continues this tendency to conflate different time periods, while also extending the area of primitive language to other peoples located at or beyond the margins of Europe (more specifically, outside the former confines of the Roman Empire): "For a long time, one attributed the Orientals' figures of style to the climate; but one has discovered images in the poems of Icelandic people, in those of ancient Scots, and in the harangues of Canadian savages, that are as daring as those in the writings of Persians and Arabs. The less civilized people are, the more figurative and sensible their language is."[34] Thus primitive languages belong to the present as much as the past, since they can still be found in places such as Iceland and Canada.

In the words of various *philosophes*, the faults of foreign languages, specifically Arabic and Hebrew, include "poverty," repetition, and excessive metaphors (both in terms of exaggeration and quantity). To begin with, the terms *pauvreté* and *richesse* are applied by Jaucourt, Rousseau, and the author of the unattributed *Encyclopédie* article "Hébraïque" to the size of a language's vocabulary. Jaucourt claims that "Hebrew . . . is the least abundant of all the Oriental languages; that is the reason why the Hebrew language expresses different things with the same word or the same thing with numerous synonyms."[35] Rousseau expresses the same idea, especially regarding the Arabic words for "camel" and "sword": "Arabic is said to have more than a thousand different words to say *camel,* more than a hundred to say *sword.*"[36] Paradoxically, they support their opinions about the poverty of Hebrew and Arabic by pointing to the large number of words that refer to one single thing—which, it seems, should convince us instead of the richness of the language.

Why is the poverty of language a problem? Partly because, as we will see, using words with multiple meanings creates too much ambiguity for the reader, which becomes a conflict of capital importance in regard to the Bible. In the article "Hébraïque" of the *Encyclopédie,* the author follows this line of reasoning: "The Hebrew language is poor in words and rich in signification; its richness has resulted from its poverty, because it was necessary to charge one single expression with various meanings, in order to supplement the dearth of words and signs . . . there are few expressions that do not make one reflect in order to judge whether it is to be taken in its natural or figurative sense."[37] Obviously, the interpretation of certain words in the Bible as literal or metaphorical had potentially explosive consequences.

Nevertheless, the religious implications were only part of the problem; critics also cite reasons that were entirely independent of religion and focused purely on questions of style. Jaucourt, for example, finds a causal connection between so-called poverty of language and two figures of rhetoric to which he objects: pleonasm and metaphor. In his opinion, since the Hebrew language has so few words (and yet so many synonyms), speakers had to turn, out of desperation, to repeating things over and over: "The pleonasm is obviously due to the narrow limits of a simple language. . . . While the expressions do not correspond entirely to the ideas of the speaker, as it often happens when using an impoverished language, he necessarily seeks to explain himself by repeating his thought in other terms, somewhat like a person whose body is hindered in one place and continually seeks a comfortable position."[38] Redundancy is one stylistic issue that appears in the parodies of biblical language that I will examine later and one that, incidentally, also emerged in the criticism of the *Iliad* in the Battle of the Ancients and the Moderns.

In regard to metaphors, the authors cited above display a distrust of words that are used outside their literal context for several reasons. Metaphors not only allow for the dangerous confusion between the literal and the metaphorical meaning of words, but they also tell us something about their language's deficiencies, particularly according to the *Encyclopédie.* The use of metaphors and images, these critics maintain, reveals a language's inability to designate both objects and abstract ideas with precision—an inadequacy that impedes progress because scientific and philosophical texts need to be precise. What metaphors and images do is muddle the listener's understanding and persuade him by lifting him up into an artificial state of emotional exaltation. As Marmontel explains in his *Poétique*, "Human understanding has three very distinct faculties: reason, sentiment, and imagination. Naked truth is enough for reason . . . but eloquence and poetry need to move the sentiment and strike the imagination."[39] The latter two wield the weapon of figurative language in a dangerous way, since "imagination is much less severe, less rebellious to persuasion and much easier to seduce."[40] To keep the powers of irrational persuasion at bay, one has to keep a defensive eye on rhetorical imagery: "imagination influences the whole soul, it is the dominant and tyrannical faculty, and . . . it even has power over reason, which the latter denies but from which it cannot free itself. . . . Should we be astonished, then, if men who are interested in persuading each other, in moving each other, have tried to cover their ideas with a material envelope that the imagination can grasp? Should we be astonished if eloquence and poetry, those two arts that aspire to dominate all minds, had recourse to the illusion of images?"[41] He then states that since it is nearly impossible to avoid metaphors, except perhaps in mathematical treatises, we have to carefully choose appropriate ones.

As Jaucourt tells us, if one does use metaphors, they should not "compromise clarity" ("nuire à la clarté") and they should be of an elevated register: "Figures became the ornament of discourse when men had acquired a vast enough knowledge of arts and sciences to create images that, without compromising clarity, were as joyful, as noble, as sublime, as the material required."[42] On the other hand, this passage suggests that bad metaphors tend to be confusing and vulgar: two reproaches to keep in mind when reading critiques of Oriental, especially biblical, language.

While other cultures indulged in excessive figurative language, French critics claimed, their own language, for better or worse, remained within the limits of rationality. The anonymous contributor of the article "Hébraïque" to the *Encyclopédie*, after repeating the ideas above concerning figurative language and the Orient, expresses regret that the French language is so cold: "A language such as French, for example, that avoids figures and allusions, that tolerates only what is natural, that finds beauty only in simplicity, is nothing but the language of man reduced to rationality. The Hebrew language, on the contrary, is the true language of poetry, of prophecy, and of revelation; a divine fire animates and transports it. What ardor there is in its hymns! what sublime images there are in the visions of Isaiah! how pathetic and touching are the tears of Jeremiah!"[43] Describing what the French language, as if personified, dislikes or shuns, this author characterizes it as homogenously natural, rational, and non-figurative, thus ignoring examples of spoken or written French that did not fit this description.[44]

Decades earlier, Anne Dacier had already made a connection between *langage figuré* and Orientals, but she took the argument to an unusual place: first, she included the Greeks (consequently the *Iliad*) among the Orientals, and second, she unequivocally praised this type of language above the "coldness" of France and the rest of western Europe. In *Des Causes de la corruption du goust*, she sees the Greek-Orientals of antiquity as the source of artistic fire, from which the present-day French have gotten too far away, geographically and chronologically, to create good poetry. She describes the Greeks as having far more imagination, which in this case has a positive value: "There are nations that are so well situated and that the sun regards so favorably that they have been capable of imagining and inventing by themselves and of reaching perfection. [The nations of the Orient] have a great deal of vivacity, imagination, and flourishes of wit, as one can still see today in the people of Greece."[45] Meanwhile, she paints an unfavorable picture of the French of her day: "there are other [nations] that, shrouded in a denser air, have never been able, except through imitation, to pull themselves out of the coarseness and the barbarism into which they were plunged from birth."[46] Dacier places the frontier that separates the warm regions of good taste from the cold regions of bad taste at the Mediterranean (so France is too cold but Greece is appropriately warm), unlike Dubos, who favored the middle ground between the English Channel and Egypt. Dacier's exclusion of France from the area of good taste anticipates the remarks in the article "Hébraïque" in which the author seems to regret the rationality of his language. Nevertheless, whether the imagery of the Orient receives praise or scorn, all critics seem to agree that it belongs to the past, that it lacks reason, and that, because of its more frequent use of rhetorical ornaments, Oriental taste represents the opposite of French taste.

Whether theorists such as Dubos openly denied the taste of others or whether they attributed bad taste to the arbitrariness of local convention, they still upheld their personal, local set of values as the truly universal standard of taste. They seemed to fixate their scorn particularly on the literature of the Middle East, far more than on Scandinavian poetry or Inca painting. In the next section, I will focus on the sources of this anti-Hebrew and anti-Arabic sentiment and how this aesthetic position was expressed in a number of parodies.

ANCIENTS VS. ASIANS

In condemning the supposedly bad taste of the Middle East, eighteenth-century critics may have simply been showing their loyalty to their classical education, particularly the works of rhetoricians such as Quintilian and Cicero. Even though the term *taste* was not used to refer to the judgment of beauty in antiquity, the ancients' designation of bad, pompous, or vulgar style, for example, often coincides with the descriptions of bad taste in eighteenth-century writings. The *philosophes* saw themselves in the role of ancient Romans, who in turn identified themselves with the ancient Greeks who, according to Quintilian and others,[47] practiced a sober and tasteful Attic style of rhetoric. Thus if the members of this lineage practiced the Attic style, then their traditional enemies, in terms of eloquence, lived to their east and practiced "Asiatic" or "Asianic" style (the difference depends on the translator).[48] Quintilian famously described the contrast between the two in *De Institutione oratoria*, or *The Orator's Education*: "This distinction between 'Attic' and 'Asianic' orators was an ancient one. The former were held to be concise and sound, the latter inflated and hollow. In the former there was nothing superfluous, the latter were especially lacking in judgment and restraint" (12.10.16). While he declares that "No one need have any doubt that the Attic manner is far and away the best" (12.10.20), Quintilian associates the Asianic style with a number of bad qualities in his discussion of the unfair accusations leveled at Cicero by overly zealous partisans of sober style: "his own contemporaries had the hardihood to attack him as bombastic, Asianic, redundant, repetitive, sometimes unsuccessful in his humour, and undisciplined, extravagant, and (heaven forbid!) almost effeminate in his Composition" (12.10.12). This opposition between foreign (especially Eastern) literary style as excessive, wordy, and effeminate and the critic's own style as manly and restrained certainly paralleled the eighteenth-century characterizations of French and Middle Eastern languages.

Like the later French critics, Quintilian attributed other people's
bad style to national character: "I prefer to think that the stylistic difference is due to the character both of the orators and of their audi-
ences. The polished and refined Athenians could not bear emptiness
and redundance, while the Asiatics, who are in other respects a more
bombastic and boastful race, were more vainglorious also in their oratory" (12.10.17). To get a closer understanding of Quintilian's standards of good Attic style, let us focus on an important passage from
book 8, which concerns the misuse of one type of rhetorical figure,
metaphor. Metaphors are especially significant in parodies of "Oriental" language, since they were considered the defining characteristics
of Middle Eastern writing, as one can see in my earlier discussion of
color and figurative language. In Quintilian's estimation, metaphors
can be faulty in the following ways:

> While moderate and timely use of Metaphor brightens out style, fre-
> quent use of it leads to obscurity and tedium, while its continuous ap-
> plication ends up as Allegory and Enigma. Some Metaphors also are
> low—like the "rocky wart [upon the mountain's head]" I mentioned
> above—and some coarse. If Cicero was right to talk of the "sink of the
> senate," meaning the foul ways of certain people, I am not therefore
> minded to approve the old orator's "you have lanced the state's abscess-
> es." Cicero did well to point out the need to guard against an ugly met-
> aphor (like "the state was neutered by Africanus' death" or "Glaucia,
> the excrement of the Senate," to quote his own examples), and against
> one which is too grand or (as happens more often) inadequate or un-
> like. . . . Excessive amounts of metaphor, especially of the same species,
> are also a fault. So too are harsh metaphors, that is to say those derived
> from distant resemblances, like the "snows on the head" or
>
> Jove spat white snow upon the wintry Alps.
>
> The biggest mistake however is made by those who believe that
> everything is appropriate in prose which is permitted to the poets,
> whose only standard is pleasure. (8.6.14–17)

These rules were updated in the 1730 treatise *Des Tropes* by César
Chesneau Dumarsais, who translated much of Quintilian's book 8
and adapted it to his public by adding examples from the Bible and
from modern writers such as Boileau and La Bruyère.

Dumarsais summarizes Quintilian's ideas about bad metaphors
into a few succinct rules, which include the following: "Metaphors
are defective 1. when they are taken from low subjects. Father De Colonia reproaches Tertullian for having said that 'the universal deluge
was the laundry of nature.' 2. When they are forced, taken from too

far, and when the connection is not natural enough or the comparison easily felt. . . . 3. One must also have consideration for different styles; there are metaphors that are appropriate for a poetic style but would be out of place in oratorical style."[49] In short, Dumarsais and Quintilian agree that metaphors should not refer to low things (such as vomit or warts); that they should not be too far-fetched; that the two terms of the metaphor should be in proportion to each other; and that the style should be appropriate for the genre, since one can be more daring in poetry than in prose.

These warnings coincide with the faults attributed to Oriental literature and consequently with the features that were exaggerated in parodies. These faults, joined with the other characteristics that are alluded to in the first part of this chapter, such as repetitiveness, will make their appearance in the following parodies of style by Montesquieu, Grimm, and Voltaire.

PARODIES OF "ORIENTAL" LANGUAGE

When critics of the eighteenth century discussed the specifically literary taste of other countries, we can see that they focused far more frequently on the "Orient," especially the Middle East, than on other parts of the world. For example, Asia was most often condemned for the visual characteristics (gaudy colors, irregular shapes) of its imported luxury items, such as furniture, fabrics, or tableware, than for its literary styles. The reason for this focus was surely that the language barrier made it nearly impossible for all but a tiny percentage of Asian texts[50] to be accessible to Europeans, while the literary productions of Africans and American natives[51] were hardly known at all in Europe. The Middle East, on the other hand, was represented in secular works such as Antoine Galland's *1001 Nights* and a collection of verses by the Persian poet Sadi,[52] although hardly any readers could verify the faithfulness of these translations. Aside from these works, the closest thing Europeans had to Middle Eastern writing was the Bible and, in rarer instances, the Koran.

Dubos, for example, could only base his contempt for Asian and Middle Eastern writing on a very fragile foundation. After proffering the usual commonplaces about commercial products from Asia, whose forms and color do not meet his standards for the "picturesque" or "pittoresque," he turns immediately to the question of literature.

> Europe is over-stocked with stuffs, china-ware, and other curiosities
> of China, and the eastern parts of Asia. Nothing can be less pictur-
> esque than the taste of the design and coloring, which prevails these
> works. There have been several translations published of the poetic
> compositions of the eastern nations. When we find a stroke in its
> proper place, or a probable adventure, we admire it; and this is as
> much as we can say of them. Wherefore all these translations, which
> seldom go thro' a second edition have only a transient vogue, for
> which they are indebted to the foreign air of the original, and to the
> inconsiderate fondness which numbers of people have for singular
> things.[53]

It is unclear whether he refers to Galland's translations or to pseudo-
Oriental tales written by Europeans, whether the texts were authen-
tic, or whether the translations are adequate. After all, in the passage
in which he praises Virgil's *Aeneid*, he states that those who cannot
read a text in its original language have no right to judge it: "He who
does not understand the language in which a poet has wrote, ought
not to be allowed to dispute with such as understand this poet, concerning his merit and the impression he makes."[54] Nevertheless, Dubos rejects "Oriental" stories, whether they are in fact from the Orient or whether they are the products of European invention.

MONTESQUIEU'S *LETTRES PERSANES*

One of the best-known Orientalizing French novels, Montesquieu's
Lettres persanes (1721), bears some of the elements of the caricatural style I describe above. Montesquieu begins the *Lettres persanes*,
as Voltaire does *Zadig*, with a reference to exaggerated "Oriental"
greetings. This prefatory text has been analyzed multiple times in
terms of narrative voice but not in terms of Montesquieu's definition
of good and bad style. In this passage, the fictional editor claims:

> My role, therefore, is simply that of translator; all my effort has been
> directed at accommodating the work to our customs and tastes; I
> have relieved the reader of as much of the Asian style as I could, and
> have saved him from a vast number of high-flown expressions, which
> would have bored him to tears. . . . I have abridged the long compli-
> ments with which Orientals are no less generous than we ourselves
> are; and I have skipped over a great many trifling details which with-
> stand the glare of public scrutiny so poorly.[55]

Like Quintilian, Montesquieu attributes to "Oriental" style the connotations of excess, both in the sense of quantity (the compliments

are too long, there are too many words) and in the sense of exaggeration, which is linked to the empty bombast of "Asianic" style. The
very phrase "bored to the skies"[56] ("ennuyé jusques dans les nuës"),
in which he playfully replaces the expected word *élevé* with *ennuyé*,
expresses the very same idea mentioned before: good style (French,
Attic) means moderation, and bad style (Hebrew, Persian, Asianic)
means an amplification that bores the reader instead of impress-
ing him. Nevertheless, it is typical of Montesquieu and of the other
Enlightenment writers to mock their own society while critiquing
foreign ones: hence the subtle turn from the "longs complimens" of
the Persians to those of the French, who are no less guilty on that
account.

In a parallel fashion, the follies of Christianity are put on display,
yet the Muslim religion also appears in its worst incarnation, representing both a childish devotion to imaginary things and, most significant for this study, a ridiculous style. The letters XV–XVII[57] between Usbek and a Muslim scholar especially emphasize this Middle
Eastern linguistic extravagance, which leads us to consider this exchange as a parody of bad taste. First, Usbek greets the mullah with
flattering words:

> You are more suited to life among the stars; no doubt you hide your-
> self lest you darken the sun; you have no blemishes like that star, but
> like the sun, you cover yourself with clouds.
>   Your learning is an abyss deeper than the ocean, your mind is
> more penetrating than Zufagar, that sword of Ali's with two points;
> you know what is happening in the nine choirs of the celestial pow-
> ers; you read the Qu'ran upon the breast of our divine Prophet, and
> when you find a passage obscure, an angel unfolds swift wings at his
> command, and descends from the throne to reveal to you its secret
> meaning.[58]

This passage belies the fictional editor's claim to have removed as
many traces of Oriental compliments as possible. Several characteristics are meant to be ridiculous in the passage above, beginning with
the stereotypical tendency that "Orientals" always make clichéd references to the sun, the moon, and the stars.[59] There is also the hyperbole of "your learning is an abyss deeper than the ocean"—a more extreme version of which can be found in the response from the mullah,
who pompously proclaims his own superiority: "the zenith of your
intellect does not reach the nadir of that of the least of our imams."[60]
Since the terms *zénith* and *nadir* denote two absolute extremes, the

highest and the lowest points possible, any comparison using these terms must necessarily be an exaggeration.

To return to Letter XVI from Usbek to the mullah, one can also point out the caricatural structure of the compliment, specifically the long series of phrases, each of which begins with "tu." The string of words, divided at regular intervals by the anaphora, are surely what Montesquieu was referring to when he condemned the monotonous style of early Christian writing in his *Essai sur le goût*. In this essay, Montesquieu professes the importance of uniformity and variety in the arts but warns that these principles are misused by "Gothic" writers such as Saint Augustine: "The same cadence or jingle repeated in every phrase is extremely disagreeable and fastidious. *Contrasts* thus multiplied, become intolerably uniform; and those oppositions that were designed to produce variety, degenerate, by perpetual repetition, into the most tedious symmetry."[61] In the passage from Usbek's letter, Montesquieu tries to demonstrate to us that just as "Oriental" writers try to dazzle readers with their hyperbole, they also employ the rhetorical technique of anaphoras, but in both cases they fail.

Furthermore, the response from the mullah in Letter XVIII contains a story whose vulgarity offends social decorum as much as its fantastic quality offends common sense. To satisfy Usbek's curiosity about the reasons behind the prohibition of eating pork among Muslims, the mullah narrates a story about how pigs came into being. On Noah's ark, he claims, the weight of animals' collected excrement made the ship tilt to one side. As a solution to this problem, the elephant was placed on the other side to produce some *ordure*, which magically transformed itself into a pig. The story further elaborates how the pig sneezed and from his nose came a rat, and so on. The important thing is the register to which this letter descends, with words such as *ordure, puanteur, éternuer,* and *sortir de son nez,* which confirms the accusations of lowness that eighteenth-century critics warn against.

The fanciful nature of this narration also brings up some problems of taste, namely the associations between the Middle East and an uncontrolled imagination. Is it an allegory or is it to be taken as a true account of events? This question leads the reader to dangerous doubts about the episode of Noah's ark and other biblical stories, whether they should be taken as truth or allegory. If one takes the story as an allegory, one can object to the presence of *ordure*, both the word and the idea, since the narrator had the choice whether to include it or not. If the events are supposed to be true, then Montesquieu obviously wants to outrage the reader's sense of verisimilitude.

The fault of lowness, which Quintilian and Dumarsais mention in regard to metaphors, appears repeatedly in the other parodies of Oriental language. More specifically, lowness manifests itself in words that designate the body and in descriptions of poverty. For instance, parodists make use of the almost animalistic words *mamelles* (breasts) and *allaiter* (to breast-feed), as opposed to the poetic and vague term *sein*, as marks of Arabic-Hebrew vulgarity. Montesquieu does it in the *Lettres persanes* in the absurd description of Mohammed's birth, after which a voice thunders from heaven: "blessed are the breasts that nurse him."[62] With an almost identical formulation, Grimm's *Petit prophète de Boehmischbroda*, which I will discuss shortly, exclaims, "my mother will bless the belly that carried me and the breasts that nourished me!"[63] Let us examine how lowness and other faults attributed to Middle Eastern style make their appearance in the parodies by Grimm and Voltaire.

GRIMM'S *LE PETIT PROPHÈTE DE BOEHMISCHBRODA*

Friedrich Melchior Grimm's 1753 satire *Le Petit prophète de Boehmischbroda* has been seen by literary historians as a strike against French music in the Querelle des Bouffons.[64] While it is true that French opera is under attack in this work, the form that this long pamphlet takes is an account of a divine vision, such as those of biblical prophets. Before discussing the parodic elements of this text, however, it would be useful to summarize its plot. It begins with the first-person narrative of a poor fiddler named Gabriel Joannes Nepomucenus Franciscus de Paula Waldstorc, who lives in his attic in Prague. Suddenly, a divine figure appears to him and transports him to the theater in Paris, where he sees a French opera. He reacts to this performance with horror and disapproval. Afterward, the divine figure who brought him to Paris demands that he write down his experiences and make them public so that he can denounce the follies of the Paris theater. From this point until the end (chapters XI–XXI), the text consists of the harangue from Waldstorc to the people of France, as dictated by the divinity who reproves them for their preference of French opera over Italian.

The overarching theme in this satire is cacophony, with its wider implications for bad taste. In the principal part of the action in the

satire, Waldstorc is subjected to the "appalling cries" and the "gar-
gling"[65] of French opera. Even from the beginning, however, Grimm
inserts some indications that we should expect ugly sounds: surely
the choice of the place-name "Boehmischbroda" in the title proceeds
from the author's desire to grate on French ears.[66] The name Waldstorc "dit Waldstoerchel" also must have had an abrasive sound, while
the word itself means *wood stork* in German—an animal whose song
is far from melodious. Grimm also subtitled his text "canticum cygni
bohemici," the swan song, which is particularly harsh, in spite of its
proverbial connotations. As in Voltaire's satires, as I will demonstrate
shortly, Grimm's proper names are meant to provoke laughter, and in
this case he mixes the ridiculous sounds of "barbaric" or provincial
Germanic names with Christian saints' names (Waldstorc's father, for
example, is named "Eustachius Josephus Wolfgangus"). The cacophonous mixture prepares us for the bad biblical style that is to follow
and it serves to pointedly emphasize the influence of Old Testament
taste on the narrative.

The text tries to offend our sensibilities by imitating the awkward
characteristics of biblical style that defy the ideals of tasteful French
poetry as described by Marmontel and others. As a reference to the
Old Testament, it is surely no accident that the *petit prophète* lives in
the Judengasse, the Jewish street, in Prague. The offensive features of
this story's style include, most prominently, lowness and repetitiveness—precisely the faults that critics warned against in descriptions
of figurative "Oriental" language. The lowness of *Le Petit prophète
de Boehmischbroda* has to do with undignified poverty, and the very
first line of the narrative demonstrates this debasing technique:

> And I was in the attic that I call my room, and it was cold, and I had
> no fire in my stove, for wood was expensive.
>   And I was wrapped in my coat, which was once blue and which
> had become white, given that it was worn out.[67]

Unlike melodramatic or pastoral depictions of humble living conditions, which rely on a certain stylized vagueness, this description is
direct and specific—and it deliberately breaks with poetic language
by mentioning money ("le bois étoit cher" and later, "il n'y eût qu'une
chandelle d'un denier"). This type of low language surely refers to the
mixture of high and low in the Bible, where one can see stereotypical-
ly crude words juxtaposed with words that are supposedly sublime.[68]

The passage I quote above also features Grimm's other, more frequently used technique, that of repetition. Parodying Old Testament rhetoric, *Le Petit prophète* begins approximately four out of every five sentences with the word *and*, with the exception of chapter XI, in which a number of sentences begin with the exclamation "O." These anaphoras also begin a large number of clauses within sentences, which bring to mind Montesquieu's pseudo-Oriental compliments that contain anaphoras that are repeated to the point of monotony. Aside from words such as *and*, longer passages are repeated absurdly in Grimm's text, such as the line about the blue coat that has turned white: "And a hand seized me by a tuft of hair, and I felt myself transported into the air, and I was on my way from Thursday to Friday, and I was wrapped in my coat, which was once blue and which had become white, given that it was worn out."[69] The comic effect in this passage relies on the fact that we have already seen the line about the blue/white coat before, the allusion to Waldstorc's poverty, and one other feature: the interruption of the action with a completely irrelevant description. This comic feature of Grimm's text surely refers to what appears to us as odd narrative techniques in the Bible, which seemingly emphasize the trivial details and bizarrely understate extraordinary events.

VOLTAIRE'S SAÜL

In this period, Grimm was thinking along the same lines as his fellow *philosophe* Voltaire, since both laughed at the trend in biblical tragedies, which was still very much alive.[70] Their shared contempt for this genre is evident in Grimm's anecdote, published in the *Correspondance littéraire*, regarding the awkward visit of an aspiring playwright, the abbé Petit, who presented Grimm and Diderot with his work *David et Bethsabée* as an homage. The *philosophes* ridiculed this man so that he would renounce his project, but he persisted in having it published. Later, Voltaire wrote his own parody of a biblical tragedy, *Saül*, partly in response to a number of biblical dramas, including Petit's.[71]

Voltaire's *Saül*, alternately labeled a *tragédie* or a *hyperdrame* but in fact more like a farce,[72] was published in 1763 and has never been performed. The play has been studied for its polemical content: critics have treated it in conjunction with Voltaire's Old Testament criticism and Pierre Bayle's controversial article "David" of his *Dictionnaire historique et critique*. By contrast, I would like to focus on this play as a pastiche of biblical style, although it may be ultimately impossible to dissociate form from content. The plot is as follows: King Saul is the victim of a conspiracy between the priest Samuel, who had originally crowned him, and David, whom Saul had raised as his protégé. Samuel is shown as a bloodthirsty zealot who practices human sacrifice and even cannibalism, and David is shown as a traitorous, rapacious man who comically adds a new wife to his household every few scenes. After several burlesque episodes of a seer with a python and the imprisoned king Agag being hacked to pieces onstage, injustice finally triumphs when David accedes to Saul's throne. Since there is no unity of time, the suddenly aged David dies in the last act and commits a final act of injustice by naming as his successor the son of his mistress Bathsheba instead of his older, legitimate sons.

One of the first stylistic features one notices in reading *Saül* is the deliberate violation of classical rules, which Voltaire had followed so punctiliously in his tragedies. Before one even reads the first line, one sees that the list of characters includes an absurd number of people, twenty-four in total, plus "la populace juive." Then one notices that each act will take place in a different city, obviously in defiance of the unity of space.[73] In case one has not yet noticed the chaotic nature of this play, the author announces: "In this tragicomedy of sorts, the unities of action, place, and time have not been observed. The author saw, like the illustrious La Motte, no need to submit to these rules. Everything happens in the time span of two or three generations, in order to make the action more tragic through the number of deaths, according to the Jewish spirit, while among us, the unity of time can only extend to twenty-four hours, and the unity of space to the walls of a palace."[74] Like those who criticized "Oriental" writing and attributed the qualities of good taste to the whole French nation, Voltaire claims that "among us," one follows the three unities, as opposed to the non-French, in this case, the Jewish people. Yet the fact that he criticizes Houdar de la Motte for following a different aesthetic contradicts his assertion about a national consensus on dramatic rules.[75]

One interesting thing about *Saül* is how closely ethics and style are related: the most morally reprehensible actions, such as the dismemberment of Agag, are always accompanied by the lowest words, such as *prépuce* or *gras*. The latter word appears in the phrase Samuel pronounces as he oversees the killing: "Yes, you are full of lard [*gras*], and your holocaust will be more pleasing to the Lord for that reason."[76] Not only is the mental image of a man being cut to pieces meant to be repugnant, but the word *gras* reduces the human body to meat.[77] By contrast, actions that are noble in Voltaire's system of eth-

ics are expressed in noble words reminiscent of his tragedies. For example, in the scene in which Saul (who is nearly the hero of this play,
in comparison to the other characters) initially liberates his prisoner
Agag, the language is neither low nor parodic:

Agag: Gentle and powerful conqueror, model of princes, who
      knows how to conquer and pardon . . . I will love in you
      the image of God who punishes and pardons.
Saül: Illustrious prince, who is made even greater by misfortune, I
      have only done my duty by saving your life.[78]

Other examples of this link between ethics and style abound: the vil-
lainous David probably utters the largest number of low words while
committing unethical acts. Even the more trivial faults, such as mar-
rying Michol to ingratiate himself with her father Saul, calls forth the
following unseemly speech:

David: . . . I had to bring your father two hundred Philistine fore-
      skins as a wedding present; two hundred foreskins are
      not so easy to find, so I had to kill two hundred men to
      finish off this deal; and then I didn't have the ass's jaw
      from Samson.[79]

We are confronted not only with the crude image of body parts but
also with the ridiculous image of an ass's jaw used as a weapon.

The joining of immorality and indecorous language, both of which
Voltaire finds in the Old Testament, culminates in the song that David
sings and dances in act IV, scene 4. "I want to sing you some bawdy
songs," he announces to his entourage, and he proceeds to sing with
his lyre:

    Dear Hebrews, sent by heaven,
    In blood you will wash your feet;
    And your dogs will fatten up
    From this blood that they will lick.
    Take care, my dear friends,
    To take all the little ones
    Who are still suckling at the breast;
    You will crush their skulls
    Against the infidel's walls
    And your dogs will fatten up
    From this blood that they will lick.[80]

It is important to note that Voltaire always scorned the Psalms and re-fused to translate them, so this is the closest to rewriting a Psalm that he comes to anywhere in his œuvre.[81] Nevertheless, Voltaire shows us three reasons why he objected to the story of Saul and of David: the violence, the chauvinism of the tribe, and the low imagery. In this scene, one of David's listeners momentarily speaks, I believe, as Voltaire's mouthpiece: Bathsheba says, disgusted, "Be done with your barracks songs; that is abominable. There is no savage who would want to sing such horrors; even the butchers of the people of Gog and Magog would be ashamed of them."[82] Her remark probably gives voice to Voltaire's outrage against the moral and aesthetic barbarity of the Old Testament.

In *Saül* as in his other comic writings about the Bible, Voltaire tries to emphasize the ugliness of certain sounds, especially proper names, to discredit the content of the passages. The cacophonous names in *Saül* often end in –g: Gog and Magog, Abisag (David's last wife), and Agag.[83] As for the sound of one character's name, "docteur Gag," which Voltaire changed from the original form *Gad*, coincides with the English word "gag" and it surely must have given its author and his English-speaking friends some comic delight. Another word Voltaire changed in order to emphasize its bizarreness to his contempo-raries is *Jerusalem*, which he writes as *Herus-Chalaïm*. The standard spelling of the city name had already been consecrated in poetry, most prominently in the much-admired epic poem *Jérusalem délivrée* by Torquato Tasso. Voltaire thus found an etymological variation of the word, just as he mocked Rousseau's *Héloïse* by calling the character *Aloïsia*, and just as he referred to the New Testament personage as *Magdeleine* instead of *Madeleine* in various works, in order to make it sound foreign and laughable.

VOLTAIRE'S "CORRECTION" OF THE SONG OF SOLOMON

Voltaire's disapproval of biblical style appears most brazenly in his adapted version of the Song of Solomon, which he sanitized in order to make it more acceptable to himself. In 1756, the duc de la Vallière wrote to Voltaire on behalf of the royal mistress and patroness of the arts, the marquise de Pompadour, who requested a poetic adaptation of the Psalms.[84] Voltaire, who had thundered his disapproval of the Psalms for years, offered instead to adapt two other books of the Old Testament: the Song of Solomon and Ecclesiastes. Voltaire's *Précis de l'Ecclésiaste* bears surprising similarities to his didactic poetry, such as the *Essai en vers sur l'homme*, and we can see in the notes that even though he put the text into French verse, he did not express any disapproval of the original text. In the notes, he translates several phrases into prose without commentary. By contrast, Voltaire's *Précis du Cantique des cantiques*[85] contains many traces of stylistic censure.

In the *Précis du Cantique des cantiques*, Voltaire does express some admiration for the Song of Solomon, though he also sees the need to correct certain excessively daring "Oriental" qualities of the poem. He praises the sentiments in the poem as "tender" and "simple," but he also insists on making it more "regular" and thus more acceptable: "The principal traits of this poem have been assembled to make a small regular work that conserves all the spirit of the original. The repetitions and the disorder, which may have been virtues in the Oriental style, are not so in ours."[86] He not only labels the faults of repetition and disorder in a poem as specifically "Oriental" faults, but later in the poem he also objects to the irrationality of some of the verses. For instance, in his translation he states, "I sleep, but my heart is awake," and in the notes he grumbles: "it is difficult to express how one can sleep and be awake at the same time. It is an Asiatic figure of speech that refers to a dream."[87] To understand this objection, we must put aside our present-day assumption that poetry lies outside the jurisdiction of reason and consider that Voltaire (following the lead of Malherbe and Boileau) believed that poetry needed to make sense grammatically as well as logically. To deviate from this classical requirement would have been to write as an "Oriental."

Most of the other changes Voltaire made to the Song of Solomon are matters of sexual modesty, specifically words that refer to the body, which he found too crudely stated in the Bible. One can see this process of censorship in the contrast between the main text (his sanitized translation in elegant verse) and his more literal translation, which he includes in the footnotes. For instance, to justify his replacement of the phrase "my breasts [*mamelles*] are better than wine"[88] (as he states in a footnote), he not only changes the speaker from the woman to the man, which he finds more "appropriate"[89] according to the *mœurs* of eighteenth-century France, but he erases the word *mamelle*. To decide how to replace it, Voltaire reflects: "Hebrew specialists say that the term that corresponds to *mamelle* has an energetic beauty in Hebrew. This word does not have the same grace in French; *tétons* is too lacking in seriousness, *sein* is too vague."[90] After these considerations, the resulting verses, reminiscent of Voltaire's early years among Regency libertine poets such as Chaulieu, are:

> The lilies, the rose buttons
> Of your budding globes
> Are to my ardent soul
> Like the beneficent wines
> Of the fertile Edom.[91]

To avoid the overly animal-like word *mamelle* and the literal act of drinking (breast milk, perhaps) evoked by the phrase "thy breasts are better than wine" or "mes mamelles sont meilleures que le vin," Voltaire separates the two terms with the more abstract term of "soul": instead of breasts being like wine, the lilies and roses (the typical skin colors of rococo figures) of the breasts are *to my soul* like wine. Voltaire complicates the syntax of the original phrase, which has the effect of distracting the reader from the bold corporeality of the original verse. Our attention is further transported away from the body by the reference to the faraway land of Idumée (Edom), which leaves us wondering whether the breasts are comparable to wine in general or specifically to the wine of this exotic region, thus chastely occupying our minds with a search for the scholarly reference.

Voltaire summarizes his views of the Song of Solomon with a sigh of mock relativism in his article "Salomon" of the *Dictionnaire philosophique*: "I confess that the 'Eclogues' of Virgil are in a different style; but each has his own, and a Jew is not obliged to write like Virgil."[92] Ultimately, though, the Song of Solomon merely falls into the category of bad "Oriental" poetry, in spite of the pleasant sentiments it occasionally expresses, in Voltaire's opinion: "It is a Jewish eclogue. The style is like that of all the eloquent works of the Hebrews, without connection, without order, full of repetition, confused, ridiculously metaphorical, but containing passages which breathe simplicity and love."[93] We will see that naïveté, like energy, is evoked as a quality that an artist can still aspire to, even when he lacks refinement, reason, or taste.

What was the deeper motive in attacking so-called Oriental style? Scholars such as David Porter[94] have argued that in eighteenth-century English critiques of Chinese porcelain, one important issue at stake was maintaining England's self-image as a commercially dominant nation. Meanwhile, when Dubos, Voltaire, and their fellows attacked Hebrew and Arabic taste in literature, we could attribute two likely motives to them. First, foreign influences may have posed a challenge to the establishment of French taste as universal, since large numbers of people felt drawn to exoticism in literature, even though works such as *1001 Nights* broke with the classical rules of composition. Second, attacking "Oriental language" allowed critics to subvert the Bible through indirect means—by attacking its style as vulgar, improbable, or exaggerated. The *philosophes* could attack not only the Old Testament itself but also the trend in adapting biblical material to genres such as theater and poetry, including poetic adaptations of Psalms by Le Franc de Pompignan and Jean-Baptiste Rousseau.

THE GOOD VS. THE BAD ORIENT

Before I finish mapping out the "Orient" as an imaginary realm of bad taste, I must address the question of Orientalism in the works of Voltaire and his fellow *philosophes*. If the literary influence of the "Orient" had to be rejected in French literature, why did the *philosophes* also write Oriental tales? It is impossible to ignore the widespread use of Asian and Middle Eastern settings in the literature of the Enlightenment, but one can distinguish between two types of views on the Orient among these authors: the "good Orient," which ingeniously encapsulated bits of wisdom in a pleasant form, and the "bad Orient," which encouraged the foolish credulity of the reading public or merely entertained it.

Voltaire explains this distinction most explicitly in *Zadig*, particularly when, in the *épître dédicatoire* to a sultana, the narrator[95] announces that this story was translated from Chaldean to Arabic for the sultan Ouloug, around the same time as the *1001 Nights*: "Ouloug preferred *Zadig*; but the sultanas were fonder of the *Thousand and One Nights*. 'How can you possibly,' wise Ouloug would say to them, 'prefer stories that make no sense and have no point?'—'That is precisely why we do like them,' would come the sultanas' reply. I flatter myself that thou wilt not be as they, and that thou wilt be a real Ouloug."[96] While taking on a mock Oriental tone, Voltaire expresses an important tenet of his own writing and of classical literature in general: the importance of both pleasing and instructing. To make his point, he shows us that he disapproves of the Orientalist fads that merely give pleasure and "that make no sense," such as the *Mille et une nuits*—or popular parodies, such as the *Mille et un quarts d'heure* or the *Mille et un jours*. On the other hand, he not only approves but makes use of Eastern literary forms that contain a kernel of moral instruction, such as the didactic poem *Gulistan* by the Persian poet Sadi.

This idea of the "good Orient" versus the "bad" appears clearly in Voltaire's treatment of religions, specifically in opposing pairs that represent, on the one hand, a foolish type of superstition and, on the other hand, rational and moderate wisdom: Islam versus Zoroastrianism, Buddhism versus Confucianism, and the supernatural aspects of Hinduism versus the Vedas.[97] In regard to the Koran, Voltaire expresses contradictory judgments that alternately praise the language as sublime and recur to the old stereotypes about exaggerated Oriental style.[98]

Other Enlightenment writers also alternated between exalting and ridiculing Middle Eastern culture in their writings—most famously Montesquieu in *Lettres persanes* but also in his lesser-known Orientalizing parodies such as *Histoire véritable* (a parody of Hinduism) and *Arsace et Isménie: Histoire orientale*. For thinkers such as Voltaire and Montesquieu to express a rigidly anti-"Oriental" point of view would mean to embrace a simpleminded nationalism and to give up the cosmopolitanism that was an important part of the Enlightenment. But to ascribe uncritically to a foreign political or aesthetic system was equally unacceptable. Their commentary on the "Orient," as found in *Lettres persanes* and *Essai sur les mœurs*, thus reveals the constant oscillation between criticizing the aspects they found objectionable (i.e., irrationality, tyranny) and praising aspects of Middle Eastern culture in a way that would put into question Europe's complacent belief in its own supremacy.

It is perhaps impossible to untangle aesthetic and ideological critique in the parodies of "Oriental" language. I will simply say that whatever ideological motives were the driving force behind these attacks (Grimm against French opera, Voltaire against the idealization of David), the means that these authors used were parodies of style. To discredit the content of the Bible, for instance, Voltaire used the weapon of taste to make it seem vulgar. The eighteenth-century critics thus punished some of their aesthetic enemies by relegating them to the realm of the exotic East, where bad taste supposedly ran wild.

CHAPTER FIVE

The Obscure, or
Enigmas and the Enigmatic

The idea that clarity and order characterize good writing seems so self-evident today that one rarely sees it as part of a polemic. In the seventeenth and eighteenth centuries, however, critics led a campaign to make clarity and order coincide with French style in order to exclude certain types of writing practiced by their contemporaries. They claimed that without these qualities, writing was not French; conversely, languages that were not French did not have these characteristics. In the article "Français" of the *Encyclopédie,* for example, Voltaire states: "The spirit [*génie*] of this language is its clarity and order, since each language has its own spirit."[1] While in other writings, such as the *Dictionnaire philosophique* and the *Discours aux Welches*, he excoriates his national tongue for its vulgarity, in this case he asserts its superiority. This is the language, he claims in the *Encyclopédie*, that has been refined and pared down by the "people of taste."[2] One can explain the apparent contradiction by considering that, in regard to clarity and order, Voltaire's *Encyclopédie* article describes his idealized vision of French rather than the language as it was actually used.

In texts such as "Français," Voltaire, Marmontel, Jaucourt, and others created the myth of the "génie de la langue française," which persists in France to this day not among the artistic avant-garde but in circles that pride themselves on their "Cartesianism"—a method of thinking and writing in a logically organized fashion. As Marc Fumaroli states in "Le Génie de la langue française," a small number of qualities have been repeatedly mentioned as specific to the French language: simplicity, wit, and especially clarity. Fumaroli remarks that ideas such as "Whatever is not clear is not French" ("Tout ce qui n'est pas clair n'est pas français") from Rivarol's 1784 essay *De l'universalité de la langue française* eventually became one of the "articles of the national credo,"[3] integral to French identity.

If clarity and order were two pillars of good taste, then the obscure and the disorderly necessarily belonged to the realm of bad taste. Why would anyone prefer the "bad" over the "good"? In the following two chapters, I will consider first clarity and then order as qualities imposed by a number of *philosophes*, and then I will delve into various types of writing that defied these principles.[4]

The present chapter will focus specifically on the requirement of clarity and how it effectively put certain types of writing outside the frontiers of acceptability. Among these, I will concentrate on two types of unclear writing: enigmas and the enigmatic. An enigma was simply a type of riddle in verse, a game that people played during social gatherings or when reading the magazine *Le Mercure de France*. These riddles were deliberately trivial, sometimes hiding an ordinary word under a grandiose description. Despite its popularity, this particular type of enigma and its variants, such as logogryphs, have practically disappeared from literary memory, although they remain safely lodged in the archives in the pages of the *Mercure* and in collections by Cotin, Ménestrier, and others.[5] Ironically, it is only through the scornful words of early modern critics that they are called to our attention at all; in fact, the frequent denunciations of the enigmas intrigued me enough to research them and to reflect upon the reasons why they must have incurred such hostility.

The other type of writing that found itself beyond the pale was referred to in the eighteenth century as the enigmatic, the mysterious, or the obscure. The *philosophes* associated the obscure with the sometimes paradoxical language of religion and with any barrier to communication, for example, in the presumably symbolic language of hieroglyphics and in the hermetic sciences. They warned against prophets and priests who sought to dazzle an ignorant populace with an elaborate cover of obscure words that only disguised a lack of meaning.

WHAT DID THEY MEAN BY CLARITY?

Eighteenth-century critics who claimed clarity was the mark of good

taste looked to their immediate predecessors in the seventeenth century such as Bouhours and Vaugelas, who in turn deferred to the rhetorical treatises of Aristotle and Quintilian. What exactly did clarity
mean for the critics of this lineage? First of all, clarity was one of the
first and most important qualities of rhetoric. Aristotle, in book III
of his *Rhetoric*, begins by stating, "In regard to style, one of its chief
merits may be defined as perspicuity [i.e., clarity]."[6] Quintilian, to emphasize the importance of clarity, puts the topic at the very beginning
of the section on style in his *Orator's Education*. Since their various
sets of rules overlap in many cases, I believe we can distill them into
a few key principles.

The first principle regards semantics: clarity requires using the appropriate word, which the French would call *le mot juste*. The right
choice can perhaps best be understood by looking at its opposite, the
types of words that must be rejected. To describe the wrong words
or "departure[s] from suitable language" (1404b), Aristotle uses the
suggestive term *foreign* or *xenos*, since "in this respect men feel the
same in regard to style as in regard to foreigners and fellow-citizens"
(1404b). He points out that people are eager to gape in awe at the foreign, and this explains why they are so impressed by unusual words;
in prose, however, one must stay within the realm of the familiar.
Searching more closely, we see that the term *foreign* covers all sorts
of semantic choices, which Aristotle lists as "strange, compound, or
coined words" (1404b). In a general sense, the words that are "foreign" are those that strike the listener as unusual or overly lofty, or
whose meaning is not immediately apparent, while familiar words
are those used commonly to designate objects.[7] In a later section, he
gives us the example of mules, which one could simply call "mules" or
to which one could give the glorious epithet of "daughters of storm-
footed steeds" (1405b).[8] The assumption that Aristotle makes is that
each thing has a common word that designates it precisely, while other words can, at best, refer to the same thing in less direct ways. Aristotle admits the possibility of two words being equally suited to
refer to one thing, such as the Greek words for "going" and "walk-
ing" (1405a), but he does not question the fundamental correlation
between words and things.

Quintilian, who also champions the use of *le mot juste*, adds that
the kinds of words to be avoided include archaic words, regional
words, or overly technical terms, lest the speaker appear pedantic.
The generally known or commonplace word is the best, in his esti-

mation. Quintilian does admit that in certain cases, the right word simply does not exist in a certain language. In Latin, for instance, he says there is a term for a person who throws a javelin, but there is no term for person who throws a ball—so some words must be replaced either by other words or by circumlocutions. This type of "abusio"[9] is necessary if the language is lacking. Quintilian includes metaphors among these misuses, since they "fit . . . words to things which do not belong to them," but he also considers them "the greatest ornament of oratory" (8.2.6).

The second rule for achieving clarity regards sentence structure, since obscurity occurs when the sentence becomes too complicated for the listener to understand. The example that Aristotle gives is the following: "As for me, I, after he had told me—for Cleon came begging and praying—set out, taking them with me" (1407a). In regard to this example, Aristotle remarks, "If the interval between 'I' and 'set out' is too great, the result is obscurity" (1407a). Like Aristotle, Quintilian rejects clauses that lengthen the interval between subject and verb, as well as other syntactical difficulties. Among the latter are arrangements of words that result in a "tangle," such as "Rocks the Italians call in the midst of the waves altars" (8.2.14) or sentences whose order makes the meaning ambiguous: "I heard that Chremes Demea struck" (8.2.16), in which we cannot see which is the subject and which is the object of the verb.

In terms of both semantics and syntax, the faults that lead to obscurity stem from a misguided desire to impress the audience. Some simply use too many words; as Aristotle complains, "Such idle chatter produces obscurity; for when words are piled upon one who already knows, it destroys the perspicuity by a cloud of verbiage" (1405a). The danger is that the audience will be swayed by words that sound exalted but which it does not understand. Aristotle adds, "the long circumlocution takes in the hearers, who find themselves affected like the majority of those who listen to the soothsayers. For when the latter utter their ambiguities, they also assent" (1407a). Quintilian also scoffs at those who exaggerate in their attempts to impress, for instance, by displaying great erudition but sounding obscure and pedantic. More generally, Quintilian insists that it is a mistake to think that common language is not good enough for oratory and to seek out something more elaborate: "Some writers too produce a medley of pointless words. In their horror of normal forms of expression, they are seduced by the appearance of elegance into wrapping up every-

thing in long-winded circumlocutions, just because they do not want
to make the simple statement" (8.2.17). In this way, he tries to crush
the pretentions of bad orators and strip language down to its bare
minimum before undertaking the topic of ornament.

It is important to note that both Aristotle and Quintilian, while
advocating clarity, do not ban metaphors or other figures completely
from language. Good style requires some ornament, Quintilian asserts, and he gives us several guidelines to help us judge the appropriateness of various figurative expressions, which I mentioned in Chapter 3. Aristotle insists throughout his *Rhetoric* that different levels of
clarity are appropriate to prose and poetry. He admits the possibility
of referring to things in "foreign" or unfamiliar ways, as long as it
happens within the poetic genre, especially epic. In regard to metaphor, he advocates appropriateness, proportion, and lack of ambiguity, but he even approves of certain enigmatic metaphors, as long as
they eventually make sense. Among the latter he includes some extreme cases, what the translator calls "smart sayings," which at first
puzzle listeners but then give them the pleasure of discovery. In one
example of a "smart saying," he cites someone who compares an arbi-
trator and an altar, which confuses his listeners until he explains that
a criminal eventually must go to one or the other (1412a). Aristotle
explains the pleasure that can be derived from momentarily enigmatic
metaphors: "Most smart sayings are derived from metaphor, and also
from misleading the hearer beforehand. For it becomes more evident
to him that he has learnt something, when, the conclusion turns out
contrary to his expectation, and the mind seems to say, 'How true it
is! but I missed it.' . . . And clever riddles are agreeable for the same
reason; for something is learnt, and the expression is also metaphorical" (1412a). This pleasure of discovery, which is produced not by
clarity but by a moment of obscurity, will be evoked by an admirer
of riddles in the seventeenth century, Claude-François Ménestrier, as
I will discuss in the next section.

The advocates for clarity in early modern France largely based their
ideas, sometimes their very phrasing, on these treatises by Aristotle
and Quintilian. Vaugelas, in his 1647 *Remarques sur la langue françoise*, shows his fidelity to Quintilian by emphasizing clear language
as the most important requirement for correct French usage.[10] Most of
Vaugelas's text consists of a list of common problems of grammar or
vocabulary; at the end, however, he devotes an entire treatise on style
to clarity, a principle he divides into "purity and clarity" ("pureté et

netteté").[11] Vaugelas defines "pureté" by scorning semantic "barbarismes" (using regional words such as *pache*[12] instead of *pacte*, or
archaic words such as *ains*) and grammatical "solecismes" (incorrect
verb conjugations such as *j'alla* for *j'allai* and other grammatical mis-
takes). The rules he establishes closely resemble Aristotle's and Quintilian's rejection of regional and archaic words. Furthermore, in the
section entitled "De la netteté du style," Vaugelas focuses more particularly on word order and ambiguity that can impede comprehension. Vaugelas was only one of many influential writers of the seventeenth century who promoted the ancient ideas of clarity: Malherbe,
Deimier, Du Plaisir, Arnauld, and Nicole, among others, also made
similar calls for clarity in their national language.[13]

   These entreaties continued to the eighteenth century through the
voices of *philosophes* like Diderot. For instance, his article "Clarté" in the *Encyclopédie* states: "In the figurative sense, it depends on
the choice and use of terms, on the order in which one has disposed
them, and on everything that helps the listener or reader understand
easily and distinctly and everything that helps the speaker or writer make his meaning or thought understood."[14] The enumeration of
these three rules of clarity (appropriate word choice, sentence structure, and lack of ambiguity) simply echo Quintilian's words: "Let us
take, as the primary virtue, Lucidity, 'proper' words, straightforward
order, no long-delayed conclusion, nothing missing and nothing too
much" (8.2.22). Similarly, Jaucourt, in the article "Style" of the *Encyclopédie*, uses Quintilian's very words: "Quintili[an] tells us that not
only should you be understood, but it should also be impossible not
to be understood."[15]

   Nevertheless, one discrepancy can be observed in the early modern critics' adoption of these classical ideas. In his *Rhetoric*, Aristotle
demonstrates the importance of clarity while drawing a line of demarcation between prose and poetry. While he strictly restrains the
prose that will be used in law courts and public forums, he is more
indulgent with poetry and looks tolerantly upon its sometimes far-
fetched language. In his *Poetics,* which deals with a different use of
language than the *Rhetoric*, he encourages poets to search precisely
for the "foreign" or lofty, unfamiliar words that he had rejected in
public address because "a diction abounding in unfamiliar usages has
dignity."[16] The common words that he judged appropriate for prose
are too "commonplace" (1458a) for poetry; however, even the poet
should not go too far in his use of elaborate language, since this ex-

cess "would result either in a riddle or in barbarism—a riddle if they were all metaphorical, barbarism if they were all importations [foreign words]" (1458a). Could it be that seventeenth- and eighteenth-century critics were overzealous in imposing Aristotle's rules of style, perhaps applying the rules that were meant only for legal harangues to all types of language, including poetry?

While the rules of clarity did not radically change between the ancients and eighteenth-century French critics, perhaps a more interesting object of inquiry involves the ways in which the rule was broken in different periods and in different countries. One can suppose, for example, that Spanish baroque poetry and German treatises on alchemy represented various types of unclear language. If we ask what the opposite of clarity is in eighteenth-century France, words that come up frequently are *galimatias*, ambiguity, mystery, and especially enigmas and the enigmatic. The latter two appear frequently together, even though they belong to two very different domains.

To examine one particular writer who was often accused of obscurity, let us turn to Montaigne once again. Despite his undeniable prominence in eighteenth-century letters, certain critics saw his archaic vocabulary and highly complicated syntax as mere faults. According to Maturin Dréano in *La Renommée de Montaigne en France au XVIIIe siècle*, word choice posed some problems. One editor named Artaud who published an abridged edition of Montaigne's *Essais* in 1700 gives a justification for omitting passages and simplifying some sentences of the original text: "We have limited ourselves to cutting or changing words that are so archaic and so obsolete that, aside from the fact that they added no beauty, they would not have been understood by many people, any more than if they had been Greek or Latin terms, which would surely not have caused anyone any pleasure. These words include: destourbier, vastité, admonester, estriver, etc."[17] The abbé Trublet, who had proposed translating Montaigne into French, also uses some of the same terms as Artaud: "that is precisely what renders him obscure. His work is full of careless faults, barbarisms, ambiguities, weak constructions."[18] On the one hand, these critics consider the chronological distance that makes Montaigne's language seem as foreign to eighteenth-century French readers as Greek. On the other hand, they treat Montaigne's text as if it were contemporary, and under that assumption they find his style lacking and in need of correction.

Aside from direct criticism of certain texts for their lack of clarity, parodies of obscure language also tended to enforce the rules stated above, turning unusual words and complicated syntax into matters of ridicule. Alexis Piron's *Métromanie*, for example, gives us an example of a bad poet whose circumlocutions leave his listeners puzzled. Damis, the poet, exclaims at one moment:

> In matters of love, the heart of a favorite of the Muses
> Is a star towards which the human understanding
> Would raise, from down below, its telescope in vain;
> Its sphere is above all intelligence.[19]

His faults include the convoluted structure of the sentence and the odd presence of the word *telescope*, which eighteenth-century critics (as well as Quintilian) would have counseled against because it belongs to a specialized technical field and thus seems too pedantic to be used in general speech. Even now, the telescope strikes us as comically out of place in a speech about love. As a response to the speech above, his impertinent valet Mondor complains:

> Sir, adjust yourself a little bit to my level,
> And, if you please, put this Hebrew into French.[20]

Mondor's reference to Hebrew in order to describe an indecipherable language is an apt choice, just as one would refer colloquially to Greek or Chinese to serve the same purpose ("It's all Greek to me" or "C'est du chinois pour moi"), since all of these examples are consistent with Aristotle's view of obscure vocabulary as foreign. In addition, the idea that unclear French equals Hebrew reminds us of the assertions by Voltaire and Rivarol that what is not clear is simply not French. And, as I argued in the previous chapter, the Hebrew language, as one of the languages of the Middle East, was considered one of the primeval sources of ambiguity and consequently of bad taste.

Like Piron, Voltaire parodies obscure writing in certain works by deliberately confounding his readers. He sometimes departs from the trenchantly clear style of his histories or his other prose texts by sprinkling perplexing terms onto his satirical works, especially in polemical treatments of religion. In these, he mentions technical terms in order to demonstrate the wide gap between the absurd theological sophistry of his day and his own ideal of a simplified form of virtue. For example, in an appropriately titled dialogue, "Galimatias dramatique," several members of various religions or sects try to convert a Chinese man. As is typical for his satires of theology, Voltaire has the representatives of each faith using obscure jargon. The Jesuit, for instance, preaches to his listener: "Our Lord wants to make all men chosen vessels; it depends on you whether you want to be vessels. . . . If you do not have contrition, you have attrition; if you lack attrition, you have your own forces and mine."[21] No less enigmatically, the Lutheran exclaims, "Believe only the Lutherans; pronounce only these words: *in, cum, sub*, and drink up."[22] The humor of these passages relies largely on the absurdly disjointed use of words such as *attrition* and *vessels*, as well as the particles *in, cum*, and *sub*, all of which seem to degenerate into nonsense or, in other words, the *galimatias* of the title. Voltaire deliberately takes these terms out of context to make them seem more incomprehensible, while readers must identify with the man whom these sectarians address. Like Zadig or l'Ingénu, the Chinese listener represents the standard of common sense, which makes him reject the mysterious terms cited above. At the end of "Galimatias dramatique," he declares that these "poor fools" should be committed to a madhouse.

While readers may find this satirical technique recurrent in Voltaire's works, the parody of obscurity takes on another form in one of his lesser-known works. A short text entitled *Pot-pourri* is surely the most extreme case of Voltaire's use of obscurity, and critics have left it largely untouched, probably because it is so incomprehensible. This prose narrative contains a number of characters who appear and disappear from the text, a shadowy plot that goes nowhere, and no obvious message, satirical or otherwise. I believe the text reaches the height of nonsense when one character proclaims: "we have read in Nostradamus these very words: *Nelle chi li po ra te ic sus res fait en bi*."[23] The text at this point crumbles into nonsense syllables, but Voltaire, who seems to have an almost insurmountable aversion to the obscure, immediately gives us the key to the meaningless syllables. Placed backward, the fragments read "*Bienfait ressuscitera Polichinelle*" or "Bienfait will resuscitate Polichinelle," referring to two characters in the story—a phrase that may not have much significance but at least is coherent. I would not presume to untangle the meaning of *Pot-pourri*; on the contrary, I would interpret it as a deliberately meaningless, hopelessly fragmented text written as a pastiche of other puzzling texts.

Aside from parodies and satires, we must also confront the issue of intentional or unintentional obscurity. Accusations of obscurity sometimes implied that the author or artist was simply incapable of composing good works—out of a lack of education, talent, or taste, or just out of pure stupidity. An example would be the unfortunate aspiring poet Damis in *Métromanie*. By contrast, the present-day myth of an esoteric genius, such as T. S. Eliot or James Joyce, whose work may seem puzzling to ordinary readers but actually contains some secret, profound truth, would have been rejected by the *philosophes*, since they subscribed to Quintilian's principle that good writing must be understandable to all and impossible to *not* be understood.

The *philosophes* grappled with the issue of obscurity in various ways, as I will demonstrate in the next sections of this chapter. In the case of riddles, or intentional play with obscurity, a number of eighteenth-century critics portrayed them as a sub-literary practice among the uneducated. In the case of the ineffable, related to the mysteries of religion or poetry, the *philosophes* wished to expose symbolic language as an instrument of charlatanism, whose practitioners try to keep an ignorant public in awe.

ON ENIGMAS

In his *Essai sur le goût*, Montesquieu links two metaphors of bad taste, the gothic cathedral and the verbal riddle: "A Gothic structure is to the eye what a riddle [*énigme*] is to the understanding; in the contemplation of its various parts and ornaments, the mind perceives the same perplexity and confusion in its ideas that arise from reading an obscure poem."[24] Even though the term *énigme* can, in an abstract sense, designate anything that puzzles us, I believe that in the statement above, Montesquieu adds the term *poëme obscur* to refer specifically to the genre of *énigmes*, the riddles in verse that were in vogue during the seventeenth and eighteenth centuries. Just as gothic cathedrals are monuments to bad taste, so are the word games called *énigmes*.

What were *énigmes*?[25] Few readers today have seen examples of these word games, although they were probably as popular in the eighteenth century as crosswords are nowadays. The game of *énigmes* reputedly began in the salons of the marquise de Rambouillet and of Valentin Conrart and were inspired by an Italian type of comic verse, the bernesque,[26] that facetiously praised an ordinary object such as an egg. At first, the enigmas' ephemeral nature made them unlikely to survive in written form, but a handful of compilations were made, for example, by the abbé Cotin, a figure famously maligned by Molière.[27]

The trend did take a more widely accessible form when the enigmas started appearing in the literary journal *Le Mercure galant*, or *Le Mercure de France*, as it was known in the eighteenth century. From their first appearance, their popularity only increased, to the extent that the journal went from including an occasional enigma every few months in the 1670s to including two enigmas per month in the eighteenth century. The enthusiasm of the reading public made itself most visible in the growing lists of names of those who had submitted the correct answer, which was printed in each issue.[28]

In order to explain enigmas to present-day readers, perhaps it would be best to give an example:

> I am composed of sweetness and charm,
> The Gods take an interest in forming me.
> Neptune from his sea offers me *je ne sais quoi,*
> Cybele her breast, Aurora her tears.
>
> Minerva from her fruits provides me with liqueur,
> Vertumnus contributes with his gifts,
> Bacchus from his grapes adds a bit of sourness,
> And with this mixture, one sees me well stocked.
>
> When someone has a banquet or a noble feast,
> They invite me immediately to join the table.
> I don't drink or eat, and I see more than one hand
> Arming itself against me. Am I not miserable?[29]

To explain how one could arrive at the correct answer of "salad," it would be useful to explain the erudite, though not particularly profound, allusions in the verses. First, the lettuce plant can only grow with the aid of the gods, since Neptune waters it, Cybele provides the earth, and Aurora presumably supplies the morning sunlight. Once the lettuce is prepared to be served, it receives olive oil from Minerva, who introduced the olive tree to humans, and vinegar, which is wine in a different form, from Bacchus. Vertumnus, Roman god of fruits and the harvest, probably adds tomatoes or other ingredients to the lettuce. In the final stanza, the salad can be described as the metaphorical guest who comes to the table but cannot eat nor drink, since it is a dish, but is instead threatened by the fork and knife of the person who eats it.

While the enigma as a genre may have a few features in common with other literary forms, the most unmistakable difference is that enigmas leave the correct word unsaid, and it is up to the reader to think of it. Renaissance *blasons* also used verse to praise or blame something *ad absurdum*, and like the enigmas, they could be about anything: household implements, food, even letters of the alphabet. However, often the titles of the *blasons* make it entirely clear what the poem is about, while the point of the enigma is that its object is unknown. Another type of *blason*, in the realm of heraldry, could be said to present to the uninitiated viewer a set of images to be decoded, but these are not exactly riddles and are not exclusively verbal. Another similar genre, emblems, can be distinguished from enigmas by their subject matter and their lack of secrecy. Emblems do not try to conceal a single word, but instead they express a maxim in verse, and their meaning is enriched by an accompanying illustration. To set them apart from other genres, it is useful to stress that enigmas are not illustrated but purely verbal and that their solution consists of a single word.

The comparison between some of these genres did occur to some contemporaries, such as Crousaz, who makes a distinction between the enigma and the emblem and favors the latter. In particular, Crousaz uses these two poetic genres to illustrate his idea that good taste is a careful balance between unity and variety. If one states an idea plainly, he claims, the statement suffers from too much unity and risks boring readers. However, if the statement is put into words that strain our comprehension too much, it sins from a lack of unity: "One would not want emblems to be confused with enigmas; confusion displeases and at the same time it is the source of error; the goal of the enigma is to exercise the mind; the emblem pleases right away and it creates an ingenious and easy pleasure."[30] The emblem is, in Crousaz's opinion, the ideal middle point between an overly plain and an overly confusing way to express oneself, because the mind is suspended in a state of ignorance only for a brief moment.

Crousaz's disposition against enigmas is mild in comparison to the outcry of critics and satirists against this poetic form. Since the beginning of the trend, opponents covered the fans of enigmas with opprobrium, mocking them for their *préciosité* and accusing them of false intellectual pretensions. We can find mockery of the enigmas as far back as 1660 in Molière's *Précieuses ridicules* and in the 1683 comedy *Le Mercure galant* by Edmé Boursault.[31] The latter play features a number of caricaturized readers of the *Mercure* who appear one after the other, each one crazed by a different aspect of the journal. One of the final readers is a ridiculous, pretentious man who wishes to have his own enigma published, an enigma whose solution is "un vent échappé par en bas."[32] Typically, he claims that his riddle is the noblest and cleverest written since the one given to Oedipus by the Sphinx.

Even Gayot de Pitaval, a proponent of enigmas who published a collection of these riddles, evidently felt the need to confront their unfavorable reputation. At the beginning of his 1717 *Recueil des énigmes les plus curieuses de ce temps*, he remarks, "I should not end this foreword without making an effort to defend the enigma from the contempt of many people, who look down on it with pity."[33] He asks skeptics not to judge the genre of enigmas after having previously seen only one bad example and expresses the wish that they will remain open-minded enough to read his collection.

The ridiculous image of the enigma-solver or enigma-writer persisted until the end of the eighteenth century. Authors Claude Crébillon and Boyer d'Argens, for example, made jabs against the trend in their novels. Crébillon, in his 1734 novel *L'Ecumoire*, ironically describes a young man of great accomplishments: "He was the finest Dancer in the World; no-body made a Bow with better Grace: He could unfold all Riddles [*énigmes*]; play'd well at all Sorts of Games."[34] These dubious skills are also highlighted by Boyer d'Argens in his novel *Lettres juives*, specifically in his description of the "demi-savants" in which Paris abounds, typified by "the man [who] would be extremely sorry if he be not thought capable of guessing at the aenigmas in the *Mercure Galant*, and composing a madrigal."[35] What these satires have in common are the accusations of effeminacy, of intellectual charlatanism, and of the absurdly disproportionate importance that ladies supposedly confer on those who have mastered the enigmas.

While it is undeniable that the writers mentioned above heaped ridicule on enigma-lovers, they do not explain the reasons for their contempt. On the other hand, the chevalier Jaucourt gives us a somewhat more straightforward explanation in the article "Enigme" of the *Encyclopédie*: "Among modern people, the enigma is a small work, normally in verse, in which, without naming the thing, someone describes its causes, its effects, and its properties, but in ambiguous terms and with ideas that spur the mind to discover what it is. I will not linger over the other rules prescribed in this literary game, because my aim is not so much to enjoin men of letters to devote sleepless nights to it, as it is to turn them away from such puerilities."[36] Specifically in regard to the enigmas that came into vogue in the seventeenth century, Jaucourt states:

> But however one may dress up the enigmas, they will never be any-
> thing more than foolish expenditures of mental energy, word games,
> deviations of language and of ideas.
>
> The somewhat distinguished men of letters of the previous cen-
> tury, who had the weakness to give in to this fad, and to allow them-
> selves to be dragged along by this torrent, would be very ashamed
> today to read their names on the list of all sorts of idle people, and
> to see that there was a time when they would have been honored to
> guess enigmas, and even more to announce to France, that they had
> had the wit to express, under a certain amount of verbiage, under a
> mysterious jargon and under ambiguous terms, a flute, an arrow, a
> fan, a clock.[37]

In short, the enigma craze that attracted even serious writers ultimately wasted mental energies for a childish purpose. Jaucourt makes
a distinction in this article between these enigmas, which were society games of the seventeenth and eighteenth centuries, and the ancient enigmas of the "Oriental kings" that Samson or the Sphinx,
for example, presented as tests. Both types of riddles are scorned by
Jaucourt, but at the end of the article, he stretches the meaning of the
word to a third type of enigma: the unanswered questions of science
and mathematics, which he considers worthier intellectual pursuits.
These enigmas, as opposed to the other two dubious sorts, are exer-
cised by real thinkers, "geniuses of a superior order,"[38] and they are
actually useful to mankind.

In considering the bad reputation of word games, however, it
would be a mistake to think that the *philosophes* themselves never
used language as a disguise. The difference is that their version of obscure language has two essential qualities: first, it contains a kernel
of wisdom (unlike *énigmes*), no matter how playful it appears on the
surface, and second, it acts as a mere veil that temporarily covers an
unambiguous, knowable truth (unlike the *énigmatique*, as I will explain in the next section). The first quality recalls Crousaz's praise of
emblems, which both please and instruct, and Jaucourt's contention
that enigmas wasted time and mental energy for no useful purpose. In
looking for a "better" sort of puzzle, then, we could turn precisely to
Renaissance emblems, since they can teach us, for example, that "All
things must perish" ("Toutes choses sont périssables") or "Whoever
harms someone else harms himself" ("Qui nuyst à aultruy il nuyst à
soymesmes").[39] It was this expectation of wisdom that made Crousaz
prefer emblems to enigmas: both leave the reader momentarily suspended in a state of puzzlement, but at least the emblem rewards him

with a piece of moral instruction in exchange for his effort. *Enigmes*, on the other hand, merely leave one with a simple and not particularly profound word, such as *fan* or *clock*.

In reference to the second quality that justified the use of obscurity, I must emphasize that the possibility of a mystery without a solution, for example, a riddle without an answer[40] or the unfathomable paradoxes of Christianity, was simply unacceptable to the *philosophes*. On the contrary, Voltaire's model of the proper use of the enigmatic involves a two-layered text, in which one statement momentarily covers another, for the purpose of eluding the censors or of displaying a flourish of wit.

One can see this technique repeatedly in *Zadig*, in which we are confronted with a number of puzzling episodes, but as in Aristotle's "smart sayings" and Crousaz's emblems, Voltaire leaves us suspended in confusion only for a moment and ultimately reveals a rational solution. In fact, Voltaire often makes the plot of this *conte* hinge on moments of puzzlement. To choose one among many such episodes, let us consider "La Danse," in which Zadig advises the king to choose a treasurer depending on how lightly he dances. The suggestion strikes the king, as well as the readers, as nonsensical. Zadig's idea leaves us in a state of confusion until we see him carry out his plan: He has each candidate wait alone in an antechamber where valuable objects are stored, and then he requires them to dance before the king. Logically, those who have stolen things are encumbered by their added weight and they dance awkwardly, while the one candidate who steals nothing can dance lightly, and thus the king can see that he is an honest man. At the end of the episode, the initial mystery is completely dispelled and the reader supposedly experiences "the pleasure of discovery," as Aristotle had remarked about "smart sayings."

The solution of this episode of *Zadig* fits with the other requirement of the "proper" use of the obscure, since it teaches us a moral lesson: dishonesty is ultimately exposed. This aspiration to a certain insight into human nature, in the style of the moralists, can be seen throughout *Zadig*. In the episode entitled "Les Enigmes," for example, Voltaire most explicitly includes the sort of riddles used by the ancient Greeks for didactic purposes. When Zadig must win a series of contests in order to ascend to the throne and be united with his beloved queen, he must answer such questions as "Which of all things in the world is at once the longest and the shortest, the quickest and the slowest, the most divisible and the most continuous, the most squandered and the most regretted, something without which nothing can be done, which obliterates what is small and gives life to what is great?"[41] The answer is "time." As we can see, the maxim-like quality of enigmas such as these justifies them in the eyes of *philosophes*, as opposed to the *Mercure*'s trivial riddles.

To consider the objection that the *énigmes* of the *Mercure* imparted no wisdom but only entertained, we should note that the issue of pleasing without instructing harks back to a battle waged in the seventeenth century over *préciosité*. While the majority of critics and authors advocated the Horatian principle of pleasing and instructing, a few put up some resistance. Among these were Honoré d'Urfé, Madeleine de Scudéry, La Calprenède, and even Corneille, during his embattled early career,[42] all of whom brazenly proclaimed that pleasing was the most important motive for writing and that instructing was unnecessary. Significantly, the first three novelists I mentioned were also associated with the *précieux* movement, as were the enigmas and other word games. When Voltaire, Jaucourt, and others expressed their contempt for *énigmes*, then, it was as much to fight against this current of *galanterie* in literature[43] as it was to put into doubt the legitimacy of the preferences of a whole segment of the reading public. The attack on gallantry was part of the *philosophes*' campaign to establish a new standard of taste based on their professional status as *gens de lettres* rather than on the standard of *bon usage* of the previous century.

The enigmas certainly called forth the participation of women and non-elites in large proportions. One study estimates that the reading public of the *Mercure*, based on responses to the enigmas, consisted of a large proportion of women, between 24 and 50 percent, depending on the year.[44] Perhaps as significant, those who composed and answered the enigmas also had no proven literary qualifications but could come from any segment of the population, including artisans and low-ranking administrators. And, as I outlined in Chapter 1, it was precisely the participation of such people—who had a profession but who enjoyed literature in their leisure time—in the literary realm that spurred the critics to attack. For this reason, I believe that the hostile language directed at enigma fans is largely directed at the imputed literary aspirations of amateurs.

THE ENIGMATIC

Aside from the fops and ladies who enjoyed playing hide-and-go-seek with language, there was another potential challenge to clarity: name-ly, the claim that certain things, by their very nature, could simply not be expressed in clear language. This threat of the *énigmatique* came from the realms of religion, poetry, and even the hermetic tradition, all of which put undue emphasis on obscure language for motives that the *philosophes* disapproved.

These early modern French critics may have demanded clarity in the name of good taste, but in previous eras, both clarity and taste had to sometimes yield to other considerations. If we look at Saint Augustine's approach to this issue, for example, we can see that ob-scurity attained a sacred status in regard to Christian doctrine. In *De Doctrina christiana*, Augustine argues to justify the ambiguities of Christian Scripture, since he and his fellow theologians had to con-front the mysteries of this body of writing without challenging its content, much less its style. Accordingly, he admonishes anyone who would reproach biblical texts for their lack of clarity or for rhetorical faults: "there is a kind of eloquence appropriate to writers who en-joy the highest authority and a full measure of divine inspiration."[45] In other words, since God could not be accused of dictating unclear texts to holy men, obscurity was now attributed to the deficiencies of readers' minds.

Rather than upholding the ideal of transparent communication from writer to reader, as classical and neoclassical writers prescribe, Augustine emphasizes the necessity of two mediating factors: first, foreign languages, and second, canonical authority. He specifically entreats scholars to learn Latin, Greek, and Hebrew in order to un-derstand Scripture. In regard to authority, Augustine advises readers to make use of officially sanctioned texts because these will prepare the reader to confront those rogue variants, which "will then be un-able to take possession of his unprotected mind and prejudice him in any way against sound interpretations or delude him by their danger-ous false-hoods and fantasies."[46] Since only some texts and interpre-tations are legitimized by the church authorities, the reader is obliged to submit to their judgment.

While Aristotle and Quintilian had found fault with the use of "foreign" words (in the literal sense as well as the vaguer sense of "un-usual"), Europeans of the Middle Ages had a different relationship to language. While ancient Greeks and Romans prized their own lan-guage as superior to those of the supposedly effeminate Persians and crude Germans, for example, medieval Europeans did not grant the same prestige to their own vernacular. In ancient Rome, if a speaker used a foreign or regional word, it was blamable not only because it confused Roman listeners but also because it came from an inferior culture. In the Middle Ages, however, scholars needed to know actual foreign and archaic languages in order to carry on their work, so if the reader did not understand a Greek or Hebrew term, this was a failing on his part, not on the part of the text. In opposition to his classical predecessors, Augustine even considers it proper that certain words remain in the original language, even in translated texts. He cites the examples of "amen, alleluia, racha, osanna," which should be kept in the original because of their "solemn authority" or because the emotions they express simply cannot be translated.[47] The classical hierarchy of the national language and foreign languages was thus reversed and the obscure became something awe-inspiring rather than contemptible.

And unlike Vaugelas, who would complain of solecisms and barbarisms in the seventeenth century, Augustine defends idiosyncrasies of Latin translations of sacred writings. What are barbarisms and solecisms, Augustine asks, but simple variations of language? He writes, "Whether you say *inter homines* or *inter hominibus* does not matter to a student intent upon things. . . . Whether one says *ignoscere* with a long or short third syllable is of little concern to someone beseeching God to forgive his sins, however he may have managed to utter the word."[48] On the contrary, he says, the real problem concerns the "boastful" scholars who are too arrogant to see past these oddities. Scripture is thus irreproachable to Augustine, and a humble faith is preferable to arrogant erudition. This inclusive attitude stands in sharp contrast to the efforts made by Vaugelas, Malherbe, and the Enlightenment *philosophes* to construct a purified version of French by drawing lines of demarcation between tasteful, correct usage and newly shameful variants.

Even if one overlooks the problems of translation and correct grammar, Christian Scripture still held some unfathomable mysteries. Rather than discrediting the religion, this type of content-based obscurity furthered Christian ideology because it challenged the minds of the faithful. "So thick is the fog created by some obscure phrases," remarks Augustine, that he believes that God created it intentionally so that intellectuals would be, first, "subdued by [the] hard work" of interpretation and, second, "rescued from boredom and reinvigorated."[49] In contrast to Augustine, however, early modern critics, such as the ones I mentioned earlier, emphasized easiness as the necessary companion to the pleasure of reading.

While the painful difficulty of reading would have been compatible with doctrines such as mortification and self-restraint, the deciphering of figurative language also held the promise of special intellectual pleasures. Saint Augustine mentions in particular one passage from the *Song of Songs*, the comparison of the beloved's teeth to a flock of sheep, which was precisely one of the images that outraged Voltaire. Augustine imposes another layer of meaning on this passage, claiming we must see this image of the teeth of Solomon's lover as an edifying metaphor for "the holy and perfect men" that serve as models to other Christians. In regard to this unusual metaphor of sheep-as-teeth-as-virtuous men, Augustine remarks, "Surely one learns the same lesson as when one hears it in plain words without the support of the imagery? And yet somehow it gives me more pleasure."[50]

For the reasons given above, enigmas, in the general sense, would find favor with medieval scholars. As Päivi Mehtonen states in *Obscure Language, Unclear Literature*,

> Enigma was not only a figure of speech; it was associated with a great many writing practices. "Imprecise and enigmatic" writing was a popular and stylistic mode in medieval literature both in Latin and in the vernaculars, in works of religious instruction and in hermeneutic tradition. . . .
>
> For the Church Fathers and scholars of the spirit, enigma was an element in Scripture worthy of preservation together with *obscura parabola quae difficile intellegitur*, "obscure allegory," "dark sayings which purport one thing and intend another," or *obscura et quasi problematica allegoriae species*—the obscure and problematic mode of allegory.[51]

One could compare this observation with Aristotle's examples of "smart sayings" and the pleasure of momentary incomprehension, but Aristotle assumed that the mysterious phrases had an eventual resolution, whereas the mysteries of Scripture could well remain forever obscure. Ultimately, however, Augustine claims that even if one does not understand the difficult passages of the Bible, one must assume that the same messages can be found stated more plainly in other parts of the Bible, and furthermore, the most important thing is to read with a certain goodwill and with fundamental principles such as love and charity in mind. These values were thus placed above any considerations of taste.

After Augustine, a number of other Christian thinkers defended the pleasures of obscurity. Among these, Normand Doiron lists Meister Eckhardt, Nicolas de Cues, Juan de la Cruz, and Pascal in his article "Le Style obscur: L'Enigme I." Specifically, Doiron refers to statements by the Spanish mystic Juan de la Cruz about the right to use mysterious language to express religious experience. Comparing Juan de la Cruz's arguments with Dante's defense of poetic language, Doiron remarks that "both mark the painful and radical impotence of words in expressing poetic plenitude, which is seen as a hypostasis of divine plenitude."[52] Not only is language portrayed here as inadequate for expressing certain profound experiences, but the justification of unclear language also involves making various types of languages (presumably such as legal, scientific, poetic, or religious) independent from each other and subject to different sets of rules. This separation is precisely what neoclassical critics will reject, submitting all types of writing to the same tasteful standards of clarity and correctness.

Alongside treatises on taste by writers such as Bouhours, the tradition of defending the potential obscurity of God's words lived on in the seventeenth century, as we can see in Pascal's *Pensées*. In this work, several fragments address the issue of God's communication through "figures." Pascal's explanation of scriptural obscurity involves the status of the "chosen ones" vis-à-vis the rest of the population, especially unbelievers. He claims that puzzling language may appear in the Bible, but only in order to repel the skeptics. Meanwhile, the virtuous can understand God's message no matter how confusing it seems to others: "There is enough light for those who only desire to see, and enough obscurity for those who have a contrary disposition."[53] Like Augustine, Pascal maintains that one advantage of obscurity is the abasement of human reason, especially its pretensions to understand all, since religious truths are beyond logic yet understandable to those who approach them with enough goodwill. Like the Spanish mystics, Pascal alludes to the ineffable: "Not all that is incomprehensible ceases to exist."[54] Just because something is beyond our intellectual limits, he claims, we should not dismiss it.

Aside from religious writers, others during the Middle Ages and Renaissance challenged the classical principle of clarity. Dante and Boccaccio, for example, defended obscurity because they claimed that poets had the right to follow different rules for manipulating language.[55] There were sporadic calls throughout Western history (Victor Hugo, Mallarmé, the surrealists) for the independence of poetic language from that of disciplines such as law or science, which would allow poets more freedom in choosing unusual words and turns of phrases. I would add that this division appeared already in the divergence between Aristotle's *Rhetoric* and his *Poetics*, particularly when he rebukes certain expressions in political addresses but accepts them in the *Iliad*, for example. This division is also very much common practice in the West of the present day, where one has decidedly different expectations about the intelligibility of, for example, a legal brief and a piece of conceptual art.

In the early modern period, however, many critics believed that literary genres (*belles-lettres*) should be submitted to the same rules of taste. Marc Fumaroli reinforces this view by arguing that correct French usage was based on legal rhetoric as much as courtly literature. He describes the rise of the French language, and specifically the ideal of clarity, as a trajectory that passes through poetic manuals as well as the legal pronouncements of François Ier.[56] Furthermore, as Päivi Mehtonen remarks in her study of obscurity, in the seventeenth century, demands for clarity came from a number of philosophical sources, sometimes even conflicting ones: rationalists and empiricists, Jansenists and Catholics. For instance, rationalists such as Descartes demanded that beliefs be based on *clear and distinct* ideas, which individuals could perceive directly, without any intervention from commentators. The latter feature of Cartesian thinking contrasted significantly with the medieval reliance on the authority of certain canonical sources that mediated between texts and readers. Meanwhile, empiricists such as Locke also challenged the assumption that obscure words had any intrinsic value, and skeptics such as Gassendi led the way for Voltaire and more radical thinkers of the eighteenth century to express the suspicion, as Mehtonen puts it, "that a text was obscure because it was at bottom inane."[57]

Gassendi, as Mehtonen points out, drew up a list of clear and obscure writers; he "distinguished two streams of natural philosophy: *perspicua* and *obscura* or *occulta*."[58] As it happens, the clear ones were also philosophically on his side and admired by other skeptics of his period: Epicurus, Aristippus, Zeno, Pyrrho.[59] The obscure ones were Homer, Hesiod, Aesop, Orpheus, Empedocles, Plato, Heraclitus the Obscure, Aristotle—a surprising list for us in the present day, since we consider some of these writers as poets and fabulists rather than "natural philosophers." Gassendi, however, submits them to the

same standards of truth. Like Gassendi, Voltaire and his fellow philosophers risked being more Catholic than the pope, so to speak, in
insisting that Aristotle's rules of composition have a larger jurisdiction than he himself had originally planned. Far from rejecting Aristotle, these critics may have been overzealous in applying some of his
rules.

Many *philosophes* of the seventeenth and eighteenth centuries addressed challenges to the principle of clarity, specifically reverence for
purportedly divine writings, by daring to speculate that the veil of puzzling words may well have hidden a great emptiness. The accusations
of a Wizard-of-Oz-like swindle perpetrated by religious figures would
come to full fruition in the works of eighteenth-century *philosophes*.
But the stakes were not only religious in nature; the opposing views
of obscure language also involved the status of the French language.
Those who tried to exclude ambiguity, imprecision, and regional variations did so in order to develop their language to serve the purposes of
good taste and consequently the glory of French civilization.

ON HIEROGLYPHICS

Curiously, many eighteenth-century discussions of clarity and obscurity eventually turned to the topic of hieroglyphics. In fact, hieroglyphics connected three of the most fundamental problems that
the *philosophes* perceived in unclear language: the charlatanism of
priests, the obsession with words in themselves, and the dangers of
alchemy.

Since Egyptian hieroglyphics were not deciphered by Europeans
until the 1820s,[60] various conflicting theories swarmed around them
in previous centuries. For instance, thinkers such as Leibniz had studied hieroglyphics, along with Chinese ideograms, as models for a perfect, universal language. Sophia Rosenfeld considers these schemes
for a utopian language in her study *A Revolution in Language* and
demonstrates how philosophers and writers looked to an imaginary
past for a model: "The search for the original language of Adam,
or, more often, a manmade philosophical language that would possess all the perfections of the lost Edenic tongue, drew the attention
of many of the most important thinkers of the era, including Bacon,
Descartes, [and] Leibniz."[61] While thinkers such as Leibniz had seen
hieroglyphics as the original language that had once allowed people
to communicate directly with each other, eighteenth-century *philos-*

ophes had a more skeptical attitude toward them. Thinkers such as Condillac and the Encyclopedists speculated about whether hieroglyphics were used to communicate or to block communication in ancient times. Curiously, both enthusiasts and skeptics had based their judgments on faulty interpretations by ancient Greek scholars such as Plotinus and more recent ones such as the seventeenth-century German Egyptologist Athanasius Kircher, who assumed that Egyptian symbols contained some mystical significance.[62]

Based on this belief, eighteenth-century scholars such as Marmontel, Jaucourt, and Rousseau set up an artificial opposition between symbolic languages (in which they included the writing of the Chinese, Aztecs, and ancient Egyptians) and languages based on a phonetic alphabet (those of Europe, even though we know now that hieroglyphics also composed a phonetic alphabet). Inevitably, this opposition entailed a hierarchization of the various systems, if not always in terms of superiority and inferiority at least in terms of primitivism and modernity, and it also contributed to their project of glorifying the French language. Enlightenment writers deemed their own language as more modern, clearer, and therefore better suited for transmitting new philosophical and scientific ideas. Clarity was an important feature of taste as well as a necessary element in building a base of scientific knowledge. This conviction appears in the writings of several authors; for example, we can return to Marmontel's *Poétique française*, particularly the segment "Du coloris ou des images" that I cited in Chapter 4. While claiming that the metaphorical language of the Orient may be better suited to expressing sentiments and imagination, Marmontel argues that it is not suited to abstract ideas: "Naked truth is enough for reason; strictly speaking, philosophical style only needs to be simple, clear, and precise."[63] While he grants that sometimes rational discourse decorates itself with rhetorical figures, he claims that the excessive use of these embellishments may end up blocking the transmission of ideas even while they may dazzle the ignorant people who admire what they do not understand.

The relationship between the two types of language was often expressed in terms of chronological progression, with symbolic languages belonging to the past and phonetic languages belonging to the present and future. As Jaucourt states in "Ecriture" of the *Encyclopédie*, one type of language had surpassed the other in the course of time:

> Letters became common writing and hieroglyphics became a secret and mysterious writing.

Indeed, this type of writing that, by representing the sound of the voice, can express all the thoughts and objects that we are accustomed to designate by these sounds seemed so simple and so fecund that it found rapid success. It spread everywhere; it became the common type of writing and it made people neglect symbolic writing, to which society became unaccustomed, to the extent that people forgot its significance.[64]

In this judgment, Jaucourt's ideas correspond to those of Jean-Jacques Rousseau, who claims in his *Essai sur l'origine des langues*:[65]

The cruder the writing, the more ancient the language is. The first manner of writing is not to depict sounds but the objects themselves, whether directly as the Mexicans did, or by allegorical figures as the Egyptians did of old. This state corresponds to passionate language, and already presupposes some degree of society and some needs to which the passions have given rise.

The second manner is to represent words and propositions by conventional characters, which can be done only when the language is completely formed and when an entire people is united by common Laws; for there is already here a double convention. Such is the writing of the Chinese: this is truly to depict sounds and to speak to the eyes.

The third is to break down the speaking voice into a certain number of elementary parts, whether vowels or articulations, with which one could form all imaginable words and syllables. This manner of writing, which is our own, must have been devised by commercial peoples who, traveling in several countries and having to speak several languages, were forced to invent characters that could be common to all of them. This is not precisely to depict speech, it is to analyze it.[66]

Finally, he states, without explaining the difference between the "savage" Mexicans and the "barbaric" Chinese: "The depiction of objects suits savage peoples; signs of words and propositions barbarous peoples; and the alphabet civilized peoples."[67] Even though he praises the passion conveyed by the pictorial languages, he still portrays, like his fellow *philosophes*, hieroglyphics as something to be surpassed and left behind once European languages come into use.[68] Condillac and Jaucourt[69] both trace an imagined history of hieroglyphics that transforms them from agents of clarity to agents of obscurity. As Sophia Rosenfeld states, Condillac based his beliefs on the writings of the Anglican bishop William Warburton, whose ideas about hieroglyphics, translated into French, appeared as "a radical, philosophical history of writing and language itself."[70] According to these thinkers, hieroglyphics began as simple signs and then became corrupted: first, primitive people needed to communicate with each other, so pictural representations came into use, such as designating "horse" by drawing a horse. Soon these drawings seemed too large and cumbersome, so people began to use an abbreviated form, or a symbolic picture that stood for an object or idea, and hieroglyphics were invented. For example, in a metonymic way, an image of a sword came to represent a tyrant, or an eye represented God's knowledge. Like Condillac, Jaucourt explains in his article "Hiéroglyphe" of the *Encyclopédie* that this system of writing was first used to transmit ideas clearly: "Indeed, they used their hieroglyphics to blatantly uncover their laws, their rules, their practices, their history; in a word, everything that had to do with civil matters."[71] Condillac and Jaucourt make distinctions between the levels of sophistication of various symbols, but the important matter to consider here is that they show that these symbols originally served as tools for communication.

Eventually, as people needed to express increasingly complex ideas, the system of hieroglyphic characters became more and more abstract and less intuitive. Consequently, only the intellectual and religious elite understood the whole system of language, while the common people were held in respectful but baffled awe. As Jaucourt states in "Hiéroglyphe," when the system of signs became an "énigme," the priests began to exploit the ignorant populace: "Thus when the art of writing was invented, the use of hieroglyphics was lost in society, to the extent that the public forgot its meaning. However, the priests carefully cultivated this knowledge because all the science of the Egyptians was entrusted to this type of writing . . . and the priests saw with pleasure that, gradually, they would be left as the only guardians of a type of writing that preserved the secrets of religion."[72] It is unclear whether the priests were withholding profound truths or merely covering an emptiness of meaning with an elaborate veil, but it was their grasp on power that concerned the Enlightenment writers.

In the final deplorable stage that Jaucourt describes, the ignorant people began to believe that these symbols actually had magical powers: "Finally, when the hieroglyphic characters became sacred, superstitious people had them engraved on precious stones and wore them as amulets and charms."[73] Instead of reading the images as merely representing an object or idea, the public began to worship them as if they were sacred objects in themselves. In other words, language that was once transparent became opaque. Even proponents of enigmas such as Ménestrier warned against the dangers of mysterious language, especially hieroglyphics, once it becomes an object of idolatry or an instrument of the occult. In these denunciations of hieroglyphics, the *philosophes* demonstrate the dangers of obscurity and the usefulness of clarity in uncovering truth.

From the virulence of most Enlightenment writers' attacks on ancient Egyptian priests, we can assume that the opinions they expressed about hieroglyphics referred to more contemporary enemies. To a certain extent but not exclusively, Egyptian esoterism represented for them the sacred mysteries of Christianity: a displacement that philosophers probably made in order to elude the censorship of the period. Their attack on obscurity was thus closely tied to their attempts to clear away any deliberate mystification set up by religious authorities.

Both fans and opponents of the obscure saw the term *enigmatic* as bridge between innocuous word games and the mysteries of Christianity. Compilers of enigmas, such as the pious Ménestrier and the more jocular Gayot de Pitaval, mention the parables and prophesies of the Bible, as well as the Trinity and the Immaculate Conception, as "énigmes." They simply placed society riddles and religious mysteries, despite their apparent disparities, next to each other in discussions of the virtues of the enigmatic. Like these two writers, their opponents also considered it logical to put the two things together—but in order to attack both. I have already discussed their mockery of the word games on the grounds of triviality, effeminacy, or pseudo-intellectualism, but the attacks on the Christian mysteries involved different stakes.

The *philosophes* covertly attacked the charlatanism of Christian authorities by railing against the obscurity of Egyptian priests in ways that sometimes echoed the denunciation of the oracles by Aristotle and Quintilian. These two writers had mentioned oracles as practitioners of suspiciously obscure language. In his *Rhetoric*, for example, Aristotle had linked deliberately ambiguous language to dishonest practices that swindled the ignorant public. The danger of unclear language was that the common people would be fooled by it, since the clouds of obscurity would blur their judgment and the unusual or "foreign" words would dazzle them into shutting off their critical faculties. Since these passages surely seemed innocuous to eighteenth-century authorities, Enlightenment writers found in them respectable precedents for their attacks on religion.

For Enlightenment writers, the rejection of obscure style implied an assault on the legitimacy of several Christian practices and doctrines. As I mentioned in the brief history of obscurity, the ambiguity of biblical language could not withstand the skeptical gaze of the proponents of clarity. If the text was incomprehensible, the latter suggested, it was surely not due to a deficiency in the reader[74] but to the possibility that the text itself was nonsense or *galimatias*. Furthermore, the accusations of secrecy among Egyptian priests were surely disguised attacks on the monopoly on interpreting sacred texts, on which the Catholic Church insisted.[75] The use of Latin, like the exclusive knowledge of hieroglyphics, also reinforced the power of the priestly class and discouraged dissent from the people, as opposed to the Protestant doctrine of individual study of the Bible, which was translated to the vernacular for that very purpose. Out of the specialized role of theologians emerged the jargon that Voltaire mocked constantly, as in the "Galimatias dramatique" I cited above. Thus we see that banning obscurity from literature on the grounds of taste provided the terms with which the *philosophes* could assail the very foundations of religion.

Nonetheless, we should also consider Diderot's idiosyncratic use of the terms *hiéroglyphes* and *emblèmes poétiques* to refer to aspects of prosody in his *Lettres sur les sourds et les muets*, in the passage concerning the difficulties of translating poetry. In this particular text, instead of presenting clarity and *hieroglyphics* as polar opposites, he describes them as different layers of poetry. First, the poem must be clear and noble, and additionally, it may contain a number of mysterious *hieroglyphs*: "discourse is not only a linkage of energetic terms that reveal one's thought with force and nobility, but it is also a network of hieroglyphics that are piled on top of each other that depict thought. I could say that, in this sense, all poetry is emblematic."[76] When he claims that only the men of taste—or even the poets themselves—are capable of understanding all the "poetic hieroglyphics," is he suggesting that experts in literature, such as himself and his fellow poets (Voltaire, Fontenelle), should usurp the role of the Egyptian priests?

THE IDOLATRY OF WORDS

Distrust of religious authorities was not the only matter at stake, however; the *philosophes* also sought to establish a certain conception of poetry that excluded any ambiguity or hermeticism, which they linked to a misguided obsession with words in themselves. Once again, hieroglyphics illustrated the problems of obscurity, since they could lead to the excess of ornament and the idolatry of words.

As discussed earlier in this chapter, the *philosophes* wanted poetry to follow the same rules of clarity as rhetoric. The image often evoked by Quintilian as well as early modern poets was that of good poetry as a healthy naked body, while bad poetry as a whore, slave, or transvestite who commits the sin of bad taste by piling on jewels and makeup.[77] The ideal of a "naked" language would call for a reading process in which words are stepping-stones to the true goal, which is meaning, and once the reader understands the meaning, the word can be discarded, so to speak.[78] The letters that compose a word, its homonyms, or the shapes of its letters were not worthy of attention according to critics such as Voltaire, although they were an integral part of certain early modern word games (anagrams, rebuses,[79] logogryphs). Admittedly, Voltaire and his fellows did insist on choosing words that gave their writing a noble style, but one could argue that the choice of particular words was still the means to an end, namely the overall impression of elegance.

To explain the problem of ornaments, let us return to Jaucourt and Condillac, who upheld the ideal of a "naked" language. In the stage of their history of hieroglyphics in which the public could no longer read the symbols, the common people allegedly began to see hieroglyphics as ornaments and consequently to place them as decorations on their monuments. What does this have to do with poetry? Condillac elides two definitions of the word *ornement* and makes an analogy between this use of symbols as architectural decoration and the use of rhetorical tropes in poetry.

In the seventeenth century, the term *hieroglyphic* was also extended to mean allegory: both designated a puzzling language involving images, whether in the literal or figurative sense, and both were thought to contain profound, even mystical, truths.[80] In Condillac's account, allegories first began as fables that were used to illustrate certain ideas, such as the hypothetical consequences of following a certain law. When these stories became overly subtle, they turned into parables, and subsequently, when they reached a level of really confusing complexity, they became enigmas. Like hieroglyphics, they became subject to exploitation by those few who had the ability to interpret them. By extension, figurative language, he claims, began to encumber the ideally transparent language of communication, only to end by making it completely incomprehensible, and this excess of ornament was symptomatic of decadence and, more specifically, the corruption of taste: "We even find that the epoch of their decadence occurred at the time when they seemed to aspire to the greatest beauties. We see figures and metaphors piling up and overloading style with ornamentations, to the point where the foundation merely seems accessory."[81] In a similar way as Montesquieu claims that barbaric taste characterizes both the crude beginning and the sickly decadence of a civilization, Condillac claims that "figures" in language belong both to primitive people and to the decadent French of the impending future.

Admittedly, ornament could not be entirely removed from the French language, at the risk of making it entirely cold. Marmontel, like Quintilian, allowed the use of figurative language on some occasions, but both critics demanded that metaphors and other tropes be held accountable to the standards of nobility, propriety, and clarity. In opposition to the poetic license claimed by Renaissance figures such as Dante and Boccaccio, as well as modern poets, the eighteenth-century critics mentioned above had no patience for verses that demanded a special set of rules. Voltaire in particular makes this point in his poem "Galimatias pindarique," in which he apostrophizes Pindar this way:

> You who possessed the talent
> To speak at length without saying anything;
> You who skilfully modulated
> Verses that no one understands,
> And that everyone must always admire.[82]

Rather than finding himself deficient in understanding Pindar's poetry or attributing to it some mysterious profundity, Voltaire boldly accuses him of "rien dire."

By making such imputations, the *philosophes* demand that incomprehensible language be dismissed with skepticism rather than admired religiously. One of the dangers of not understanding hieroglyphics, as Jaucourt had mentioned, was that people would forget to see them as mere signifiers and instead focus undue attention on them, as in the case of magical amulets. An analogy could be made between this warning against amulets and the effort to prevent people from becoming obsessed with words in themselves.

Roland Barthes, in *Le Degré zéro de l'écriture*, observes this essential difference between classical language and the modern conception of poetry, which values the density of the word or "la densité du Mot": "In classical [language], connections lead the word on, and at once carry it towards a meaning which is an ever-deferred project."[83] In modern times, by contrast, the word "shines with an infinite freedom and prepares to radiate towards innumerable uncertain and possible connections."[84] Classical language, in other words, valued a word only for its utility within a grammatical structure whose purpose was to transmit a coherent message to the reader. Modern writing, especially poetry, deliberately broke up this system in order to isolate each word and make it an end in itself; while we are reading, the purpose of the writer is still in suspension, so we have to consider the various definitions, ambiguities, sounds, and other features of the word, which may or may not prove to be important later to the understanding of the poem. While Barthes does bring to light an important distinction between two ways of looking at language, it is interesting to see that he attributes each type of language to a specific era of French history. He portrays the "classical doctrine" as triumphant in the two centuries preceding the Revolution, which plays into the hands of the proponents of good taste, who wished to convey to posterity that their aesthetic was the only French aesthetic of their time. A more specialized study of the eighteenth century, however, reveals various currents of opposition to the ideas of Voltaire and of the Encyclopedists within the same period, including those who enjoyed word games and religious mysticism, both of which favored the "densité du Mot."

Rather than advocating an ideal of transparent language whose sole purpose is to communicate, Ménestrier, for example, lists several ways in which people have looked at words or even individual letters. In his *Philosophie des images énigmatiques* (1694), he considers various games with words, such as rebuses, anagrams, and writing words backward, which involve focusing attention on features of words apart from their utility as signifiers, such as their shape, the letters that compose them, and the accidents of homonyms. Ménestrier even examines cases in which people have assigned meaning to certain individual letters, which implicates Christian mysticism as much as the frivolous appeal of word games. For example, certain "mysterious and enigmatic letters of the Greek alphabet,"[85] he claims, have acquired a certain mystical significance: A and Ω represent the beginning and the end, T the cross, and Θ death. Instead of phonetic units, these letters become objects of intense speculation in themselves, not unlike the *énigmes* of the *Mercure* whose solution was a single letter.

While Ménestrier discusses games in a neutral or even praising tone, he denounces any excesses that deviate from the accepted symbolism of Christianity and lead to superstitious beliefs. Even anagrams and names written backward, he warns us, approach the sinful territory of black magic, when used in the Kabbalah or in alchemy: "these affected obscurities would be blameable in any other compositions but enigmas,"[86] he explains.

Even Saint Augustine, in *De Doctrina christiana*, warns readers against the idolatrous practice of granting magical powers to signs, letters of the alphabet, or amulets. He considers mysterious language acceptable if the signs (i.e., words) veiled orthodox Christian truths, but he evidently worries about potential excesses of interpretation or an obsession with signs. In reference to these "contracts about meaning arranged and ratified with demons,"[87] Augustine remarks: "To this category belong all the amulets and remedies which the medical profession also condemns, whether these consist of incantations, or certain marks which their exponents call 'characters.' . . . The purpose of these practices is not to heal the body, but to establish certain secret or even overt meanings."[88] For example, he mentions, like Ménestrier, that people may attribute special meanings to certain Greek letters: "So (by way of example) the single letter which is written like a cross means one thing to Greeks and another to Latin-speakers, and has meaning not by nature but by agreement and convention."[89] Thus Augustine maintains that signs such as words or letters are only important to the extent that they point to a meaning, so we must not give undue attention to the signs themselves.[90]

ALCHEMY

This intense focus on words, including hieroglyphics, brings us to the third problem that the *philosophes* found in obscurity: the occult practices of alchemy. This aspect of obscurity most emphatically shows us that one of the major motives in Ménestrier's writing of *La Philosophie des images énigmatiques* was to distinguish the "improper use of enigmas" ("mauvais usages des énigmes")[91] from their proper use, as Michel Charles remarks in his presentation of this text. As I stated above, in Ménestrier's opinion, some of the same practices that offered trivial entertainment, in the case of word games, or access to profound truths, in the case of Christian symbols or parables, could have dangerous consequences in other contexts. For example, he denounces some non-Christian prophets whose language was enigmatic, specifically "Nostradamus, pretending to be a prophet, composed impertinent enigmas, which are full of nonsense and of words with neither rhyme nor reason."[92] He also elaborates on misguided popular beliefs about hieroglyphics, which were mixed up with alchemy.[93]

As Ménestrier explains in a section entitled "Des Enigmes suspectes, décriées et dangereuses," mysteries can come from two sources, one light and one dark. Since God divided people into "children of light and children of darkness, it is the same for the works of the human mind."[94] His idea of good enigmas include the playful riddles in verse, as well as certain kinds of science, which corresponds to Jaucourt's comment that people should devote their mental efforts to solving the enigmas of science. But the institutionally accepted type of science, "permitted sciences,"[95] as Ménestrier calls it, coexisted with another type of science, the "forbidden sciences," which include "magic, judicial astrology, wands for finding sources of water and metals, chiromancy, talismans."[96] Ménestrier deplores that "these dark sciences, that are obviously connected with demons,"[97] happen to share many features of "good" enigmas.

For Ménestrier, it was important to separate legitimate Christianity from the superstitious practices of the alchemists, but for the *philosophes*, it was more useful to merge religion with alchemy as much as possible. Thus in Voltaire's article with the absurdly long title "Hermès, ou Ermès, ou Mercure Trismégiste, ou Thaut, ou Taut, ou Thot" of the *Dictionnaire philosophique*, he tries to prove how closely related Christian Scripture is to the Hermetic myth of God's creation of the world through the Word.

While Ménestrier rejected alchemy on the grounds of religious virtue, the Enlightenment writers ridiculed the "dark arts" in order to uphold the mission of the modern scientific method. For instance, the unnamed author of the *Encyclopédie* article "Hermétique" taunts practitioners of alchemy or hermetic science for considering themselves superior to the "most profound metaphysicists, the most sublime physicists, the Descartes, the Newtons, the Leibnizes."[98] The author of the article remarks that alchemists should be blamed for their love of the obscure, the secret, or the occult: "The hermetic philosophers intentionally write very obscurely, by occupation, out of *esprit de corps*; they even profess it."[99] But he is not fooled into thinking that they have anything to hide: "I believe I can deduce from the small number of observations that I have just reported on the alchemical writings, without even deciding on the worthlessness of this practice or on the frivolity of the alleged pretexts for defending the obscurity of the doctrine, that it would be, I would say, a very bizarre mania to occupy yourself with deciphering hermetic enigmas; that it is even very probable that these enigmas have no meaning."[100] The accusation of emptiness hidden under an elaborate veil recalls the skeptics' questioning of religious texts and Voltaire's mockery of Pindar.

Modern science, the author of "Hermétique" declares, requires open communication, not the secrecy that was valued in the past. He particularly compares the alchemists' tendency to guard "the obscurity of their writings"[101] to the secret language of hieroglyphics: "they even enveloped them in hieroglyphics or emblems that were just as unintelligible."[102] The author claims that such practices may have appealed to other "centuries" and "nations," but things have now changed: "certainly this taste is not of our century or of our nation; our philosophy is communicative and likes what is obvious."[103] Thus the author seeks to create an illusion of consensus by claiming that his opponents' ideology simply does not exist in eighteenth-century France, much as other critics claimed that other aesthetic systems were not French.

While the difference between alchemy and institutional science is obvious to us in the present day, I believe it is worthwhile to consider that clarity as a principle of good style may have included alchemy among its many enemies that had to be excluded from eighteenth-century France. In terms of good style, enigmas represented to Voltaire and to the Encyclopedists a needless detour from a preferable alternative of a clear, linear statement. The call for clarity among the *philosophes* seemed to combine principles of style with a political agenda, specifically the demand to make ideas, whether moral, scientific, or of any other domain, as comprehensible as possible to a large public. Excess ornament and wit could only act as a barrier between the writer and reader or between orator and listener, so language had to be streamlined in order for everyone to enjoy the benefits of knowledge. Clear writing style, like transparency in government and religion, would allow for a more just and more immediate relationship between the authorities (intellectual, political) and the public.[104] The enemy to be eradicated was the middle layer that interposed itself between legitimate power and those it governed—the "demi-savants" mocked by Boyer d'Argens, secretive priests, and incomprehensible language.

But as Elena Russo argues in *Styles of Enlightenment*, the seemingly universal principle of clarity upheld by philosophers such as Rousseau and Diderot represented only one party that simply tried to disqualify its rivals by accusing them of obscure style and calling them fops or *beaux-esprits*. One could consider that these so-called *beaux-esprits*, whom Russo defends against the scorn with which literary history has treated them, did not fail in the standards of the *philosophes* but simply followed a different set of values. Rather than aiming for a style that transmits emotions or ideas with as little interference as possible from writer to reader, the *beaux-esprits* preferred to revel in ambiguity, disguises, and wordplay. Marivaux is the best-known practitioner of this style, and he was certainly accused of producing *galimatias* by the prominent *philosophes*. Among those who resisted clarity out of principle, one could also include the fans of enigmas, who took pleasure in delving into obscurity in order to discover a solution.

I believe that another important consideration in this conflict between clarity and its opposites is that while the *philosophes* defended a transparent sort of communication, it had to be one-sided. One of the horrors of enigmas in the *Mercure* was surely that the poem was simply incomplete without a reader's answer[105]—and that sometimes readers even grew confident enough to write their own enigmas as responses. The voice of the public seems monstrous even to the *philosophes* whose ideas were considered dangerously democratic.

CHAPTER SIX

The Disorderly

Like clarity, order seems so self-evident as to be indisputable. Under this assumption, the proponents of clarity and order characterized these principles as *the* defining features of the French language, ostensibly dismissing any rival aesthetics. The thought that one should prefer the orderly over the disorderly seems so reasonable that we forget that conversation, magazines, travel narratives, and other forms of communication had their particular reasons for not ordering knowledge schematically. The critics themselves, such as Montesquieu and Diderot, sometimes seemed to revel in disordered plots, whether because they imitated the vagaries of human thought or because they deliberately played with readers' expectations. Yet they saw order as a necessary feature in language and literature, particularly if it was to dominate the world of letters, as they proclaimed. In this chapter, I will demonstrate how critics such as Buffon enforced the principle of order through discussions of good and bad taste in writing style and how they excluded particular genres because of their random patterns.

THE DANGERS OF RANDOM PATTERNS

For theorists such as Crousaz, André, and Montesquieu, good taste unequivocally demanded order. To a large extent, theorists simply put emphasis again on the ancient rhetorical skill of *dispositio*, or the proper arrangement of the various sections of a speech. Some critics made a subtle distinction between *ordre* and *uniformité*, and all required that order be counterbalanced by its opposite value, diversity or variety. Crousaz, for example, states that beauty depends principally on a balance between uniformity and variety. He defines uniformity as the ability to relate a number of objects to one single main object. The mind, he states, contemplates a number of things, but it searches for "similar traits, which allows it to connect several things to one main object and to reduce a large number to one single category."[1] According to Crousaz, however, too much uniformity bores us, while too much variety confuses us. From the perfect balance between the two, the other basic qualities of beautiful objects emerge: "regularity, order, proportion: three things that necessarily please the human mind and that, in truth, deserve to be loved."[2] In contrast to uniformity, Crousaz defines order as a methodical way of proceeding from one topic to another related one, particularly in oratory or in works of literature, rather than jumping around indiscriminately.

This definition of order coincides with André's statement that in literature, ideas have to follow each other through a series of relations. He remarks that "order is absolutely necessary in a speech" because "the truths" must be put in order, "so that the first ones clarify the following ones, and that the latter, in turn, give to the former, by a natural progression, a kind of new shine."[3] It is significant that André chooses the term *enchaînement* to describe the process of moving from one subject to the next, since this image of a chain will figure prominently in Diderot and d'Alembert's Preliminary Discourse to the *Encyclopédie* in which they justify their method of ordering their material, as well as in Montesquieu's famous, if little-understood, reference to the "chaîne secrète" embedded in his *Lettres persanes*.

In his *Essai sur le goût*, Montesquieu repeats Crousaz's ideas about the balance between order and variety, but he especially focuses on the effect of order on the human mind (or soul): "It is not sufficient to exhibit to the mind a multiplicity of objects; it is farther requisite, that they be exhibited with order and arrangement; for then it retains what it has seen, and also forms to itself some notion of what is to follow. One of the highest mental pleasures is what we receive from a consciousness of the extent of our views, and the depth of our penetration."[4] Montesquieu refers to the mind (or the *âme*) as if it were a particularly susceptible person when he warns us that a lack of order can sadden and demoralize it. Confronted by a disorderly work, he claims, the mind "retains nothing, foresees nothing; it is dejected by the confusion that reigns in its ideas, and by the comfortless void that succeeds the abundance and variety of its vain recourses."[5] To encourage the *âme*, the work of art or literature has to strike the perfect balance between the amusement offered by variety and the comforting certainty of order.

Like Montesquieu, Diderot had a complex approach to order. Lester Crocker notes that throughout his career, Diderot oscillated between advocating order and praising disorder in relation to artistic beauty. For instance, Diderot described disorder as essential to the creative process of the artist in the articles "Eclectisme" and "Génie" of the *Encyclopédie*. But this "pre-romantic"[6] idealization of disorder concerns the production of art and not the reception of art, which does depend on order. Crocker states, "His most abstract effort, the article 'Beau,' which he wrote for the *Encyclopédie*, is itself the product of an orderly, rigorously systematic intellect."[7] Not only does Diderot argue in a systematic way in this article, according to Crocker, but he puts a special emphasis on the importance of order in the arts. As Crocker remarks, "In all places and times, the abstractions which designate 'order, proportion, relationships, harmony' are the constituents of the idea of beauty"; in other words, "they are universals."[8] Indeed, Diderot argues in this text that the idea of order is not imposed by convention but born from a necessity in the human mind.

While the principles of clarity and order are frequently mentioned in the writings of eighteenth-century French critics, one treatise in particular focused especially on applying order to writing: Buffon's *Discours sur le style*. This treatise, which Buffon first presented as a speech when he was inducted into the Académie Française in 1753, enjoyed such acclaim that schoolchildren for at least the following century knew it as a standard text about rhetoric.[9] The subject of the *Discours sur le style* is how to write well, with taste and genius; and its main recommendation for achieving good style is order. While others had expressed these ideas before Buffon, I would like to concentrate on what this treatise rejects as it upholds the principle of order, namely, orality, femininity, and false wit. The attack on these three characteristics implies the de-legitimization of what Marc Fumaroli calls the "oral genre" of conversation.

The first major principle that Buffon defends in this treatise is the superiority of written over oral expression. Why does Buffon champion the written over the oral? He accuses the spoken language of having too great an influence on the emotions, since the speaker can make use of gestures, as well as different volumes and tones of voice. In this matter, Buffon defies the whole tradition of oratory that preceded him. According to Buffon, a speaker's immediate transmission of emotion to his listeners bypasses the faculty of reason: "It is the body that speaks to another body."[10] With his example of an orator who seeks to "move the multitudes and carry them away,"[11] Buffon evokes the image of an unruly mob, assuming that common people are helplessly gullible. By contrast, he addresses his fellow academicians as a small elite characterized by "a delicate taste,"[12] who can only be persuaded through the combination of their reason and their sentiment. In his opinion, writing appeals to the reader's mind, which is a fairer form of persuasion, while speaking exerts an unfair sort of persuasion, comparable to Marmontel's "seduction" through figurative language, which can inflame the imagination too much. Admittedly, it is ironic that Buffon's defense of the written word was originally a speech, but one supposes that the irony was dispelled as soon as it was distributed in print.

The ability to speak well, according to Buffon, requires less willpower than the ability to write well, since he depicts oratory as an almost involuntary activity. He discredits speech as "that natural facility . . . which is a mere talent, a quality attributed to anyone with strong passions, a supple voice, and a prompt imagination."[13] Unlike persuasive speakers, according to Buffon, good writers have deliberately studied their art and achieved a profound understanding of their subject. Accordingly, Buffon designates "the enlightened centuries"[14] as valuing reason and order in writing.

Second, Buffon states that order is essential to style: "Style," he states, "is only the order and the movement that one puts into one's thoughts."[15] He repeats the ideas expressed previously by critics such as Crousaz—in particular, the principle of *uniformité*, according to which all parts of the work must be connected to one single main topic—by stating, "the whole subject is one."[16] As in Crousaz's and André's description of order, Buffon also demands that one "tightly link"[17] one idea to the subsequent one. Buffon insists that the force of one's ideas will make them fall into place and it will become clear which ideas are more important. From there, one can place them at proper "intervals" and create transitions between them: "by constantly recalling these first lineaments, one will determine the proper intervals that separate the main ideas, and then there will appear the ideas of lesser and of medium importance that will serve to fill these intervals."[18] These rules of good writing should seem familiar to any present-day composition class.

In explaining the process of good composition in the *Discours sur le style*, Buffon situates good and bad writing on a sexual schema, as can be seen in the running metaphor of heat, fertility, and masculinity, all three of which were interrelated in ancient medical discourse. Buffon constantly draws a distinction between a writer of *génie* and the multitude of lesser writers. While in the present day, the term *genius* tends to refer to an exceptional level of talent, in the *Discours sur le style* it still retains its ancient etymology, which was related to male fecundity. Christine Battersby, in her study *Gender and Genius*,[19] notes that the term *genius* referred, in ancient Rome, to a household god that protected the patrilineal family and was thus connected to the word *generation* in the sense of conceiving progeny. In subsequent centuries it eventually became intermingled with a similar-sounding term, *ingenuity*, which denoted good judgment and artistic skill. Because of this coincidental similarity between the two words, Battersby contends that among the intellectuals from the Renaissance to the Romantic Age, artistic creativity was proclaimed to be closely tied to male sexual potency. Therefore, as Battersby claims, many writers and artists justified the exclusion of women from the realm of the arts, under the presumption that their female bodies and minds lacked genius because they lacked the male generative faculties.

Battersby's insights into the discourse surrounding the term *genius* are particularly pertinent to Buffon's treatise. The idea of generation in terms of lineage concerns Buffon particularly, since he establishes his concept of genius, which is necessary for good writing, in terms of fecundity and sterility. A good writer, he says, "will distinguish the sterile from the fecund ideas."[20] In regard to those who try to write without any order and with too much wit, Buffon remarks: "this is the fault of minds that are cultivated but sterile."[21] In his whole treatise, the fertile minds of good writers bear fruit in the form of works that will survive for many generations, while the sterile witticisms of bad writers will die out. In other words, "The well-written works will be the only ones that will be passed on to posterity," but those that "only concern small things—if they are written without taste, without nobility, and without genius, will perish,"[22] as if he were indeed talking about the chances that a family's seed would be passed on to the future.

According to the system of ancient science that Buffon's metaphors constantly refer to, fertility is a force within the healthy male body, while the female body is infertile by nature.[23] Fertility is created in the male body by the presence of heat, which, according to scientists such as Galen, Hippocrates, and Aristotle, brings about "coction," or cooking, of vital spirits. These vital spirits create sexual potency as well as intellectual creativity. These ideas lived on in the early modern era in the writings of Juan Huarte,[24] the influential Spanish doctor who wrote the *Examen de ingenios* of 1575 (translated as *L'examen des esprits* or *The examination of mens wits*).[25] Huarte particularly insisted on the necessary link between gender differences and the quantity of heat, and by consequence the level of fertility and intellectual activity, even stating categorically that a woman with a brain sufficiently dry and warm for intellectual activity could not be classified as a female.

We can see how these ancient ideas make their appearance in Buffon's description of genius as depending on heat and fertility. The metaphorical language that Buffon uses to describe an author's "possession" of his material is suggestive of sexual activity. With one's *génie* (whose grammatical gender is masculine), he proclaims, one must "embrace," "penetrate," and "seize" one's subject.[26] Then, when a good writer is being productive, he will feel the pleasure of creating life: he will be eager to make his material "bloom" and "heat will be produced from this pleasure, it will spread everywhere, and will give life to each expression."[27] In contrast to this generative heat, Buffon describes unsuccessful attempts at literary creation as useless sparks of mere *bel-esprit*. While he describes good writing with images of fire, he states: "Nothing is more opposed to heat than the desire to put witticisms everywhere; nothing is more contrary to the light that creates a body and spreads uniformly throughout a text, than these sparks that only come from the force of striking words against each other, which only dazzle us for a few instants and then leave us in darkness."[28] This passage conveys its message on several levels: first, the literal one about useless wit; then the metaphorical one, referring to the forging of metal, with images of sparks and fire; and a third, more subliminal, metaphorical level that refers to sexual potency. In the literal sense, Buffon warns us that authors or speakers who try to be witty too often prove to be deficient in substance: this is the frequent complaint in the eighteenth century about *beaux-esprits* that Elena Russo deals with in *Styles of Enlightenment*. In reference to sparks of wit or flickering ("papillotage"), Russo remarks, "Common

to the denunciation of those visual effects (which were also used metaphorically to describe a type of discursive style) was the mistrust of
everything that drew attention to details . . . to the detriment of the
unity of composition. More dazzling than enlightening, the diamonds
of style radiated a cold light that did not illuminate the mind but tick-
led the imagination in a purely sensuous, meaningless way."[29] Buffon's
metaphor of fire contrasts with such images of sparks or a spray of
light, or the "faux brilliant" of wit. If one applies the images of sparks
to the ancient medical discourse I mention above, one can interpret
"the desire to put witticisms everywhere," or more ambiguously expressed in French, "le désir de mettre partout des traits saillans" as
sexual promiscuity, which leads to dissipation and infertility.[30]

In the *Discours sur le style*, Buffon's frequent use of the words
nerfs and *nerveux* reveals further connections to the masculine body:
for example, "the more of this thin and brilliant wit one puts in a
text, the less nerve, the less light, the less heat and style there will
be."[31] While in the eighteenth century, nerves were seen increasingly
as receptors of feeling, a more ancient conception of nerves had to do
with sinews, tendons, or muscles. According to the medical definition in the *Encyclopédie*, "nerfs" are tubes that originate in the brain
and distribute animal spirits throughout the body. This idea does not
explain why Buffon asserts that good style is "strong, nervous, and
concise,"[32] however. But the article *nerf (anatomie)* in the *Supplément* of the *Encyclopédie* places an important remark at the beginning: "the noun *nerve* has been applied to very different body parts
among the Ancients . . . not only did they give this name to ligaments
and tendons, but even to muscles."[33] The author cites Celsius and Aristotle as examples. Furthermore, according to both encyclopedias,
certain technical terms used by artisans seem to have preserved some
of the old usage of *nerf*. For example, the original *Encyclopédie* contains a brief definition of *nerveux (maréchalerie)* in regard to animals: "a nervous horse is one that has a great deal of force,"[34] and
nerf (maréchalerie) claims that this word tends to (wrongly) designate
one particular tendon of the horse's leg, while other technical uses
of the term, such as *nerf de cerf* or *nerf de bœuf* are defined as "the
genital part."[35] These associations for the word *nerf* allow Buffon to
describe good style as muscular or virile, while he portrays bad style
with images of limp-wristed effeminacy.

If one links one's ideas tightly, as in a chain, then "the style becomes firm, nervous, and concise; if one allows one's ideas to follow

each other slowly and to be joined only by the coincidence of words, however elegant they may be, the style will be vague, loose, and dawdling."[36] When writing lacks masculinity, then, it reaches a dead end, because it produces useless pleasures that do not last. Without a plan or "lineament,"[37] he says, the writer "throws irregular sallies and discordant figures to chance."[38] These images of oddly shaped figures thrown by the wayside perhaps suggest wasted seed (as in Tissot's medical treatise *L'Onanisme*), menstruation, or monstrous births. According to Aristotle, Huarte, and others, women's sexual fluids, without male intervention, lack sufficient heat to create anything but grotesquely shaped discharge, as in menstruation or as a sort of expulsion of misshapen embryos.[39] Battersby summarizes these theories: "The woman reveals her lack of formative force through the unshaped matter which is expelled each month as blood."[40] If Buffon intended to describe bad literary productions as expelled half-formed creatures, he would be echoing Alexander Pope's *Dunciad*, "Round him much Embryo, much Abortion lay / Much future Ode, and abdicated Play."[41] In short, good writing depends on masculinity and heat, while effeminacy can only lead to inadequate compositions that will never live on for posterity.

AGAINST CONVERSATION

One can see the *Discours sur le style*'s denunciation of orality and disorder as a covert attack on, among other things, conversation—a practice that was by nature spoken and unstructured. In this sense, Buffon, like his fellow *philosophes*,[42] was participating in a more general move away from the worldliness of the seventeenth century and toward the professionalization of literature. The contentious transfer of aesthetic authority, particularly the authority to make judgments of taste, from the aristocratic amateurs of the seventeenth century to the *gens de lettres* of the eighteenth century has been well documented by scholars such as Marc Fumaroli, Dena Goodman, Faith Beasley, and Joan De Jean. These scholars have focused on the declining reputation of salon culture, where conversations took place, as a major change in aesthetic standards.

Conversation was one of the most important literary practices of this aristocratic salon culture, and Marc Fumaroli goes so far as to call it an "oral genre" and an "institution."[43] But in what ways did conversation no longer conform to the new rules of good taste defended by Buffon and his fellows? First, conversation followed no pre-determined plan but rather the caprice of the interlocutors and the contingency of the moment. Second, the purpose of conversation was pleasure above all, in contrast to the famous classical dictum of pleasing and instructing. While in the seventeenth century, even thinkers such as Descartes and Pascal had made concessions to this etiquette,[44] eighteenth-century *philosophes* expressed increasing impatience with their submission to the salons' rules of politeness, even if they actually depended to some extent on the protection of the salons and their members.[45]

In the early modern era as in the present day, conversation's ephemeral nature makes it difficult to contemplate it as an object of study. In some remarks about the "genre" of conversation in general, Roland Barthes deems that it poses a challenge to the scientific aspirations of the linguistic studies of his time: "Conversation is one of those things that pose a discreet challenge to science, because they are non-systematic and derive their value, one could say, from their formal limpness."[46] Nevertheless, we are at least able to reconstruct conversations to some extent through written sources of the period. There existed a number of texts that presumably taught people the rules,[47] even though good conversation was ideally learned through direct experience in elite circles. In other cases, fictional texts sometimes contain dialogues that were meant to re-create the conversational experience. Among these we could include passages from Madeleine de Scudéry's novels *Clélie* and *Le Grand Cyrus*, which Delphine Denis has mined to rediscover the rules of elegant speech among the so-called *précieuses*.[48]

If indeed conversation was an "oral genre," it defined itself in contrast to the more schematized oral genres, such as oratory and scholastic debate. For instance, anything resembling a scholarly dissertation was ruled out from worldly conversations, according to the interlocutors of Scudéry's dialogues. Significantly for the issue of order and disorder, Delphine Denis maintains that, according to Scudéry, speakers must seem impassioned, which results in a disorderly speech: certain figures of rhetoric "aim to demonstrate the passion of the speaker; the disorder of the phrase, which sometimes accumulates synonymous terms without any connections, suggests emotion in order to provoke emotion."[49] Since disorder and pleasure characterized conversation, some could see it as a threat to morality.

Women in particular were said to be gifted for conversation in the seventeenth and eighteenth centuries. Dubos, for example, assumes that "men are more capable than women of strong and close application,"[50] but to compensate, women are better at acting and at declamation because they can conjure up their sensibility much more easily than men: "As women have a quicker and more docile sensibility, and a greater flexibility, as it were in their hearts than men; they succeed better than our sex in performing what Quintilian requires of those who attempt to declaim. They are much easier affected with such passions as they chuse to imitate."[51] This so-called natural talent that women have for oral expression, which Dubos admires in the early part of the century, becomes a matter of suspicion in Buffon's *Discours*.

Both the proponents and the enemies of eloquence described the ability to touch the audience's emotions as a bodily phenomenon. The requirements for good conversation also involved the body, particularly women's supposed ability to perceive the nuances of the reactions among the people surrounding them. In theory, these characteristics made women the perfect arbiters among a number of speakers, ensuring the perfect balance between politeness and liveliness. However, this special role granted to women also had its negative side. Unlike intellectual males, whose minds could supposedly concentrate on a single subject for a protracted amount of time, women's minds were thought to be constituted in a way that made them flit from one topic to another. According to the stereotype, women were condemned to be eternal dilettantes and never experts in any scholarly subject. This belief found justification in medical discourse, as Alexandre Wenger states in *La Fibre littéraire: Le discours médical au XVIIIe siècle*: "According to the common representation of women, which is confirmed as much by women writers as it is by physicians, female intelligence is sparkling and lively, but easily carried away; subject to contingency, to the moment, and to emotion. Women have a passionate character; they feel strongly, but always in an ephemeral way."[52] This characterization of women was sometimes extended to the men who frequented salons, as we can see in the criticism of false wit, as well as in the scorn for enigmas that I treated in the previous chapter.

Based on ideas about the feminine constitution, eighteenth-century writers often blamed the general intellectual decadence on the influence of superficial conversations. Alexandre Wenger remarks upon one physician in particular, Louis de La Caze, who warns against the intellectual weakening of society in general: "[La Caze] explains, in

a somewhat twisted way, that the primary cause is the female constitution itself, since men, aware that women never focus their mind
on a single object for long, have adopted as a first rule of politeness
to vary their subjects of conversation, which explains that these conversations are 'now all disjointed.'"[53] Not only medical treatises but
texts by *philosophes* cited the female influence as putting a limit on
any profound scholarly reflection. For instance, we can see the impatience with conversation that Montesquieu is starting to feel early in
the century: "We can no longer tolerate anything that has a determi-
nate object: the military men no longer tolerate military affairs; men
of study, their studies; and so on. . . . It is the interaction with women
that has brought us to this point, since it is in their character not to be
attached to anything that is fixed. So we have become like them. Now
there is only one sex, and we are all women in our minds."[54]

This criticism anticipates Jean-Jacques Rousseau's lengthier denunciation of the female organizer of intellectual gatherings in his *Lettre
à d'Alembert*, as Dena Goodman comments in *The Republic of Letters*. Thus we see that worldly gatherings of men and women who en-
gaged in conversation, once seen as the tribunals of good taste, began
to appear in eighteenth-century texts as the places where good taste
was weakened and dispersed. The new good taste represented by Buffon involved order, rationality, and the written word.

RANDOMNESS IN WRITING

Not all written sources were equally orderly, however, since the practice of conversation was reflected in several types of text that also
suffered from a reputation of bad taste among critics. Among these,
we can include *ana*, *abrégés*, compilations, almanacs, and magazines
such as the *Mercure*. Daniel Mornet, who deals with order as much as
with clarity in his *Histoire de la clarté française*, blames the desire in
the eighteenth century to simply compile knowledge without sorting
it out for the presence of these genres. In this case, he follows Diderot's and d'Alembert's argumentation in the Preliminary Discourse to
the *Encyclopédie*, which maintained that at one stage in the French
cultural development, intellectuals did nothing but gather knowledge, especially from ancient texts, without judgment. Mornet suggests, however, that this compiling activity continued up to the eighteenth century: "One misunderstands the history of French thought
in the eighteenth century if one confines it to the history . . . of strictly

literary genres. . . . In the provinces especially, far from the theater, the opera, and the fashionable salons, when one ceases to be ignorant and indifferent, one acquires two tastes and curiosities: that of charming and gallant literature, fugitive poems, madrigals and songs, and that of indefatigable erudition that compiles, compiles, compiles, always more intent on the quantity than on the quality."[55] I will concentrate on two written genres represented in this passage by Mornet: the compilations found in *ana* and the gallant literature of the *Mercure de France*.

Mornet judges that the genre of *ana* is particularly responsible for assembling useless fragments of knowledge without a greater plan. He qualifies *ana* as "crumbs of science," "empty and puerile curiosities," and "chatter."[56] Few people nowadays are aware of the genre of *ana*, which received so much scorn in the eighteenth century. These texts, whose titles combined the names of well-known figures, such as the philologist Scaliger, with the ending *-ana*, bore titles such as Scaligeriana, Huetiana, Arlequiniana, and Socratiana. The *Dictionnaire de Trévoux*'s very definition of the word includes quotations that tell us of this genre's generally bad reputation:

> ANA . . . This word does not mean anything and is only a Latin ending for plural neuter adjectives; but because for some time people have used these kinds of Latin adjectives for the titles of books, including French ones, that are collections of the memorable words or sentiments of some scholars or intelligent men, people call these books *-ana books*, or simply *ana*, so one says, "All of these *-ana* books," or "All of these *ana* greatly displease me." The *-ana* books often have people say things that they never thought, or that they should never had said.[57]

Several researchers divide the *ana* genre into several stages, from actual erudite summaries (*Huetiana*) to excerpts from a writer's works (*Sevigniana*) and, finally, collections of bons mots and anecdotes (*Encyclopediana*, *Arlequiniana*, etc.) Jean Pie Namur, author of a bibliography of *ana*, sees this division chronologically, as a sign of the decadence of taste: "reading *ana* must have been instructive, if taste, reason, truth, had always guided the composition of this sort of work; but because of the success of *ana*, the public soon saw itself flooded with them."[58] Taking a more neutral stance, Bernard Beugnot suggests in "Forme et histoire: Le statut des *ana*" that future research on *ana* could take several directions. One of these is the oral aspect of this genre, which is implied not only by their "désordre" but because the sources and the form of these *ana* have close ties to conversation. In support of this idea, he cites the *Dictionnaire de Trévoux*'s remark that many of the anecdotes must be taken from conversations or "entretiens": "Numerous indeed are those—*Menagiana, Anonimiana, Naudeana et Patiniana, Segraisiana, Longuerana, Boloeana*—whose complete title includes the word 'conversation.'"[59] Whatever their source, we can see that *ana* were vulnerable to the same critiques as conversation, for example, that they were disorderly and futile entertainments.

Aside from these *ana*, magazines also suffered from a bad reputation because of the way they organized material. Out of all of the literary genres that were attacked for their disparateness, the *Mercure* stands out because it presents an interestingly deliberate aesthetic of disorder. In some years, the journal boldly proclaims its heterogeneity and in other years it submits to the pressure of order. The importance of the conversational model, rejected by Buffon, is apparent as soon as one glances at the first issue of the *Mercure*, which in its first incarnation was called *Le Mercure galant*. In the editor's preface, or the address from "Le Libraire au lecteur," he boasts that this text contains a number of disparate fragments, so it "must contain something to please everyone, because of the diversity of material with which it is filled."[60] This heterogeneity is underlined by its fictional epistolary form. At the beginning of the main text of this issue, the reader encounters a fictional narrator who claims to address a lady of his acquaintance who happens to be outside of Paris. He states that he wishes to give her news of the city but that the main purpose of his news is to please, not instruct: "it is of little importance to me whether they are useful to others, as long as they amuse you: that is my only goal."[61] The model is that of a correspondence, which can be seen as a written form of long-distance conversation. While this first issue took the form of a letter, later issues based their format more explicitly on conversation. For example, the March 1677 issue precedes its articles with a fictional social setting: "We had assembled to play a game at the home of an amiable duchess and, while waiting for some ladies who were to join us, since the most important things are ordinarily the first that come up as the subjects of conversation, we put news of the war on the table."[62] Because the contents of the journal follow the non-linear path of conversation, then, it is understandable that the topics addressed should not be held to a rigid schema. The capricious change from subject to subject is certainly reflected in the table of contents. One sample from the *Mercure* of September 1745 includes the following list:

> New Memoirs of Foreign Missions.
> The Bourgeois Cook.
> The Day at Fontenoy, Ode by M. Fréron, extract.
> Explanation of an Altarpiece.
> Letters to the Editors of the *Mercure*.
> Question.
> Madrigal.
> New Engravings.
> View of the Battle of Fontenoy.
> Answers to the Enigmas and Logogryphs.[63]

This type of promiscuous mixture of poetry, political news, games, and other sundry items can be found in any issue of the *Mercure* of the seventeenth to mid-eighteenth century. Several critics saw this heterogeneity as a problem, and eventually some of these critics would attempt to take over the journal and impose order on it.

In Chapter 5 I discussed the bad reputation of the *Mercure* specifically in regard to its enigmas, but there were also many complaints about its form. One eighteenth-century chronicler of the newly founded field of journalism describes the reasons why the *Mercure* was so widely scorned. Denis-François Camusat, in his 1734 *Histoire critique des journaux*, remarks that one major problem that many critics saw in the *Mercure* was that "Since its birth, this work was a jumble of all sorts of things. News, promotions to state honors, nominations for benefices, marriages, baptisms, deaths, theatrical performances, gallant stories, medals, inductions to academies, sermons, legal speeches, judgments, brief poems, enigmas, songs, dissertations, sometimes scholarly and sometimes playful, everything went in, everything found a place."[64] This disparate list becomes almost a topos in its own right, since we also see it frequently in the texts about bibliomania and metromania (for example, Villier's list of bad genres in publication or the long list of subjects Cydalise plans to tackle in her book in *Les Philosophes*). In each example, the author seeks to show the foolishness of putting these separate objects together when it would be wiser to concentrate on one single topic. In other cases, the author dismisses the genres listed by piling them up and making them look ridiculously trivial.

Louis-Sébastien Mercier complains at length about the *Mercure* in his *Tableau de Paris*, first by characterizing its contributors as small-minded provincials, and then by claiming that the decision to publish certain pieces is not based on quality but on *hasard* or chance. He describes the scene he imagines of the clerk of the *Mercure* receiving submissions and choosing one according to size:

> The clerk, with an indifferent hand, opens the packages that fall on his desk and pile up with each post. . . . Songs, madrigals, epistles, stanzas, etc., rain on him, and the tired clerk no longer takes the trouble to break open the seals. . . . He stuffs and buries all of these pieces in enormous boxes, where they sleep, waiting for someone to fish one out when needed. Woe to the piece that is too long or too short for the page that someone wants to fill! Even if it were excellent, they would reject it in order to choose another one that fits exactly into the empty space.[65]

This attack on its apparently random selection of pieces is part of Mercier's more general criticism of the quality of the journal.

According to Camusat, an early historian of the field of journalism, some critics even compared the *Mercure* to a menstrual period, referring to its monthly apparition, its association with a female readership, and its general distastefulness. He cites one satire that expresses this thought:

> The foolish book that one sees in the hand of the bourgeois,
> One delivery with each cycle of the moon —
> Would that be the sewer of the French Parnassus?
> No, but according to the laws
> That are common to the feminine sex,
> The French muse has her monthly periods.[66]

These satirical verses, trivial as they may be, still illustrate the metaphorical link between good writing and procreation.[67]

The larger consequence of the *Mercure*'s faults, as the writer of the preface states (he claims Camusat died before finishing his history of journalism, so he has taken over), is that journals ultimately lead to "the corruption of taste and the decadence of literature"[68] because they hire bad authors who "compose without taste, without discernment, without science."[69] Journals harm readers, he claims, because they make young people think they know a subject after only reading a small piece about it, and these people go on to wield their newfound literary judgment, but without any qualifications.

The critiques may have been applicable when Camusat wrote his history, but the situation changed later in the eighteenth century. The *Mercure* appeared, from its foundation in 1672 to the Revolution, in various guises that mostly depended on the vision of the successive editors. It wavered from a "gallant" tone, which was often enhanced by especially trivial content (love poems, comic anecdotes, etc.), random order, and contributors from a mixture of backgrounds, to a stricter order of subjects and a list of contributors from the ranks of the *philosophes*. In the second half of the century, protégés of Voltaire, such as Marmontel, the abbé Raynal, and La Harpe, took over the *Mercure* and tried to impose some order on the material, in terms of categorizing the pieces rather than placing them at random. At other times, however, editors had recourse to the original *Mercure* aesthetic and allowed the pieces to fall where they might.

In the early eighteenth century, the editors of the *Mercure* defend the disorderly and effeminate model, even when they claim to change it. They abandon the conversational model, which had so strongly dominated the early *Mercure galant* but only for the sake of even more variety. The joint editors of the *Mercure*, Dufresny, Laroque, and Fuzelier, claimed in the preface of the June 1721 issue that the former model was too uniform in terms of authorial voice. They, in turn, were privileging a multivoiced *Mercure*, and they claimed that their journal would benefit from an even more decentered sense of critical judgment, deferring to "friends" who would choose the pieces according to merit. In keeping with the conversational model of the previous century, nevertheless, they emphasize pleasure as the ultimate goal of the journal: "Reading a collection that is diverse in its expression as it is in its material will be more amusing than reading a book that would come every month repeating the same language to the public."[70] Finally, as if out of defiance, the editors defend the chaotic nature of the journal against the criticism with which we are now familiar: "we have to fight against the relentless censors . . . there are even some who persist in considering the variety that constitutes its character as a fault. Are they unaware that this journal is made for everyone and that it must serve nourishment that appeals to all tastes?"[71] Nevertheless, the editors claim that the articles will follow a certain set order based on the following categories: political news, legal notices, arts and letters, and poetry.

In a later period, when several members of the so-called philosophical party took control of this journal, they focused even more on the principles of order and strove to invest some authority into their choice of material. The abbé Raynal, known for collaborating with Diderot to compose his monumental Enlightenment work *His-*

toire des deux Indes, took on the job of editor of the *Mercure* from 1750 to 1754. Then Marmontel acted as editor from 1758 to 1762 and La Harpe from 1772 to 1778, until the *Mercure* was bought by Panckoucke and took a more political turn during the Revolutionary period. These editors claimed to respond to criticism of the *Mercure* by dividing the journal strictly into sections (political news, book reviews, poetry, etc.) and by selecting their materially more carefully. The *Mercure*, specifically that of La Harpe, received praise from Voltaire, who claimed it was finally being brought in line with good taste: "You lend beautiful wings to this Mercury, which was not even gallant in the time of Vizé[72] and which is becoming, thanks to your care, a monument to taste, reason, and genius. . . . It is what I had advised long ago to journalists."[73] Finally, an erudite man, according to Voltaire's standards, could impose order and quality on this much-criticized journal.

Although critics such as Marmontel and La Harpe tried to reform the structure and content of the *Mercure*, its reputation remained tarnished in the 1780s of Louis-Sébastien Mercier, who complains in *Le Tableau de Paris*,

> Previously, the *Mercure* merely distributed banalities; suddenly, it
> became uncivil and harsh in the hands of a pedant. Then it was dis-
> figured by dryness and stupidity, and the profession of underliner was
> mistaken for the profession of critic. One is astonished to see juvenile
> or unknown writers judging the arts with a ridiculous or monotonous
> emphasis and the Don Quixotes of good taste fighting for the cause
> without understanding it. Some futile remarks, some petty nitpicking,
> that's what you find in it. Oh, how many minor authors in Paris are
> capable of dissertating on small nothings![74]

It is unclear whether the "pedant" Mercier refers to was Raynal, but we can venture a guess that Marmontel, who would have been in his twenties during his term as editor, is the "juvenile" ("imberbe") judge of literature that he names the "Don Quixote of good taste." Perhaps the Quixotic mission was the attempt to improve the journal at all.

We can more fully understand the indignation caused by the *Mercure* by comparing it to two contemporary publications: the scientific journal *Le Journal des savants* and the *Encyclopédie*. The *Journal des savants* displayed much more uniformity than the *Mercure* in both authorial voice and in the format and content of each article. Rather than representing multiple authorial voices, as the *Mercure* does, the articles in the *Journal des savants* give the impression of

proceeding from a single source. Whatever the editorial policy may
have been in reality, there is nothing equivalent to the *Mercure*'s so-
licitation of letters, poems, and other pieces from readers or from
"everybody" ("tout le monde"), as one of the early editors states. The
uniformity of voice in the *Journal des savants* reflects the uniformity
of subject matter, since the journal is composed almost exclusively of
one type of article: book reviews. By contrast, the *Mercure* included
book reviews, but they were interspersed among an unpredictable as-
sortment of poems, enigmas, letters to the editor, sheet music, archeo-
logical treatises, and other pieces. Since the *Journal des savants* had
proposed a scientific mission from the outset, the depth and difficulty
of the material far exceed that of the typical *Mercure* article. The
Journal thus executed its mission to instruct, while the *Mercure*, at
least until the mid-1700s, remained true to its primary aim to please.

A starker contrast that present-day scholars will inevitably draw
is the one between the *Mercure* and the *Encyclopédie*. As editors of
this latter work, d'Alembert and Diderot not only took great pains to
justify distributing their articles within the seventeen volumes by alphabetical order, but they also made it possible for readers to place
each topic within the all-inclusive schema of human knowledge. This
knowledge took the shape of their famous Tree of Human Knowledge
or the "Arbre des connaissances humaines" that was based on Francis Bacon's division of knowledge between imagination, reason, and
memory, along with their respective subfields. Unlike the *Mercure*,
the *Encyclopédie* did not demonstrate a conversational exchange between people of different backgrounds, with a permeable separation
between readers and writers; instead, all of its material proceeded
from the authority of learned experts on each field, chosen by the
main editor, Diderot. Although the alphabetical order of the articles
necessarily juxtaposed disparate topics, the editors insisted on the article's place in their tree of knowledge according to the subject category mentioned in parentheses after the title of the article. A typical
series of articles would include, for example, the following entries,
which are ordered alphabetically but seem, at first glance, to refer to
random fields of knowledge:

    racinaux (architecture)
    racine (botany)
    rack ou arak (modern history)
    Rackelsburg (geography)
    racle (nautical arts)

The reader could look up the subject in parentheses, however, in the tree of knowledge in order to put it into context. Thus the Encyclopedists succeeded in bringing potential randomness within the realm of order.

Michel Foucault, in *Les Mots et les choses*, discusses Buffon's taxonomic order along with the rival taxonomy of Linnaeus, which supposedly exemplify eighteenth-century schemas of categorization. However, another rivalry strikes me as more pertinent in the context of taste, that of randomness and order. The trouble with conversation, *ana*, and magazines lies ostensibly in their tasteless lack of logical order, a critique that opens the way for the imposition of a professional, authoritative, often characterized as male, system on literature. On the other hand, conversation and texts such as the *Mercure* threatened the position of the intellectual because they were participative, decentered practices, often marked as female.[75]

Ultimately, the reason why critics warn us against disorder is that it represents non-productive pleasure. From the sparks of wit that fail to generate fertile heat to the perhaps pointless anecdotes of *ana*, disorder is equivalent to sexual pleasure without procreation. Appropriately, André Pessel, in a study of the conversations of *précieuses*, sees the ritual of salon conversation as modeled on an erotic exchange of "the caress and the pleasure"[76] between partners but without lasting results: "One could also say that conversation is a derision of maternity: the woman is sterile and engenders nothing but discourse."[77] The scorn of unproductive pleasure among authors such as Buffon recalls the comedies I treated in Chapter 1 such as Palissot's *Les Philosophes* and Piron's *La Métromanie*, which satirize would-be authors who must choose between an improbable literary career and a conventional bourgeois life of marriage and, presumably, parenthood. Disorder thus fulfills its louche potential as moral disorder or vice.

In various contexts, *disorder* can refer to different ills: the moral disorders of vice, the bodily disorders of illness, random patterns, or simply messiness. All of these meanings were brought together in the *philosophes'* battle against disorder, in their campaign to establish "ordre et clarté" as the defining characteristics of the French language and consequently of French culture.

Conclusion

In 1834, Victor Hugo defiantly renounced good taste, specifically the good taste of eighteenth-century France, in a long, polemical poem entitled "Réponse à un acte d'accusation." The violent language of this piece reveals to what extent he assumes that taste had exerted an oppressive power over poetic creativity. In this poem, Hugo represents the norms of rhetoric and poetics as a number of arrogant aristocrats, while he imagines the words that did not fit the rules of decorum as the long-suffering populace. "Poetry was a monarchy,"[1] he proclaims, and he takes on the role of the monarchy's destroyer when he cries, "I am that Danton! that Robespierre!"[2] He incites the lowly words, for example *cochon* and *nez*, to revolt against their masters in a reenactment of the events of 1789. And it is no coincidence that those whom he attacks by name in this poem are exactly the authors whose ideas I have discussed in this study.

Hugo begins by announcing "I trampled good taste and ye olde ffrench verse / Under my feet"[3] and proceeds to call out the authors who, he claims, have ruled despotically over the world of letters. He takes aim at Aristotle, Vaugelas, Racine, and Dumarsais, and he enjoins the "people" to "throw out the Bouhours, the Batteux, and Brossettes / That have put thumbscrews on the human mind!"[4] Boileau, who served as a model for eighteenth-century *philosophes*, is not spared; he appears as one of the legendary members of the Académie Française, an institution that legitimized the authority of many of the defenders of good taste. Boileau is guilty by association, since Hugo implies that the despotic rule of the Académie Française both parallels and proceeds from royal power: "Gold-lilied, Tristan-and-Boileau, blue-backdropped, / Forty Academy chairs with the throne in the middle."[5] Furthermore, Hugo depicts an *Art poétique*, possibly Boileau's, being hanged from a lamppost, recalling many incidents during the Revolution in which people suffered the same fate at the hands of the mob.

Another proponent of good taste, Voltaire, appears several times, once as the author of *Mérope*, a tragedy for which he was much admired, and another time as a bully who is tormenting Corneille. Hugo describes an amusing situation in which Corneille finds a low word, a member of the "stylistic riffraff,"[6] in his works and decides to keep it: "Corneille, / If he found one cowering in his lines, / Let it stay— didn't stoop to pick it up."[7] Notwithstanding the English translation, the original French verse makes an explicit reference to the famously tasteful phrase "qu'il mourût," when Hugo's imaginary Corneille refuses to send away the vulgar word with the phrase "qu'il s'en aille." It is apparent here that while Hugo condemns the elitism of Voltaire and other critics, he favors Corneille as a "bonhomme,"[8] slightly humiliated by his fellow writers but still one of the "great ones" that Hugo favors.

Aside from caricaturing famous critics, Hugo attacks specific phrases such as the "qu'il mourût" and common motifs, such as that of clarity, found in eighteenth-century writings on taste. For instance, he evokes Boileau's biblical example of the sublime, "Let there be light" but subverts it: "I, hideous creature, said: / 'Let darkness be!'— and voilà! there was darkness."[9] The technique of undercutting the metaphors of taste continues throughout the poem and culminates in the apparition of a muse, who embodies several elements of so-called bad taste. In her emotion, she "sweep[s] from zenith to nadir," a hyperbole that we had seen parodied by Montesquieu in the *Lettres persanes*, and she dazzles with "a hurricane of sparks," which recalls Buffon's scorn of false brilliance. Rather than submit to the restraints of moderation, she revels in unreason and excess; she thus represents the return of so-called bad taste in a more egalitarian world that does not put limits on creativity.

In this poem, Hugo demonstrates to us not only that he was well versed in the previous century's conceptions of taste but also that the educational system that formed him had already absorbed these ideas enough to impose them as a dogma. He emphasizes this point by associating the rigid conventions of literature with his schooldays, particularly in the line "when I left school and Latin verse and school-work."[10] Thus we see that the eighteenth-century campaign for what the French call "classical" taste successfully implanted itself in the minds of future generations. Even though Hugo and future avant-garde writers overtly rejected these norms, they still had to struggle with them in order to free themselves to create, and they had to ac-knowledge their power and ubiquity, especially in the pedagogical realm.

Even now, French classical taste is a matter of national pride. While I have no desire to deny the value of classicism and its productions, I still find it fascinating to examine how the edifice of taste, perhaps Voltaire's Temple of Taste, was built over the remains of rejected au-thors, styles, words, and genres. If we can unearth these remains, just as archaeologists dig for the relics of past civilizations, we will have a better understanding of classical taste itself and a more complete view of the literary landscape of eighteenth-century France.

Even in recent times, the sociologist Pierre Bourdieu felt the need to challenge the assumption of a transcendent good taste that is un-fettered by social considerations. In 1979 Bourdieu exposed some of the underpinnings of taste in contemporary France in his study *La Distinction* by proving how the reception of culture largely depends on levels of education, which in turn depend largely on social class. His findings show that what the bourgeois and the intellectual elite consider high art mostly remains the preference of those classes, while other classes make other choices. This idea, he admits, seems at once perfectly obvious and at the same time defies the belief that taste is in the realm of "the denial of the social." Some of his contemporaries, he claims, "strive to repress the clear relation between taste and edu-cation,"[11] refusing to see the relativism of cultural reception in their society.

In regard to the eighteenth century, I have not used Bourdieu's methods to document what type of people enjoyed which literary works; I have focused instead on the rhetorical means by which cer-tain critics excluded particular genres and styles in order to construct the ideal of good taste. More specifically, I hope to have elucidated the strategies that Dubos, Montesquieu, Batteux, Voltaire, Marmon-tel, and like-minded writers employed to defend their vision of what French literature should be. What French literature "should be" in-volved qualities such as decorum, order, clarity, and nominal defer-ence to the rules of the ancients, principally Quintilian and Aristotle. But when what French literature "should be" clashed with what French literature was—namely, what was actually produced, sold, and read—these critics wielded the scalpel of taste to delineate the image of France's cultural heritage that they wished to present to posterity and to the world.

It is perhaps because of this defamation in their time that we have now largely forgotten how diverse the literary production of the period really was. For example, poetic rewritings of Psalms, chivalric novels, literary magazines, and the works of Montaigne and Marot apparently enjoyed some popularity during the eighteenth century, but they were accused of bad taste by eighteenth-century critics. Indeed, the fact that the eighteenth-century critics' canon of classic French literature—Corneille, Racine, Molière, Boileau—does not differ greatly from ours shows us the success of their campaign. Nevertheless, a few authors, such as the abbé Prévost and Marivaux, managed to survive the scorn of Voltaire and other critics to become present-day classics. And in recent decades, using widely different methods, the research of Robert Darnton and Joan DeJean has looked beyond the canon to rediscover best-selling authors such as Louis-Sébastien Mercier and Françoise de Graffigny, who had not been included in the *philosophes'* vision of great literature.[12]

When we look at the French literary canon that we have inherited, it is evident that the problems of taste of the past still affect us today. Let us consider two lists of books: on the one hand, the table of contents of Lagarde et Michard's anthology of eighteenth-century works, used for pedagogical purposes, and on the other, Robert Darnton's "forbidden best-seller" list of 1779. The first shows us the French classics that we are used to—Montesquieu, Voltaire, Diderot, and Rousseau. The second shows us something different—sentimental novels by Madame Riccoboni, works of pornography such as *Thérèse philosophe*, novels by Louis-Sébastien Mercier, and the less edifying works of Voltaire, such as *La Pucelle d'Orléans*. To the latter list, we could add the saints' lives and other religious publications that would surely feature prominently in a best-seller list of non-forbidden works of the period.

How do we reconcile this difference? The Great Books answer would be that the first category, the canon represented by Lagarde et Michard, includes authors who simply endured through the ages because of the high quality of their writing, while those who were forgotten, at least until DeJean and Darnton rediscovered them, deserved their obscurity. But who decided on this selection and when? By what standards were they deemed worthy of the canon, and who set those standards? My claim is not that the quality of Riccoboni's writing surpasses that of Diderot's: judgments such as these are not the object of this study. Instead, I hope that the present work will contribute to the understanding of the process by which highly popular types of literature were cast aside during the formation of the French literary legacy in the eighteenth century—through satire, through theories of beauty, and with the help of two damning words from which there is seemingly no redemption: *bad taste.*

NOTES

INTRODUCTION

1. Mary Douglas, *Thought Styles: Critical Essays on Good Taste* (London: Sage, 1996), 50.

2. The sociologist Hebert Gans, for example, proposed the idea of coexisting "taste cultures and publics" within a society, an idea that denies the previous distinction between high and low culture by refusing to make judgments about which culture is superior and which is inferior. Herbert Gans, *Popular Culture and High Culture: An Analysis and Evaluation of Taste* (1974; New York: Basic Books, 1999).

3. Luc Ferry, *Homo aestheticus: L'invention du goût à l'âge classique* (Paris: Grasset, 1990).

4. The word *aesthetic* allegedly appears for the first time in Alexander Gottlieb Baumgarten, *Meditationes philosophicae de nonnullis ad poema pertinentibus* (Magdeburg: Grunerti, 1735) and then as the title of his work *Aesthetica* in 1750. In an article entitled "L'Esthétique: Problèmes de définition," Baldine Saint Girons helpfully explains the origin of the neologism *aesthetics* and its divergent meanings in eighteenth-century German philosophy. She begins by exposing the problem that has created some confusion among students of aesthetics: "From the beginning, aesthetics is marked by ambiguity: is it the science of knowledge through the senses . . . , the science of the beautiful . . . , or the science of art?" ["D'emblée, l'esthétique est marquée d'équivoques: est-ce la *science de la connaissance sensible* . . . , la *science du beau* . . . ou la *science de l'art*?"] Baldine Saint Girons, "L'Esthétique: Problèmes de définition," *L'Esthétique naît-elle au XVIIIe siècle?* ed. Serge Trottein (Paris: Presses Universitaires de France, 2000), 83. The first meaning, related to perception, plays an important role in Kant's *Critique of Pure Reason*, while the second meaning—the science of the beautiful—concerns his *Critique of Judgment*. Aesthetics as the judgment of art, the third definition, was more relevant to Hegel, for example, than it was to Kant.

Saint Girons mentions that the French word *esthétique* appears for the first time in the supplement to the *Encyclopédie* in 1776 and then is forgotten, only to reappear in the nineteenth century. Nonetheless, for practical purposes, I will use the term *aesthetic* to refer to the judgment of beauty and of art in eighteenth-century French texts.

5. Luc Ferry and several other scholars have speculated about the first metaphorical use of the word *taste*, that is, not in the sense of how food tastes to the tongue but as the more abstract judgment of beauty or of artistic productions. While no definitive answer has been agreed on, Ferry states that the works of the seventeenth-century Spanish author Baltasar Gracián were instrumental in coining the term *gusto* (or taste) to refer to the critical faculty. See Ferry, 26–27.

6. "L'autonomisation du champ intellectuel et artistique a constitué la condition permettant de penser l'ordre esthétique proprement dit, et donc favorisé l'émergence de l'esthétique moderne." Annie Becq, *La Genèse de l'esthétique française moderne, 1680–1814* (Pisa: Pacini, 1984; Paris: Albin Michel, 1994), 25.

7. Geoffrey Turnovsky, *The Literary Market: Authorship and Modernity in the Old Regime* (Philadelphia: University of Pennsylvania Press, 2010).

8. Jürgen Habermas, *The Structural Transformation of the Public Sphere: An Inquiry into a Category of Bourgeois Society* (Cambridge, Mass.: MIT Press, 1991), 36.

9. Joan DeJean, in *Ancients Against Moderns*, objects to Habermas's views because, she asserts, the "public use of reason" did not begin in eighteenth-century coffeehouses but earlier in salons and in the pages of the *Mercure galant*. She claims that the various seventeenth-century *querelles* challenge Habermas's idea of the "monopoly of interpretation" under Louis XIV. Joan DeJean, *Ancients Against Moderns: Culture Wars and the Making of a Fin de Siècle* (Chicago: University of Chicago Press, 1997).

10. Habermas, 40.

11. Ibid., 41.

12. Ibid.

13. Ibid.

14. Ibid., 37.

15. Charles Batteux, *A Course of the Belles Lettres: Or the Principles of Literature* (London: Printed for B. Law and Co., T. Caslon, J. Coote, S. Hooper, G. Kearsly, and A. Morley, 1761), 68. "Il ne peut y avoir en général qu'un seul bon goût . . . et tous ceux qui ne l'approuvent point, ont nécessairement le goût mauvais." Charles Batteux, *Les Beaux-arts réduits à un meme principe* (Paris: Durand, 1746), 102.

16. Thomas Crow, *Painters and Public Life in Eighteenth-Century Paris* (New Haven, Conn.: Yale University Press, 1985), 5.

17. It is typical of this viewpoint that La Harpe's *Lycée* covered only Greek, Roman, and French literature as if they all belonged to one continuous history.

18. Charlotte Guichard cites Diderot's objections to private commissions of art by wealthy individuals, which he accused of being "anti-patriotique," versus the more public forum of the Louvre's salons. Guichard mentions Diderot's beliefs about the importance of publicly accessible art in the formation of the national taste, which he expresses in the introduction to his *Salon de 1769*. Charlotte Guichard, *Les Amateurs d'art à Paris au XVIIIe siècle* (Seyssel: Champ Vallon, 2008), 314. Ironically, the two opposing groups, the amateurs (aristocrats who supported the arts, whose views were represented by the comte de Caylus, the Doublet-Bachaumont circle, and La Font de Saint Yenne) and the *philosophes* (who favored the king, his mistress the marquise de Pompadour, and her bourgeois family who influenced artistic policy) both saw themselves as the defenders of the heroic "grand goût" and accused the other group of promoting effeminate taste.

19. Vol. 2 of *The works of the Marchioness de Lambert* (Dublin: J. Potts, 1770), 5. "D'un sentiment très-délicat dans le Cœur, & d'une grande justesse dans l'Esprit." Anne-Thérèse, marquise de Lambert, vol. 1 of *Œuvres* (Paris: Ganeau, 1748), 147.

20. Lambert, II:4. "C'est la Nature qui le donne; il ne s'acquiert pas; le monde délicat seulement le perfectionne" (Lambert, I:145).

21. "le sentiment enseigne bien mieux si l'ouvrage touche . . . que toutes les dissertations composées par les critiques pour en expliquer le mérite et pour en calculer les perfections et les défauts. La voïe de discussion et d'analise, dont se servent ces messieurs, est bonne à la verité, lorsqu' il s'agit de trouver les causes qui font qu'un ouvrage plaît ou qu' il ne plaît pas, mais cette voïe ne vaut pas celle du sentiment lorsqu' il s' agit de décider cette question." Jean-Baptiste Dubos, vol. 2 of *Réflexions critiques sur la poésie et sur la peinture* ([1719]; Paris: P.-J. Mariette, 1733), 324. When he uses the term *critique* in a negative way, as we can see in this quotation, it is not clear how Dubos distinguished this type of critic from other critics such as himself.

22. The developments in the field of taste that I describe have some interesting parallels and divergences with developments in the field of visual arts of the same period, especially in regard to the authority of taste. Just as the *mondains* saw their aesthetic authority slip from their hands to those of the *gens de lettres*, the *amateurs* of the art world begin to encounter opposition from the same *gens de lettres* in the second half of the eighteenth century. Thomas Crow informs us that many prominent painters of the early eighteenth century had aligned themselves with the aristocratic *amateurs* such as the comte de Caylus. Consequently, they sided with their patrons in their fight to maintain the latter's political privileges and parliamentary rights, against encroachments from Louis XV's absolutist monarchy. One can see how this campaign would be compatible with Montesquieu's political theory, which favored a strong aristocracy that would act as a barrier to the potential excesses of monarchical power, as he expressed in his *Esprit des lois*. It is not entirely improbable that

the belief in the aristocracy's benevolent political power in relationship to the king and to the people finds a parallel in Dubos's and Lambert's placement of the right to make artistic judgments in the aristocracy.

By contrast, the next wave of aesthetic philosophy favored the power of the king. Annie Becq notes that the majority of *philosophes*—Voltaire, d'Alembert, Marmontel—actually chose to oppose the aristocrats and parliamentarians during the parliamentary crises of the second half of the eighteenth century. Partly due to their affiliation with the Académie Française, a royal institution, partly due to resentment over the Parliament of Paris's past injustices, they preferred the direct patronage of the court, whether they served Louis XV, his mistress Mme. de Pompadour, or royal ministers. Not only did most of the *philosophes* take a stand in favor of the monarchy and against aristocrats and their privileges, but they also published invectives against the aristocrat/ amateur party's influence on the arts. Charlotte Guichard, in *Les amateurs d'art à Paris au XVIIIe siècle*, sees the hostility of the *philosophes*, notably Diderot, against the *amateurs*, as opposition to any obstacles between the artist and the public. Diderot believed, as Guichard points out, in replicating an ancient patriotic ideal in which the philosopher or the artist would communicate directly with his audience and incite it to virtues such as devotion to the state. The amateurs who amassed private collections, in Diderot's mind, were not only unnecessary intermediaries between the artist and the public but also corrupted art through their commissions of paintings of effeminate or petty subjects, especially those of François Boucher.

23. Montesquieu tends to be grouped with Diderot and the other *philosophes* because of their collaboration in the *Encyclopedia* and because of the common ground they shared in many aspects of political philosophy. However, one could also separate them based on their difference in age, since Montesquieu died in 1755, when Rousseau's and Diderot's careers were beginning. Other differences include their attitudes toward taste that I deal with in this study and their opinions regarding aristocratic privilege vis-à-vis the monarch.

24. [César Chesneau, Dumarsais,] "Philosopher," The Encyclopedia of Diderot & d'Alembert Collaborative Translation Project, trans. Dena Goodman (Ann Arbor: Scholarly Publishing Office of the University of Michigan Library, 2002). "Le monde est plein de personnes d'esprit & de beaucoup d'esprit, qui jugent toujours; toujours ils devinent, car c'est deviner que de juger sans sentir quand on a le motif propre du jugement. . . . Le philosophe . . . juge & parle moins, mais il juge plus surement & parle mieux" ("Philosophe," *Encyclopédie, ou dictionnaire raisonné des sciences, des arts et des métiers*, ed. Robert Morrissey (Chicago: University of Chicago ARTFL Encyclopédie Project, Spring 2010 Edition), XII:509–10).

25. Voltaire, "Men of Letters," *Encyclopedia*. "passent des épines des Mathématiques aux fleurs de la Poésie, & qui jugent egalement bien d'un livre de Métaphysique & d'une piece de théatre" (Voltaire, "Gens de lettres," *Encyclopédie*, VII:599).

26. Voltaire, "Men of Letters," *Encyclopedia*. "Un *homme de lettres* n'est pas ce qu'on appelle *un bel esprit*: le bel esprit seul suppose moins de culture, moins d'étude, & n'exige nulle philosophie; il consiste principalement dans l'imagination brillante, dans les agrémens de la conversation, aidés d'une lecture commune. Un bel esprit peut aisément ne point mériter le titre *d'homme de lettres*; & l'*homme de lettres* peut ne point prétendre au brillant du bel esprit" (Voltaire, "Gens de lettres," *Encyclopédie*, 600).

Elena Russo, in *Styles of Enlightenment: Taste, Politics and Authorship in Eighteenth-Century France* (Baltimore: Johns Hopkins University Press, 2006), explains the declining reputation of the word *wit*, or *bel-esprit*, from the seventeenth to the eighteenth centuries.

27. Classical scholar and husband of Anne Dacier.

28. Martinus Scriblerus was a caricature of an erudite fool invented by the satirists Jonathan Swift, Alexander Pope, and the other members of the Scriblerus Club.

29. Voltaire, *The Temple of Taste*, in vol. 36 of *The Works of Voltaire: A Contemporary Version with Notes* (Paris: E. R. DuMont, 1901), 42.

> Le teint jauni, les yeux rouges et secs,
> Le dos courbé sous un tas d'auteurs grecs,
> Tout noircis d'encre, et coiffés de poussière.
> Je leur criai de loin par la portière:
> "N'allez-vous pas dans le Temple du Goût
> Vous décrasser?"—"Nous, messieurs? point du tout;
> Ce n'est pas là, grâce au ciel, notre étude:
> Le goût n'est rien; nous avons l'habitude
> De rédiger au long de point en point
> Ce qu'on pensa; mais nous ne pensons point."

Voltaire, *Le Temple du goût*, in vol. 9 of *Complete Works* (Oxford: Voltaire Foundation, 1999), 126.

30. Pierre Bourdieu, *The Rules of Art: Structure and Genesis of the Literary Field* (Cambridge: Polity Press, 1996), 224. "Un des enjeux centraux des rivalités littéraires (etc.) est le monopole de la légitimité littéraire, c'est-à-dire, entre autres choses, le monopole du pouvoir de dire avec autorité qui est autorisé à se dire écrivain . . . le monopole du *pouvoir de consécration* des producteurs ou des produits." Pierre Bourdieu, *Les Règles de l'art: Genèse et structure du champ littéraire* (Paris: Seuil, 1992), 311. Bourdieu uses the word *etc.* to remind us that he refers to writers and to artists who practice other media, such as painters and sculptors.

1. TOO MANY BOOKS

1. Louis Bollioud de Mermet, *Crazy book-collecting or bibliomania* (New York: Duprat & Co., 1894), 5. "Jamais on ne vit tant de livres de toutes les especes, de toutes les formes, & jamais on n'a vu si peu de lecteurs dont l'étude sérieuse, & l'instruction solide soient le véritable but." Louis Bollioud-Mermet, *De la bibliomanie* (La Haye: n.p., 1761), 7.

2. Bernhard Metz, "Bibliomania and the Folly of Reading," *Comparative Critical Studies* 5.2–3 (2008): 249–69. Metz finds that the word *bibliomane* is explicitly used in satires written by the nineteenth-century writers Charles Nodier (also a librarian) and Gustave Flaubert, among others. There is even one Italian comedy about a bibliomaniac by Alberto Nota, entitled *Il Bibliomane* (1822–27). In regard to ancient Rome, Metz counts scrolls among "books."

3. As Neil Kenny remarks in his study that compares book collecting and the beginnings of *histoire littéraire*, "Bibliomania began to be identified as a phenomenon in France in the second half of the seventeenth century. It spectacularly inflated the prices of livres rares et curieux on the Paris market throughout the eighteenth century, especially from about 1720." Kenny bases this statement on the research of Jean Viardot and other historians of the book. Neil Kenny, "Books in Space and Time: Bibliomania and Early Modern Histories of Learning and 'Literature' in France," *MLQ: Modern Language Quarterly* 61.2 (June 2000): 254.

4. Alexandre Wenger, *La Fibre littéraire: Le discours médical sur la lecture au XVIIIe siècle* (Geneva: Droz, 2007).

5. Natania Meeker, "*Lire et devenir:* The Embodied Reader and Feminine Subjectivity in Eighteenth-Century France," *The Eighteenth Century* 47.1 (Spring 2006): 39–57.

6. "la démocratisation des lettres. . . . C'est la quantité—le *trop*—qui fait l'épidémie, car les ouvrages qui inondent le marché réveillent chaque jour la curiosité de nouveaux lecteurs, dépourvus de compétences critiques particulières" (Wenger, 36).

7. Jean Marie Goulemot, *Forbidden Texts: Erotic Literature and Its Readers in Eighteenth-Century France* (Philadelphia: University of Pennsylvania Press, 1994), 35. "Les manuels des confesseurs rappellent l'extrême attention qu'il faut porter aux lectures, et on ne peut comprendre l'existence de la censure si l'on oublie l'influence (néfaste bien évidemment) du livre qu'elle sous-entend." Jean Marie Goulemot, *Ces Livres qu'on ne lit que d'une main: Lecture et lecteurs de livres pornographiques au XVIIIe siècle* (Aix-en-Provence: Alinea, 1991), 47.

8. In terms of physiology, women had the added disadvantage of their bodily nature, since their nerves or "fibers" supposedly reacted more violently to stimuli. Young people, on the other hand, suffered from their general inexperience and from their virginity, which dangerously restrained the proper flow of their vital fluids. See Wenger and Meeker.

9. "Celui qui écrit sur l'art de bâtir, imitera Caramuel, qui ne s'est pas renfermé dans ce qui concerne uniquement l'Architecture, mais qui a traité en même tems de plusieurs matieres de Théologie, de Mathématiques, de Géographie, d'Histoire, de Grammaire, &c." ("Livre," *Encyclopédie,* IX:607).

10. Chartier notes that in a sample of inventories of people's property af-

ter death, taken from the mid-eighteenth century, 19 percent of servants are counted as having books among their possessions, compared with merchants (15 percent) and artisans (12 percent). Roger Chartier, *Lectures et lecteurs dans la France d'Ancien Régime* (Paris: Seuil, 1987), 168.

11. "l'édition française connaissait une nouvelle période de prospérité. Financiers et nouveaux riches s'empressaient d'acheter des livres, qu'ils préféraient luxueux, bien illustrés et traitant de sujets profanes, pour ne pas dire légers." Henri-Jean Martin, *Le Livre français sous l'Ancien Régime* (Paris: Promodis/Editions du Cercle de la Librairie, 1987), 85.

12. Bollioud-Mermet, *Bibliomania*, 9–10. "Ils se vantent d'avoir acquis une quantité prodigieuse de volumes. J'aimerois bien mieux qu'ils fussent pourvus de génie, de talents, & de doctrine; & ce qui est plus nécessaire encore, de bon sens, d'innocence, & de vertus. Mais ces choses-là ne sont pas vénales comme les livres: & si l'on pouvoit les vendre, je ne sais s'ils se présenteroit beaucoup d'acheteurs" (Bollioud-Mermet, *Bibliomanie*, 13–14).

13. Bollioud-Mermet, *Bibliomania*, 5; Bollioud-Mermet, *Bibliomania*, 7.

14. Bollioud-Mermet, *Bibliomania*, 36. "que la presse n'a pas daigné tirer de leur obscurité et dont la rareté ne peut être attribuée qu'au mépris qu'on en a conçu!" (Bollioud-Mermet, *Bibliomanie*, 66).

15. Bollioud-Mermet, *Bibliomania*, 10. "On n'est point du tout curieux de science, ni de sagesse, on veut seulement en montrer l'écorce & la superficie" (Bollioud-Mermet, *Bibliomanie*, 14).

16. Bollioud-Mermet, *Bibliomania*, 47. "livres d'un genre bizarre et singulier, où il n'y a rien à gagner pour l'instruction, rien à espérer pour la culture et l'esprit, rien même pour l'amusement des lecteurs polis et délicats!" (Bollioud-Mermet, *Bibliomanie*, 87–88).

17. Bollioud-Mermet, *Bibliomania*, 47–48. "fables, contes, romans, histoires de chevalerie, aventures galantes, poésies burlesques, facéties, bons mots, œuvres macaroniques, traités de magie, de sorcellerie, art divinatoire, mémoires de procédures scandaleuses, chroniques médisantes, libelles diffamatoires et tant d'autres écrits dictés par une imagination déréglée et par la liberté cynique" (Bollioud-Mermet, *Bibliomanie*, 87–88).

18. Pierre de Villiers, *Entretiens sur les contes de fées, et sur quelques autres ouvrages du temps pour servir de préservatif contre le mauvais goût* (Paris: Jacques Collombat, 1699). The title can be roughly translated as Conversations about Fairy Tales and Other Works of Our Times, to Serve as a Preservative Against Bad Taste.

19. "fourrer bien ou mal dans les titres des livres le terme de Caractere, celui de Mœurs, & celui de ce Siecle" (Villiers, 197).

20. Bollioud-Mermet, *Bibliomania*, 40. "ce que je déplore est qu'en cette matière comme en toute autre, les moindres particuliers veulent s'égaler aux Souverains. Ils osent affecter surtout cette ridicule ambition dans les choses du goût" (Bollioud-Mermet, *Bibliomanie*, 73).

21. "L'amour des livres n'est estimable que dans deux cas; 1°. lorsqu'on sait les estimer ce qu'ils valent, qu'on les lit en philosophe, pour profiter de ce qu'il peut y avoir de bon, & rire de ce qu'ils contiennent de mauvais; 2°. lorsqu'on les possede pour les autres autant que pour soi, & qu'on leur en fait part avec plaisir & sans réserve" (d'Alembert, "Bibliomanie," *Encyclopédie*, II:228).

22. Several scholars have called our attention to Diderot's disapproval of private collectors, who selfishly keep artworks from the public realm, as opposed to the king, who shares his art with the public in the exhibitions at the Louvre's Salons. See Julia Simon, *Mass Enlightenment: Critical Studies in Rousseau and Diderot* (Albany: State University of New York Press, 1995) and Paula Rea Radisich, "Deconstructing Dissipation," *Eighteenth-Century Studies* 29.2 (1995–96): 222–24. Both researchers compare Diderot's complaints about art sales and the state of the art market by citing Krzysztof Pomian, *Collectors and Curiosities, Paris and Venice, 1500–1800*, trans. Elizabeth Wiles-Porter (Cambridge: Polity Press, 1990).

23. Bollioud-Mermet, *Bibliomania*, 20. "Le nombre de livres nécessaires à chaque citoyen est borné. Tout ce qui passe au delà est superflu, ou trop ambitieux" (Bollioud-Mermet, *Bibliomanie*, 34).

24. Bollioud-Mermet, *Bibliomania*, 23."Rien ne paroît, en effet, plus déplacé que de trouver des traités de théologie chez un géometre, & des méthodes de physique chez un orateur" (Bollioud-Mermet, *Bibliomanie*, 39).

25. Bollioud-Mermet, *Bibliomania*, 14. "l'homme non lettré" (Bollioud-Mermet, *Bibliomanie*, 22).

26. Bollioud-Mermet, *Bibliomania*, 15. "Tel qui par le commerce ou par les emplois de finance a fait une fortune considérable, après avoir acquis, à force d'argent, l'avantage de devenir noble, veut encore paraître homme de tous les goûts" (Bollioud-Mermet, *Bibliomanie*, 24).

27. Bollioud-Mermet, *Bibliomania*, 5–6. "des hommes qu'un défaut d'éducation a privés des avantages de l'étude: à qui leurs emplois en ôtent même le loisir & le goût: qui affectent néanmoins de former des bibliothèques" (Bollioud-Mermet, *Bibliomanie*, 7–8).

28. Metz, 249–50.

29. Bollioud-Mermet, *Bibliomania*, 53. "Quand même la vanité, le luxe envahiroient toutes les professions, infecteroient tous les états, le leur doit être exempt de cette contagion" (Bollioud-Mermet, *Bibliomanie*, 98).

30. "J'ai oüi dire à un des plus beaux esprits de ce siecle, qu'il étoit parvenu à se faire, par un moyen assez singulier, une bibliotheque très-choisie, assez nombreuse, & qui pourtant n'occupe pas beaucoup de place. S'il achette, par exemple, un ouvrage en douze volumes, où il n'y ait que six pages qui méritent d'être lûes, il sépare ces six pages du reste, & jette l'ouvrage au feu. Cette maniere de former une bibliotheque m'accommoderoit assez" (d'Alembert, "Bibliomanie," *Encyclopédie*, II:228).

31. Curiously, a number of the nineteenth-century satires of bibliomania that Metz describes end with libraries being destroyed by fire.

32. Louis-Sébastien Mercier, vol. 2 of *Memoirs of the year two thousand five hundred* (London: G. Robinson, 1772), 5. "sacrifice expiatoire offert à la vérité, au bon sens, au vrai goût." Louis-Sébastien Mercier, vol. 1 of *L'An deux mille quatre cent quarante, rêve s'il en fut jamais* (N.p., 1786), 327–28.

33. "le livre peut être obstacle autant qu'appui dans la recherche de la vérité" (Chartier, 196–97).

34. Bollioud-Mermet, *Bibliomania*, 8. "progrès de l'étude . . . art aussi ingénieux qu'admirable de l'imprimerie" (Bollioud-Mermet, *Bibliomanie*, 11).

35. Bollioud-Mermet, *Bibliomania*, 28–29. "C'est une question encore indécise que de savoir si l'invention de l'imprimerie a plus contribué aux progrès des lettres et à la perfection de la morale qu'elle ne leur a nui" (Bollioud-Mermet, *Bibliomanie*, 52).

36. Bollioud-Mermet, *Bibliomania*, 11. "J'aimerois autant voir un aveugle de naissance s'empresser à faire une collection de tableaux" (Bollioud-Mermet, *Bibliomanie*, 17).

37. "Il versifiera donc! Le beau genre de vie! / Ne se rendre fameux qu'à force de folie! / Etre, pour ainsi dire, un homme hors des rangs, / Et le jouet titré des petits et des grands! / Examinez les gens du métier qu'il embrasse. / La paresse ou l'orgueil en ont produit la race. / Devant quelques oisifs, elle peut triompher; / Mais, en bonne police, on devrait l'étouffer." Act V, scene 4 of Alexis Piron, *La Métromanie*, in vol. 1 of *Théâtre du XVIIIe siècle* (Paris: NRF Gallimard, 1972), 1118.

38. Molière, in *Le Misanthrope,* also refers to the inordinate love of writing poetry as an itch or a rash, when the title character, Alceste, sneers at the poetic efforts of the fop Oronte: "il faut qu'un galant homme ait toujours grand empire / Sur les démangeaisons qui nous prennent d'écrire." Act I, scene 2, in vol. 2 of *Œuvres complètes* (Paris: Gallimard Pléiade, 1971), 157.

39. "une démangeaison / Qui fait honte à la rime, autant qu'à la raison" (Piron, 1029).

40. "Nœuds vulgaires." Charles Palissot de Montenoy, *Les Philosophes,* in vol. 2 of *Théâtre du XVIIIe siècle* (Paris: NRF Gallimard, 1974), 156.

41. These scheming *philosophe* characters were explicitly based on Rousseau, Diderot, and their colleagues.

42. "je crois qu'en effet / Un ouvrage excellent s'annonce au moindre trait. / C'est un je ne sais quoi . . . dont notre âme est saisie . . . / Cela se sent . . . enfin c'est l'attrait du génie" (Palissot, 168).

43. For an extensive study of the expression and its use, see Richard Scholar, *The Je-Ne-Sais-Quoi in Early Modern Europe: Encounters with a Certain Something* (Oxford: Oxford University Press, 2005).

44. *Carondas*: Mais apprenez-moi donc comment cela se fit; / Il faut que
          vous sachiez tout ce qui s'est écrit / . . . / Quoi! vous n'avez
          pas lu le savant Vossius?
   Cydalise: Non, jamais.
   Carondas: Casaubon?
   Cydalise: Encor moins.
   Carondas: Grotius?
   Cydalise: Point du tout. Sont-ce là les livres d'une femme?
                  . . .
   Carondas: Vous connaissez du moins Thalès, Anaxagore?
   Cydalise: Non.
   Carondas: *Le Fils naturel?*
   Cydalise: Pour celui-là, d'accord. / Ce sont de
          ces écrits qu'il faut citer d'abord.   (Palissot, 167–68)

45. J'y traite en abrégé de l'esprit, du bon sens,
Des passions, des lois et des gouvernements;
De la vertu, des mœurs, du climat, des usages;
Des peuples policés et des peuples sauvages;
Du désordre apparent, de l'ordre universel,
Du bonheur idéal et du bonheur réel.
J'examine avec soin les principes des choses.
L'enchaînement secret des effets et des causes.
J'ai fait exprès pour vous un chapitre profond;
Je veux l'intituler: *Les devoirs tels qu'ils sont.*
Enfin c'est en morale une encyclopédie,
Et Valère l'appelle un livre de genie. (Palissot, 157)

46. "Nous savons lui prescrire / Comment il faut penser, parler, juger,
écrire; / Nous le déciderons aisément" (Palissot, 160).

47. Regarding the nineteenth century, he cites the words of the author-li-
brarian Charles Nodier, who, exasperated by the unqualified praise of printing, wrote an article ironically entitled "De l'utilité morale de l'instruction
pour le peuple" (1830), in which he dissociates the idea of the perfectibility
of man and the growth of the book trade. In this article he argues, as Martin
summarizes it, "l'art typographique n'a pas émancipé les peuples mais les a
pervertis" (Martin, 20). In short, Nodier has recourse to the same arguments
as Villiers and Bollioud-Mermet: the common man, far from benefiting from
instruction, uses his newly found literacy to read inferior works. Those that
Nodier particularly frowns on include "des livres d'ascétisme et de mysticité
qui fascinent [le peuple]," the opposite extreme, "livres obscènes et impies
qui l'énervent et l'abrutissent," or *gazettes* and *almanachs* (Martin, 21).

48. Charles-Louis de Secondat, baron de Montesquieu, *Reflections on
the causes of the rise and fall of the Roman Empire* (Glasgow: Robert Urie,
1758), 161. "L'invention de l'imprimerie, qui a mis les livres dans les mains
de tout le monde, celle de la gravure, qui a rendu les cartes géographiques si
communes, enfin, l'établissement des papiers politiques, font assez connaître

à chacun les intérêts généraux pour pouvoir plus aisément être éclairci sur les faits secrets." Charles-Louis de Secondat, baron de Montesquieu, *Considérations sur les causes de la grandeur des Romains et de leur decadence*, in vol. 2 of *Œuvres complètes* (1721; Oxford and Naples: Voltaire Foundation and Istituto italiano per gli studi filosofici, 2000), 264.

49. Jean-Antoine-Nicolas de Caritat, marquis de Condorcet, *Outlines of an historical view of the progress of the human mind* (Philadelphia: Lang and Ustick, 1796), 149. "Enfin, l'imprimerie n'a-t-elle pas affranchi l'instruction des peuples de toutes les chaînes politiques et religieuses?" Jean-Antoine-Nicolas de Caritat, marquis de Condorcet, *Esquisse d'un tableau historique des progrès de l'esprit humain* (1794; Paris: Boivin et Cie, 1933), "Huitième époque," 119.

50. Condorcet, *Outlines*, 254. "L'art de l'imprimerie s'était répandu sur tant de points; il avait tellement multiplié les livres; on avait su les proportionner si bien à tous les degrés de connaissances, d'application, et même de fortune; on les avait pliés avec tant d'habileté à tous les goûts, à tous les genres d'esprit; ils présentaient une instruction si facile, souvent même si agréable; ils avaient ouvert tant de portes à la vérité, qu'il était devenu presque impossible de les lui fermer toutes; qu'il n'y avait plus de classe, de profession à laquelle on pût l'empêcher de parvenir" (Condorcet, "Neuvième époque," 163–64).

51. Condorcet, *Outlines*, 183, 184. "Cette instruction, que chaque homme peut recevoir par les livres dans le silence et la solitude, ne peut être universellement corrompue" (Condorcet, "Huitième époque," 119).

52. "L'imprimerie a fondé le règne du genre humain." Germaine de Staël, *Des circonstances actuelles qui peuvent terminer la révolution et des principes qui doivent fonder la république en France* (Paris: Librarie Fischbacher, 1906), 192. The title of the treatise can be translated as Of the Current Circumstances That Can End the Revolution and of the Principles That Must Found the Republic in France.

53. "perfectibilité de l'esprit humain" (Staël, 193).

54. "la découverte de l'imprimerie est un présent divin fait aux hommes." Louis-Sébastien Mercier, vol. 5 of *Le Tableau de Paris* (Amsterdam: n.p., 1783), 319.

55. An additional reason for this neglect is that our current eighteenth-century canon was influenced by nineteenth-century ideals of democracy and progress. As Antoine Compagnon showed in his *Troisième République des lettres* (Paris: Seuil, 1983), nineteenth-century French professors shaped the canon by selecting the eighteenth-century literature that fit the patriotic needs of the period.

56. Voltaire, *The History of the Russian Empire under Peter the Great*, vol. 34 of *Works*, 6. "Un libraire de Hollande commande un livre comme un manufacturier fait fabriquer des étoffes; et il se trouve malheureusement des écrivains que la nécessité force de vendre leur peine à ces marchands,

comme des ouvriers à leurs gages; de là tous ces insipides panégyriques et ces libelles diffamatoires dont le public est surchargé: c'est un des vices les plus honteux de notre siècle." Voltaire, *Histoire de l'empire de Russie sous Pierre le Grand*, in vol. 46 of *Œuvres complètes* (Oxford: Voltaire Foundation, 1999), 387.

57. Voltaire, *Dialogues, and essays literary and philosophical* (Glasgow: Robert Urie, 1764), 215. "Commerce du papier imprimé." Voltaire, "Des Mensonges imprimés," vol. 31B of *Œuvres complètes* (Oxford: Voltaire Foundation, 1994).

58. Voltaire, *Dialogues*, 204. "Chacun veut lire, ou pour fortifier cette âme, ou pour l'orner, ou pour se vanter d'avoir lu" (Voltaire, "Mensonges," 352).

59. Voltaire, *Dialogues*, 215. "une bibliothèque immense, dans laquelle il n'y aurait pas dix pages de vérité" (Voltaire, "Mensonges," 373).

60. Voltaire, *Dialogues,* 277–78. "Après les temps fabuleux viennent ce qu'on appelle les temps héroïques: les premiers ressemblent aux Mille et une nuits, où rien n'est vrai; les seconds aux romans de chevalerie, où il n'y a de vrai que quelques noms et quelques époques. Voilà déjà bien des milliers d'années et de livres à ignorer, et de quoi mettre l'esprit à l'aise. Viennent enfin les temps historiques, où le fond des choses est vrai, et où la plupart des circonstances sont des mensonges. Mais parmi ces mensonges n'y a-t-il pas quelques vérités? oui, comme il se trouve un peu de poudre d'or dans les sables que les fleuves roulent" (Voltaire, "Mensonges," 379–80).

61. "ce ne fut ni sur Homère, ni sur Virgile, ni sur quelque auteur de cette volée que l'imprimerie naissante s'essaya. On commença par de petits ouvrages de peu de valeur, de peu d'étendue et du goût d'un siècle barbare." Denis Diderot, vol. 8 of *Œuvres complètes* (Paris: Hermann, 1976), 482.

62. "ouvrages estimés," "livres savants" (Diderot, *Œuvres completes*, VIII:483–84).

63. "tems ténébreux" (Diderot and d'Alembert, "Discours préliminaire," *Encyclopédie*, I:xx).

64. D'Alembert and Diderot, "Preliminary Discourse," *Encyclopedia*. "Le pays de l'érudition et des faits est inépuisable; on croit, pour ainsi dire, voir tous les jours augmenter sa substance par les acquisitions que l'on y fait sans peine. Au contraire le pays de la raison et des découvertes est d'une assez petite étendue; et souvent au lieu d'y apprendre ce que l'on ignoroit, on ne parvient à force d'étude qu'à desapprendre ce qu'on croyoit savoir" (Diderot and d'Alembert, "Discours préliminaire," *Encyclopédie*, I:xx).

65. "une foule de poëtes, d'orateurs, et d'historiens latins" (Diderot and d'Alembert, "Discours préliminaire," *Encyclopédie*, I:xx).

66. Jean-Jacques Rousseau, *Discourse on the Sciences and Arts*, vol. 2 of *The Collected Writings of Rousseau* (Hanover, N.H.: University Press of

New England, 1990), 20. "l'art d'éterniser les extravagances de l'esprit humain." Jean-Jacques Rousseau, *Œuvres complètes*, vol. 3 (Paris: NRF Gallimard/Pléïade, 1964), 27–28.

67. The idea also plays an important part in his educational treatise *Emile*.

68. Rousseau, *Sciences*, 21. "Mais si le progrès des sciences et des arts n'a rien ajoûté à nôtre véritable félicité; s'il a corrompu nos mœurs, et si la corruption des mœurs a porté atteinte à la pureté du goût, que penserons-nous de cette foule d'auteurs élémentaires qui ont écarté du temple des muses les difficultés qui défendoient son abord, et que la nature y avoit répandües comme une épreuve des forces de ceux qui seroient tentés de savoir?" (Rousseau, *Sciences et arts*, 28–29).

69. Rousseau, *Sciences*, 21. "Que penserons-nous de ces compilateurs d'ouvrages qui ont indiscrettement brisé la porte des sciences et introduit dans leur sanctuaire une populace indigne d'en approcher; tandis qu'il seroit à souhaiter que tous ceux qui ne pouvoient avancer loin dans la carriére des lettres, eussent été rebuttés dès l'entrée, et se fussent jettés dans des arts utiles à la societé. Tel qui sera toute sa vie un mauvais versificateur, un geométre subalterne, seroit peut-être devenu un grand fabricateur d'étoffes" (Rousseau, *Sciences et arts*, 29).

70. Rousseau, *Sciences*, 21. "Délivre-nous des lumières et des funestes arts de nos pères, et rends-nous l'ignorance, l'innocence et la pauvreté . . . !" (Rousseau, *Sciences et arts*, 28).

71. See Voltaire's demands in his 1739 *Conseils à un journaliste*, where he specifies the extensive knowledge that a journalist must have if he is to distinguish himself as an *homme de lettres* rather than a hack.

72. Jean-Baptiste Dubos, vol. 2 of *Critical reflections on poetry, painting, and music* (London: J. Nourse, 1748), 77–78. "Celui qui n'est pas pilote, dit Horace, n'ose s'asseoir au gouvernail. On ne se mêle point de composer des remedes, quand on n'a pas étudié la vertu des simples. Il n'y a que les medecins qui ordonnent la saignée aux malades. Ce n'est même qu'après un apprentissage qu'on exerce les plus vils métiers, mais tout le monde capable ou non, veut faire des vers" (Dubos, *Réflexions*, II:104).

73. Clement Greenberg, "Avant-garde and Kitsch," in *Pollock and After: The Critical Debate* (1961; New York: Routledge, 2000), 52.

74. Ibid., 56.

75. Matei Calinescu, *Five Faces of Modernity: Modernism, Avant-Garde, Decadence, Kitsch, Postmodernism* (Durham, N.C.: Duke University Press, 1987), 227.

76. Max Horkheimer and Theodor W. Adorno, "The Culture Industry: Enlightenment as Mass Deception," in *Dialectic of Enlightenment* (1944; New York: Continuum, 1994), 134.

2. WHAT IS GOOD TASTE?

1. "il est bien plus aise de dire ce que ce n'est pas que le *goût*, & le bon ou mauvais *goût*, que de marquer précisément ce que c'est." "Goust," in vol. 3 of *Dictionnaire universel françois et latin, vulgairement appelé Dictionnaire de Trévoux* (Paris, 1721), 286.

2. "il n'est pas difficile d'établir que l'esprit & le *goût* ne sont pas la même chose. . . . Il est bien aisé de remarquer aussi que le *goût* ne vient pas du sçavoir; on peut avoir beaucoup de connoissances, de grandes lumieres, & un très mauvais *gout*" ("Goust," 286).

3. Subsequent editions of the *Dictionnaire de Trévoux* in the eighteenth century dispense with the list of quotations but they maintain the rest of the article.

4. "M[adeleine de] SCUD[éry]. Le bon *goût* est un sentiment naturel qu'on ne sçauroit apprendre, ni enseigner: il faut qu'il soit né avec nous. Ainsi il ne faut pas traitter de haut en bas ceux qui ne l'ont point: on n'a pas de piéces en main pour convaincre qu'ils ont tort. S[aint-] EVR[emond]. Le bon *goût* ne vient que d'une connoissance exquise, & juste, à bien juger du bien, & du mal, pour toute sorte de bienséance, & d'agrémens: on ne l'acquiert qu'avec beaucoup de soins, & de réfléxions. LE CH[evalier]. DE M[éré]. Les mauvais Auteurs gâtent le *goût* du public, en l'accoutumant à des choses fades, & insipides" ("Goust," 285–86).

5. "le bon Goût est ce qui est conforme à la *nature*; ce qui est approuvé par la *raison*; ce qui n'est, *ni outré, ni affecté*; ce qui plaît à nos *sens*; ce qui séduit notre *cœur*; ce qui nous *intéresse*; ce en quoi nous ne trouvons *rien qui nous choque, rien qui nous révolte*; ce que *les fameux Artistes ont le plus universellement pratiqué*; ce que *les vrais connoisseurs estiment*. Tout ce qui n'a pas ces qualités ne peut être que de mauvais goût" (emphasis added). Louis Bollioud-Mermet, *De la corruption du goust dans la musique française* (Lyon: A. Delaroche, 1746; New York: AMS Press, 1978), 48.

6. Zeuxis was a celebrated painter in Greece during the fifth century B.C. According to legend, he could not find a single woman who was perfect enough to pose for a portrait of Helen, so he assembled a number of models and copied different body parts from each one in order to depict the perfect beauty. Numerous eighteenth-century artists chose this legend as a subject of their paintings. For a recent study of the Zeuxis story, see Elizabeth C. Mansfield, *Too Beautiful to Picture: Zeuxis, Myth, and Mimesis* (Minneapolis: University of Minnesota Press, 2007).

7. "Mais comment choisir dans la Nature ce qui doit être reproduit? Comme décider que telle 'partie' est plus belle qu'une autre si l'on n'a pas d'abord défini la beauté? On en revient ainsi au point de départ, et tout le livre de Batteux se réduirait à une tautologie—pour être belle, une œuvre d'art doit imiter la belle nature—s'il n'était admis une fois pour toutes que

l'Antiquité possède le privilège du bon goût." Jean Ehrard, *L'Idée de nature en France à l'aube des Lumières* (Paris: Flammarion, 1970), 185–86.

8. Boileau, in Chant III of his *Art poétique*, states:

Achille déplairoit moins boüillant et moins promt.
J'aime à lui voir verser des pleurs pour un affront.
À ces petits defauts marquez dans sa peinture,
L'esprit avec plaisir reconnoist la *nature*.
Qu'il soit sur ce modele en vos écrits tracé.
Qu'Agamemnon soit fier, superbe, interessé.
Que pour ses dieux Enée ayt un respect austere.
Conservez à chacun son propre caractere. (emphasis added)

Nicolas Boileau-Despréaux, *Œuvres* (Paris: Gallimard
Pléïade, 1966), 171.

9. Eighteenth-century usage of the word *intéresser* supposes a stronger feeling of empathy than we associate with it in our time. The 1762 edition of the *Dictionnaire de l'Académie Française* includes the following definition of the word *intéresser*: "Émouvoir, toucher de quelque passion." Later theorists, such as Kant, will claim that the appreciation of beauty is based on the exact opposite of interest: *dis*interest, or a judgment that is detached from considerations of personal profit or physical satisfaction.

10. Much has been written on this question of how to bridge the gap between individual experience and communal judgments of art. Critics have especially concentrated on how Immanuel Kant wrestled with this problem in his *Critique of Judgment*. For example, see Ferry, *Homo aestheticus*.

11. Antoine Houdar de La Motte, who spearheaded the Modern movement in the Querelle d'Homère, was one of the rare eighteenth-century critics who dared to suggest that the *Iliad* was boring or otherwise faulty.

12. Richard Scholar makes the link between the idea of grace and an aesthetically elusive ideal in *The Je-Ne-Sais-Quoi in Early Modern Europe* (Oxford: Oxford University Press, 2005).

13. André and other theoreticians made exceptions for superior artists, such as Shakespeare or Michelangelo, who sometimes knowingly broke rules.

14. Robert Darnton, *The Literary Underground of the Old Régime* (Cambridge, Mass.: Harvard University Press, 1982).

15. The *Mercure* was founded in 1672 with the royal privilege. It was one of the first journals that ever existed in France, along with the *Gazette de France*, which disseminated information from the government, and the *Journal des Savants*, which was devoted to scientific discoveries. The success of the *Mercure* surely inspired a number of publications in other countries: *Der Teutsche Merkur* in Germany, the *Mercurio peruano* in Peru, which borrowed its title, and other journals with more limited formats, such as fashion magazines and readings specifically for women.

16. Ernst Cassirer, *The Philosophy of the Enlightenment*, trans. James

P. Pettegrove and Fritz C. A. Koelin (Princeton, N.J.: Princeton University Press, 1968).

17. George Dickie, in *The Century of Taste: The Philosophical Odyssey of Taste in the Eighteenth Century* (Oxford: Oxford University Press, 1996), expresses great impatience with the way in which Kant studies have come to overshadow the field of eighteenth-century aesthetics, to the detriment of the thinkers who preceded him, such as Hutcheson or Addison.

18. Claude Chantalat, *A la Recherche du goût classique* (Paris: Klincksieck, 1992).

19. See Denise Gigante, *Taste: A Literary History* (New Haven, Conn.: Yale University Press, 2005); David Marshall, *The Frame of Art: Fictions of Aesthetic Experience, 1750–1815* (Baltimore: Johns Hopkins University Press, 2005); and Dickie, *The Century of Taste,* among others.

20. "On voit ainsi que le même mot est utilisé à la fois pour suggérer les mérites du jugement et ceux de la chose jugée, de la même façon qu'au sens propre il évoque la délicatesse du palais et la saveur exquise des aliments qui le flattent." Chantalat, 22.

21. Lambert, *Works,* II:5. "Le Goût a pour objet l'Agréable: la Beauté a des regles, l'Agréable n'en a point. Le Beau sans l'Agréable ne peut plaire; il tient au Goût: voilà pourquoi il plaît plus que le Beau; il est arbitraire & variable comme lui" (Lambert, *Œuvres,* I:145–46).

22. Wladyslaw Folkierski, *Entre le classicisme et le romantisme* (Paris: Champion, 1925), 38.

23. Folkierski points out that Descartes's one notable remark about beauty can be found in his 1649 work *Des Passions de l'âme,* in which he compares the judgment of good and evil to that of beauty and ugliness. Descartes values the former type of judgment more highly because it is based on the "internal senses," unlike the idea of beauty, which is based on the inferior "external sense" of vision. See Folkierski, 36, and René Descartes, *Les Passions de l'âme,* part 2, article LXXXV, "De l'Agrément et de l'Horreur" (Paris: Vrin, 1994), 126–27.

24. Blaise Pascal, *Pensées,* ed. Philippe Sellier (Paris: Bordas, 1991), fragment #486, p. 380.

25. His other publications included treatises on geometry and algebra, and several treatises on logic. See Jacqueline La Harpe, *Jean-Pierre de Crousaz et le conflit des idées au siècle des lumières* (Berkeley: University of California Press, 1955), 24–25.

26. "Le bon goût nous fait d'abord estimer par sentiment ce que la Raison auroit approuvé, après qu'elle se seroit donné le tems de l'examiner assez pour en juger sur de justes idées." Jean-Pierre de Crousaz, *Traité du beau* (1715; Amsterdam: Chez l'Honoré et Chatelain, 1724), book 1, 170.

27. "[S]i j'assemble trois lignes également posées pour faire un Triangle equilatéral, ou desquelles deux le soient également & une troisiéme differemment, pour faire un Isoscele; si je pose 4 lignes égales pour faire un quarré:

si j'en assemble un plus grand nombre, formans entr'elles des Angles égaux, pour avoir des Polygones, ces diversités entremêlées d'égalité formeront dans ces figures une régularité qu'on estime & qu'on aime" (Crousaz, 22).

28. "colifichets gothiques" (Crousaz, 29).

29. "Le mauvais goût . . . nous fait sentir avec plaisir ce que la Raison n'approuveroit pas" (Crousaz, 171).

30. Denis Diderot, "Beautiful," *Encyclopedia.* "le système le plus suivi, le plus étendu, & le mieux lié que je connoisse" (Denis Diderot, "Beau," *Encyclopédie* II:173).

31. Aside from the obvious influence of Descartes, Annie Becq insists particularly on the influence of Malebranche on André's category of *beauté essentielle*, which may be even independent of God's will (Becq, 416–17).

32. "J'appelle Beau, dans un ouvrage d'esprit, non pas ce qui plaît au premier coup d'œil de l'imagination dans certaines dispositions particulières des facultés de l'âme, ou des organes du corps mais ce qui a droit de plaire à la raison, & à la réflexion par son excellence propre, par sa lumière ou par sa justesse, &, si l'on me permet ce terme, par son agrément intrinsèque." Yves-Marie André, *Essai sur le beau* (1741; Amsterdam: Chez J. H. Schneider, 1759), 79.

33. „Le pere André distribue avec beaucoup de sagacité & de philosophie le beau en général dans ses différentes especes; il les définit toutes avec précision: mais on ne trouve la définition du genre, celle du beau en général [essentiel], dans aucun endroit de son livre" (Diderot, „Beau," *Encyclopédie,* II:173).

34. „Je dis en second lieu qu'il y a un beau naturel, dépendant de la volonté du Créateur, mais indépendant de nos opinions & de nos goûts" (André, 13–14).

35. Batteux, 106. „Que dirait-on d'un peintre qui représenterait les hommes, petits, maigres, bossus, boiteux, etc. comme ils sont souvent dans la nature?" (Batteux, 162).

36. Batteux, 69. „Et comme cette position du même modele peut se varier à l'infini, & que ces variations peuvent encore se multiplier par les points de vue qui sont aussi infinis; il s'ensuit que le même objet peut être représenté sous un nombre infini de faces toutes différentes, & cependant toutes régulières & entierement conformes à la Nature & au bon Goût" (Batteux, 104).

37. Batteux, 68. „Il ne peut y avoir en général qu'un seul bon goût, qui est celui qui approuve la belle nature, et tous ceux qui ne l'approuvent point, ont nécessairement le gout mauvais" (Batteux, 102).

38. Batteux, 43. „Est-ce l'autorité des hommes, ou plutot n'est-ce point la voix de la nature qui opère ces changements? Qu'un homme, qui ait le gout exquis, soit attentif à l'impression que fait sur lui l'ouvrage de l'art, qu'il sente distinctement, et qu'en conséquence il se prononce: il n'est guère possible que les autres hommes ne souscrivent à son jugement. Ils éprouvent le meme

sentiment que lui, si ce n'est au meme degré, du moins sera-t-il de la meme espece; et quels que soient le préjugé et le mauvais gout, ils se soumettent, et rendent secrètement hommage à la nature" (Batteux, 65–66).

39. Dubos, *Critical Reflections*, II:10. "l'heureuse disposition des organes" (Dubos, *Réflexions*, II:16).

40. Dubos, *Critical Reflections*, II:11. "J'ai supposé que le sang de celui qui compose s'échauffât; car les peintres et les poëtes ne peuvent inventer de sang froid: on sçait bien qu'ils entrent en une espece d'enthousiasme, lorsqu'ils produisent leurs idées" (Dubos, *Réflexions*, II:14).

41. His use of the terms *warm* and *cold* refers to a theory from ancient medicine that assumed that vital spirits were warmed up in the body; bodily heat agitated the vital spirits, which led the brain to be more productive. The idea can be traced from Hippocrates, Aristotle, and Galen to Juan Huarte and then to eighteenth-century writers such as Montesquieu and Buffon. I will have occasion to explore this idea further in the fourth and sixth chapters, specifically regarding the faulty genius and bad taste of women and the people of other countries.

42. Dubos, *Critical Reflections*, I:3. "La matiere que j'ose traiter est présente à tout le monde. Chacun a chez soi la regle ou le compas applicable à mes raisonnemens" (Dubos, *Réflexions*, I:3).

43. Dubos, *Critical Reflections*, II:245. "C'est que je ne comprens point le bas peuple dans le public capable de prononcer sur les poëmes ou sur les tableaux. . . . Le mot de public ne renferme ici que les personnes qui ont acquis des lumieres, soit par la lecture, soit par le commerce du monde" (Dubos, *Réflexions*, II:334–35).

44. Dubos, *Critical Reflections*, II:353–54. "Les opinions dont l'étendüe et la durée sont fondées sur le sentiment propre, et pour ainsi dire, sur l'expérience intérieure de ceux qui les ont adoptées dans tous les temps, ne sont pas sujettes à être détruites" (Dubos, *Réflexions*, II:488).

45. Terry Eagleton, *The Ideology of the Aesthetic* (London: Blackwell, 1990), 19.

46. Montesquieu originally wrote his *Essai sur le goût* as an article for the *Encyclopédie*, but it was later printed as an independent text. As it was printed in the *Encyclopédie* in 1757, the article "Goût" contains Montesquieu's text, along with Voltaire's and d'Alembert's articles on the same subject. Montesquieu's article was included in his collected works beginning in 1758, according to Annie Becq's critical introduction to the *Essai*, and it has been published as an independent text several times since.

47. Charles de Secondat, baron de Montesquieu, *An Essay on Taste*, in Alexander Gerard, *An Essay on Taste: To which are annexed, three dissertations on the same subject, by Mr de Voltaire, Mr D'Alembert, and Mr de Montesquieu* (Edinburgh: A. Millar, A. Kincaid, and J. Bell, 1764), 251. "Les sources du beau, du bon, de l'agréable, &c. sont donc dans nous-

mêmes; & en chercher les raisons, c'est chercher les causes du plaisir de notre ame" Montesquieu, *Essai sur le goût*, in vol. 9 of *Œuvres complètes* (Oxford: Voltaire Foundation, 2006), 487.

48. I translated the following passage: "La Poésie, la Peinture, la Sculpture, l'Architecture, la Musique, la Danse, les différentes sortes de jeux, enfin les ouvrages de la nature & de l'art, peuvent lui donner du plaisir; voyons pourquoi, comment & quand ils les lui donnent; rendons raison de nos sentimens; cela pourra contribuer à nous former le *goût*, qui n'est autre chose que l'avantage de découvrir avec finesse & avec promtitude la mesure du plaisir que chaque chose doit donner aux hommes" (Montesquieu, *Goût*, 488). The printed edition had removed some key phrases from the original: "It derives pleasure from poetry, painting, sculpture, architecture, music, dancing; in a word, from the various productions of nature and art. Let us, therefore, inquire into the reasons that render these objects pleasing, as also into the manner of their operation, and the times and circumstances in which they produce their agreeable effects, and thus give an account of our various feelings" (Montesquieu, *Taste*, 251).

49. Although some categorize Montesquieu along with other *philosophes* such as Voltaire, Diderot, and Rousseau, and although these *philosophes* held him in high esteem, it is nonetheless important to note that he belonged to an earlier generation. Montesquieu died in 1755, when the other *philosophes'* careers were just beginning their ascent. Voltaire was an exception; he had an unusually long career, which extended nearly over the whole eighteenth century.

50. Sylvain Menant, *L'Esthétique de Voltaire* (Paris: SEDES, 1995).

51. "au jugement de convention il oppose un impressionisme intégral, fondé sur l'indépendance du connaisseur, la fraîcheur et l'acuité de son impression." Raymond Naves, *Le Goût de Voltaire* (1938; Geneva: Slatkine Reprints, 1967), 494.

52. Voltaire, "Taste," *Encyclopedia*. "c'est un discernement prompt comme celui de la langue et du palais, et qui prévient comme lui la réflexion; il est comme lui sensible et voluptueux à l'égard du bon; il rejette comme lui le mauvais avec soulèvement" (Voltaire, "Goût," *Encyclopédie*, VII:761).

53. Voltaire, "Taste," *Encyclopedia*. "incertain et égaré, ignorant même si ce qu'on lui présente doit lui plaire, et ayant quelquefois besoin comme lui d'habitude pour se former" (Voltaire, "Goût," *Encyclopédie*, VII:761).

54. Voltaire, "Taste," *Encyclopedia*. "Un jeune homme sensible, mais sans aucune connaissance . . . sera ému à la première représentation qu'il verra d'une belle tragédie; mais il n'y démêlera ni le mérite des unités. . . . Ce n'est qu'avec de l'habitude et des réflexions qu'il parvient à sentir tout d'un coup avec plaisir ce qu'il ne démêlait pas auparavant" (Voltaire, "Goût," *Encyclopédie*, VII:761).

55. Voltaire, "Taste," *Encyclopedia*. "le sentiment des beautés et des défauts dans tous les arts" (Voltaire, "Goût," *Encyclopédie*, VII:761).

56. "Of the Standard of Taste" was first published in 1757 as part of David Hume's *Four Dissertations*.

57. "Il constate, en 1754, l'existence en son siècle d'une nouvelle espèce de rhétoriques et poétiques: 'Les premières, scolastiques, détaillées . . . les secondes générales et qui se bornent à bien exposer les premiers principes de l'art. Les troisièmes philosophiques et qui contiennent des réflexions fines sur les causes du plaisir ou du dégoût que donnent les ouvrages d'éloquence et de poésie.'" Annie Becq, "Les Arts poétiques en France au XVIIIe siècle," *Etudes littéraires* 22.3 (1990): 45–55. She cites from the abbé Trublet, vol. 3 of *Essais sur divers sujets de littérature et de morale* (Paris: Briasson, 1735), 204–5.

58. Jaucourt, d'Alembert, and Buffon, who occasionally wrote about literary style, were also experts in other fields, such as medicine and mathematics.

59. Dumarsais, *Des Tropes*, ed. M. Fontainier, avec une introduction de M. Gérard Genette (1818; Geneva: Slatkine Reprints, 1967). The complete edition of *Des Tropes* was originally published in 1757.

60. See Michel Cardy, *The Literary Doctrines of Jean-François Marmontel*, Studies on Voltaire and the Eighteenth Century 210 (Oxford: Voltaire Foundation, 1982).

61. "Il n'y a donc qu'un juge suprême, un seul juge qui, en fait de *goût*, soit sans appel: c'est la nature. Heureusement presque tout est soumis à cet arbitre universel." Jean-François Marmontel, *Essai sur le goût*, in *Eléments de littérature* (1787; Paris: Desjonquères, 2005), 36.

62. "il sent tout ce qu'il doit sentir, il le sent au degré où il doit le sentir, et, autant que sa langue peut le permettre, il le dit comme il doit le dire. Pas un tour qui ne rende le mouvement de sa pensée, pas une epithète ambitieuse ou superflue; pas une hyperbole excessive; pas une fausse métaphore, quoique tout y soit en images; pas un trait de sensibilité qui ne soit juste et pénétrant, Pourquoi cela? Parce que la nature est toujours vraie, et que tout ce qui est exagéré, maniéré, forcé, mis hors de sa place est de l'art" (Marmontel, *Goût*, 38).

63. "Entre l'état de l'homme sauvage et l'état de l'homme civilisé, et dans le passage de l'un à l'autre, est l'état de l'homme barbare [i.e., l'homme inculte]. Le sauvage, comme je l'ai conçu, serait l'homme de la nature; le barbare, au contraire, est un homme dénaturé; sa raison, ses mœurs, ses idées, ses sentiments sont pervertis par des conventions et par ses habitudes, tout aussi artificielles que les modes du luxe et de la vanité. . . .

Tirer les hommes de la barbarie, c'est donc commencer par les rendre à la nature" (Marmontel, *Goût*, 144).

64. Denis Diderot, "Beautiful," *Encyclopedia*. "J'appelle donc beau hors de moi, tout ce qui contient en soi de quoi réveiller dans mon entendement l'idée de rapports; & beau par rapport à moi, tout ce qui réveille cette idée" (Diderot, "Beau," *Encyclopédie*, II:176).

65. Diderot, "Beautiful," *Encyclopedia*. I added quotation marks to make this passage clearer. "si je lui dis que c'est la réponse d'un homme consulté sur ce qu'un autre doit faire dans un combat, il commence à appercevoir dans le répondant une sorte de courage . . . & le qu'il mourût commence à l'intéresser. Si j'ajoûte qu'il s'agit dans ce combat de l'honneur de la patrie; que le combattant est fils de celui qu'on interroge; que c'est le seul qui lui reste; que le jeune homme avoit à faire à trois ennemis, qui avoient déjà ôté la vie à deux de ses freres; que le vieillard parle à sa fille; que c'est un Romain: alors la réponse qu'il mourût, qui n'étoit ni belle, ni laide, s'embellit à mesure que je développe ses rapports avec les circonstances, & finit par être sublime" (Diderot, "Beau," *Encyclopédie*, II:177).

66. John D. Lyons, *Before Imagination: Embodied Thought from Montaigne to Rousseau* (Stanford, Calif.: Stanford University Press, 2005), 181.

67. Lester G. Crocker, *Diderot's Chaotic Order: Approach to Synthesis* (Princeton, N.J.: Princeton University Press, 1974), 54.

68. "l'homme de goût," "lecteurs ordinaires." Denis Diderot, *Lettre sur les sourds et les muets*, in *Esthétique-Théâtre*, vol. 4 of *Œuvres* (Paris: Laffont, 1996), 35, 37.

69. "il y a mille gens de bon sens contre un homme de goût, et mille personnes de goût contre une d'un goût exquis" (Diderot, *Sourds*, 141).

70. Dubos, *Critical Reflections*, II:258. "Le sentiment dont je parle est dans tous les hommes, mais comme ils n'ont pas tous les oreilles et les yeux également bons, de même ils n'ont pas tous le sentiment également parfait. Les uns l'ont meilleur que les autres, ou bien parce que leurs organes sont naturellement mieux composez, ou bien parce qu'ils l'ont perfectionné par l'usage fréquent qu'ils en ont fait et par l'expérience" (Dubos, *Réflexions*, II:352).

71. Dubos, *Critical Reflections*, II:258. "Il arrive donc que ceux qui ont la vûë courte, hésitent quelque-temps à se rendre au sentiment de celui qui a les yeux meilleurs qu'eux, mais dès que la personne qui s'avance s'est approchée à une distance proportionnée à leur vûë, ils sont tous d'un pareil avis. De même tous les hommes qui jugent par sentiment, se trouvent d'accord un peu plûtôt ou un peu plus tard sur l'effet et sur le mérite d'un ouvrage" (Dubos, *Réflexions*, II:352–53).

72. For a detailed discussion of the debate, see Jacqueline Lichtenstein, *La Couleur éloquente: Rhétorique et peinture à l'âge classique* (Paris: Flammarion, 1989), 153–82.

73. Dubos, *Critical Reflections*, I:394. "œil plus voluptueux" (Dubos, *Réflexions*, I:487).

74. Dubos, *Critical Reflections*, I:394. "expressions touchantes" (Dubos, *Réflexions*, I:487).

75. Dubos, *Critical Reflections*, I:396. "La prédilection qui nous fait donner la préférence à une partie de la peinture sur une autre partie, ne dépend

donc point de notre raison, non plus que la prédilection qui nous fait aimer
un genre de poësie preferablement aux autres. Cette prédilection dépend de
notre goût, et notre goût dépend de notre organisation, de nos inclinations
présentes, et de la situation de notre esprit" (Dubos, *Réflexions*, I:489).

76. Batteux, 42. "Comme la plupart n'y pensent que quand ils sont rem-
plis de préjugés, ils ne peuvent démeler la voix de la nature dans une si grande
confusion. Ils prennent le faux gout pour le vrai; ils lui en donnent le nom"
(Batteux, 120).

77. Recent critics have illuminated the analogy of aesthetic taste and the
taste of food. See Carolyn Korsmeyer, *Making Sense of Taste: Food and Philosophy* (Ithaca, N.Y.: Cornell University Press, 1999).

I would add a few observations taken from French sources, namely the
connection between *goût* and *ragoût* (a sort of stew). Cartaud de la Vilate's
idea of good taste coincides with Voltaire's: one immediately enjoys the flavor
of the *ragoût*, but a good connoisseur must also know in detail what elements
it contains. Dubos, on the other hand, accepts the first part of this tasting of
the *ragoût*, the immediate enjoyment, but rejects the second part, the reasoning over how it is composed. Trublet rejects the analogy between food and
art: if a *ragoût* tastes bad to you, no one can explain to you why it should
taste good, while in matters of art, you can be convinced through reason.

78. Voltaire, "Taste," *Encyclopedia*. "Comme le mauvais *goût* au physique consiste à n'être flatté que par des assaisonnements trop piquants et
trop recherchés, aussi le mauvais *goût* dans les arts est de ne se plaire qu'aux
ornements étudiés, et de ne pas sentir la belle nature" (Voltaire, "Goût,"
Encyclopédie, VII:761).

79. For an excellent study of the concept of the feeling of disgust in re-
lation to literature, see Winfried Menninghaus, *Die Ekel*, translated into
English as *Disgust: The Theory and History of a Strong Sensation* (Albany:
SUNY Press, 2003).

80. Voltaire, "Taste," *Encyclopedia*. "Le *goût* dépravé dans les arts est
de se plaire à des sujets qui révoltent les esprits bien faits; de préférer le burlesque au noble, le précieux et l'affecté au beau simple et naturel: c'est une
maladie de l'esprit" (Voltaire, "Goût," *Encyclopédie*, VII:761).

81. "Le style est une empreinte de l'ame, où l'on voit les divers caractéres
de ses passions. Le langage des Dogmatiques est fastueux, celui des Pirrho-
niens modeste & circonspect. Platon parloit avec enflûre; Socrate étoit toûjours modéré & penchoit vers la raillerie. . . . Le contraste si marqué entre ces
quatre hommes célebres, Mrs. Arnaud, Claude, Nicole, & Jurieux est l'effet
de la contrariété de leurs humeurs." François Cartaud de la Vilate, *Essai
historique et philosophique sur le goût* (Paris: Chez Maudouyt, 1736), 260.

82. "Le Goût délicat est un discernement exquis, que la nature a mis dans
certains organes, pour démêler les différentes vertus des objets qui rélevent
du sentiment" (Cartaud de la Vilate, 235).

83. "Si c'est un malheur d'être blessé de la plûpart des objets qui nous environnent, le Goût délicat est un présent bien funeste. Les organes les plus fins sont les plus exposés. Avec des yeux ordinaires on trouve beaux certains objets, sur qui une vûë plus exacte a lieu d'exercer son chagrin" (Cartaud de la Vilate, 237).

84. Lambert, II:3–4. "Il y a cependant une justesse de Goût, comme il y a une justesse de Sens. . . . Comme on ne peut en donner de regle assurée, on ne peut aussi convaincre ceux qui y font des fautes: dès que leur sentiment ne les avertit pas, vous ne pouvez plus les instruire" (Lambert, I:145).

3. THE BARBARIC, OR OF TIME AND TASTE

1. Dubos, *Critical Reflections,* II:95. "la supériorité de certains siecles sur les autres siecles est trop connuë pour qu'il soit besoin que nous nous arrêtions à la prouver. Il s'agit uniquement de remonter, s'il est possible, aux causes qui donnent tant de supériorité à un certain siecle sur les autres siecles" (Dubos, *Réflexions,* II:128).

2. Homi K. Bhabha, *Nation and Narration* (London: Routledge, 1990), 5.

3. Ibid., 2.

4. While this narrative equates "the world" with Western Europe, Voltaire is a scrupulous enough historian to tell different stories for other regions, such as India, Persia, and China, in *Essai sur les mœurs et l'esprit des nations* (Paris: Garnier, 1990). The problem is not addressed by Dubos, Marmontel, La Harpe, or any of the other critics I mention in this chapter.

5. Voltaire, *The Age of Louis XIV,* vol. 22 of *The Works of Voltaire: A Contemporary Version with Notes* (Paris: E. R. Dumont, 1901), 5. "Mais quiconque pense, et, ce qui est encore plus rare, quiconque a du goût, ne compte que quatre siècles dans l'histoire du monde. Ces quatre âges heureux sont ceux où les arts ont été perfectionnés, et qui, servant d'époque à la grandeur de l'esprit humain, sont l'exemple de la postérité." Voltaire, *Siècle de Louis XIV,* vol. 14 of *Œuvres complètes* (Paris: Garnier, 1877–83), 154.

6. Voltaire, *Temple of Taste,* 47. "chargé des antiquailles / Que nos très gothiques aïeux/ Entassaient autour des murailles / De leurs temples, grossiers comme eux" (Voltaire, *Le Temple du goût,* 131).

7. In his *Essai sur les mœurs,* Voltaire contrasts societies that granted a high value to the individual rights of people and those in which people were killed, tortured, or oppressed for political reasons. I refer to *humanism* here in the present-day sense of "any system of thought or ideology which places humans, or humanity as a whole, at its centre, *esp.* one which is predominantly concerned with human interests and welfare, and stresses the inherent value and potential of human life" (*Oxford English Dictionary,* 2009). This present-day use of the word *humanism* comes closer to the eighteenth-

century concept of *droit naturel* than it does to the use of *humanisme*, which referred mostly to the study of classical texts.

8. See Bouhours, *Entretiens d'Ariste et Eugène*, 109–22. Fénelon makes remarks about the "barbaric" mixture of Latin, Gaulish, and Frankish during the Middle Ages and expresses doubts about Montaigne's and Marot's style in *Lettre à l'Académie*. François de Salignac de La Mothe-Fénelon, vol. 6 of *Œuvres complètes* (Geneva: Slatkine Reprints, 1971).

9. Dubos, *Critical Reflections*, II:99–100. "Les annales du genre humain font mention de quatre siecles dont les productions ont été admirées par tous les siecles suivans. Ces siecles heureux où les arts ont atteint une perfection à laquelle ils ne sont point parvenus dans les autres, sont celui qui commença dix années avant le regne de Philippe pere d'Alexandre le grand, celui de Jules Cesar et d'Auguste, celui de Jules II et de Leon X enfin celui de notre roi Louis XIV" (Dubos, *Réflexions*, II:134–35).

10. "ces brigands que le Nord a vomis, / Désolateurs de l'Europe éplorée, / Et des beaux arts farouches ennemis." Charles Palissot de Montenoy, *La Dunciade*, vol. 3 of *Œuvres* (Liège: Plomteux, 1777), 111.

11. "cahos [*sic*] d'ignorance profonde" (Palissot, *La Dunciade*, 115).

12. "âge de barbarie" (Palissot, *La Dunciade*, 116).

13. "siècles affreux" (Palissot, *La Dunciade*, 117).

14. "Sœur du Chaos, je regnais avant toi; / Je commandais la nature entiere, / Quand sur le Pinde on ignorait ta loi. / Longtems la nuit preceda la lumiere, / Et le destin te fit naître après moi" (Palissot, *La Dunciade*, 153). In this assertion she echoes the original *Dunciad* by Alexander Pope, in which the goddess of Dulness has similar origins: "In eldest time, e'er mortals writ or read, / E'er Pallas issued from the Thund'rer's head, / Dulness o'erall possessed her ancient right, / Daughter of Chaos and Eternal Night" (I, lines 6–10). Alexander Pope, *The Dunciad*, vol. 5 of *The Poems of Alexander Pope* (New Haven, Conn.: Yale University Press, 1963), 269. The idea of a primeval goddess of night (who is attended by fear, ignorance, etc.) probably has its origins in Hesiod's *Theogony*.

15. Rémy Saisselin, *Taste in Eighteenth-Century France* (Syracuse, N.Y.: Syracuse University Press, 1965), 76.

16. "Voltaire cherche les siens, les porteurs dans tous les temps et dans tous les lieux du flambeau de la raison, à savoir des principes et des valeurs de la modernité éclairée de son temps considérés comme universels." Diego Venturino, "Généalogies du Grand Siècle," in *Voltaire et le Grand Siècle,* Studies on Voltaire and the Eighteenth Century 2006:10, ed. Jean Dagen and Anne-Sophie Barrovecchio (Oxford: Voltaire Foundation, 2006), 3.

17. For overviews of this literary battle, see Marc Fumaroli's extensive introduction to the anthology *La Querelle des Anciens et des Modernes* (Paris: Gallimard, 2001) or DeJean, *Ancients against Moderns*.

18. Voltaire, "Ancients and Moderns," *A Philosophical Dictionary,* in

vol. 5 of *The Works of Voltaire: A Contemporary Version with Notes* (Paris: E. R. Dumont, 1901), 166. "La raison et le goût veulent, ce me semble, qu'on distingue dans un ancien comme dans un moderne le bon et le mauvais, qui sont très souvent à côté l'un de l'autre." Voltaire, "Anciens et Modernes," in *Dictionnaire philosophique*. vol. 17 of *Œuvres complètes* (Paris: Garnier, 1877–83), 234.

19. Even though the term *barbarian* comes from the Greek epithet for non-Greek-speaking peoples, eighteenth-century writers who use this term as an insult conflate it with the term for the "barbarians" who invaded Rome centuries later, including the Gothic tribe. J.G.A. Pocock distinguishes between the Greek use and the "neo-Latin" use of *barbarian* in vol. 4 of *Barbarism and Religion* (Cambridge: Cambridge University Press, 2005), 14.

20. "La maniere gotique n'est la manière d'un peuple particulier c'est la maniere de la naissance ou de la fin de l'art." Montesquieu, "De la maniere gothique," vol. 9 of *Œuvres complètes*, 91. Ursula Haskins Gonthier, in "Montesquieu's 'De la manière gothique,'" remarks upon the strangeness of Montesquieu's qualification of even Egyptian and early Roman art as *gothique*. Her essay is in *Medievalism and "manière gothique" in Enlightenment France*, Studies on Voltaire and the Eighteenth Century 2006:05, ed. Peter Damian-Grint (Oxford: Voltaire Foundation, 2006), 335–40. Gonthier argues that "Gothic art is seen in this treatise as the characteristic expression of the despotic state" (336) but that Montesquieu gives a more favorable impression of the government by the Gothic tribes in the *Esprit des lois*.

21. "une maniere qui ne reconnoît aucune regle, qui n'est dirigée par aucune étude de l'antique, & dans laquelle on n'apperçoit qu'un caprice qui n'a rien de noble; cette maniere barbare a infecté les beaux Arts, depuis 611 jusqu'en 1450, tems à jamais mémorable, où on commença à rechercher le beau dans la nature & dans les ouvrages des anciens." Jaucourt, "Gothique (manière)," *Encyclopédie*, VII:749.

22. Montesquieu, *Taste*, 266. "Un bâtiment d'ordre gothique est une espece d'enigme pour l'œil qui le voit, et l'âme est embarrassée, comme quand on lui présente un poëme obscur" (Montesquieu, *Goût*, 494).

23. "C'est par cette raison que les colifichets gothiques sont tombés dès que le goût est devenu meilleur; on a préféré une simplicité dans les parties, qui laissait voir d'abord les proportions qu'elles ont les unes avec les autres, à une infinité de petits ornemens & d'enjolivemens qui amusoient, qui détournoient l'attention du principal" (Crousaz, 29).

24. Montesquieu echoes Shaftesbury's remarks in *Characteristics of Men, Manners, Opinions, Times* (1711; Cambridge: Cambridge University Press, 1999) that Saint Augustine and "his sorry race" practiced an unacceptable style. Shaftesbury complains, "A saint-author of all men least values politeness" and is not guided by "the Standard of good Company." The Christian

author, he complains, merely concerns himself with his moral sins, when he really is a sinner against "grammar, good argument, and good sense" (75).

25. Montesquieu, *Taste*, 271–72. "quelques écrivains, qui dans chaque phrase mettent toûjours le commencement en contraste avec la fin par des antitheses continuelles, tels que S. Augustin et autres auteurs de la basse latinité, et quelques-uns de nos modernes, comme Saint-Evremont: le tour de phrase toûjours le même et toujoûrs uniforme déplaît extrèmement; ce contraste perpetuel devient symmétrie, et cette opposition toûjours recherchée devient uniformité" (Montesquieu, *Goût*, 497).

26. Example of antitheses: Voltaire disapproves of Houdar de La Motte's line "Que ne vaincra-t-il point, il s'est vaincu lui-même" in *Discours aux Welches*, in vol. 25 of *Œuvres complètes* (Paris: Garnier, 1879), 239.

In Saint Augustine's *Confessions* (Oxford: Oxford University Press, 1998), we find antitheses such as: "Our heart is restless until it rests in you" (book I, section i, p. 3), "you are wrathful and remain tranquil. You will a change without any change in your design. You recover what you find, yet have never lost . . . you are never avaricious, yet you require interest . . . you pay off debts, though owing no money to anyone; you cancel debts and incur no loss [etc.]" (I:4, p. 5).

27. Walter Ong discusses the origins of this distinction between the barbaric and the civilized in ancient Greek culture, and he points out that later European nations internalized this contempt for the non-Greeks, including parts of their own cultures. According to Ong, this mentality led Europeans "to give their cultures some kind of continuity with Greco-Roman culture, [and to] 'fix . . .' their histories (as in the legend deriving the British race from a Brutus supposed to be Aeneas' great-grandson) and even their political institutions (as in the case of the quasi-fictitious concept of the Holy Roman Empire)." See his "The Barbarian Within," in *The Barbarian Within and Other Fugitive Essays and Studies* (New York: Macmillan, 1962), 263.

28. Nicolas Boileau, *The Art of Poetry*, in *Selected Poems*, trans. Burton Raffel (New Haven, Conn.: Yale University Press, 2007), 45. "O le plaisant projet d'un poète ignorant, / Qui de tant de héros va choisir Childebrand! / D'un seul nom quelquefois le son dur et bizarre / Rend un poème entier ou burlesque ou barbare." Canto III of the *Art poétique* (Boileau, *Œuvres complètes*, 174).

29. Voltaire, *Discourse to the Welsh*, vol. 37 of *Works*, 89. "des Vandales, que vous avez appelés du nom sonore de Bourgonsions ou de Bourguignons, gens d'esprit d'ailleurs et fort propres, qui oigaient leurs cheveux avec du beurre fort." Voltaire, *Discours aux Welches*, vol. 25 of *Œuvres complètes* (Paris: Garnier, 1877–83), 230.

30. Voltaire, *Welsh*, 90. "ce fut alors que la contrée des Welches porta le nom mélodieux de Frankreich, ancien nom de la France" (Voltaire, *Welches*, 237).

31. Voltaire, *Welsh*, 99–100. "mots welches et tudesques" or "secs et barbares" (Voltaire, *Welches*, 237).

32. "peuples celtes, ou keltes, espèce de sauvages, dont on ne connaît que le nom." Voltaire, "Franc ou Franq; France, François, Français," *Dictionnaire philosophique*, vol. 19 of *Œuvres complètes* (Paris: Garnier, 1877–83), 184.

33. "un reste de l'ancien patois s'est encore conservé chez quelques rustres dans cette province de Galles, dans la basse Bretagne, dans quelques villages de France" (Voltaire, "Franc," 184).

34. "Il importe peu de connaître quelques restes de ces ruines barbares, quelques mots d'un jargon, qui ressemblait, dit l'empereur Julien, au hurlement des bêtes. Songeons à conserver dans sa pureté la belle langue qu'on parlait dans le grand siècle de Louis XIV" (Voltaire, "Franc," 187).

35. Voltaire, *Welsh*, 103–4. "Je suis bien loin de nier que Pascal, Bossuet, Fénelon, aient été très éloquents. C'est lorsque ces génies parurent que vous cessâtes d'être Welches, et que vous fûtes Français" (Voltaire, *Welches*, 240).

36. Voltaire, *Welsh*, 113. "un autre fléau . . . une secte de gens durs qui se disent solides, . . . d'hommes lettrés ennemis des lettres, qui veulent proscrire la belle antiquité et la fable" (Voltaire, *Welches*, 246).

37. Voltaire, *Welsh*, 113. "Gardez-vous bien de les croire ô Français! vous redeviendrez Welches" (Voltaire, *Welches*, 246).

38. "On ne voit rien de si pitoyable que les poésies de cinq ou six siècles . . . on ne voit que de misérables ouvrages, faits par des gens qui n'avoient que des idées prises de l'Ecriture sainte. (L'application unique de plusieurs moines à l'Ecriture a fait faire bien des mauvaises ouvrages profanes . . .) Mais, dès que l'on commença à lire les Anciens, que l'on eût perdu un siècle à les commenter et à les traduire, on vit paroître des auteurs." Montesquieu, *Pensées*, fragment #120, in Montesquieu, vol. 9 of *Œuvres complètes*, 123.

39. "Je crois que nous étions gâtés par les idées de l'Ecriture sainte qu'on vouloit toujours transporter dans les poésies." Montesquieu, *Pensées*, fragment #128, p. 126.

40. See J.G.A. Pocock's study of Edward Gibbon's *Decline and Fall of the Roman Empire*, entitled *Barbarism and Religion*.

41. Katherine Astbury, "Masculinity and Medievalism in the Tales of Baculard d'Arnaud" in *Medievalism and "manière gothique" in Enlightenment France*, Studies on Voltaire and the Eighteenth Century 2006:05, ed. ed. Peter Damian-Grint (Oxford: Voltaire Foundation, 2006), 50.

42. Studies of this serial collection of novels include Roger Poirier, *La Bibliothèque universelle des romans: Rédacteurs, textes, public* (Geneva: Droz, 1976) and Angus Martin, *La Bibliothèque universelle des romans, 1775–1789* (Oxford: Voltaire Foundation, 1985).

43. The *Bibliothèque bleue* was a collection of cheap and widely distrib-

uted publications printed on blue paper. See Lise Andries, "La *Bibliothèque bleue* et la redécouverte des romans de chevalerie au dix-huitième siècle," in *Medievalism and "manière gothique" in Enlightenment France*, 52–67, and Lise Andries and Geneviève Bollème, eds., *La Bibliothèque bleue* (Paris: Laffont, 2003).

44. Lionel Gossman, *Medievalism and the Ideologies of the Enlightenment: The World and Work of La Curne de Sainte-Palaye* (Baltimore: Johns Hopkins University Press, 1968), 257–58.

45. Aside from the popularity of novels, Gossman also points out the link between interest in chivalry and nostalgia for aristocratic privilege as a resistance to absolutism.

46. Dubos, *Critical Reflections*, I:117. "Les romans de chevalerie et de bergerie ont encore fomenté chez les françois le goût qui leur fait demander de l'amour par tout" (Dubos, *Réflexions*, I:131).

47. Dubos, *Critical Reflections*, I:141. "Ces pieces écrites depuis quarante-huit ans nous paroissent des poëmes gothiques composez cinq ou six generations avant nous" (Dubos, *Réflexions*, I:169).

48. Dubos, *Critical Reflections*, I:142. "Ces farces, dont le sujet éternel est le train de vie de gens de mauvaises mœurs et d'un certain étage, sont autant contre les regles que contre la bienséance" (Dubos, *Réflexions*, I:170).

49. Dubos, *Critical Reflections*, I:142. "Il n'est qu'un certain nombre de personnes qui aïent assez frequenté les originaux dont on expose des copies, pour juger si les caracteres et les évenemens sont traitez dans la vraisemblance. On se lasse de la mauvaise compagnie sur le théatre comme on s'en lasse dans le monde" (Dubos, *Réflexions*, I:170).

50. Voltaire, *Age*, 6. "Les arts, toujours transplantés de Grèce en Italie, se trouvaient dans un terrain favorable, où ils fructifiaient tout à coup. La France, l'Angleterre, l'Allemagne, l'Espagne voulurent à leur tour avoir de ces fruits; mais, ou ils ne vinrent point dans ces climats, ou bien ils dégénérèrent trop vite" (Voltaire, *Siècle*, 156).

51. Voltaire, *Age*, 7. "ni des Michel-Ange, ni des Palladio . . . quelques épigrammes et quelques contes libres composaient toute notre poésie" (Voltaire, *Siècle*, 156).

52. "Réduisant la Renaissance à un phénomène exclusivement italien, il a vu dans le 'Siècle de Louis-le-Grand' l'héritier direct du 'Siècle de Léon X' et des Médicis. Tous ses efforts ont tendu à rompre les liens entre notre XVIe et notre XVIIe siècles, pour isoler celui-ci de la tradition nationale, et l'inscrire dans la perspective des quatre grands siècles de l'Humanité. De même coup, il a précipité dans les ténèbres 'gothiques' la mémoire de notre Renaissance." Claude Faisant, *Mort et résurrection de la Pléiade* (Paris: Champion, 1998), 234–35.

53. "Descartes n'était pas né. La langue n'avait ni pureté ni correction. . . . Le théâtre français, devenu depuis le premier du monde, n'existait pas. Amyot en prose et Marot en poésie se distinguaient surtout par

un caractère de naïveté qui est encore senti aujourd'hui parmi nous; mais la noblesse et la régularité d'une diction soutenue, les convenances du style proportionnés au sujet, étaient des mérites ignorés." Jean-François de la Harpe, vol. 5 of *Lycée, ou Cours de littérature ancienne et moderne* (Paris: Chez Depelafol, 1825), 30. Of sixteen volumes, the first four are devoted to ancient Greek and Latin literature. Volume 5 begins with a forty-page overview of the Middle Ages and Renaissance, and then turns to Pascal and Racine. Volumes 5–14 discuss this part of the seventeenth century and the eighteenth century.

54. "langage bizarre et obscur," "au fond, il a, parmi beaucoup de fatras et d'ordures, des traits et même des morceaux pleins d'un verve satirique, originale et piquante" (La Harpe, V:31).

55. "Entre Euripide et Racine, il devait s'écouler de longs siècles de barbarie" (Marmontel, *Goût*, 54).

56. "Les erreurs de l'esprit, les écarts de l'imagination, les fictions absurdes, les compositions déréglées, n'ont pas été l'effet de l'ignorance, mais de la dépravation . . . . Les ébauches les plus grossières, les productions les plus informes de l'art naissant, lui ont paru merveilleuses. Les poésies de Ronsard, les tragédies de Jodelle ont été, dans leur temps, des chefs-d'œuvre inimitables. . . . L'art s'est persuadé que son mérite consistait dans des tours de force et d'adresse, dans de vaines subtilités, dans de puérils raffinements, dans une recherche pénible de sentiments outrés, d'expressions étranges, d'antithèses forcées, d'hyperboles extravagantes" (Marmontel, *Goût*, 45).

57. Dubos, *Critical Reflections*, II:124–25. "Est-ce parce que Ronsard et ses contemporains ne sçavoient pas les langues anciennes qu'ils ont fait des ouvrages dont le goût ressemble si peu au goût des bons ouvrages grecs et romains? Au contraire, le plus grand de leurs défauts est de les avoir imitez trop servilement ; c'est d'avoir voulu parler grec et latin avec des mots françois" (Dubos, *Réflexions*, II:169)."

58. D'Alembert and Diderot, "Preliminary Discourse," *Encyclopedia*. "au lieu d'enrichir la Langue Françoise, on commença par la défigurer. Ronsard en fit un jargon barbare, hérissé de Grec & de Latin: mais heureusement il la rendit assez méconnoissable, pour qu'elle en devînt ridicule" (d'Alembert and Diderot, "Discours préliminaire," I:xxi).

59. D'Alembert and Diderot, "Preliminary Discourse," *Encyclopedia*. "Bientôt l'on sentit qu'il falloit transporter dans notre Langue les beautés & non les mots des Langues anciennes. Réglée & perfectionnée par le goût, elle acquit assez promptement une infinité de tours & d'expressions heureuses" (d'Alembert and Diderot, "Discours préliminaire," I:xxi).

60. The verse appears in the first canto of Boileau's *Art poétique* (160).

61. D'Alembert and Diderot, "Preliminary Discourse," *Encyclopedia*. "Malherbe, nourri de la lecture des excellens Poëtes de l'antiquité, & prenant comme eux la Nature pour modele, répandit le premier dans notre Poësie une

harmonie & des beautés auparavant inconnues" (d'Alembert and Diderot, "Discours préliminaire," I:xxi –xxii).

62. "Ronsard gâta la langue en transportant dans la poésie française les composés grecs dont se servaient les philosophes et les médecins . . . Malherbe répara un peu le tort de Ronsard. La langue devint plus noble et plus harmonieuse par l'établissement de l'Académie française, et acquit enfin dans le siècle de Louis XIV la perfection où elle pouvait être portée dans tous les genres" (Voltaire, "Franc," 184).

63. Voltaire, *Age of Louis XIV*, 368–69. "Il aurait corrompu la langue française, si le style marotique, qu'il employa dans ses ouvrages sérieux, avait été imité. Mais heureusement ce mélange de la pureté de notre langue avec la difformité de celle qu'on parlait il y a deux cents ans, n'a été qu'une mode passagère" (Voltaire, chapter 32 of *Siècle de Louis XIV*, 552).

64. R. Anthony Lodge, in *French: From Dialect to Standard* (London: Routledge, 1993), describes this transition from the sixteenth to the seventeenth centuries: "The style of the Pléiade involved the use of a wide range of vocabulary items (including dialectalisms, italianisms, etc.), convoluted syntax (often influenced by Italian) and multilayered meanings." Malherbe, by contrast, represented "restricted vocabulary (shunning dialectalisms, archaisms, loan-words, etc.), a rigorously explicit syntax (*précision*) and unambiguous surface meanings (*clarté*)" (174).

65. "Mais qui la prenait au sérieux?" René Bray, *La Formation de la doctrine classique en France* (Paris: Nizet, 1945), 15.

66. Among other texts, see the article "Touraine" in the *Encyclopédie*, which reports a dubious anecdote that makes her seem as foolish as Molière's *précieuses ridicules*.

67. "Les Italiens & les Espagnols sont plus riches que nous en *diminutifs;* il semble que la langue françoise n'aime point à être riche en babioles & en colifichets, dit le P. Bouhours. On ne se sert plus aujourd'hui de ces mots qui ont la terminaison de *diminutifs*, comme *hommelet, rossignolet, montagnette, campagnette, tendrelet, doucelet, nymphelette, larmelette,* &c. . . .

Les Italiens & les Espagnols font encore d'autres *diminutifs* des premiers *diminutifs;* par exemple, de *bambino*, un petit enfant, ils ont fait *bambinello, bamboccio, bambocciolo,* &c. C'est ainsi qu'en latin de *homo* on a fait *homuncio,* & d'*homuncio, homunculus,* & encore *homulus.* Ces trois mots sont dans Cicéron. Le P. Bouhours dit que ce sont des pygmées qui multiplient, & qui font des enfans encore plus petits qu'eux" (Dumarsais, "Diminutif," *Encyclopédie*, IV:1010).

68. "n'ont rien négligé en leur tems pour introduire ces termes dans notre langue" (Dumarsais, "Diminutif," *Encyclopédie*, IV:1010).

69. "elle s'en déclare hautement la protectrice; cependant notre langue n'a point reçu ces *diminutifs;* ou si elle les reçut en ce tems-là, elle s'en défit aussi-tôt. Dès le tems de Montagne on s'éleva contre tous ces mots si mignons,

favoris de sa fille d'alliance: elle eut beau entreprendre leur défense & crier au meurtre de toute sa force, avec tout cela la pauvre demoiselle eut le déplaisir de voir ses chers *diminutifs* bannis peu-à-peu; & si elle vivoit encore, je crois, poursuit le P. Bouhours, qu'elle mourroit de chagrin de les voir exterminés entierement" (Dumarsais, "Diminutif," *Encyclopédie*, IV:1010).

70. Marc Fumaroli may show some unfounded optimism when he makes it seem that there is a smooth continuity from Montaigne to seventeenth-century literature and when he assumes Montaigne's prose received a uniformly positive reception. See "Le Génie de la langue française," in vol. 3, part 2 of *Les Lieux de mémoire*, ed. Pierre Nora (Paris: NRF Gallimard, 1992), 679–743.

71. Michel Delon's *L'Idée d'énergie au tournant des Lumières (1770–1820)* (Paris: Presses Universitaires de France, 1988) explores the double-sided nature of the concept of energy. On the one hand, it carried positive connotations in regard to artistic creation, but it also implied a disregard for decorum and even clarity, particularly for critics such as La Harpe (150).

72. "Le *français* acquit de la vigueur sous la plume de Montaigne; mais il n'eut point encore d'élévation et d'harmonie" (Voltaire, "Franc," 184).

73. "Montaigne était sans doute un esprit d'une trempe fort supérieure. . . . Avouons d'abord les défauts: c'est par là qu'il faut commencer avec les gens qu'on aime. . . . Sa diction est incorrecte, même pour le temps, quoiqu'il ait donné à la langue des expressions et des tournures qu'elle a gardées comme de vieilles richesses; il abuse de la liberté de converser, et perd de vue le point de la question établie" (La Harpe, V:31–32).

74. "son livre n'est presque plus un livre françois," Maturin Dréano, *La Renommée de Montaigne en France au XVIIIe siècle* (Angers: Editions de l'Ouest, 1952), 117. Montaigne's *Essays* were put on the Vatican's Index and banned in France from 1669. Pierre Coste edited a complete edition of the *Essays*, in the original French, which was published in London in 1724, and this edition can be found reprinted multiple times during the eighteenth century.

75. "L'abbé Trublet se reprenait aussitôt à discuter sur la langue de Montaigne. 'Celle-ci est ce qu'on appelle communément du Gaulois. Or mettre du Gaulois en François, c'est à la lettre traduire. Les mots gaulois ont été jadis françois, mais aujourd'hui, ils ne le sont pas plus que des mots italiens ou espagnols, si on en excepte la terminaison qui est toujours françoise'" (Dréano, 124–25).

76. Sarah Benharrech, "Lecteur, que vous êtes bigearre!: Marivaux et la 'querelle de Montaigne,'" *MLN* 120.4 (2005): 925–49.

77. "Si Montaigne avait vécu de nos jours, que de critiques n'eût-on pas fait de son style! Car il ne parlait ni français, ni allemand, ni breton, ni suisse. Il pensait, il s'exprimait au gré d'une âme singulière et fine." Pierre Carlet de Marivaux, *Le Cabinet du philosophe* (1734), in *Journaux et Œuvres diverses*

(Paris: Garnier, 1969), 388, http://artfl.uchicago.edu/cgi-bin/philologic/navigate.pl?newfrantext1.578.

78. Voltaire, *The Age of Louis XIV* (London: Dent; New York: Dutton, 1935), 357. "La saine philosophie ne fit pas en France d'aussi grands progrès qu'en Angleterre et à Florence . . . . Toutes les grandes inventions et les grandes vérités vinrent d'ailleurs. Mais dans l'éloquence, dans la poésie, dans la littérature, dans les livres de morale et d'agrément, les Français furent les législateurs de l'Europe. Il n'y avait plus de goût en Italie. La véritable éloquence était partout ignorée" (Voltaire, *Louis XIV*, 539). This passage is found in chapter 32, "Des Beaux arts," which is omitted from the edition of the *Age of Louis XIV* of the *Works of Voltaire: A Contemporary Version with Notes* (Paris: E. R. Dumont, 1901).

79. "Concluons que le siècle du génie fut aussi le siècle du *goût*; ajoutons, et d'un *goût* plus délicat, plus fin, plus éclairé que celui de Rome et d'Athènes" (Marmontel, *Goût*, 60).

80. "On conçoit bien pourtant qu'il y eut d'abord, dans ce concours d'écrivains et de connaisseurs, une infinité de prétentions manquées et de fausses lueurs d'esprit, de talent et de *goût*. Chaque société eut ses prédilections, chaque bel esprit eut son cercle, chaque talent ses ennemis. . . . Les tribunaux les plus célèbres étaient souvent les plus injustes. Ici, Pradon avait des mécènes, et Racine des détracteurs; là, Chapelain était admiré en récitant des vers de *La Pucelle*; ailleurs, c'étaient les Scudéry qu'on exaltait, en déprimant Corneille; Boursault avait des partisans qui le préféraient à Molière. Tout semblait confondu" (Marmontel, *Goût*, 59–60).

81. "C'était dans ce moment de fermentation et de trouble que l'esprit public s'épurait, comme le vin en jetant son écume. Tout ce que demande l'opinion pour se rectifier, tout ce que demande le *goût* pour se polir, c'est du mouvement . . . les partialités cessent, les préventions se dissipent, l'opinion se fixe à la fin; et regardez au fond du creuset, la vérité y reste pure comme l'or" (Marmontel, *Goût*, 60).

82. "Ce n'est donc pas ce flux et reflux de sentiments contraires, de jugements épars, d'opinions hétérogènes, qui décident du *goût* de tout un siècle; c'est leur résultat, c'est l'ensemble et la somme de l'opinion publique. Tout le monde avait eu ces torts; le public seul enfin se trouva juste" (Marmontel, *Goût*, 60).

83. "Dieu dit: Que la lumière se fasse; et la lumière se fit" (Boileau, 340).

84. In this passage Voltaire echoes Fénelon's words in *Lettre à l'Académie*, where the latter also complains: "Pour faire un bon vers, on l'accompagne d'un autre vers foible, qui le gâte. Par exemple je suis charmé quand je lis ces mots: *qu'il mourût*. Mais je ne puis souffrir le vers que la rime amène aussitôt: *ou qu'un beau désespoir alors le secourût*" (Fénelon, 635).

85. "Qu'il mourût / Ou qu'un beau désespoir alors le secourût," "Voilà ce fameux *qu'il mourût*, ce trait du plus grand sublime, ce mot auquel il n'en

est aucun de comparable dans toute l'antiquité. Tout l'auditoire fut si transporté qu'on n'entendit jamais le vers faible qui suit." Voltaire, *Commentaires
sur Corneille*, vol. 54 of *Complete Works* (Banbury: Voltaire Foundation,
1975), 272.

86. Tzvetan Todorov, *Theories of the Symbol* (Oxford: Blackwell, 1982),
122. "*Qu'il mourût* n'est pas beau en ce qu'il imite mais par la place qu'il
occupe dans un ensemble de relations." Tzvetan Todorov, *Théories du symbole* (Paris: Seuil, 1977), 153.

87. Voltaire, "Ancients and Moderns," 167. "ce vers tel qu'on n'en trouve
pas un seul ni dans Homère, ni dans Sophocle, ni dans Euripide qui en ap-
proche" (Voltaire, "Anciens et Modernes," 234).

88. The authors who mention the competition between Racine and Pradon, with Racine winning out, include Boileau, Houdar de la Motte, Dubos,
the marquis d'Argens, Le Sage, Marmontel, Jean-Jacques Rousseau, and La
Harpe. In Palissot's *Dunciade*, the Goddess of Stupidity supports Pradon.

89. Voltaire, *Preface to Mariamne*, in vol. 19 of *The Works of Voltaire:
A Contemporary Version with Notes*, 236. "il arriva que les deux *Phèdres*
semblèrent d'abord avoir une égale destinée; mais l'impression régla bientôt
le rang de l'une et de l'autre: Pradon selon la coutume des mauvais auteurs,
eut beau faire une préface insolente dans laquelle il traitait ses critiques de
malhonnêtes gens: Sa pièce tant vantée par sa cabale et par lui, tomba dans
le mépris qu'elle mérite" Voltaire, *Mariamne*, vol. 2 of *Œuvres complètes*
(Paris: Garnier, 1877–83), 165.

90. Dubos, *Critical Reflections*, II:299. "La Phedre de Pradon, que le public méprise tant aujourd' hui, et pour dire encore plus, qu'il a si parfaitement
oubliée" (Dubos, *Réflexions*, II:410).

91. Voltaire, *Preface to Mariamne*, 236. "sans la *Phèdre* de monsieur Racine, on ignorerait aujourd'hui que Pradon en a composé une" (Voltaire, *Mariamne*, 165).

92. Dubos, *Critical Reflections*, II:301. "Quant à la Phedre de Pradon,
on se souvient encore qu'une cabale composée de plusieurs autres, dans lesquelles entroient des personnes également considerables par leur esprit et par
le rang qu' elles tenoient dans le monde, avoit conspiré pour élever la Phedre
de Pradon et pour humilier celle de Racine" (Dubos, *Réflexions*, II:413).

93. "contre ceux qui envoyaient leurs laquais applaudir à la *Phèdre* de
Pradon, et qui louaient les loges à la *Phèdre* de Racine pour les laisser vides,
et pour faire accroire qu'elle était tombée." Voltaire, *Les Honnêtetés littéraires*, in *Œuvres de 1767*, vol. 63B of the *Complete Works* (Oxford: Voltaire
Foundation, 2008), 73.

94. Dacier begins her treatise *Des Causes de la corruption du goust* with
an attack on Desmarets de Saint-Sorlin, author of *Clovis ou la France chres-
tienne* of 1654: "Il y a cinquante ans que l'Auteur des Visionnaires [Desma-
rets], homme qui ne manquoit pas d'esprit ni même de savoir, mais sans goût,

& dont l'imagination déréglée lui faisoit produire une infinité de mauvaises choses, & tres peu de passables, s'éleva contre ce grand Poëte [Homère], voici comment. Plein de bonne opinion de sa capacité & de son génie, il se croyoit fort au dessus de tout ce que l'antiquité a eu de plus grand; & pour le prouver il donna son poëme de *Clovis*. Ce Poëme fut reçu comme il meritoit." Anne Dacier, *Des Causes de la corruption du goust* (Amsterdam: Pierre Humbert, 1715), 4.

95. Voltaire, *The Maid of Orleans*, vol. 41 of *Works*, 161. "la louche énigme," "les absurdes mensonges." Voltaire, *La Pucelle d'Orléans*, in vol. 7 of *Complete Works* (Geneva: Voltaire Foundation, 1970), 520. The poem was first published with Voltaire's approval in 1762.

96. Voltaire, *Maid*, 161. "aux Scudéri, le Moine, Desmarets" (Voltaire, *Pucelle*, 520).

97. This note by Voltaire does not appear in the English translation. "[Georges de] Scudéri, auteur d'*Alaric*, poème épique. Le Moine, auteur de *Saint Louis*, ou louisiade, poème épique. Desmarets de Saint-Sorlin, auteur de *Clovis*, poème épique; ces trois ouvrages sont de terribles poèmes épiques" (Voltaire, *Pucelle*, 520).

98. Voltaire, *Maid*, 160–61. "Amas confus de moderne et d'antique . . . / damnable édifice [qui] / Fut fabriqué par un tel artifice / Que tout mortel qui dans ces lieux viendra / Perdra l'esprit tant qu'il y restera" (Voltaire, *Pucelle*, 520–21).

99. Jean-Claude Bonnet, "Le Débat sur le 'Grand Siècle' à l'Académie au début du XIXe siècle," in *Un Siècle de deux cents ans? Les XVIIe et XVIIIe siècles: Continuités et discontinuités*, ed. Jean Dagen and Philippe Roger (Paris: Desjonquères, 2004), 108–18.

100. "A un effort inouï, succèderait une fatale léthargie. Il était donc entendu que le XVIIIe siècle serait la fatigue ou le repos du génie" (Bonnet, 112–13).

101. Marc-André Bernier, "Les Lumières au prisme de la décadence des lettres et du goût," in *Les Songes de Clio: Fiction et histoire sous l'Ancien Régime*, ed. Sabrina Vervacke, Éric Van der Schueren, and Thierry Belleguic (Québec: Presses de l'Université Laval, 2006), 201–13.

102. "bien loin de proposer de l'histoire un tableau exaltant, voire exalté, des progrès succésifs des lumières et du bon goût," "sous la figure de la *décadence*" (Bernier, 203).

103. For example, Voltaire praises improvements in the standard of living in his poem *Le Mondain*, and he contrasts scientific advances with the decadence in statesmanship in the dialogue *Les Anciens et les modernes, ou la toilette de madame de Pompadour*.

104. "grossièreté" and "rusticité" (Dacier, 14).

105. "nous avons croupi encore plus long-temps dans notre barbarie, parce que nous n'avons pas pris soin de connoître ces parfaits modeles que

les Latins & Grecs nous avoient laissez; & que nous n'avons pas plûtôt commencé à les étudier, qu'on a vû cette grossiereté s'éclipser peu à peu, & la politesse & la propreté de ces Originaux chasser enfin la rusticité & le poison de nos Ouvrages . . . c'est imitation seule qui a introduit le bon goût parmi nous" (Dacier, 14–15).

106. "Nous avons vû d'une maniere convainquante que c'est l'étude des Grecs & des Latins qui nous a tirez de la grossiereté où nous étions; & nous allons voir que c'est l'ignorance & le mépris de cette même étude qui nous y replonge. En effet, on n'a pas eû plûtôt négligé ces excellents Originaux . . . qu'on a vû des flots de méchants Ouvrages inonder Paris & tout le Royaume" (Dacier, 14–16).

107. Montesquieu, "De la maniere gothique," 91.

108. "la décadence des lettres après un règne florissant": "On dirait que chaque climat n'ait pu donner qu'une seule moisson, et que, le sol épuisé une fois par sa propre fécondité, il ait fallu des siècles de repos pour le renouveler et le rendre fertile" (Marmontel, *Goût*, 69).

109. "ce que l'art a de plus heureux, de ce que la nature a de plus beau" (La Harpe, I:8).

110. "[ils] se jettent en foule dans toutes les innovations bizarres et monstrueuses que le mauvais goût peut inspirer, et que le caprice et la nouveauté font quelquefois réussir. Alors, l'art, les artistes et les juges sont également corrompus; c'est l'époque de la decadence" (La Harpe, I:8).

111. Domna Stanton, "The Fiction of *Préciosité* and the Fear of Women," *Yale French Studies* 62 (1981): 107–34.

4. ON FOREIGN TASTE

1. In reference to Spain, see Bray, 28–33. Bray claims that Italy enjoyed a prestigious reputation among French writers of the seventeenth century, but he refers almost exclusively to scholars such as Vida, Scaliger, and Castelvetro (Bray, 34–48). If one looks at texts by seventeenth-century writers such as Bouhours and Bellegarde, however, one sees that they also denounce poets such as Marino and protest against the frivolity and *mollesse* of Italian literary language. In *Entretiens d'Ariste et Eugène*, Bouhours attacks Italy and Spain but puts Hebrew on par with French and does not mention Arabic at all. The latter were targets more often for the eighteenth century.

2. Sadek Neaimi, in *L'Islam au siècle des Lumières* (Paris: L'Harmattan, 2003), tells us that since the Middle Ages only a few Christian scholars had taken an interest in the Orient, mostly in order to refute Islam, but popular interest in a pleasingly "exotic" Orient only began in the mid-seventeenth century, exemplified by Racine's *Bajazet* (23).

3. The Jesuits' *Lettres édifiantes et curieuses* were published serially from 1706 to 1776.

4. Jean Chardin, *Journal du voyage du chevalier Chardin en Perse et aux Indes Orientales* (London, 1686); Jean-Baptiste Tavernier, *Les Six voyages de Jean-Baptiste Tavernier . . . qu'il a fait en Turquie, en Perse et aux Indes* (Paris, 1677).

5. For more about the sources of Dubos's connection between climate and national character, see Alfred Lombard, *L'Abbé Du Bos, un initiateur de la pensée moderne* (1913; Geneva: Slatkine Reprints, 1969), 243–47. According to Lombard, the earliest treatises of climate theory can be found in Hippocrates' *Airs Waters Places*; these ideas were developed by Jean Bodin in the sixteenth century in his *République* and his *Méthode*, and they were further elaborated by seventeenth-century authors such as Jean Chardin (*Voyage . . . en Perse*) and Fontenelle (*Réflexions sur la poétique*). Dubos himself cites as sources Juan Huarte (*Examen de ingenios/Examen des esprits*) and John Barclay (*Icon animorum/Tableaux des esprits*).

6. Dubos, *Critical Reflections*, II:177. "Comme deux graines venuës sur la même plante donnent un fruit dont les qualitez sont differentes, quand ces graines sont semées en des terroirs differens, ou bien quand elles sont semées dans le même terroir en des années differentes: ainsi deux enfans qui seront nez avec leurs cerveaux composez précisément de la même maniere, deviendront deux hommes differens pour l'esprit et pour les inclinations, si l'un de ces enfans est élevé en Suede et l'autre en Andalousie" (Dubos, *Réflexions*, II:238).

7. Dubos, *Critical Reflections*, II:110. "tout le monde sçait qu'il n'est sorti des extrémitez du nord que des poëtes sauvages, des versificateurs grossiers et de froids coloristes. La peinture et la poësie ne se sont point approchées du pole plus près que la hauteur de la Hollande" (Dubos, *Réflexions*, II:148).

8. Dubos, *Réflexions*, II:15.

9. Dubos, *Critical Reflections*, II:111. "au-delà du cinquante-deuxième degré de latitude Boréale, ni plus près de la ligne que le vingt-cinquième degré" (Dubos, *Réflexions*, II:150).

10. Dubos, *Critical Reflections*, II:109. "où les arts et les lettres ne fleurissent pas" (Dubos, *Réflexions*, II:147).

11. Dubos, *Critical Reflections*, II:8. "dépendance réciproque" (Dubos, *Réflexions*, II:10–11).

12. Dubos refers to France and Italy both as centers of good taste; this conflation parallels his argument in his historical work *Réflexions critiques de l'établissement de la monarchie française dans les Gaules* (1734), in which he seeks to blur the lines between Gauls, Romans, and Franks. He shows the Romans as culturally superior and the Gauls adhering willingly to the Romans through the language and institutions.

13. Dubos, *Critical Reflections*, II:115. "On remarque que les hommes nez en Europe et sur les côtes voisines de l'Europe, ont toujours été plus propres que les autres peuples aux arts, aux sciences et au gouvernement po-

litique. Par tout où les europeans, ont porté leurs armes, ils ont assujetti les naturels du païs" (Dubos, *Réflexions*, II:156).

14. Dubos, *Critical Reflections*, II:116–17. "S'il se rencontre quelque sphinx d'une beauté merveilleuse, on peut croire qu'il soit l'ouvrage de quelque sculpteur grec qui se sera diverti à faire des figures égyptiennes, comme nos peintres se divertissent quelquefois à imiter dans leurs ouvrages, les figures des bas-reliefs et des tableaux des Indes et de la Chine. Nous-mêmes n'avons-nous pas eu des ouvriers qui se sont divertis à faire des sphinx? On en compte plusieurs dans les jardins de Versailles, qui sont des originaux de nos sculpteurs modernes" (Dubos, *Réflexions*, II:57–58).

15. Dubos, *Critical Reflections*, II:119. "comme le génie manquoit à ces peuples [of Latin America], ils étoient malgré leur dexterité, des artisans grossiers. Ils n'avoient ni les regles du dessein les plus simples, ni les premiers principes de la composition, de la perspective et du clair-obscur. . . . Dans la suite ils ont vû des meilleurs tableaux d'Italie, dont les espagnols ont transporté un grand nombre dans le nouveau monde. Ces maîtres leur ont encore enseigné comme il falloit se servir des pinceaux et des couleurs, mais sans pouvoir en faire des peintres intelligens" (Dubos, *Réflexions*, II:161).

16. Dubos, *Critical Reflections*, II:119. "la vivacité des couleurs brillantes" (Dubos, *Réflexions*, II:162).

17. Dubos, *Critical Reflections*, II:293. "A force de voir des tableaux durant la jeunesse, l'idée, l'image d'une douzaine d'excellens tableaux se grave et s'imprime profondément dans notre cerveau encore tendre. Or, ces tableaux qui nous sont toujours présens, et dont le rang est certain, dont le mérite est décidé, servent, s'il est permis de parler ainsi, de pieces de comparaison, qui donnent le möien de juger sainement à quel point l'ouvrage nouveau qu'on expose sous nos yeux" (Dubos, *Réflexions*, II:402).

18. Dubos, *Critical Reflections*, II:296. "Comme nous avons vû en France plus de poëtes excellens que de grands peintres, le goût naturel pour la poësie a eu plus d'occasions de s'y cultiver" (Dubos, *Réflexions*, II:406).

19. "Combien de beautés arbitraires n'ont-elles pas été inventées . . . ! On porte, en Europe, des pendans d'oreilles; on y joint, dans le Mogol, des pendans de nez. En France, on se poudre les cheveux, et on les frise pour les mettre en boucles; en Canada on se les graisse pour les laisser pendre sur les épaules. Dans le Nouveau Monde, on voit des peuples entiers qui se peignent le visage de vert, de bleu, de rouge, de jaune, de mille couleurs étrangères" (André, 34).

20. "Que leur a-t-on demandé dans tous les temps, depuis la naissance des lettres jusqu'à nos jours? que leur a-t-on demandé dans toutes les nations, depuis les extrémités de l'orient, qui a vu naître l'éloquence, jusqu'à celles de l'Occident, qui l'a vu portée à sa perfection? et aujourd'hui, qu'est-ce que toute la terre leur demande comme par le cri général de la raison? La vérité, l'ordre, l'honnête et le décent, voilà, Messieurs (je ne crains pas d'en être ja-

mais démenti par le bon goût), voilà le beau essentiel que nous cherchons tout naturellement dans un ouvrage d'esprit" (André, 82).

21. "Cette société s'étend: ce n'est plus un cercle, c'est une ville, un pays, tout un peuple; et par une longue cohabitude le *goût* y devient uniforme" (Marmontel, *Goût*, 36).

22. "C'est alors qu'il commence à prendre une sorte d'autorité, et si la nation est réellement plus éclairée, plus cultivée que ses voisines, si elle est plus fertile en objets d'agrément, elle aura quelque droit de servir de modèle dans l'art de plaire et de jouir" (Marmontel, *Goût*, 36).

23. "mais encore chaque nation peut-elle prétendre, de son côté, savoir aussi ce qui lui est convenable . . . son *goût* ne sera pas le *goût* de ses voisins, mais ce sera le bon *goût* pour elle . . . il ne sera point prouvé pour elle que le *goût* dominant soit meilleur que le sien" (Marmontel, *Goût*, 36).

24. "Ainsi les convenances qui intéressent le *goût* ne sont pas toutes accidentelles et factices; il en est d'immuables, il en est d'éternelles comme les essences des choses . . . pour les convenances essentielles et immuables, il doit y avoir un *goût* indépendant, comme elles, de toute espèce de convention; la nature les a établies, la nature les fait sentir" (Marmontel, *Goût*, 36–37).

25. "qu'*il ne faut pas disputer des goûts*" (André, 66). André refers to the famous Latin proverb "de gustibus non est disputandum."

26. Jean-Jacques Rousseau, *Essay on the Origin of Languages and Writings Related to Music* (Hanover, N.H.: University Press of New England, 1998), 294. "appel[er] les choses de leur vrai nom." Jean-Jacques Rousseau, *Essai sur l'origine des langues*, in vol. 5 of *Œuvres complètes* (Paris: NRF Gallimard, 1995), 381. The text was first published posthumously in 1781.

27. Marmontel gives several examples, such as "un esprit lumineux" or describing a man's enraged state by saying "il rugit." Marmontel, vol. 1 of *Poétique françoise* (Paris: Lesclapart, 1763), 170.

28. "C'est un artifice de la poésie, de peindre une idée avec des couleurs étrangères à son objet, afin de rendre cet objet sensible s'il ne l'est pas assez" (Marmontel, *Poétique*, I:163).

29. French peasants are sometimes included among the savages who use metaphors: "Quiconque voudra faire attention au peuple dans son langage, il le verra presque toujours porté à parler *figurément*. Ces expressions, *une maison triste, une campagne riante, le froid d'un discours, le feu de ses yeux,* sont dans la bouche de ceux qui courent le moins après les métaphores, & qui ne savent pas même ce que c'est qu'une métaphore" (Jaucourt, "Figure," *Encyclopédie*, VI:766).

30. "Les premiers hommes étant simples, grossiers & plongés dans les sens, ne pouvoient exprimer leur conception des idées abstraites, & les opérations réfléchies de l'entendement, qu'à l'aide des images sensibles, qui, au

moyen de cette applications, devenoient métaphore" (Jaucourt, "Figure," *Encyclopédie*, VI:766).

31. Rousseau, *Languages*, 294. "Le langage figuré fur le prémier à naitre, le sens propre fut trouvé le dernier. On n'appella les choses de leur vrai nom que quand on les vit sous leur véritable forme. D'abord on ne parla qu'en poësie; on ne s'avisa de raisonner que longtems après" (Rousseau, *Langues*, 381).

32. As Edward Saïd remarks in *Orientalism* (New York: Vintage Books, 1994), it is typical for European countries to fail to make a distinction between the foreign cultures of the present day and of the distant past.

33. Diderot remarks in the *Lettre sur les sourds et muets*, "Si l'on examine l'hébreu avec attention, on prendra nécessairement des dispositions à le reconnaître pour le langage des premiers habitants de la terre," without giving further proof of this conviction (Diderot, *Sourds*, 40).

34. "On a longtems attribué les figures du style oriental au climat; mais on a trouvé des images aussi hardies dans les poësies des islandois, dans celles des anciens écossois, et dans les harangues des sauvages du Canada, que dans les écrits des persans et des arabes. Moins les peuples sont civilisés, plus leur langage est figuré, sensible" (Marmontel, *Goût*, 168).

35. "l'hebreu . . . est la moins abondante de toutes les langues orientales; de-là vient que la langue hébraïque exprime des choses différentes par le même mot, ou une même chose par plusieurs synonymes" (Jaucourt, "Figure," *Encyclopédie*, VI:765).

36. Rousseau, *Languages*, 296n. "On dit que l'Arabe a plus de mille mots différens pour dire un *chameau*, plus de cent pour dire *glaive*" (Rousseau, *Langues*, 382n).

37. "[L'hébreu] est une langue pauvre de mots & riche de sens; sa richesse a été à la suite de sa pauvreté, parce qu'il a fallu nécessairement charger une même expression de diverses valeurs, pour suppléer à la disette des mots & des signes . . . il y a peu d'expressions où l'on n'ait besoin de quelque réflexion, pour juger s'il faut la prendre au sens naturel ou au sens figuré" ("Hébraïque," *Encyclopédie*, VIII:88).

38. "Le pléonasme se doit visiblement aux bornes étroites d'un langage simple. . . . Lorsque les expressions ne répondent pas entièrement aux idées de celui qui parle, comme il arrive souvent en se servant d'une langue qui est pauvre, il cherche nécessairement à s'expliquer en repétant sa pensée en d'autres termes, à peu près comme celui dont le corps est gêné dans un endroit, cherche continuellement une place qui le satisfasse" (Jaucourt, "Figure," *Encyclopédie*, VI:765–66).

39. "L'entendement humain a trois facultés bien distinctes: la raison, le sentiment et l'imagination. La vérité toute nue suffit à la raison. . . . Mais l'éloquence et la poësie ont le sentiment à émouvoir et l'imagination à frapper" (Marmontel, *Goût*, 165–66).

40. "l'imagination est beaucoup moins sévère, moins rebelle à la persuasion et bien plus facile à séduire" (Marmontel, *Goût,* 166–67).

41. "l'imagination influe sur tout l'ame, qu'elle en est la faculté dominante et tyrannique, et . . . elle a sur la raison même un empire que celle-ci désavoue, mais dont elle ne peut s'affranchir. . . . Faut-il donc s'étonner si les hommes intéressés à se persuader, à s'émouvoir mutuellement, ont tâché de revêtir leurs idées d'une enveloppe matérielle que l'imagination pût saisir? Faut-il s'étonner si l'éloquence et la poésie, ce deux arts qui aspirent à dominer tous les esprits, ont eu recours à l'illusion des images?" (Marmontel, *Goût,* 167–68).

42. "Les *figures* devinrent l'ornement du discours, quand les hommes eurent acquis des connaissances assez étendues des Arts & des Sciences, pour en tirer des images qui, sans nuire à la clarté, étoient aussi riantes, aussi nobles, aussi sublimes que la matiere le demandoit" (Jaucourt, "Figure," *Encyclopédie,* VI:766).

43. "Une langue telle que la françoise, par exemple, qui fuit les figures & les allusions, qui ne souffre rien que de naturel, qui ne trouve de beauté que dans le simple, n'est que le langage de l'homme réduit à la raison. La *langue hébraïque* au contraire est la vraie langue de la Poésie, de la prophétie, & de la révélation; un feu céleste l'anime & la transporte: quelle ardeur dans ses cantiques! quelles sublimes images dans les visions d'Isaïe! que de pathétique & de touchant dans les larmes de Jérémie!" ("Hébraïque," *Encyclopédie,* VII:88–89).

44. In *Entretiens d'Ariste et Eugène,* Bouhours's interlocutors also list the qualities that do not fit their ideal of the French language. "Ceux qui n'appellent jamais les choses par leur nom, et qui ne parlent que par metaphore, ne parlent pas trop bien françois. Ils sont aussi éloignez du caractere de nôtre langue, repliqua Eugene, que les masques, qui courent les ruës pendant le carnaval avec des habillemens bizarres, sont éloignez de nos modes" (53–54).

45. "Il y a des Nations si heureusement situées, & que le Soleil regarde si favorablement, qu'elles ont été capables d'imaginer & d'inventer d'elles-mêmes, & d'arriver à la perfection; [les Nations de l'Orient] ont beaucoup plus de vivacité, d'imagination & de fleurs d'esprit, comme on le voit encore aujourd'hui par les Peuples de la Grece" (Dacier, 12).

46. "il y en a d'autres [nations] qui ensevelies dans un air plus épais, n'ont jamais pû, que par le secours de l'imitation, se tirer de la grossiereté & de la barbarie où leur naissance les a plongées" (Dacier, 12).

47. In the introduction to Quintilian's *The Orator's Education,* the editor, Donald Russell, comments on the Attic/Asian distinction: "Few topics in this area have been more discussed than this, ever since Wilamowitz's article in <u>Hermes</u> 1900, 1–52 (reprinted in Stark (1968) 350–401), which remains a classic statement of the problems. The most important ancient texts are:

Cicero, *Brutus* 51, 325; *Orator* 27, 212, 230–231; Dionysus of Halicarnassus, *Ancient orators*, preface (LCL 1.4–14); Tacitus, *Dialogues* 18." Quintilian, *The Orator's Education*, ed. and trans. Donald A. Russell (Cambridge, Mass.: Harvard University Press, 2001), 189–90.

48. Since Quintilian indicates that the areas he refers to are the cities conquered by the Greeks, the terms *Asianic* or *Asiatic* must refer not to present-day Asia but to ancient Persia, or the area covering present-day Turkey and Iran.

49. "Les métaphores sont défectueuses, 1. Quand elles sont tirées de sujets bas. Le P. De Colonia reproche à Tertulien d'avoir dit que *le déluge universel fut la lessive de la nature.* 2. Quand elles sont forcées, prises de loin et que le raport n'est point assez naturel ni la comparaison assez sensible . . . 3. Il faut aussi avoir égard aux convenances des diférens styles, il y a des métaphores qui conviènent au style poëtique, qui seroient déplacées dans le style oratoire" (Dumarsais, 170–72).

50. One exception: the fables of the Indian writer Bidpaï (or Pilpay), to whom Jean de La Fontaine and Voltaire allude in their works, were available since the seventeenth century. The stories of Bidpaï, along with those of the Ethiopian Luqman (or Lokman), also appeared in 1724, translated by the same Antoine Galland who introduced the *1001 Nights* to the French public.

51. Authors such as the Mexican mystic Sor Juana Inés de la Cruz and the Peruvian-Spanish nobleman Garcilasso de la Vega "the Inca" achieved some fame in Europe, but they followed the norms of Spanish writing. Garcilasso's history of the Incas was translated into French in 1633 and notably served as a source for Françoise de Graffigny's novel *Lettres d'une Péruvienne.*

52. One work of this thirteenth-century poet, *Gulistan, ou L'empire des roses,* was translated into French as early as 1634 by André Du Ryer, and it continued to be published in France throughout the seventeenth and eighteenth centuries. Du Ryer, who was a French diplomat in Turkey and in Egypt, also translated the Koran into French in 1647.

53. Dubos, *Critical Reflections,* II:118. "L' Europe n'est que trop remplie aujourd'hui d'étoffes, de porcelaine, et des autres curiositez de la Chine et de l'Asie orientale. Rien n'est moins pittoresque que le goût de dessein et de coloris qui regne dans ces ouvrages. On a traduit plusieurs compositions poëtiques des orientaux. Quand on y trouve un trait mis en sa place, ou bien une avanture vraisemblable, on l'admire. C'est en dire assez. Aussi toutes ces traductions, qui ne se réimpriment gueres n'ont qu'une vogue passagere qu'elles doivent à l'air étranger de l'original, et à l'amour inconsideré que bien des gens ont pour les choses singulieres" (Dubos, *Réflexions,* II:159–60).

54. Dubos, *Critical Reflections,* II:371. "celui qui ne sçait pas la langue dans laquelle un poëte a écrit, ne doit pas être reçu à disputer contre ceux qui entendent ce poëte, concernant son mérite et l'impression qu'il fait" (Dubos, *Réflexions,* II:513–14).

55. Montesquieu, *Persian Letters* (Oxford: Oxford University Press, 2008), 3. "Je ne fais donc que l'office de Traducteur: toute ma peine a été de mettre l'Ouvrage à nos mœurs: J'ai soulagé le Lecteur du langage Asiatique autant que je l'ai pû; & l'ai sauvé d'une infinité d'expressions sublimes, qui l'auroient ennuyé jusques dans les nües. . . . J'ai retranché les longs com-plimens, dont les Orientaux ne sont pas moins prodigues que nous; & j'ai passé un nombre infini de ces minuties, qui ont tant de peine à soutenir le grand jour." Montesquieu, *Lettres persanes*, in vol. 1 of *Œuvres complètes* (Oxford and Naples: Voltaire Foundation and Istituto italiano per gli studi filosofici, 2004), 138. Montesquieu's alleged model for his *Lettres persanes* was the novel *L'Espion dans les cours des princes chrétiens* (also known as *L'Espion turc*) by the Italian Jean-Paul Marana, which first appeared in France in 1684. Marana's narrator also claims to have merely translated the papers of the Turkish spy and also remarks unfavorably on the supposedly typical Oriental style: "On trouvera au reste plusieurs tours d'expression qui ont quelque chose de guindé, & qui ne sont pas fort du genie de notre Langue. On auroit pu les changer si on avoit voulu; mais quoiqu'on n'ait pas regardé ces endroits comme des beautez, on a jugé néanmoins qu'ils étoient nécessaires pour la bienséance. On traduit un *Arabe* & un *Mahometan*. Il est de la bienséance de le faire parler comme tel; & il seroit ridicule de le faire parler par-tout comme un Académicien moderne." Jean-Paul Mara-na, vol. 2 of *L'Espion turc dans les cours des princes chrétiens* (London, 1742), v.

56. The translator of this English edition chooses the expression "bored to tears."

57. In the critical edition of *Lettres persanes*, which I cite here, letters XV–XVIII are the equivalent of letters XVI–XVII in other editions.

58. Montesquieu, *Persian Letters*, 22–23. "Tu es bien plus fait pour le sé-jour des étoiles. Tu te caches sans doute de peur d'obscurcir le Soleil. Tu n'as point de taches comme cet Astre; mais, comme lui, tu te couvres de nuages. Ta science est un abîme plus profond que l'Océan; ton esprit est plus perçant que Zufagar, cette épée de Hali qui avait deux pointes; tu sais ce qui se passe dans les neuf chœurs des Puissances célestes; tu lis l'Alcoran sur la poitrine de notre divin Prophète; et, lorsque tu trouves quelque passage obscur, un Ange, par son ordre, déploie ses ailes rapides et descend du Trône pour t'en révéler le secret." Letter XV from Usbek to Mollak Méhémet-Hali (Montesquieu, *Lettres persanes*, 173–74).

59. For example, Voltaire claims in his *Essai sur les mœurs*, in support of the idea that Arabs and Hebrews have no taste in poetry, "Nous savons assez que le bon goût n'a jamais été connu dans l'Orient ... Otez aux Arabes, aux Persans, aux Juifs, le soleil et la lune, les montagnes et les vallées, les dragons et les basilics, il ne leur reste presque plus de poésie" (I:252).

60. Montesquieu, *Persian Letters*, 24. "le zénith de votre esprit ne va pas

au nadir de celui du moindre des immaums." Letter XVII (XVIII in other editions) (Montesquieu, *Lettres persanes*, 177).

61. Montesquieu, *Taste*, 271–72. "Le tour de phrase, toujours le même et toujours uniforme, déplaît extrêmement; ce contraste perpétuel devient symétrie, et cette opposition toujours recherchée devient uniformité" (Montesquieu, *Goût*, 497).

62. Montesquieu, *Persian Letters*, 51. "heureuses les mamelles qui l'allaiteront." Letter XXXIX (XXXVII in other editions), from Hagi Ibbi au juif Ben Josué, Prosélyte Mahométan (Montesquieu, *Lettres persanes*, 235).

63. "ma mère bénira le ventre qui m'a porté & les mamelles qui m'ont allaité!" Friedrich Melchior Grimm, *Le Petit prophète de Boehmischbroda* (1753; La Haye, 1774), 5.

64. Grimm and his fellow *philosophes* Jean-Jacques Rousseau and Denis Diderot supported Italian opera, which put more emphasis on melody and on humble, comic material, such as Pergolese's *La Serva padrona*. Fans of French opera preferred music with more emphasis on harmony and on elevated subject matter, as exemplified by Rameau and Lully.

65. "cris épouvantables," "gargarisme" (Grimm, 15–16).

66. Many German words must have grated on French ears, if we agree with Marmontel's description of *douceur* and *rudesse* in the French language. In his *Poétique française*, he states that the most "doux" of languages would ideally contain only one consonant and one vowel per syllable. By contrast, words with several consonant sounds that are difficult for the tongue to form in sequence can be considered "rude" or harsh: "car dans une syllabe composée de plusieurs consonnes qui semblent se presser autour d'une voyelle, *sphinx, trop, grecs, Cecrops,* la réunion précipitée de toutes ces articulations en un tems syllabique rend l'action de l'organe pénible et confuse" (Marmontel, *Poétique*, I:212).

67. "Et j'étois dans mon grenier que j'appelle ma chambre, & il faisoit froid, & je n'avois point de feu dans mon poële, car le bois étoit cher. / Et j'étois envelopé dans mon manteau qui autrefois étoit bleu & qui est devenu blanc, attendu qu'il est usé" (Grimm, 3–4).

68. Let us glance briefly, for example, at Isaiah 1:6–8, noting the disconcerting presence of words such as *ointment* and *cucumbers*: "From the sole of the foot even unto the head there is no soundness in it; but wounds, and bruises, and putrefying sores: they have not been closed, neither bound up, neither mollified with ointment. Your country is desolate, your cities are burned with fire: your land, strangers devour it in your presence, and it is desolate, as overthrown by strangers. And the daughter of Zion is left as a cottage in a vineyard, as a lodge in a garden of cucumbers, as a besieged city."

69. "Et une main me saisit par le toupet, & je me sentis transporté dans les airs, & je fus en chemin depuis le Jeudi jusqu'au Vendredi, & j'étois en-

veloppé dans mon manteau qui autrefois étoit bleu, & qui est devenu blanc, attendu qu'il étoit usé" (Grimm, 8).

70. Mireille Herr, in *Les Tragédies bibliques au XVIIIe siècle* (Paris: Champion and Geneva: Slatkine, 1988), states that literary critics had as-' sumed that the biblical tragedy was an unpopular genre in the eighteenth century, but she proves the opposite with support from library inventories and other sources.

71. See introduction to *Saül*, in Voltaire, vol. 56A of *Complete Works* (Oxford: Voltaire Foundation, 2001), 365.

72. Mireille Herr calls Voltaire's *Saül* a farce and "une suite de tableaux comiques ou grotesques" (149).

73. The unities of time and action had been outlined by Aristotle in his *Poetics*, but the unity of space was established in seventeenth-century France.

74. "On n'a pas observé dans cette espèce de tragi-comédie l'unité d'action, de lieu et de temps. On a cru avec l'illustre la Motte devoir se soustraire à ces règles. Tout se passe dans l'intervalle de deux ou trois générations pour rendre l'action plus tragique par le nombre des morts selon l'esprit juif, tandis que parmi nous l'unité de temps ne peut s'étendre qu'à vingt-quatre heures, et l'unité de lieu dans l'enceinte d'un palais" (Voltaire, *Saül*, 465–66).

75. Russell Goulbourne cites this passage to prove that one of Voltaire's principal targets was the *drame bourgeois*. *Voltaire Comic Dramatist*, Studies on Voltaire and the Eighteenth Century 2006:03 (Oxford: Voltaire Foundation, 2006), 241.

76. "Oui, tu es gras, et ton holocauste en sera plus agréable au Seigneur." Act I, scene 3 (Voltaire, *Saül*, 477).

77. In a climax of horror and absurd dark humor, Samuel commands "qu'on brûle les restes de cet infidèle, et que ses chairs servent à nourrir nos serviteurs," further emphasizing the link between the high (tragedy, humanity) and the low (smoked meats).

78. "AGAG: Doux et puissant vainqueur, modèle des princes, qui savez vaincre et pardonner . . . j'aimerai en vous l'image du Dieu qui punit et pardonne.
SAÜL: Illustre prince, que le malheur rend encore plus grand, je n'ai fait que mon devoir en sauvant vos jours." Act I, scene 2 (Voltaire, *Saül*, 471–72).

79. "DAVID: . . . il me fallut apporter à votre père deux cents prépuces de Philistins pour présent des noces: deux cents prépuces ne se trouvent pas si aisément, je fus obligé de tuer deux cents hommes pour venir à bout de cette entreprise; et je n'avais pas la mâchoire d'âne de Samson." Act II, scene 2 (Voltaire, *Saül*, 481–82).

80. "Je veux vous faire des chansons gaillardes . . .
Chers Hébreux par le ciel envoyés
Dans le sang vous baignerez vos pieds;
Et vos chiens s'engraisseront
De ce sang qu'ils lécheront.

Ayez soin, mes chers amis,
De prendre tous les petits
Encore à la mamelle,
Vous écraserez leur cervelle
Contre le mur de l'infidèle;
Et vos chiens s'engraisseront
De ce sang qu'ils lécheront."

Act IV, scene 5 (Voltaire, *Saül*, 523–24).

81. The editors of this critical edition of *Saül*, Henri Lagrave and Marie-Hélène Cotoni, cite as sources for this song: Psalms 67 and 136, as well as 1 Kings 21:23–24, 1 Kings 22:35–38, and 2 Kings 9:33–36.

82. "Finissez donc vos airs de corps de garde; cela est abominable: il n'y a point de sauvage qui voulût chanter de telles horreurs: les bouchers des peuples de Gog et Magog en auraient honte." Act IV, scene 5 (Voltaire, *Saül*, 523–24).

83. Admittedly, it is difficult to prove definitively that these sounds struck Voltaire as ugly; we can only draw this conclusion from his descriptions of supposedly nonmelodious French words that he lists in the article "Franc." Among the words he lists as derived from Celtic, he includes many that end with the –g sound: *bègue, dogue, gogue, morgue, nargue.*

To eliminate such alleged barbarity and to make the French language more beautiful, he calls for a reform of language in the same article: "si on assemblait une société d'hommes qui eussent l'esprit et l'oreilles justes, et s'il s'agissait de réformer la langue, qui fut si barbare jusqu'à la naissance de l'Académie, on adoucirait la rudesse de plusieurs expressions, on donnerait de l'embonpoint à la sécheresse de quelques autres, et de l'harmonie à des sons rebutants. *Oncle, ongle, radoub, perdre, borgne,* plusieurs mots terminés durement, auraient pu être adoucis."

84. William Hanley, in "The Censure of Voltaire's Biblical Verse," *Australian Journal of French Studies* 21.1 (1984), remarks, "Why did he write the *Précis*? Initially, the suggestion that he adapt and translate Biblical verses came from the Duc de La Vallière, transmitting with insistence the wish of Mme de Pompadour in 1756. [letters D6760, D6844] The King's mistress wished to be seen as having undergone a religious conversion, and Voltaire was asked to contribute to that impression by providing French versions of the Psalms . . . , which the Duc promised to have published at the Imprimerie royale. Though he chose not to do the Psalms, according to the Comte d'Argental the *Précis de l'Ecclésiaste* was written for Mme de Pompadour" (27).

85. The Song of Solomon is known as the *Cantique des cantiques* ("Canticle of canticles") in French.

86. "On a rassemblé les principaux traits de ce poëme pour en faire un petit ouvrage régulier qui en conservât tout l'esprit. Les répétitions et le désordre, qui étaient peut-être un mérite dans le style oriental, n'en sont point

un dans le nôtre." Voltaire, *Précis du Cantique des cantiques*, in vol. 9 of *Œuvres complètes* (Paris: Garnier, 1877), 496.

87. "Je dors, mais mon coeur veille," "Il est difficile d'exprimer comment à la fois on dort et on veille. C'est une figure asiatique qui exprime un songe" (Voltaire, *Cantique*, 503).

88. "mes mamelles sont meilleures que le vin" (Voltaire, *Cantique*, 501).

89. "convenable" (Voltaire, *Cantique*, 501).

90. "Les hébraïsants disent que le terme qui répond à mamelle est d'une beauté énergique en hébreu. Ce mot n'a pas en français la même grâce; tétons est trop peu grave, sein est trop vague" (Voltaire, *Cantique*, 501).

91. "Les lis, les boutons de rose / De tes deux globes naissants / Sont à mon âme enflammée / Comme les vins bienfaisants / De la fertile Idumée" (Voltaire, *Cantique*, 501).

92. Voltaire, "Solomon," *Philosophical Dictionary*, vol. 13 of *Works*, 247. "J'avoue que les églogues de Virgile sont d'un autre style; mais chacun a le sien, et un Juif n'est pas obligé d'écrire comme Virgile." Voltaire, "Salomon," *Dictionnaire philosophique*, vol. 36 of *Complete Works* (Oxford: Voltaire Foundation, 1994), 512.

93. Voltaire, "Solomon," 247–48. "C'est une églogue juive. Le style est comme celui de tous les ouvrages d'éloquence des Hébreux, sans liaison, sans suite, plein de répétitions, confus, ridiculement métaphorique; mais il y a des endroits qui respirent la naïveté et l'amour" (Voltaire, "Salomon," 512).

94. See David Porter, "Monstrous Beauty: Eighteenth-Century Fashion and the Aesthetics of the Chinese Taste," *Eighteenth-Century Studies* 35.3 (Spring 2002): 395–411.

95. He gives the narrator the name of Sadi, the Persian poet I mentioned above, whom Voltaire admired.

96. Voltaire, *Candide and Other Stories* (Oxford: Oxford University Press, 1990), 124. "Ouloug aimait mieux la lecture de *Zadig*; mais les sultanes aimaient mieux les Mille et un. Comment pouvez-vous préférer, leur disait le sage Ouloug, des contes qui sont sans raison, et qui ne signifient rien? C'est précisément pour cela que nous les aimons, répondaient les sultanes. Je me flatte que vous ne leur ressemblerez pas, et que vous serez un vrai Ouloug." Voltaire, *Zadig*, in *Œuvres complètes*, vol. 30B (Oxford: Voltaire Foundation, 2004), 115.

97. This series of contrasting pairs appears most prominently in the *Essai sur les mœurs et l'esprit des nations*.

98. For example, Voltaire remarks: "Parmi les déclamations incohérentes dont ce livre [le Koran] est rempli, selon le goût oriental, on ne laisse pas de trouver des morceaux qui peuvent paraître sublimes. Mahomet, par exemple, parlant de la cessation du déluge, s'exprime ainsi: 'Dieu dit: Terre, engloutis tes eaux; cieux, puise les ondes que tu as versées: le ciel et la terre obéirent.'

Sa définition de Dieu est d'un genre plus véritablement sublime" (Voltaire, *Essai sur les mœurs*, I:271).

5. THE OBSCURE, OR ENIGMAS AND THE ENIGMATIC

1. "Le génie de cette langue est la clarté et l'ordre: car chaque langue a son génie" (Voltaire, "Français," *Encyclopédie*, VII:286).

2. "gens de goût" (Voltaire, "Français," *Encyclopédie*, VII:287).

3. "articles du *Credo* national" (Fumaroli, "Génie," 967).

4. Delphine Denis has recently explored various kinds of obscurity in the literature of early modern France: see Delphine Denis, ed., *L'Obscurité: Langage et herméneutique sous l'Ancien Régime* (Louvain: Academia Bruylant, 2007).

5. François Colletet and Gayot de Pitaval also produced compilations of *énigmes*.

6. Aristotle, *The "Art" of Rhetoric*, trans. John Henry Freese (Cambridge, Mass.: Harvard University Press, 1994), vol. 22 of the *Works of Aristotle*, book III, chapter 2, Bekker page 1404b.

7. However, low words, even if they are accurate, must also be avoided for the sake of decency. Aristotle had stated the necessity of selecting the most beautiful words to include in metaphors, for example, preferring "'rosy-fingered morn' [rather than] 'purple-fingered,' or, what is still worse, 'red-fingered'" (1405b). Quintilian, too, cautions us to stay away from "words that are obscene, disgusting, or low" (8.2.1).

8. This was a technique early moderns used not by mistake but for comic effect—for example, the writers of enigmas and Boileau in *Le Lutrin*.

9. Quintilian uses the word *abusio* and adds the Greek term *katachresis* (8.2.6). The term *abusio* does not always have negative connotations; Quintilian defines it as a word that "lends the nearest name to things that have no name" (8.6.34) and the translator adds, in parentheses, "'misuse.'"

10. Wendy Ayres-Bennett, in *Vaugelas and the Development of the French Language* (London: MHRA, 1987), states that Quintilian was one of Vaugelas's greatest influences.

11. Claude Favre de Vaugelas, *Remarques sur la langue françoise, utiles à ceux qui veulent bien parler et bien escrire* (Paris: Camusat, 1747), 567.

12. The *Dictionaire critique de la langue française* by Jean-François Féraud (Marseille: J. Moss, 1787) comments on *pache*: "On l'a dit aûtrefois pour *pacte*, et le peuple le dit encôre en certaines Provinces."

13. A brief overview of clarity in sixteenth- and seventeenth-century France is provided by Normand Doiron in "Le Style obscur: L'Enigme I," *Littératures classiques* 28 (Autumn 1996): 211–37.

14. "Au figuré, c'est l'effet du choix & de l'emploi des termes, de l'ordre selon lequel on les a disposés, & de tout ce qui rend facile & nette à l'enten-

dement de celui qui écoute ou qui lit, l'appréhension du sens ou de la pensée de celui qui parle ou qui écrit" (Diderot, "Clarté," *Encyclopédie*, III:505).

15. Jaucourt, "Style," *Encyclopedia*. "Il faut, dit Quintilien, non seulement qu'on puisse nous entendre, mais qu'on ne puisse pas ne pas nous entendre" (Jaucourt, "Style," *Encyclopédie*, XV:553).

16. Aristotle, *On the Art of Poetry*, chapter 22, in Aristotle, Horace, Longinus, *Classical Literary Criticism* (London: Penguin, 1965), 63 (1458a).

17. "On s'est contenté de retrancher ou de changer des mots qui sont si vieillis et si hors d'usage qu'outre qu'ils ne faisoient aucune beauté, ils n'auroient pas plus été entendus de bien des gens que si c'étoient des termes grecs ou latins, ce qui n'auroit sans doute fait aucun plaisir. Tels sont: destourbier, vastité, admonester, estriver, etc." (Artaud, cited by Dréano, 22).

18. "c'est là principalement ce qui le rend obscur. Il est plein de négligences, de barbarismes, d'équivoques, de constructions louches" (Trublet, cited by Dréano, 117–18).

19. "En fait d'amour, le coeur d'un favori des Muses / Est un astre vers qui l'entendement humain / Dresserait d'ici-bas son télescope en vain: / Sa sphère est au-dessus de toute intelligence" (Piron, 1059).

20. "Monsieur, à ma portée ajustez-vous un peu, / Et, de grâce, en français, mettez-moi cet hébreu" (Piron, 1059).

21. "Notre Seigneur veut faire de tous les hommes des vases d'élection; il ne tient qu'à vous d'être vases. . . . Si vous n'avez pas la contrition, vous avez l'attrition; si l'attrition vous manque, vous avez vos propres forces et les miennes." Voltaire, "Galimatias dramatique," in vol. 24 of *Œuvres complètes* (Paris: Garnier, 1879), 75.

22. "Ne croyez que les luthériens: prononcez seulement ces mots, *in, cum, sub*, et buvez du meilleur" (Voltaire, "Galimatias dramatique," 76).

23. "nous avons lu dans Nostradamus ces propres paroles: *Nelle chi li po ra te ic sus res fait en bi.*" Voltaire, *Pot-pourri*, in *Romans et contes* (Paris: Garnier, 1960), 415.

24. Montesquieu, *Taste*, 266. "Un bâtiment d'ordre gothique est une espèce d'énigme pour l'œil qui le voit, & l'ame est embarrassée, comme quand on lui présente un poëme obscur" (Montesquieu, *Goût*, 494).

25. Parts of this section were published as an article. Jennifer Tsien, "Between Cleverness and Folly: The Enigmas of the *Mercure galant*," *Cahiers du dix-septième* 11.1 (2006): 193–218.

26. Created by Francesco Berni (1498–1535). For more information, see, for example, Richard A. Mazzara, "Saint-Amant and the Italian Bernesque Poets," *French Review* 32.3 (January 1959): 231–41.

27. A caricature of Cotin appears under the name of "Trissotin" in Molière's *Précieuses ridicules*. Among primary sources, one can look at the enigmas printed each month in the journal *Le Mercure galant*, later named *Le Mercure de France*. Earlier versions of the enigmas, which were practiced

in salons, appear in a collection by Florence Vuilleumier-Laurens: Charles Cotin, *Les Enigmes de ce temps* (Paris: Société des Textes Français Modernes, 2003). A more general study of word games can be found in Laure Hesbois, *Les Jeux de langage* (Ottawa: Éditions de l'Université d'Ottawa, 1986).

28. As the years pass, the list becomes longer and the names become more and more bizarre when readers create enigmatic pseudonyms. Examples of names listed in the *Mercure* (May 1690) as those who have submitted the correct answer include: les Prisonniers du Fort-l'Evêque, la Jolie Solitaire de la rue saint Honoré, la Brebis Amoureuse et son Pasteur Mouton bellant, le Captif délivré de la Barbarie, and Innocence reconnue de la rue Maçon.

29. Je suis un composé de douceur & de charmes,
Les Dieux pour me former s'interessent pour moy,
Neptune par sa mer m'offre je ne sçay quoi,
Cybelle par son sein, l'Aurore par ses larmes.

Minerve par ses fruits fournit une liqueur;
Vertumne par ses dons se met de la partie;
Bacchus par ses raisins y mesle un peu d'aigreur,
Et de tout leur mélange on me voit assortie.

Fait-on quelque Regal, quelque noble festin,
On m'invite aussi-tost pour venir à la table;
Je n'y bois, ny ne mange, & vois plus d'une main
Qui s'arme contre moy; suis-je pas miserable?
        Le Mercure galant (March 1689): 297–98.

30. "On ne veut pas que l'on confonde l'Embleme avec l'Enigme; la confusion deplaît, elle est en même tems l'effet et la source de l'Erreur; l'Enigme a pour but d'exercer; l'Embleme va tout droit à plaire, & à faire un plaisir ingénieux & aisé" (Crousaz, 28).

31. An alternate title to the play is *La Comédie sans titre*, which Boursault took on after the editor of the *Mercure* protested. Edmé Boursault, *La Comédie sans titre, ou Le Mercure galant*, vol. 3 of *Théâtre des auteurs du second ordre* (Paris: Belin, 1813), 95.

32. Boursault, 95.

33. "Je ne dois pas finir cet Avertissement sans m'efforcer de défendre l'Enigme du mépris de plusieurs personnes qui la regardent en pitié du haut de leur esprit." François Gayot de Pitaval, *Recueil des énigmes les plus curieuses de ce temps* (Paris: Legras, 1717), xii.

34. Claude-Prosper Jolyot de Crébillon, vol. 1 of *The Skimmer: or, The History of Tanzai and Neadarne* (London: F. Galicke, 1735), 203. "C'étoit le plus beau danseur du monde, personne ne faisoit la révérence de meilleure grace: il devinoit toutes les énigmes, jouoit bien tous les jeux." Claude-Prosper Jolyot de Crébillon, *L'Ecumoire*, in vol. 2 of *Œuvres* (1734; London [Frankfurt]: Varrentrap, 1779), 161, http://artfl.uchicago.edu/cgi-bin/philologic/navigate.pl?newfrantext.574.

35. Jean-Baptiste de Boyer d'Argens, vol. 1 of *The Jewish Spy: Being a*

*philosophical, historical and critical correspondence, by letters which lately
pass'd between certain Jews in Turkey, Italy, France, &c.* (Dublin: Nelson
and Saunders, 1753), 58. "Tel homme . . . seroit au desespoir qu'on ne le crût
pas en état de deviner les énigmes du *Mercure galant*, et de composer un madrigal." Jean-Baptiste de Boyer, marquis d'Argens, vol. 1 of *Lettres juives, ou
Correspondance philosophique, historique et critique entre un juif voïageur
en différens Etats de l'Europe et ses correspondans en divers endroits* (La
Haye: P. Paupie, 1738), 83.

36. "L'*énigme* parmi les modernes, est un petit ouvrage ordinairement en
vers, où sans nommer une chose, on la décrit par ses causes, ses effets & ses
propriétés, mais sous des termes & des idées équivoques pour exciter l'esprit
à la découvrir. Je ne m'arrêterai pas à rapporter les autres regles qu'on pres-
crit dans ce jeu littéraire, parce que mon dessein est bien moins d'engager les
gens de Lettres à y donner leurs veilles, qu'à les détourner de semblables pué-
rilités" (Jaucourt, "Enigme," *Encyclopédie*, V:690).

37. "Mais quelque décoration qu'on ait donnée aux *énigmes*, elles ne seront presque jamais que de folles dépenses d'esprit, des jeux de mots, des
écarts dans le langage & dans les idées.

Les gens de lettres un peu distingués du siecle passé, qui ont eu la foiblesse
de donner dans cette mode, & de se laisser entraîner au torrent, seroient bien
honteux aujourd'hui de lire leurs noms dans la liste de toutes sortes de gens
oisifs, & de voir qu'un tems a été qu'ils se faisoient un honneur de deviner
des *énigmes*; & plus encore d'annoncer à la France, qu'ils avoient eu assez
d'esprit pour exprimer, sous un certain verbiage, sous un jargon mystérieux
& des termes équivoques, une flûte, une fleche, un éventail, une horloge"
(Jaucourt, "Enigme," *Encyclopédie*, V:690).

38. "des génies d'un ordre supérieur" (Jaucourt, "Enigme," *Encyclopédie*, V:691).

39. These two devises are taken from Gilles Corrozet, *Hecatomgraphie*
(Paris: Denis Janot, 1540).

40. The prime example of the riddle without an answer appears in Lewis Carroll's *Alice in Wonderland* when the dormouse asks Alice during the
Mad Hatter's tea party: "Why is a raven like a writing-desk?" The dormouse
never provides the answer, to the chagrin of Alice and of many readers.

41. Voltaire, *Zadig*, 192–93. "Quelle est de toutes les choses du monde la
plus longue et la plus courte, la plus prompte et la plus lente, la plus divisible
et la plus étendue, la plus négligée et la plus regrettée, sans qui rien ne se peut
faire, qui dévore tout ce qui est petit, et qui vivifie tout ce qui est grand?"
(Voltaire, *Zadig*, 223).

42. On the principle of "plaire et instruire" and on the resistance against
it, see Bray, 64–69. On the ideal of pleasing without instructing, see Denis,
La Muse galante, 243.

43. In the past few decades, researchers such as Alain Viala and Delphine

Denis have made efforts to restore the status of *galanterie*, in spite of its reputation as frivolous. In his article "'Qui t'a fait *minor?*' Galanterie et Classicisme," *Littératures Classiques* 31 (1997), Viala argues that the gallant aesthetic, represented by the paintings of Watteau or the style of Fontenelle and the
Mercure galant, has not been treated fairly by scholars: "l'histoire et la critique
littéraires admettent aujourd'hui que parmi les courants de sensibilité, de civi-
lité et d'esthétique du XVIIe, le courant galant a eu un rôle important; mais il a
été longtemps laissé dans l'obscurité, mais il est encore tenu pour mineur face
à l'esthétique classique" (116). See also Denis, *La Muse galante*; and Viala, *La
France galante: Essai historique sur une catégorie culturelle, de ses origines
jusqu'à la Révolution* (Paris: Presses Universitaires de France, 2008).

44. Janet Letts, "Responsive Readers of the *Mercure Galant,* 1680–
1710," *Cahiers du dix-septieme* 5.2 (Fall 1991): 211–28.

45. Saint Augustine, *De Doctrina christiana* (Oxford: Clarendon Press,
1995), III:26.

46. Ibid., II:24.

47. Ibid., II:34–35.

48. Ibid., II:45–46.

49. Ibid., II:10.

50. Ibid., II:11–12. In this passage, Augustine is paraphrasing Cicero's
Orator, where the latter speculates about why metaphorical speech is more
enjoyable than plain speech. *On the Ideal Orator,* trans. James M. May and
Jakob Wisse (Oxford: Oxford University Press, 2001), III:159–60.

51. Päivi Mehtonen, *Obscure Language, Unclear Literature: Theory and
Practice from Quintilian to the Enlightenment,* trans. Robert MacGilleon
(Helsinki: Finnish Academy of Science and Letters, 2003), 73.

52. "Tous deux marquent la douloureuse et radicale impuissance des mots
à exprimer la plénitude poétique, regardée comme une hypostase de la plénitude divine" (Doiron, 229).

53. Blaise Pascal, *Pensees: The Provincial Letters,* trans. W. F. Trotter
(New York: The Modern Library, 1941), 138. "Il y a assez de lumière pour
ceux qui ne désirent que de voir, et assez d'obscurité pour ceux qui ont une
disposition contraire" (Pascal, *Pensées,* fragment #274, p. 268).

54. Pascal, 136. "Tout ce qui est incompréhensible ne laisse pas d'être"
(Pascal, *Pensées,* fragment #262, p. 265).

55. Mehtonen, 104.

56. Fumaroli, "Génie," 923.

57. Mehtonen, 165.

58. Ibid., 160.

59. The passage that Mehtonen refers to can be found in Pierre Gassendi,
Petri Gassendi Opera Omnia in sex tomos divisa (Lyon: Laurent Anisson
and Jean-Baptiste Devenet, 1658; Stuttgart-Bad Canstatt: Friedrich Frohm-
ann, 1964), 1.13b–17a.

60. Jean-François Champollion was the first to successfully decipher hieroglyphics in the 1820s. See Madeleine V. David, *Le Débat sur les écritures et l'hiéroglyphe aux XVIIe et XVIIIe siècles* (Paris: SEVPEN, 1965).

61. Sophia Rosenfeld, *A Revolution in Language: The Problem of Signs in Late Eighteenth-Century France* (Stanford, Calif.: Stanford University Press, 2001), 29.

62. The name *hieroglyphics*, with the Greek prefix *hier-* denoting sacredness, had its source in a misunderstanding by ancient Greeks, beginning with Diodorus.

63. "la vérité toute nue suffit à la raison: le style philosophique n'a besoin à la rigueur que d'être simple, clair et précis" (Marmontel, *Poétique*, I:165).

64. "Les lettres sont devenues l'*écriture* commune, & les hiéroglyphiques devinrent une *écriture* secrete & mystérieuse. En effet, une *écriture* qui en représentant les sons de la voix peut exprimer toutes les pensées & les objets que nous avons coûtume de désigner par ces sons, parut si simple & si féconde qu'elle fit une fortune rapide. Elle se répandit par-tout; elle devint l'*écriture* courante, & fit négliger la symbolique, dont on perdit peu-à-peu l'usage dans la société, de maniere qu'on en oublia la signification" (Jaucourt, "Ecriture," *Encyclopédie*, V:359).

65. It is true that this work was not published during Rousseau's lifetime, but Jaucourt and Rousseau belonged to the same intellectual milieu, so we can assume that the text circulated in manuscript form or that they discussed these ideas together, along with other contributors to the *Encyclopédie*, such as Marmontel.

66. Rousseau, *Languages*, 297. "Plus l'ecriture est grossiere, plus la langue est antique. La premiere maniere d'écrire n'est pas de peindre les sons, mais les objets mêmes, soit directement, comme faisoient les Mexicains, soit par des figures allégoriques, comme firent autrefois les Egyptiens. Cet etat répond à la langue passionnée, & suppose déjà quelque société & des besoins que les passions ont fait naître. La seconde maniere est de représenter les mots & les propositions par des caracteres conventionnels, ce qui peut le faire que quand la langue est tout-à-fait formée & qu'un peuple entier est uni par des loix communes; car il y a déjà ici double convention: telle est l'ecriture Chinois; c'est-là véritablement peindre les sons & parler aux yeux. La troisieme est de décomposer la voix parlante à un certain nombre de parties élémentaires, soit vocales, soit articulées, avec lesquelles on puisse former tous les mots & toutes les syllabes imaginables. Cette maniere d'écrire, qui est la notre, a du être imaginée par des peuples commerçans qui voyageant en plusieurs pays & ayant à parler plusieurs langues, furent forcés d'inventer des caracteres qui pussent être communs à toutes. Ce n'est pas précisément peindre la parole, c'est l'analyser" (Rousseau, *Langues*, 384).

67. Rousseau, *Languages*, 297. "La peinture des objets convient aux

peuples sauvages; les signes des mots et des propositions, aux peuples barbares, et l'alphabet, aux peuples policés" (Rousseau, *Langues*, 385).

68. Jacques Derrida was concerned with the implications of Rousseau's
teleological vision of European phonetic languages succeeding other systems.
See Jacques Derrida, *De la grammatologie* (Paris: Minuit, 1967), particularly
the critique of Rousseau in the chapter "La Violence de la lettre," 157–89.
Derrida questions the assumption that writing (presumably phonetic) made
scientific progress possible, an idea that could have been taken directly from
Jaucourt or Marmontel when they rejected "Oriental" languages as irrational, sensual, and unfit for philosophical treatises.

69. See Etienne Bonnot de Condillac, *Essai sur l'origine des connaissances
humaines* (Amsterdam: P. Mortier, 1746), notably part 2, section 1, chapter
14, entitled "De l'origine de la fable, de la parabole et de l'énigme." See also
the articles "Ecriture" and "Hiéroglyphe" by Jaucourt in the *Encyclopédie*.

70. Rosenfeld, 38.

71. "En effet, ils employerent leurs *hiéroglyphes* à dévoiler nuement leurs
loix, leurs réglemens, leurs usages, leur histoire, en un mot tout ce qui avoit
du rapport aux matieres civiles" (Jaucourt, "Hiéroglyphe," *Encyclopédie*,
VIII:205).

72. "Aussi quand on eut inventé l'art de l'écriture, l'usage des *hiéroglyphes*
se perdit dans la société, au point que le public en oublia la signification. Cependant les prêtres en cultiverent précieusement la connoissance, parce que
toute la science des Egyptiens se trouvoit confiée à cette sorte d'écriture . . .
& les prêtres virent avec plaisir, qu'insensiblement ils resteroient seuls dépo-
sitaires d'une écriture qui conservoit les secrets de la religion" (Jaucourt,
"Hiéroglyphes," VIII:206).

73. "Enfin, quand les caracteres *hiéroglyphiques* furent devenus sacrés, les
gens superstitieux les firent graver sur des pierres précieuses, & les porterent
en façon d'amuletes & de charmes" (Jaucourt, "Hiéroglyphes," VIII:206).

74. Strictly in regard to Christian mysteries, Ménestrier follows the church
doctrine that Mehtonen had explained, that obscurity was not in God but
in our minds: "C'est la Religion, qui a consacré les Enigmes par l'obscurité
de ses Misteres, qui sont au dessus de la penetration de l'esprit humain. . . .
Cette obscurité [est] dans la faiblesse de nos esprits." Claude-François Ménestrier, *La Philosophie des images énigmatiques* (Lyon: Chez Hilaire Baritel, 1694), preface (n.p.).

75. The application of this doctrine, which was established at the Coun-
cil of Trent, is explained in "Hermeneutics," in *The Catholic Encyclopedia*
(New York: Robert Appleton Company, 1910).

76. "le discours n'est seulement un enchaînement de termes énergiques qui
exposent la pensée avec force et noblesse, mais que c'est encore un tissu d'hiéroglyphes entassés les uns sur les autres qui la peignent. Je pourrais dire en ce
sens que toute poésie est emblématique" (Diderot, *Sourds,* 34).

77. For example, Quintilian (8.3.19–20) and Boileau's Satire XII, "L'Equivoque."

78. One challenge to this distinction between naked and ornamented language was Saint Augustine's contention that all language was metaphorical because it always stood for something else, namely, the thing it designated.

79. Nevertheless, Voltaire's theory and practice, or his public and private statements, sometimes contradicted each other. For instance, he created some rebuses for his private communication with Frederick II of Prussia.

80. David, 20–21.

81. Condillac, *Essay,* 183–84. "On trouvera même l'époque de leur décadence dans ces tems où elles paroissent vouloir s'approprier de plus grandes beautés. On verra les figures et les métaphores s'accumuler et surcharger le stile d'ornemens, au point que le fond ne paroîtra plus que l'accessoire" (Condillac, *Essai,* 194).

82. "Toi qui possédas le talent / De parler beaucoup sans rien dire: / Toi qui modulas savamment / Des vers que personne n'entend, / Et qu'il faut toujours qu'on admire." Voltaire, vol. 8 of *Œuvres complètes de Voltaire* (Paris: Garnier, 1877–85), 486–88.

83. Roland Barthes, *Writing Degree Zero and Elements of Semiology* (Boston: Beacon Press, 1970), 47. In this passage, the translator changes "langage classique" (which could be oral or written) to "classical speech" (only oral). "Dans le langage classique, ce sont les rapports qui mènent le mot puis l'emportent aussitôt vers un sens toujours projeté." Roland Barthes, *Le Degré zéro de l'écriture, suivi de Nouveaux essais critiques* (1953; Paris: Seuil, 1972), 37.

84. Barthes, *Writing Degree Zero,* 47. "brille d'une liberté infinie et s'apprête à rayonner vers mille rapports incertains et possibles" (Barthes, *Le Degré zéro,* 37).

85. "lettres misterieuses & énigmatiques dans l'Alphabet Grec" (Ménestrier, 34).

86. "ces obscuritez affectés seroient blâmables en toutes autre composition que celle des Enigmes" (Ménestrier, 63).

87. Augustine, II:74, 91.

88. Ibid., II:75.

89. Ibid., II:93.

90. "Now that I am discussing signs, I must say, conversely, that attention should not be paid to the fact that they exist, but rather to the fact that they are signs, or, in other words, that they signify. For a sign is a thing which of itself makes some other thing come to mind, besides the impression that it presents to the senses. So when we see a footprint we think that the animal whose footprint it is has passed by" (Augustine, II:57).

91. Michel Charles, "La Poétique de l'énigme: Présentation, notes et commentaire de Michel Charles," *Poétique* 45 (February 1981): 28. These pages

contain excerpts of Ménestrier's *Poétique de l'énigme*, which is part of his *Philosophie des images énigmatiques*, accompanied by a commentary by Michel Charles.

92. "Nostradamus qui pour faire le Prophète a composé des Enigmes impertinentes, remplies de fadaises et de mots qui n'ont ni rime ni raison" (Ménestrier, 33).

93. Both hieroglyphics and alchemy were believed to have been founded by the Greek god Hermes Trismegiste, whose alter ego was the Egyptian god Thoth. A connection between Hermes and his Roman counterpart Mercury, then, to the title of the *Mercure galant* would perhaps be too far-fetched.

94. "Enfans de lumiere & Enfans des tenebres[,] il en est de même des ouvrages de l'esprit humain" (Ménestrier, 249).

95. "sciences permises" (Ménestrier, 250).

96. "sciences deffendues," "magie, astrologie judiciaire, baguette pour trouver les sources & les metaux, chiromancie, talismans" (Ménestrier, 250).

97. "ces sciences noires, qui ont un commerce evident avec les demons" (Ménestrier, 251).

98. "plus profonds métaphysiciens, des plus sublimes physiciens, des Descartes, des Newton, des Leibnitz" ("Hermétique," *Encyclopédie*, VIII:169).

99. "Les *philosophes hermétiques* écrivent donc très-obscurement à dessein, par état, par esprit de corps; ils en font profession" ("Hermétique," *Encyclopédie*, VIII:169).

100. "Je crois pouvoir déduire du petit nombre d'observations que je viens de rapporter sur les écrits alchimiques, que sans décider même de la nullité de l'art & de la frivolité des prétextes allégués pour défendre l'obscurité de la doctrine, que ce seroit, dis-je, une manie bien bisarre que celle de s'occuper à pénétrer le sens des énigmes *hermétiques;* qu'il est très-probable même que ces énigmes n'ont pas un sens" ("Hermétique," *Encyclopédie*, VIII:171).

101. "l'obscurité de leurs écrits" ("Hermétique," *Encyclopédie*, VIII:171).

102. "ils les ont encore enveloppés sous des hyéroglyphes ou des emblèmes tout aussi peu intelligibles" ("Hermétique," *Encyclopédie*, VIII:171).

103. "certainement ce goût n'est ni de notre siecle ni de notre nation; notre philosophie est communicative & amie de l'évidence" ("Hermétique," *Encyclopédie*, VIII:171).

104. Rousseau's ideal of unmediated communication, transcending language itself, is the subject of Jean Starobinski's eminent work *Jean-Jacques Rousseau: La transparence et l'obstacle* (Paris: Gallimard, 1971).

105. Tzvetan Todorov, in his structural study of riddles or *devinettes*, among which one could count *énigmes*, insists on the dialogic aspect of this genre. He includes riddles among other forms of literature, specifically "genres dialogiques," challenging the system of institutionalized genres. *Les Genres du discours* (Paris: Seuil, 1978), 227.

6. THE DISORDERLY

1. "des traits ressemblans, qui le mettent en état de rapporter plusieurs choses à un seul chef, & d'en reduire un grand nombre à une seule classe" (Crousaz, 18).

2. "la régularité, l'ordre, la proportion, trois choses qui plaisent necessairement à l'Esprit humain & qui effectivement méritent qu'on les aime" (Crousaz, 22).

3. "l'ordre est absolument nécessaire, dans un discours," "les vérités," "en sorte que les premières éclairent les suivantes, et que celles-ci, à leur tour, donnent aux premières, par leur suite naturelle, une espèce de nouvel éclat" (André, 69).

4. Montesquieu, *Taste*, 262. "Il ne suffit pas de montrer à l'ame beaucoup de choses, il faut les lui montrer avec ordre; car pour lors nous nous ressouvenons de ce que nous avons vu, & nous commençons à imaginer ce que nous verrons; notre ame se félicite de son étendue & de sa pénétration" (Montesquieu, *Goût*, 493).

5. Montesquieu, *Taste*, 263. "l'ame ne retient rien, ne prévoit rien; elle est humiliée par la confusion de ses idées, par l'inanité qui lui reste; elle est vainement fatiguée & ne peut goûter aucun plaisir" (Montesquieu, *Goût*, 493).

6. Crocker, 57.

7. Ibid., 52.

8. Ibid., 53.

9. In the introduction to one edition of the *Discours sur le style*, the editor remarks, "Le *Discours*, commenté et appris par cœur par des générations d'élèves des classes de rhétorique au XIXe siècle, a connu des dizaines d'éditions dans ce siècle. Baudelaire, Flaubert, Barbey d'Aurevilly le citent avec éloge." Georges-Louis Leclerc, comte de Buffon, *Discours sur le style* (Castelnau-le-Lez: Editions Climats, 1992), 12.

10. "C'est le corps qui parle au corps." Georges-Louis Leclerc, comte de Buffon, *Discours sur le style*, in *Œuvres* (Paris: NRF Gallimard/Pléïade, 2007), 422. By contrast, Sophia Rosenfeld recounts in *A Revolution in Language* how late eighteenth-century philosophers and Revolutionary politicians valued the ideal of direct communication, from body to body, without the interference of words.

11. "émouvoir la multitude et l'entraîner" (Buffon, 422).

12. "un goût délicat" (Buffon, 422).

13. "cette facilité naturelle de parler qui n'est qu'un talent, une qualité accordée à tous ceux dont les passions sont fortes, les organes souples et l'imagination prompte" (Buffon, 422). These characteristics of the "naturally" good speaker recall the backhanded compliments that eighteenth-century critics gave to writers of the past. Montaigne and Marot, for example, were said to have a "naïve" style that flowed from their pen almost unintentionally.

14. "les siècles éclairés" (Buffon, 422).

15. "Le style n'est que l'ordre et le mouvement qu'on met dans ses pensées" (Buffon, 422).

16. "tout sujet est un" (Buffon, 423).

17. "enchaîne étroitement" (Buffon, 422).

18. "c'est en se rappelant sans cesse ces premiers linéaments, qu'on déterminera les justes intervalles qui séparent les idées principales, et qu'il naîtra des idées accessoires et moyennes qui serviront à les remplir" (Buffon, 422).

19. Christine Battersby, *Gender and Genius: Towards a Feminist Aesthetics* (London: The Women's Press, 1989).

20. "distinguera les pensées stériles des pensées fécondes" (Buffon, 422).

21. "ce défaut est celui des esprits cultivés, mais stériles" (Buffon, 425).

22. "Les ouvrages bien écrits seront les seuls qui passeront à la postérité," "ne roulent que sur de petits objets; s'ils sont écrits sans goût, sans noblesse et sans génie, ils périront" (Buffon, 427).

23. The theory was propounded by Aristotle in *On the Generation of Animals*. See the summary by David C. Lindberg in *The Beginnings of Western Science* (Chicago: University of Chicago Press, 1992), 64–66.

24. I previously mentioned Juan Huarte in Chapter 3 as the intermediary between the ancient theories of climate and those of Dubos and Montesquieu.

25. Juan Huarte de San Juan, *Examen de ingenios para las ciencias* (Madrid: Esteban Torre, 1977). Evelyne Berriot-Salvatore deals with his influence in France, especially in regard to the concept of gender, in "Le Discours de la médecine et de la science," in *Histoire des femmes en occident,* vol. 3, ed. Arlette Farge and Natalie Zemon Davis (Paris: Plon, 1991), 359–95.

26. "embrasser," "pénétrer," and "saisir" (Buffon, 423). Another version of this statement is more explicitly sexual: "Pour bien écrire, il faut que la chaleur du cœur se réunisse à la lumière de l'esprit. L'âme . . . ne peut manquer de se mouvoir avec plaisir vers l'objet présenté; elle l'atteint, le saisit, l'embrasse, et ce n'est qu'après en avoir pleinement joui, qu'elle est en état d'en faire jouir les autres par l'expression de ses pensées" (Buffon, 1499).

27. "faire éclore," "la chaleur naîtra de ce plaisir, se répandra partout, et donnera la vie à chaque expression" (Buffon, 424).

28. "Rien ne s'oppose plus à la chaleur, que le désir de mettre partout des traits saillans; rien n'est plus contraire à la lumière, qui doit faire un corps et se répandre uniformément dans un écrit, que ces étincelles qu'on ne tire que par force en choquant les mots les uns contre les autres, et qui ne nous éblouissent pendant quelques instants que pour nous laisser ensuite dans les ténèbres" (Buffon, 424).

29. Russo, 151.

30. Several eighteenth-century sources confirm this link between too much sexual activity and bodily weakness, intellectual weakness, and even infertility. Among these sources we can include the influential text by the physician Samuel-Auguste Tissot, *L'Onanisme* [1760]. The *Encyclopédie*

also advances the same claims in articles such as "Semence, maladies de la": "La trop fréquente évacuation de la liqueur séminale produit des cardialgies, des anxiétés, la lassitude des lombes, le tremblement, le vertige, la froideur de tout le corps, la foiblesse, l'orgasme, la phthisie dorsale, & sinalement l'impuissance" (XIV:940) and "Non-naturelles, choses": "Il y a aussi des humeurs . . . comme . . . la semence & le lait, dont l'évacuation est utile & même nécessaire dans les circonstances qui l'exigent, mais dont la trop grande perte est aussi tres-désavantageuse à la santé, & peut occasionner de grandes maladies" (XI:223–24).

31. "Plus on mettra de cet esprit mince et brillant dans un écrit, moins il y aura de nerf, de lumière, de chaleur et de style" (Buffon, 425).

32. "fort, nerveux et concis" (Buffon, 422).

33. "Le nom de *nerf* a été pris pour des parties très différentes chez les anciens . . . non-seulement ils ont donné le nom aux ligamens & aux tendons, mais aux muscles même." "Nerf," in vol. 4 of *Supplément au Dictionnaire des sciences, des arts et des métiers* (Paris: Chez Panckoucke, 1777), 26.

34. "un cheval *nerveux*, est celui qui a beaucoup de force" ("Nerveux [maréchalerie]," *Encyclopédie*, XI:105).

35. "c'est le membre qui sert à la génération" ("Nerf de cerf," *Encyclopédie*, XI:102); "la partie génitale" ("Nerf de bœuf," *Encyclopédie*, XI:102).

36. "le style devient ferme, nerveux et concis; si on les laisse se succéder lentement, et ne se joindre qu'à la faveur des mots, quelque élégants qu'ils soient, le style sera diffus, lâche et traînant" (Buffon, 422).

37. Buffon, 422.

38. "jette à l'aventure des traits irréguliers et des figures discordantes" (Buffon, 423).

39. Marie-Hélène Huet, in *Monstrous Imagination* (Cambridge, Mass.: Harvard University Press, 1993), explains how early modern medicine explained monstrous births, particularly in regard to ancient ideas of fertility and gender.

40. Battersby, 29.

41. Pope, 278.

42. Even though Buffon was not an intimate member of Voltaire's or Diderot's circles, and even though the latter were known to joke about him, the *philosophes* still deferred to him in many scientific matters. This acknowledgment of his authority is reflected in their hundreds of references to Buffon's *Histoire naturelle* in the *Encyclopédie* in articles such as "Accouchement," "Animal," "Eunuque," and "Fleuve," as well as in engravings of animals.

43. Marc Fumaroli, *Trois institutions littéraires* (Paris: Gallimard, 1994). The three institutions he refers to are the Académie Française, conversation, and "le génie de la langue française." The section entitled "Conversation" (110–210) also appears in Pierre Nora, ed., *Les Lieux de mémoire*, vol. 3,

part 2 (Paris: NRF Gallimard, 1992), 679–743. I will refer to page numbers in the latter edition.

44. Fumaroli mentions the importance of Descartes's opening statement of the *Discours de la méthode* as "Le bon sens est la chose du monde la mieux partagée" as a concession to *mondain* culture, as well as his choice to write in French, not Latin. Pascal weighs the pros and cons of the *esprit de finesse* and *esprit de géométrie*, giving them almost equal value.

45. See Dena Goodman, *The Republic of Letters: A Cultural History of the Enlightenment* (Ithaca, N.Y.: Cornell University Press, 1994) and Turnovsky (86–96) on D'Alembert's rhetorical defiance of the salon culture, in spite of his actual position vis-à-vis women such as the marquise du Deffand.

46. "La conversation est l'un de ces objets qui portent un défi discret à la science parce qu'ils sont asystématiques et tirent leur valeur, si l'on peut dire, de leur mollesse formelle." Roland Barthes, introduction to the issue of *Communications* entitled "La Conversation" (Paris: Seuil, 1979), n.p.

47. Jacqueline Hellegouarc'h created an anthology that includes some of these treatises from the seventeenth and eighteenth centuries in *L'Art de la conversation* (Paris: Classiques Garnier, 1997).

48. Domna Stanton, in "The Fiction of *Préciosité* and the Fear of Women," presents a convincing argument that the term *précieux* was only used pejoratively by the opponents of figures such as Scudéry and the marquise de Rambouillet, rather than the participants themselves.

49. "Ces figures visent donc d'abord à témoigner de la passion du locuteur; le *désordre* de la phrase, qui accumule parfois sans liaison les termes synonymes, suggère l'émotion pour mieux la provoquer." Delphine Denis, *La Muse galante: Poétique de la conversation dans l'œuvre de Madeleine de Scudéry* (Paris: Champion; Geneva: Slatkine, 1997), 233–34.

50. Dubos, *Critical Reflections*, I:340. "les hommes [sont] plus capables que les femmes d'une application forte et d'une attention suivie" (Dubos, *Réflexions*, I:416).

51. Dubos, *Critical Reflections*, I:339–40. "Comme les femmes ont une sensibilité plus soudaine, et qui est plus à la disposition de leur volonté, que la sensibilité des hommes, comme elles ont, pour parler ainsi, plus de souplesse dans le coeur que les hommes, elles réussissent mieux que les hommes à faire ce que Quintilien exige de tous ceux qui veulent se mêler de déclamer. Elles se touchent plus facilement qu'eux des passions qu'il leur plaît d'avoir" (Dubos, *Réflexions*, I:415).

52. "La représentation commune—accréditée aussi bien par les femmes-écrivains que par les médecins—veut que l'intelligence féminine soit pétillante et vive, mais emportée, soumise au contingent, au moment et à l'émotion. Les femmes ont un caractère passionné; elles éprouvent vivement, mais toujours de manière éphémère" (Wenger, 74). Wenger's statements are confirmed by the treatises of eighteenth-century physicians such as Pierre-Jean-Georges

Cabanis and Pierre Roussel. Cabanis describes the nature of women thus: "Incapables de fixer assez longtems leur attention sur une seule chose, elles ne peuvent éprouver les vives et profondes jouissances d'une méditation forte; elles en sont même incapables. Elles passent rapidement d'un sujet à l'autre; et il ne leur en reste que quelques notions partielles, incomplètes, qui forment presque toujours dans leur tête les plus bizarres combinaisons." *Rapports du physique et du moral de l'homme* (1802; Paris: Caille et Ravier, 1815), 306.

Roussel states that "On sçait qu'en général elles ont une plus grande facilité de parler que les hommes" (25). He also sees a link between flightiness and *finesse*: "C'est à cette disposition qui rend les organes de la femme plus actifs que forts, & qui leur donne plus de sensibilité que de consistance, qu'elle doit cette finesse de tact & cette pénétration qui consistent à saisir dans les objets qui la frappent rapidement, une infinité de nuances, de choses de détail, & de rapports déliés qui échappent à l'homme le plus éclairé" (29). *Système physique et moral de la femme* (Paris: Chez Vincent, 1775).

53. "Or, explique-t-il de façon assez retorse, la cause première en est la constitution féminine elle-même car les hommes, conscients que les femmes ne fixent jamais longtemps leur esprit sur un même objet, ont adopté comme première règle de politesse de varier leurs sujets de conversation, ce qui explique que ces dernières 'sont aujourd'hui toutes décousues'" (Wenger, 154).

54. "On ne peut plus souffrir aucune des choses qui ont un objet déterminé: les gens de guerre ne peuvent souffrir la guerre; les gens de cabinet, le cabinet; ainsi des autres choses. . . . C'est le commerce des femmes qui nous a menés là: car c'est leur caractère de n'être attachées à rien de fixe. Aussi sommes-nous devenus comme elles. Il n'y a plus qu'un sexe, et nous sommes tous femmes par l'esprit." Montesquieu, *Pensées*, fragment #1062, pp. 153–54.

55. "On comprend mal l'histoire de la pensée française au XVIIIe siècle quand on l'enferme dans l'histoire . . . des genres proprement littéraires. . . . En province notamment, loin de la Comédie, de l'Opéra et des salons à la mode, quand on cesse d'être ignare et indifférent, on a deux goûts et curiosités: celui de la littérature aimable et galante, poésies 'fugitives,' madrigaux ou chansons, et celui de l'érudition infatigable qui compile, compile, compile, toujours plus soucieuse de la quantité que de la qualité" (Mornet, 30–31).

56. "miettes de science," "curiosités vides et puériles, " and "bavardages" (Mornet, 28).

57. "ANA . . . Ce mot ne signifie rien, & n'est qu'une terminaison Latine de noms adjectifs neutres pluriels; mais parce que depuis quelque temps on a formé de ces sortes d'adjectifs Latins des titres à des livres, même François, qui sont des Recüeils des mots ou sentimens mémorables de quelques savants, ou gens d'esprit, on appelle ces livres des livres en *ana*, ou simplement des *ana*, ainsi l'on dit, Tous ces livres en *ana*, ou tous ces *ana*, me déplaisent fort. Les livres en *ana* font souvent dire aux gens des choses auxquelles ils n'ont

jamais pensé, ou qu'ils devroient n'avoir jamais dites" ("Ana," *Dictionnaire de Trévoux*, 1771).

58. "la lecture des *ana* aurait dû être instructive et amusante, si le goût, la raison, la vérité, avaient toujours servi de guide dans la composition de ces sortes d'ouvrages; mais le succès des *ana* fut cause que le public s'en vit bientôt inondé." [Jean Pie] Namur, *Bibliographie des ouvrages publiés sous le nom d'ana* (Bruxelles: Delevigne et Callewaert, 1839), viii.

59. "Nombreux sont en effet ceux—*Menagiana, Anonimiana, Naudeana et Patiniana, Segraisiana, Longuerana, Boloeana*—dont le titre complet comporte le nom 'conversations.'" Bernard Beugnot, "Forme et histoire: Le statut des *ana*," in *Mélanges offerts à Georges Couton* (Lyon: Presses Universitaires de Lyon, 1981), 92.

60. "Ce livre doit avoir dequoy plaire à tout le monde, à cause de la diversité des matieres dont il est remply." *Le Mercure galant*, vol. 1 (Paris, 1672), n.p.

61. "il m'importe peu qu'elles soient utiles à d'autres, pourveu qu'elles vous divertissent: c'est mon unique but" (12–13).

62. "On s'estoit assemblé pour une Partie de Jeu chez une aimable Duchesse, & en attendant quelques Dames qui en devoient estre, comme les choses les plus importantes sont d'abord l'ordinaire des sujets des Conversations, on mit sur le tapis les Affaires de Guerre." *Le Nouveau Mercure Galant* (March 1677): 1–3.

63. "Nouveaux Mémoires des Missions Etrangeres.
La Cuisiniere bourgeoise.
La Journée de Fontenoy, Ode par M. Fréron, Extrait.
Explication d'un Canon d'Autel.
Lettre aux Auteurs du Mercure.
Question.
Madrigal.
Estampes nouvelles.
Vûe de la Bataille de Fontenoy.
Mots des Enigmes & Logogryphes."

64. "Cet ouvrage fut dés sa naissance un ramas de toutes sortes de choses. Nouvelles, Promotions aux Dignités de l'Etat, Nominations aux Benefices. Mariages, Baptêmes, & Morts, Spectacles, Histoires galantes, Médailles, Receptions aux Academies, Sermons, Plaidoiés, Arrêts, petites Piéces de Poësie, Enigmes, Chansons, Dissertations, quelquefois savantes & quelquefois enjouées, tout y entra, tout y trouva place." Denis-François Camusat, vol. 2 of *Histoire critique des journaux* (Amsterdam: J.-F. Bernard, 1734), 99.

65. "Le commis, d'une main indifférente, ouvre les paquets qui à chaque courier tombent sur son bureau et s'y amoncelent. . . . Chansons, madrigaux, épîtres, stances, etc. pleuvent, et le commis lassé ne se donne plus la peine de briser les cachets. . . . Il entasse et ensevelit toutes ces pieces dans d'énormes

cartons, où elles dorment, en attendant qu'on en pêche une au besoin. Malheur à celle qui est trop longue ou trop courte pour la page qu'on veut remplir! Fût-elle excellente, on la rejette pour choisir celle qui s'ajuste précisément à l'espace vuide." Louis-Sébastien (Mercier, *Tableau*, IV:14–15).

66. "Le so[t] livre qu'on voit dans la main du Bourgeois / Reglement à toutes les lunes, / Seroit-ce pas l'égout du Parnasse François? / Non, mais c'est que selon les Loix / Au sexe feminin communes, / La Muse Françoise a ses mois (Camusat, II:205).

67. Aristotle explains in *Generation of Animals* (Cambridge, Mass.: Harvard University Press, 1979) that blood in men is heated up ("coction") to become semen, while women's menstrual blood proves that they are unable to accomplish the same: "Now it is impossible that any creature should produce two seminal secretions at once, and as the secretion in females which answers to semen in males is menstrual fluid, it obviously follows that the female does not contribute any semen to generation; for if there were semen, there would be no menstrual fluid; but as the menstrual fluid is in fact formed, therefore there is no semen" (727a).

68. "la corruption du goût & la décadence des belles lettres" (Camusat, I:xiv).

69. "composent sans gout, sans discernement, sans science" (Camusat, I:xiv).

70. "La lecture d'un Recueil diversifié par les expressions comme il l'est par les matieres, sera plus amusante que celle d'un Livre qui viendroit tous les mois repeter au Public le même langage" (*Mercure galant*, June 1721, vi).

71. "nous avons à combattre des Censeurs opiniâtres. . . . Il en est même qui s'obstinent encore à lui compter comme un défaut la variété qui constitue son caractere. Ignorent-ils que ce journal est fait pour tout le monde, & qu'il doit des mets à tous les goûts?" (*Mercure galant*, June 1721, viii, ix).

72. Donneau de Visé was the first editor of the *Mercure* from 1672 to 1674.

73. "Vous prêtez de belles ailes à ce Mercure, qui n'était pas même galant du temps de Vizé et qui devient, grâce à vos soins, un monument de goût, de raison et de génie. . . . C'est ce que j'avais conseillé, il y a longtemps aux journalistes." *Mercure* (May 1772): 122. Quoted in Claude Bellanger and Jacques Godechot, eds., *Histoire générale de la presse française*, vol. 1 (Paris: Presses Universitaires de France, 1969), 210.

74. "Anciennement le mercure distribuoit des fadeurs; il devint tout-à-coup incivil et dur entre les mains d'un pédant. Ensuite la sécheresse et la sottise le défigurerent, et l'art du sousligneur fut pris pour l'art du critique. On est étonné de voir des écrivains imberbes ou sans nom, jugeant les arts avec une emphase ridicule ou monotone, et Don-Quichottes du bon goût, s'escrimer pour sa cause sans le connoître. Quelques futiles remarques, quelques

chicanes minutieuses, voilà tout ce qu'on y trouve. Oh, combien de petits auteurs à Paris sont habiles à disserter sur des riens!" (Mercier, *Tableau*, IV:17).

75. I say "marked as" a gender, because in reality, specific women such as Anne Dacier may have written in a schematic order, while men may have used looser structures, as did some editors of the *Mercure*.

76. "la caresse et la jouissance." André Pessel, "De la conversation chez les précieuses," in "La Conversation" issue of *Communications* (Paris: Seuil, 1979), 20. Pessel's sources are those very texts by de Pure, Somaize, etc., that Domna Stanton warned against using because they satirized *préciosité* rather than documented them reliably, but his conclusions do not seem to contradict the ideas suggested by researchers such as Delphine Denis, who analyzes the words of the so-called *précieuses* themselves.

77. "On dira aussi de la conversation qu'elle est dérision à l'égard de la maternité: la femme est stérile à n'engendrer que des discours" (Pessel, 15).

CONCLUSION

1. "La poésie était la monarchie." Victor Hugo, „Réponse à un acte d'accusation"/"Reply to a Bill of Indictment," in *Les Contemplations: The Selected Poems of Victor Hugo: A Bilingual Edition* (Chicago: University of Chicago Press, 2001), verse 35, pp. 164–65.

2. "Oui, je suis ce Danton! je suis ce Robespierre!" (Hugo, v. 141, pp. 170–71).

3. "J'ai foulé le bon goût et l'ancien vers françois / Sous mes pieds" (Hugo, v. 3–4, pp. 162–63).

4. "Au panier les Bouhours, les Batteux, les Brossettes! / A la pensée humaine ils ont mis les poucettes" (Hugo, v. 113, pp. 168–69). Claude Brossette was the founder of the Académie de Lyon.

5. "Fleurs de lys d'or, Tristan et Boileau, plafond bleu, / Les quarante fauteuils et le trône au milieu" (Hugo, v. 163–64, pp. 172–73).

6. "Populace du style" (Hugo, v. 50, pp. 166–67).

7. "Si Corneille en trouvait un blotti dans son vers, / Il le gardait, trop grand pour dire: Qu'il s'en aille; / Et Voltaire criait: Corneille s'encanaille!" (Hugo, v. 56–58, pp. 166–67).

8. Hugo, v. 59, pp. 166–67.

9. "hideux, j'ai dit à l'ombre: Sois! / Et l'ombre fut" (Hugo, v. 4–5, pp. 162–63).

10. "Quand je sortis du collège, du thème, / Des vers latins, farouche, espèce d'enfant blême" (Hugo, v. 29–30, pp. 164–65).

11. Pierre Bourdieu, *Distinction: A Social Critique of the Judgment of Taste* (Cambridge, Mass.: Harvard University Press, 1984). "la dénégation du social . . . s'acharnent à refouler l'évidence de la relation entre le goût et

l'éducation." Pierre Bourdieu, *La Distinction: Critique sociale du jugement* (Paris: Minuit, 1979), 9.

12. Robert Darnton, *The Forbidden Best-Sellers of Pre-Revolutionary France* (New York: Norton, 1995); Joan DeJean, "Classical Reeducation: Decanonizing the Feminine," *Yale French Studies* 75 (1988): 26–39.

BEFORE 1800

André, Yves-Marie. *Essai sur le beau.* 1741. Amsterdam: Chez J. H. Schneider, 1759.

Argens, Jean-Baptiste de Boyer, marquis d'. *The Jewish Spy: Being a philosophical, historical and critical correspondence, by letters which lately pass'd between certain Jews in Turkey, Italy, France, &c.* 4 vols. Dublin: Nelson and Saunders, 1753.

———. *Lettres juives, ou Correspondance philosophique, historique et critique entre un juif voïageur en différens Etats de l'Europe et ses correspondans en divers endroits.* 6 vols. La Haye: P. Paupie, 1738.

Aristotle. *The "Art" of Rhetoric.* Trans. John Henry Freese. Vol. 22 of the *Works of Aristotle.* Cambridge, Mass.: Harvard University Press, 1994.

———. *The Generation of Animals.* Cambridge, Mass.: Harvard University Press, 1979.

Aristotle, Horace, Longinus. *Classical Literary Criticism.* Trans. T. S. Dorsch. London: Penguin, 1965.

Augustine, Saint. *De Doctrina Christiana.* Oxford: Clarendon Press, 1995.

Batteux, Charles. *Les Beaux-arts réduits à un même principe.* Paris: Durand, 1746.

Boileau[-Despréaux, Nicolas]. *Œuvres complètes.* Paris: NRF Pléiade, 1966.

———. *Selected Poems.* Trans. Burton Raffel. New Haven, Conn.: Yale University Press, 2007.

Bollioud-Mermet, Louis. *De la bibliomanie.* La Haye: n.p., 1761.

———. *De la corruption du goust dans la musique française.* Lyon: A. Delaroche, 1746. New York: AMS Press, 1978.

———. *Crazy book-collecting or bibliomania.* New York: Duprat, 1894.

Bouhours, Dominique. *Entretiens d'Ariste et Eugène.* Paris: Mabre-Cramoisy, 1671.

Boursault, Edmé. *La Comédie sans titre, ou le Mercure galant*. In vol. 3 of *Théâtre des auteurs du second ordre*. Paris: Belin, 1813.

Buffon, Georges-Louis Leclerc, comte de. *Discours sur le style*. Castelnau-le-Lez: Editions Climats, 1992.

———. *Œuvres*. Paris: NRF Gallimard/Pléïade, 2007.

Cabanis, Pierre-Jean-Georges. *Rapports du physique et du moral de l'homme*. 2 vols. 1802. Paris: Caille et Ravier, 1815.

Camusat, Denis-François. *Histoire critique des journaux*. 2 vols. Amsterdam: J.-F. Bernard, 1734.

Cartaud de la Vilate, François. *Essai historique et philosophique sur le goût*. Paris: Chez Maudouyt, 1736.

Condillac, Etienne Bonnot de. *Essai sur l'origine des connaissances humaines*. Amsterdam: P. Mortier, 1746.

———. *Essay on the Origin of Human Knowledge*. Cambridge: Cambridge University Press, 2001.

Condorcet, Jean-Antoine-Nicolas de Caritat, marquis de. *Esquisse d'un tableau historique des progrès de l'esprit humain*. Paris: Boivin et Cie, 1933.

———. *Outlines of an historical view of the progress of the human mind*. Philadelphia: Lang and Ustick, 1796.

Crébillon, Claude-Prosper Jolyot de. *L'Ecumoire*. In vol. 2 of *Œuvres*. London [Frankfurt]: Varrentrap, 1779. http://artfl.uchicago.edu/cgi-bin/philologic/navigate.pl?newfrantext.574.

———. *The Skimmer, or The History of Tanzai and Neadarne*. 2 vols. London: F. Galicke, 1735.

Crousaz, Jean-Pierre de. *Traité du beau*. 1715. 2 vols. Amsterdam: Chez l'Honoré et Chatelain, 1724.

Dacier, Anne. *Des Causes de la corruption du goust*. Amsterdam: Pierre Humbert, 1715.

Dictionnaire universel françois et latin vulgairement appelé Dictionnaire de Trévoux. Trévoux and Paris, 1721 and 1771.

Diderot, Denis, and Jean le Rond d'Alembert, eds. The Encyclopedia of Diderot & d'Alembert Collaborative Translation Project. Ann Arbor: Scholarly Publishing Office of the University of Michigan Library, 2006.

———. *Encyclopédie, ou dictionnaire raisonné des sciences, des arts et des métiers*, ed. Robert Morrissey. Chicago: University of Chicago ARTFL Encyclopédie Projet. Spring 2010 edition. http://encyclopedie.uchicago.edu/.

———. *Esthétique-Théâtre*. Vol. 4 of *Œuvres*. 5 vols. Paris: Laffont, 1996.

———. *Œuvres complètes.* 25 vols. Paris: Hermann, 1976.

Dubos, Jean-Baptiste. *Critical Reflections on Poetry, Painting and Music.* 3 vols. London: J. Nourse, 1748.

———. *Réflexions critiques sur la poésie et sur la peinture.* 1719. 3 vols. Paris P.-J. Mariette, 1733.

Dumarsais, César Chesneau. *Des Tropes.* 1730. Ed. M. Fontainier, with an introduction by Gérard Genette. 1818. Geneva: Slatkine Reprints, 1967.

Fénelon, François de Salignac de La Mothe-. *Lettre à l'Académie.* Vol. 6 of *Œuvres complètes.* 10 vols. Geneva: Slatkine Reprints, 1971.

Gerard, Alexander. *An Essay on Taste: To which are annexed, three dissertations on the same subject, by Mr de Voltaire, Mr D'Alembert, and Mr de Montesquieu.* Edinburgh: A. Millar, A. Kincaid, and J. Bell, 1764.

Grimm, Friedrich Melchior. *Le Petit prophète de Boehmischbroda.* 1753. La Haye, 1774.

Huarte de San Juan, Juan. *Examen de ingenios para las ciencias.* Madrid: Esteban Torre, 1977.

La Harpe, Jean-François de. *Lycée, ou Cours de littérature ancienne et moderne.* 16 vols. Paris: Chez Depelafol, 1825.

Lambert, Anne-Thérèse, marquise de. *Œuvres.* 2 vols. Paris: Ganeau, 1748.

———. *The works of the Marchioness de Lambert.* 2 vols. Dublin: J. Potts, 1770.

Marivaux, Pierre Carlet de. *Journaux et Œuvres diverses.* Paris: Garnier, 1969. http://artfl.uchicago.edu/cgi-bin/philologic/navigate. pl?newfrantext1.578.

Marmontel, Jean-François. *Eléments de littérature.* 1787. Paris: Desjonquères, 2005.

———. *Poétique françoise.* 2 vols. Paris: Lesclapart, 1763.

Ménestrier, Claude-François. *La Philosophie des images énigmatiques.* Lyon: Chez Hilaire Baritel, 1694.

Mercier, Louis-Sébastien. *L'An deux mille quatre cent quarante, rêve s'il en fut jamais.* 3 vols. N.p., 1786.

———. *Memoirs of the year two thousand five hundred.* 2 vols. London: G. Robinson, 1772.

———. *Le Tableau de Paris.* 12 vols. Amsterdam: n.p., 1782–83.

Montesquieu, Charles de Secondat, baron de. *Œuvres complètes.* 22 vols. Oxford and Naples: Voltaire Foundation and Istituto italiano per gli studi filosofici, 1997–.

———. *Persian Letters.* Oxford: Oxford University Press, 2008.

———. *Reflections on the causes of the rise and fall of the Roman Empire.* Glasgow: Robert Urie, 1758.

Palissot de Montenoy, Charles. *La Dunciade*. In vol. 3 of *Œuvres*. 6 vols. Liège: Plomteux, 1777.

———. *Les Philosophes*. In vol. 2 of *Théâtre du XVIIIe siècle*. 2 vols. Paris: NRF Gallimard, 1974.

Pascal, Blaise. *Pensées*. Ed. Philippe Sellier. Paris: Bordas, 1991.

———. *Pensees: The Provincial Letters*. Trans. W. F. Trotter. New York: The Modern Library, 1941.

Piron, Alexis. *La Métromanie*. Vol. 1 of *Théâtre du XVIIIe siècle*. 2 vols. Paris: NRF Gallimard, 1972.

Quintilian. *The Orator's Education*. Ed. and trans. Donald A. Russell. Cambridge, Mass.: Harvard University Press, 2001.

Rousseau, Jean-Jacques. *The Collected Writings of Rousseau*. Hanover, N.H.: University Press of New England, 1990.

———. *Œuvres complètes*. 10 vols. Paris: NRF Gallimard/Pléiade, 1964.

Shaftesbury. *Characteristics of Men, Manners, Opinions, Times*. Cambridge: Cambridge University Press, 1999.

Staël, Germaine de. *Des circonstances actuelles qui peuvent terminer la révolution et des principes qui doivent fonder la république en France*. Paris: Librarie Fischbacher, 1906.

Supplément au Dictionnaire des sciences, des arts et des métiers. Paris: Chez Panckoucke, 1776–77.

Vaugelas, Claude Favre de. *Remarques sur la langue françoise, utiles à ceux qui veulent bien parler et bien escrire*. Paris: Camusat, 1747.

Villiers, Pierre de. *Entretiens sur les contes de fées, et sur quelques autres ouvrages du temps pour servir de préservatif contre le mauvais goût*. Paris: Jacques Collombat, 1699.

Voltaire. *The Age of Louis XIV*. London: Dent. New York: Dutton, 1935.

———. *Candide and Other Stories*. Oxford: Oxford University Press, 1990.

———. *Complete Works*. Oxford: Voltaire Foundation, 1968–.

———. *Dialogues, and essays literary and philosophical*. Glasgow: Robert Urie, 1764.

———. *Essai sur les mœurs et l'esprit des nations*. 2 vols. Paris: Garnier, 1990.

———. *Œuvres complètes*. 52 vols. Paris: Garnier, 1877–83.

———. *Romans et contes*. Paris: Garnier, 1960.

———. *The Works of Voltaire: A Contemporary Version with Notes*. 42 vols. Paris: E. R. Dumont, 1901.

AFTER 1800

Barthes, Roland. *Le Degré zéro de l'écriture, suivi de nouveaux essais critiques.* 1953. Seuil, 1972.

———. Introduction to the issue "La Conversation" of *Communications*, 1979.

———. *Writing Degree Zero and Elements of Semiology.* Boston: Beacon Press, 1970.

Battersby, Christine. *Gender and Genius: Towards a Feminist Aesthetics.* London: The Women's Press, 1989.

Becq, Annie. "Les Arts poétiques en France au XVIIIe siècle." *Etudes littéraires* 22.3 (1990): 45–55.

———. *La Genèse de l'esthétique française moderne, 1680–1814.* Pisa: Pacini, 1984. Paris: Albin Michel, 1994.

Bellanger, Claude, and Jacques Godechot, eds. *Histoire générale de la presse française.* 5 vols. Paris: Presses Universitaires de France, 1969.

Benharrech, Sarah. "Lecteur, que vous êtes bigearre!: Marivaux et la 'querelle de Montaigne.'" *MLN* 120.4 (2005): 925 49.

Bernier, Marc-André. "Les Lumières au prisme de la décadence des lettres et du goût." In *Les Songes de Clio: Fiction et histoire sous l'Ancien Régime,* ed. Sabrina Vervacke, Éric Van der Schueren, and Thierry Belleguic. Québec: Presses de l'Université Laval, 2006.

Beugnot, Bernard. "Forme et histoire: Le statut des ana." In *Mélanges offerts à Georges Couton,* 85–101. Lyon: Presses Universitaires de Lyon, 1981.

Bhabha, Homi K. *Nation and Narration.* London: Routledge, 1990.

Bonnet, Jean-Claude. "Le Débat sur le 'Grand Siècle' à l'Académie au début du XIXe siècle." In *Un Siècle de deux cents ans? Les XVIIe et XVIIIe siècles: Continuités et discontinuités,* ed. Jean Dagen and Philippe Roger. Paris: Desjonquères, 2004.

Bourdieu, Pierre. *La Distinction: Critique sociale du jugement.* Paris: Minuit, 1979.

———. *Distinction: A Social Critique of the Judgment of Taste.* Cambridge, Mass.: Harvard University Press, 1984.

———. *Les Règles de l'art: Genèse et structure du champ littéraire.* Paris: Seuil, 1992.

———. *The Rules of Art: Structure and Genesis of the Literary Field.* Cambridge: Polity Press, 1996.

Bray, René. *La Formation de la doctrine classique en France.* Paris: Nizet, 1945.

Calinescu, Matei. *Five Faces of Modernity: Modernism, Avant-Garde, Decadence, Kitsch, Postmodernism.* Durham, N.C.: Duke University Press, 1987.

Cassirer, Ernst. *The Philosophy of the Enlightenment.* Trans. James P. Pettegrove and Fritz C. A. Koelin. Princeton, N.J.: Princeton University Press, 1968.

The Catholic Encyclopedia. 17 vols. New York: Robert Appleton Company, 1907–22.

Chantalat, Claude. *A la Recherche du goût classique.* Paris: Klincksieck, 1992.

Charles, Michel, ed. "La Poétique de l'énigme: Présentation, notes et commentaire de Michel Charles." *Poétique* 45 (February 1981): 28–51.

Chartier, Roger. *Lectures et lecteurs dans la France d'Ancien Régime.* Paris: Seuil, 1987.

Crocker, Lester G. *Diderot's Chaotic Order: Approach to Synthesis.* Princeton, N.J.: Princeton University Press, 1974.

Crow, Thomas. *Painters and Public Life in Eighteenth-Century Paris.* New Haven, Conn.: Yale University Press, 1985.

Dagen, Jean, and Anne-Sophie Barrovecchio, eds. *Voltaire et le Grand Siècle.* Studies on Voltaire and the Eighteenth Century 2006:10. Oxford: Voltaire Foundation, 2006.

Damian-Grint, Peter, ed. *Medievalism and "manière gothique" in Enlightenment France.* Studies on Voltaire and the Eighteenth Century 2006:05. Oxford: Voltaire Foundation, 2006.

Darnton, Robert. *The Forbidden Best-Sellers of Pre-Revolutionary France.* New York: Norton, 1995.

———. *The Literary Underground of the Old Régime.* Cambridge, Mass.: Harvard University Press, 1982.

David, Madeleine V. *Le Débat sur les écritures et l'hiéroglyphe aux XVIIe et XVIIIe siècles.* Paris: SEVPEN, 1965.

DeJean, Joan. *Ancients Against Moderns: Culture Wars and the Making of a Fin de Siècle.* Chicago: University of Chicago Press, 1997.

———. "Classical Reeducation: Decanonizing the Feminine." *Yale French Studies* 75 (1988): 26–39.

Delon, Michel. *L'Idée d'énergie au tournant des Lumières (1770–1820).* Paris: Presses Universitaires de France, 1988.

Démoris, René, and Florence Ferran. *La Peinture en procès: L'invention de la critique d'art au siècle des Lumières.* Paris: Presses de la Sorbonne Nouvelle, 2001.

Denis, Delphine. *La Muse galante: Poétique de la conversation dans l'œuvre de Madeleine de Scudéry.* Paris: Champion and Geneva: Slatkine, 1997.

———, ed. *L'Obscurité: Langage et herméneutique sous l'Ancien Régime.* Louvain: Academia Bruylant, 2007.

Derrida, Jacques. *De la grammatologie*. Paris: Minuit, 1967.

Doiron, Normand. "Le Style obscur: L'Enigme I." *Littératures classiques* 28 (Autumn 1996): 211–37.

Douglas, Mary. *Thought Styles: Critical Essays on Good Taste*. London: Sage, 1996.

Dréano, Maturin. *La Renommée de Montaigne en France au XVIIIe siècle*. Angers: Editions de l'Ouest, 1952.

Eagleton, Terry. *The Ideology of the Aesthetic*. London: Blackwell, 1990.

Ehrard, Jean. *L'Idée de nature en France à l'aube des Lumières*. Paris: Flammarion, 1970.

Faisant, Claude. *Mort et résurrection de la Pléïade*. Paris: Champion, 1998.

Farge, Arlette, and Natalie Zemon Davis, eds. *Histoire des femmes en occident*. Paris: Plon, 1991.

Ferry, Luc. *Homo aestheticus: L'invention du goût à l'âge classique*. Paris: Grasset, 1990.

Folkierski, Wladyslaw. *Entre le classicisme et le romantisme*. Paris: Champion, 1925.

Fumaroli, Marc. "Le Génie de la langue française." In vol. 3, part 2 of *Les Lieux de mémoire*, ed. Pierre Nora, 679–743. Paris: NRF Gallimard, 1992.

———. *Trois institutions littéraires*. Paris: Gallimard, 1994.

Gans, Herbert. *Popular Culture and High Culture: An Analysis and Evaluation of Taste*. 1974. New York: Basic Books, 1999.

Goodman, Dena. *The Republic of Letters: A Cultural History of the French Enlightenment*. Ithaca, N.Y.: Cornell University Press, 1994.

Goulbourne, Russell. *Voltaire Comic Dramatist*. Studies on Voltaire and the Eighteenth Century 2006:03. Oxford: Voltaire Foundation, 2006.

Goulemot, Jean Marie. *Forbidden Texts: Erotic Literature and Its Readers in Eighteenth-Century France*. Philadelphia: University of Pennsylvania Press, 1994.

———. *Ces Livres qu'on ne lit que d'une main: Lecture et lecteurs de livres pornographiques au XVIIIe siècle*. Aix-en-Provence: Alinea, 1991.

Greenberg, Clement. "Avant-garde and Kitsch." In *Pollock and After: The Critical Debate*. New York: Routledge, 2000.

Guichard, Charlotte. *Les Amateurs d'art à Paris au XVIIIe siècle*. Seyssel: Champ Vallon, 2008.

Habermas, Jürgen. *The Structural Transformation of the Public Sphere: An Inquiry into a Category of Bourgeois Society*. 1962. Cambridge, Mass.: MIT Press, 1991.

Hanley, William. "The Censure of Voltaire's Biblical Verse." *Australian Journal of French Studies* 21.1 (1984): 26–42.

Herr, Mireille. *Les Tragédies bibliques au XVIIIe siècle.* Paris: Champion and Geneva: Slatkine, 1988.

Horkheimer, Max, and Theodor W. Adorno. *Dialectic of Enlightenment.* Trans. John Cumming. New York: Continuum, 1994.

Howells, Robin. *Playing Simplicity: Polemical Stupidity in the Writing of the French Enlightenment.* Oxford: Peter Lang, 2002.

Hugo, Victor. "Réponse à un acte d'accusation"/"Reply to a Bill of Indictment." In *Les Contemplations. The Selected Poems of Victor Hugo: A Bilingual Edition.* Chicago: University of Chicago Press, 2001: 162–77.

Kenny, Neil. "Books in Space and Time: Bibliomania and Early Modern Histories of Learning and 'Literature' in France." *MLQ: Modern Language Quarterly* 61.2 (June 2000): 253–86.

Letts, Janet. "Responsive Readers of the *Mercure Galant*, 1680–1710." *Cahiers du dix-septieme* 5.2 (Fall 1991): 211–28.

Lindberg, David C. *The Beginnings of Western Science.* Chicago: University of Chicago Press, 1992.

Lodge, R. Anthony. *French: From Dialect to Standard.* London: Routledge, 1993.

Lombard, Alfred. *L'Abbé Du Bos: Un initiateur de la pensée moderne.* 1913. Geneva: Slatkine Reprints, 1969.

Lyons, John D. *Before Imagination: Embodied Thought from Montaigne to Rousseau.* Stanford, Calif.: Stanford University Press, 2005.

Martin, Henri-Jean. *Le Livre français sous l'Ancien Régime.* Paris: Promodis/Editions du Cercle de la Librairie, 1987.

Meeker, Natania. "*Lire et devenir*: The Embodied Reader and Feminine Subjectivity in Eighteenth-Century France." *The Eighteenth Century* 47.1 (Spring 2006): 39–57.

Mehtonen, Päivi. *Obscure Language, Unclear Literature: Theory and Practice from Quintilian to the Enlightenment.* Trans. Robert MacGilleon. Helsinki: Finnish Academy of Science and Letters, 2003.

Menant, Sylvain. *L'Esthétique de Voltaire.* Paris: SEDES, 1995.

Metz, Bernhard. "Bibliomania and the Folly of Reading." *Comparative Critical Studies* 5.2–3 (2008): 249–69.

Mornet, Daniel. *Histoire de la clarté française, ses origines, son évolution, sa valeur.* Paris: Payot, 1929.

Morrissey, Robert. *La Rêverie jusqu'à Rousseau: Recherches sur un topos littéraire.* Lexington, Ky.: French Forum, 1984. http://isbndb.com/d/publisher/french_forum.html.

Namur, [Jean Pie]. *Bibliographie des ouvrages publiés sous le nom d'ana.* Bruxelles: Delevigne et Callewaert, 1839.

Naves, Raymond. *Le Goût de Voltaire.* 1938. Geneva: Slatkine Reprints, 1967.

Neaimi, Sadek. *L'Islam au siècle des Lumières.* Paris: L'Harmattan, 2003.

Ong, Walter. "The Barbarian Within." In *The Barbarian Within and Other Fugitive Essays and Studies.* New York: Macmillan, 1962.

Pessel, André. "De la conversation chez les précieuses." *Communications* (1979): 14–30.

Pocock, J.G.A. *Barbarism and Religion.* 5 vols. Cambridge: Cambridge University Press, 2005.

Porter, David. "Monstrous Beauty: Eighteenth-Century Fashion and the Aesthetics of the Chinese Taste." *Eighteenth-Century Studies* 35.3 (Spring 2002): 395–411.

Rosenfeld, Sophia. *A Revolution in Language: The Problem of Signs in Late Eighteenth-Century France.* Stanford, Calif.: Stanford University Press, 2001.

Russo, Elena. *Styles of Enlightenment: Taste, Politics and Authorship in Eighteenth-Century France.* Baltimore: Johns Hopkins University Press, 2006.

Saint Girons, Baldine. "L'esthétique: Problèmes de définition." In *L'esthétique naît-elle au XVIIIe siècle?* Ed. Serge Trottein. Paris: Presses Universitaires de France, 2000.

Saisselin, Rémy. *Taste in Eighteenth-Century France.* Syracuse, N.Y.: Syracuse University Press, 1965.

Scholar, Richard. *The Je-Ne-Sais-Quoi in Early Modern Europe: Encounters with a Certain Something.* Oxford: Oxford University Press, 2005.

Stanton, Domna. "The Fiction of *Préciosité* and the Fear of Women." *Yale French Studies* 62 (1981): 107–34.

Todorov, Tzvetan. *Les Genres du discours.* Paris: Seuil, 1978.

———. *Théories du symbole.* Paris: Seuil, 1977.

———. *Theories of the Symbol.* Oxford: Blackwell, 1982.

Turnovsky, Geoffrey. *The Literary Market: Authorship and Modernity in the Old Regime.* Philadelphia: University of Pennsylvania Press, 2010.

Viala, Alain. *La Naissance de l'écrivain: Sociologie de la littérature à l'âge classique.* Paris: Minuit, 1985.

———. "'Qui t'a fait minor?' Galanterie et Classicisme." *Littératures Classiques* 31 (1997): 115–34.

Wenger, Alexandre. *La Fibre littéraire: Le discours médical sur la lecture au XVIIIe siècle.* Geneva: Droz, 2007.

INDEX

ACKNOWLEDGMENTS

This book began during a conversation at the café of the New York Public Library one afternoon in 2003, when my former professor and future colleague Philippe Roger asked me, "What are you going to do next?" I presented him with several ideas that I had been toying with; the one he liked best, he said, was the one about Bad Taste. And so, through several years of research and a few major changes in life, including a move from New York to Virginia, I developed the idea into a book. Along the way, I was fortunate to receive support, both moral and material, from many sources.

First of all, I must express my gratitude to Elena Russo for her faith in my work and for coming to the rescue at a critical point in my writing process. She and Josué Harari helped me guide my manuscript to the beginning stages of publication and eventually into the capable hands of Jerome Singerman. During the writing process, the University of Virginia offered generous travel and summer research funds and a year of sabbatical leave, all of which accelerated the completion of my book. I am particularly grateful to Dean Meredith Jung-En Woo for her encouragement and kind support. Rita Felski also deserves thanks for her excellent advice and Nathan Brown for the long hours he spent helping me put the manuscript into its final shape.

I wish to thank my family and my friends, especially Elisabeth Ladenson, Philippe Roger, and Sophia Rosenfeld, for accompanying me through the rockiest stretches of my academic path. During these times, Edna-Jakki Miller taught me how to be a stronger woman. Finally, Mark Ilsemann, my husband, deserves my gratitude for guiding my heart toward certainty, even when my mind drifted toward skepticism.